COGNITIVE PROCESSES

second edition

Lyle E. Bourne, Jr.
University of Colorado

Roger L. Dominowski
University of Illinois–Chicago

Elizabeth F. Loftus
University of Washington

Alice F. Healy
University of Colorado

PRENTICE-HALL, INC., ENGLEWOOD CLIFFS, NEW JERSEY 07632

Library of Congress Cataloging-in-Publication Data

Main entry under title:

Cognitive processes.

    Bibliography: p.
    Includes index.
    1. Cognition. 2. Human information processing
I. Bourne, Lyle Euguen
BF311.C5518 1986   153   85-12262
ISBN 0-13-139833-4

Editorial/production supervision and
interior design: Debbie Ford
Cover design: Wanda Lubelska Design
Manufacturing buyer: Barbara Kelly Kittle

Printed in the United States of America

10 9 8 7 6 5 4 3 2 1

ISBN 0-13-139833-4 01

Prentice-Hall International (UK) Limited, *London*
Prentice-Hall of Australia Pty. Limited, *Sydney*
Prentice-Hall Canada Inc., *Toronto*
Prentice-Hall Hispanoamericana, S.A., *Mexico*
Prentice-Hall of India Private Limited, *New Delhi*
Prentice-Hall of Japan, Inc., *Tokyo*
Prentice-Hall of Southeast Asia Pte. Ltd., *Singapore*
Editora Prentice-Hall do Brasil, Ltda., *Rio de Janeiro*
Whitehall Books Limited, *Wellington, New England*

Contents

Preface

The field of cognitive psychology continues to grow in breadth and depth as researchers generate new findings and propose new ideas. We have incorporated the data and theories that have emerged since the publication of the first edition to produce an up-to-date account of cognition. Our coverage of the field has been broadened, and the text has been substantially reorganized and rewritten. The overall scope of the changes is suggested by the fact that two-thirds of the references are new. Two chapters have been added, one concerning sensory memory and pattern recognition, the other attention and short-term memory. Our treatment of abstraction and categorization has been reorganized to provide an integrated discussion of the various theories of concept structure and concept acquisition. The chapter on language has been expanded and gives special emphasis to multi-level comprehension processes. Other new sections focus on topics such as reconstructive processes in memory, problem-solving expertise, decision making, and possible sources of cognitive development.

Like its predecessor, this book was created with the aim of giving students a comprehensive, richly-illustrated, and understandable discussion of cognitive processes. Basic concepts and principles are explained, using examples, and experimental findings are explicitly related to the general topics being considered. Well-established findings and theories form the core of a coherent description, but we have also pointed out ambiguities and uncertainties where they exist, and we have sought to provide balanced coverage of more controversial issues. For example, alternative views of the structure and formation of concepts are compared, and the strengths and weaknesses of alternative models of semantic-knowledge structures are discussed. An extensive list of references has been included to assist readers who desire more detailed study of topics of special interest.

The general orientation of the text is that human beings may be viewed as information processors who are both subject to certain constraints and capable of considerable flexibility. The first chapter presents an overview and a brief history of cognitive psychology. Chapters 2 through 4 deal with the many facets of human memory, including iconic and echoic memories, pattern recognition, attention, short-term memory, and the encoding and retrieval processes that are involved in learning, remembering, and forgetting various kinds of material. Chapters 5 through 7 focus on knowledge structures, their acquisition and utilization: concepts, semantic networks, schemas, and linguistic structures of varying degrees of complexity. Chapters 8 and 9 concern relatively complex, goal-oriented behavior—problem solving, reasoning, judgment, and decision making; the influence of processing limitations, strategies, and the nature of a person's knowledge base is emphasized. Chapter 10 reviews cognitive development with particular attention given to the processes that might play major roles in understanding the massive changes that occur between infancy and adulthood. Chapter 11 presents a selection of applications of cognitive theories and findings to phenomena such as eyewitness testimony, classroom learning, and schizophrenic thought. In this way we hope to encourage the reader to perceive the potential usefulness of knowledge about cognitive processes.

We would like to thank Robert G. Crowder and several anonymous reviewers for their incisive comments on earlier versions of the manuscript. Their suggestions might not always have been followed, but they are appreciated nonetheless.

L. E. B., Jr.
R. L. D.
E. F. L.
A. F. H.

ONE

Introduction
and Brief History

Outline

Cognitive psychology is the study of the human mind, its capabilities and limitations expressed in behavior. While studies of the human mind are by no means new in psychology, it is only fairly recently, say, in the last twenty years or so, that true and significant progress has been made. This book attempts to describe that progress, to summarize our present state of knowledge, and to set the stage for investigating the many significant problems that remain to be solved.

Cognitive psychologists approach their discipline from a basically scientific perspective. Mind, on the other hand, is a relatively imprecise concept. There are vast differences of opinion about the mind, even among psychologists. At one time in psychology, the mind was considered to be the fundamental, if not the only concern of psychology. At another time, the concept was banished and most psychologists refused even to use the term. Such is the checkered history of this field, a matter that we will have more to say about later.

Currently, the concept of mind is of considerable interest to psychologists, especially those who call themselves cognitive psychologists. Cognitive psychologists study the structure and processes of the human mind. There is a strong tendency among cognitive psychologists to view the human mind as a calculational device and cognition as a system for processing information. We adopt this orientation despite its inadequacies, many of which will become clearer as we move along. We find such a framework to be the most useful of those currently available for organizing and discussing the major topics of this area.

We begin by briefly looking at some of the more extreme examples of what the human mind can accomplish. You may find these examples extraordinary; nonetheless they are real. They illustrate what a mind, perhaps even an otherwise ordinary mind, can do if pushed to the limit. They are not merely curiosities; they represent the kind of activity that a complete science of cognition must eventually come to grips with.

Some Capabilities of the Human Mind

A MENTAL CALCULATOR

I. M. L. Hunter (1968) describes the unusual powers of rapid mental calculation possessed by Professor A. C. Aitken, a distinguished mathematician at Edinburgh University. He gives the following example. Professor Aitken is asked to express the fraction 4/47 as a decimal. In Hunter's words:

> He is silent for 4 seconds, then begins to speak the answer at a nearly uniform rate of 1 digit every three-quarters of a second. "0—8—5—1—0—6—3—8—2—9—7—8—7—2—3—4—0—4—2—5—5—3—1—9—1—4, that's about as far as I can carry it." The total time between the presentation of the problem and this moment is 24 seconds. He discusses the problem for 1 minute and then continues the answer at the same rate as before. "Yes, 1—9—1—4—8—9, I can get that." He pauses for 5 seconds, "3—6—1—7—0—2—1—2—7—6—5—9—5—7—4—4—5—8, now that is the repeating point. It starts again at 085. So if that is 46 places, I am right." (p. 341)

This is indeed a remarkable performance! One might rightly wonder whether any other human being is capable of such mental "gymnastics." Hunter's report gives the impression that Aitken has a computer for a brain and can grind out answers to arithmetic questions of this sort with little conscious effort. Actually, a more intense study of what it is that Professor Aitken is doing reveals a much more ordinary basis. Professor Aitken has no unusual memory capacity nor is he more intelligent than everyone else. True enough, he knows how to perform numerical calculations in his head about as well as any person who has ever lived. But his ability derives from intense and prolonged practice, not from any unique natural talent. His calculational feats rest upon a broad knowledge of number facts and highly developed manipulative skills that can be performed mentally, and in a very rapid fashion, on those number facts.

practice

IDIOTS SAVANTS

Seemingly incredible calculational skills like those of Aitken are not restricted to individuals with unique training or superior intellect. They sometimes crop up in otherwise borderline individuals. Extreme cases of this sort have been labeled *idiots savants* (wise idiots). One example, reported by Scheerer, Rothmann, and Goldstein (1945), was an eleven-year-old boy with an intelligence test score falling technically within the mentally retarded range (IQ = 50) who nonetheless evidenced some remarkable cognitive accomplishments. His most impressive skill was calendar calculations. Given a person's birthday, he could immediately say on what day of the week it fell during the previous year. He could name the day of the week for any date beginning with the year 1880. He could give the date for the second Tuesday in April 1940 or the last Thursday in December 1934. His answers to these and similar questions were virtually immediate; his recall of the birthdates of real people was also almost perfect.

Idiots savants show outstanding cognitive accomplishments in very narrow areas, while often falling below normal in others. The area is not always mathematical or calculational. Yoshihiki Yamamoto is a well known Japanese artist who has produced highly prized paintings even though his IQ is under 50. Yamamoto was fortunate enough to be placed in a special school during his youth where a curriculum could be developed around his extraordinary artistic talents. The quality of Yamamoto's artistic work is generally conceded to be genius-level, yet he is mentally retarded on the basis of his functioning in other areas (Morishima & Brown, 1977).

Finally, Brink (1980) has described the case of Mr. Z who is retarded in language and mathematical skills yet has an amazing capacity to repair and modify mechanical and electrical devices. Without instruction, he has dismantled, reassembled, and modified several complex ten-speed bicycles. He can copy any picture or drawing with incredible accuracy and speed, even though his creative artistic talents are nonexistent. He has an amazing array of magical tricks that even professional magicians have not been able to reproduce.

It is probably true that extremely high skill can be developed in almost any cognitive area. To date, at least seven categories have been identified: calendar calculation, mathematical ability, mechanical dexterity, memory for facts, musical talent, painting and drawing, and, on rare occasion, an ability to make extraordinarily fine sensory discriminations. What is baffling about *idiots savants* is that these skills seem to be entirely limited to one kind of activity. They represent another riddle for cognitive psychologists to solve. However, the number of such cases is relatively small and there has been little opportunity to study them in depth.

MNEMONISTS

It will come as no surprise to learn that some people have better memories than others. Every once in a while, you may run into somebody who seems to have a truly outstanding memory. Almost all of us have been impressed at one time or another with a friend or acquaintance who remembers everyone he or she has ever met and is never at a loss for a person's name, no matter how much time has gone by since their last meeting. Does such a person have a unique and different kind of mind or is it just a trick that everyone could master with practice?

The famous Russian psychologist, A.R. Luria (1968) studied a man whom he called S over a span of many years. S appeared to remember volumes of information of a variety of sorts after only brief and apparently effortless examination. Moreover, he could recall this material at will no matter how much time had passed. This case history has become a classic and is fascinating to read. S's memory feat appeared to depend largely on his use of mental imagery. That is, when he wanted to learn something, S formed an image of it. If there were several items to remember, he distributed images in different locations of a mental map. Commonly, he would distribute items to be remembered along some roadway he visualized in his mind. When the time came to recall these materials S would recreate the map image and then take a mental walk through it. As he encountered each successive location in the image the object to be remembered would automatically spring to mind.

S used what are called mnemonic devices to enhance his memory. Many people do, but S seemed to have perfected the art. The particular device illustrated has sometimes been called the method of loci (see Figure 1-1), in reference to the positioning of items to be remembered at different places or loci in a complex image (see Chapter 4). But S is not the only mnemonist who has been examined by cognitive psychologists nor is the method of loci the only device that mnemonists use. Hunt and Love (1972) studied a mnemonist called VP, whose ability to recall was at least in part dependent upon being multilingual—he could keep confusable items straight in memory by encoding them into different languages.

Mnemonics are devices that anyone can use to enhance memory. They constitute an important topic in contemporary cognitive psychology. We are beginning to understand how people use imagery, their basic storehouse of knowledge, and their language to form stable memories of their experiences. People who are extremely good at mnemonics, like S and VP, perfect one or more systems for remembering an amount of material which would seem, on the surface, to be impossible.

Figure 1-1. The method of loci. This is a mnemonic technique that almost anyone can learn to use to improve memory. The trick is to associate the words to be learned, such as the grocery list, with a well-known series of landmarks. For example, use distinctive items along the route you usually take home. Here the subject associates tomatoes with his mailbox, the newspaper with a big oak tree, hot dogs with a deep pothole in the road, bananas with his driveway, bread with the garage door, and so on. Each item is associated, by imagery, with its own familiar landmark. To retrieve the items later, just take a mental trip along your route home. Try it. It works! Luria's S developed this technique into an art. He could remember vast sets of new material by the method of loci.

SHORT- AND LONG-TERM MEMORY

We will be concerned in this book with the distinction cognitive theory commonly makes between short-term and long-term memory. Short-term memory refers to holding information that is necessary only for some immediate use, for example, looking up the telephone number of the local taxi and remembering it only long enough to dial. Long-term memory refers to the capacity to store information for activities that may occur at some unspecified time in the future. There is evidence to suggest that all information must pass through short-term memory on its way to more permanent storage in long-term memory; that is, we must process new information in some immediate sense before it is in a form suitable for more permanent representation. Older people often report difficulty in storing new information in long-term memory. A senile person is able to recall events in his or her life that happened before senility set in, but the memory bank seems closed to new inputs.

Certain types of brain damage appear to create a similar memory deficit. Milner (1966) describes a study of a young man, HM, who had lost part of his temporal lobes and hippocampus in a brain operation. Prior to the operation, his IQ was 104, about normal. After the operation, he tested at 118, significantly above normal. There are reasons for this change, but the point is that the operation did *not* result in a reduction of intelligence. This individual could remember events in his life prior to the operation as well as anybody. However, after the operation, new experiences seemed not to stick in long-term memory. Says Milner,

> Ten months before I examined him, his family had moved from their old house to one a few blocks away on the same street. He still has not learned the new address, though remembering the old one perfectly, nor can he be trusted to find his way home alone. He does not know where objects constantly in use are kept; for example, his mother still has to tell him where to find the lawn mower, even though he may have been using it only the day before. She also states that he will do the same jigsaw puzzle day after day without showing any practice effect, and that he will read the same magazines over and over again without finding their content familiar. (1959, p. 49)

The man described his own life as "like walking through a dream," not really remembering where he was or how he got there. He remarked that, for him, every day was unique. It was as if today was continually pushed out of his short-term memory, one item at a time, and tomorrow never came and could not be remembered even if it did.

What is striking about this patient is that he could remember events that happened before brain damage, but events that occurred after the operation were retained but for a brief period of time. The theoretical conception of memory as having both short-term and long-term storage helps us to interpret this kind of result. Apparently, whatever else the brain damage did, it obliterated those processes which are responsible for converting factual information into long-term memories. Interestingly enough, however, HM was capable of acquiring new skills, even though he showed no conscious awareness of the process. How neurological structures provide the underpinning for transfer from short- to long-term memory is currently an issue of intense experimental examination by cognitively oriented biological psychologists.

INTERACTION OF SHORT-
AND LONG-TERM MEMORY

One should understand that long- and short-term memory, despite their demonstrated independence, can interact in fairly dramatic ways. Chase and Ericsson (1981) present an analysis of a single subject (SF) who has become exceedingly skillful at using his long-term memory apparently to enhance the capacity of his short-term memory. Over the course of two years of training, involving over 250 hours of practice in the laboratory, SF has steadily increased his digit span, a standard test of short-term memory, from 7 digits, which is about normal for adults, to over 80 digits (see Figure 1–2). The contrast between ordinary and expert memory

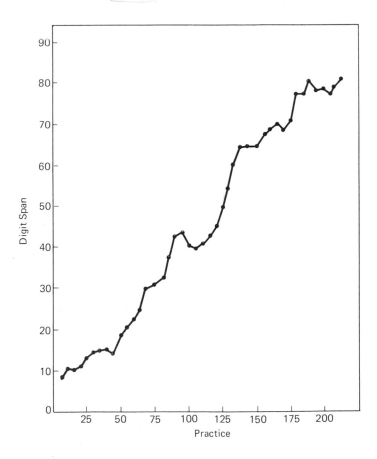

Figure 1–2. Growth in digit span for the subject, SF. Even after 200 days of practice, this learning curve shows no signs of leveling off. (Redrawn from Figure 1, p. 608, in Ericsson, K.A. & Chase, W.G. Exceptional memory. [1982]. *American Scientist, 70,* 607–615.)

performance is astounding. For most people, the digit span is stable over a wide range of materials. This relative stability is taken by many cognitive psychologists to imply a fundamental property of human memory called the limited capacity of short-term memory. Capacity limitations place severe constraints on people's ability to process information and to solve problems. But SF appears to defy this limitation. How is it possible to by-pass the limits of short-term memory?

It is first important to note that SF's ability did not develop overnight. Rather, it is a consequence of long and tedious practice. According to Chase and Ericsson, the skill that SF has developed depends very heavily on his ability to make use of information already permanently present in his long-term memory and to retrieve and utilize that information in an exceptionally rapid and efficient way. SF, as it turns out, is a runner. He has an extensive knowledge of running times for various kinds of track events. As digits are read to him on any given trial, he rapidly encodes these digits into chunks of three or four numbers, corresponding to what he knows about running times. For example, the numbers 3492 might be encoded as "3 minutes, 49.2 seconds, a near record time for the one mile distance." SF, in other words, breaks down the strings of digits into chunks he can understand as related to running times. He has developed a skill of accessing his extensive knowledge of running time numbers almost instantaneously and using that knowledge to recode a long string of digits into something more manageable. Thus, SF's exceptional "short-term memory" is really attributable to his ability to use semantic knowledge already permanently in long-term memory. The sheer magnitude of SF's memory feat is something for which cognitive psychology will have to develop explanations. We describe this feat here, however, to illustrate the interrelatedness of what might otherwise appear to be completely independent memory structures.

We should emphasize that SF's performance really does not disprove the fundamental limitation on human short-term memory. Nor does it demonstrate any expansion of short-term memory per se. Rather, it illustrates a way around the ordinary limitations on our processing capacity. To convince you that SF's short-term memory has not changed all we need to do is to switch to another memory task. If, instead of asking SF to remember a string of digits, we present a string of letters, H-R-D-N-C-G-P, his performance drops to normal. That is, for any kind of material other than items to which he can apply his vast knowledge of running times in a rapid skillful way, SF's capacity is not different from yours or ours.

FLASHBULB MEMORY

Psychologists typically distinguish between an emotional/motivational component and an intellectual component of behavior. Indeed, these components are treated in different chapters of any general psychology book. Furthermore, specialized texts are commonly devoted to one or the other aspect of behavior, not both. As a case in point, the present book is largely about intellectual aspects of behavior. Everything we have discussed thus far has been completely independent of any emotional involvement.

One should not get the impression from this that emotion and motivation have nothing to do with the intellect. Indeed, there are very important interactions.

For example, it is perfectly clear that knowledge is not enough to create behavior. One must be motivated to act on knowledge if any observable performance is to result. The influence of emotions is often even more startling. In preceding sections, we have discussed various phenomena associated with the memories of certain unique individuals. One dramatic kind of memory phenomenon that just about everybody exhibits, however, derives from emotional experience. This phenomenon is referred to by Brown and Kulick (1977) as flashbulb memory, the memory for circumstances in which one first learned of a very surprising and emotion-arousing event. These authors found the circumstances surrounding the news of President John Kennedy's assassination to be a memory that almost everyone has with great perceptual clarity. That is, when asked, people who were adult at the time can typically tell where they were, what they were doing at the time, who told them, what the immediate aftermath was, how they felt about it, and possibly other idiosyncratic concomitants of the event. For younger readers, the shooting of President Reagan or of John Lennon, events which occurred after the original Brown-Kulick report, probably produce the same effect.

Two principal factors contribute to the establishment of flashbulb memory. One is a high level of surprise and the other is a high level of emotional arousal. If these two variables do not attain high enough levels, no flashbulb memory results. If they do attain the critical levels, then the event is retained with unique clarity.

The retention of surprising, emotional events may be biologically significant and thus have high selection value. It is possible that evolution has provided human beings and possibly other animals with an innate basis for a flashbulb memory. Whether or not these speculations are true, flashbulb memory illustrates more clearly than any other phenomenon the tight interrelationship between cognitive and emotional processes.

CREATIVE INSIGHT

There are reports from several eminent scientists about how they discovered the solution to a problem they had been working on during a time when they were not even thinking about the problem. One such scientist is Otto Loewi, who won the Nobel Prize for discovering how nerve impulses are transmitted by chemical agents. Loewi described how the critical experiment was revealed to him during a state of near-sleep. He had come up with the general idea of a chemical transmission mechanism for nerve impulses seventeen years earlier, but had put the idea aside for the lack of a way to test it. Fifteen years later, he developed a technique to detect fluids secreted by a frog's heart. Then, one night two years after that:

> I awoke, turned on the light, and jotted down a few notes on a tiny slip of thin paper. Then I fell asleep again. It occurred to me at 6 o'clock in the morning that during the night I had written down something most important, but I was unable to decipher the scrawl. The next night, at 3 o'clock, the idea returned. It was the design of an experiment to determine whether or not the hypothesis of chemical transmission that I had uttered seventeen years ago was correct. I got up immediately, went to the laboratory, and performed a single experiment on a frog heart according to the nocturnal design. (Loewi, 1960, p. 17)

Thus, the solution to a long-standing problem occurred to Loewi in a moment of insight. He was asleep, not trying to solve any problem, yet nonetheless a solution came to mind (see Figure 1–3). He isolated two frog hearts, only one of which had its nerves intact. He stimulated the vagus nerve of the first heart. The vagus nerve has an inhibitory effect and thus the heartbeat slowed down. He immediately removed some of the salt solution in which the heart was bathed and applied it to the second heart. It also slowed down. By this procedure, Loewi unequivocally showed that nerves influence the heart and other tissues by releasing specific chemical substances from their terminals.

How can we establish the conditions for insight? While the process may seem magical, some important suggestions are beginning to appear in research. If a complete set of conditions could be discovered, think of the importance this would have for all the creative work that remains to be done.

MIND OVER MATTER

There have been numerous reports of cases in which an individual demonstrates extraordinary control over his or her own bodily functions. You have heard of the Indian yogi who can sleep on a bed of nails. Another yogic practice is to sit in a tub and draw water up into the lower intestine to cleanse it. At the Men-

Figure 1-3. Otto Loewi's solution to the problem of neural transmission occurred to him during a dream. Apparently, creative insight does not require immediate active effort.

ninger Foundation, an Indian yogi voluntarily threw his heart into fibrillation—that is, he made it beat at about 300 beats per minute—for 17 seconds. At this rate the heart will not pump any blood, and so his pulse disappeared. Reports of such unusual actions have been largely ignored in the scientific literature but are now being looked at intensely by cognitive psychologists because of the rapidly developing field of biofeedback research.

If an instrument is used to inform a person exactly what some part of the body, normally inaccessible to consciousness, is doing, the person often can find ways of changing and controlling the activity. For example, if the activity of a single muscle fiber is electronically amplified and displayed either visually or in auditory form, the subject can learn to relax or to activate the fiber. Likewise, if a sound is used to indicate when an alpha rhythm appears in the electronic recording of brain activity (EEG), many subjects seem to be able to learn to decrease or increase the amount of their alpha rhythm. The essence of biofeedback techniques is that they make available to consciousness information that is ordinarily not present. Having that information, people can try various strategies to see what effects they have on the "involuntary" process. A person can thus achieve cognitive control over bodily activity, essentially what we mean by mind over matter.

COMMENT

What the human mind can accomplish when pushed to the limit is truly remarkable. But we would be remiss if we left the reader with the impression that the mind is remarkable only in the extreme. Indeed even ordinary, everyday mental accomplishments of human beings can be astoundingly complex. Consider, for example, the extent of knowledge and skill required to use your native language. Your vocabulary alone amounts to some 50,000 or so entries, and that is only a small part of being able to speak intelligibly. Think for a moment about how many people you know by name or face. If you try to list them you will not only be impressed, but probably also run out of time and patience before coming close to exhausting your knowledge. Some estimates place the real number again in the tens of thousands for an adult. The point is that we do not have to limit our discussion to unusual or abnormal abilities to provide a convincing case for the truly staggering magnitude of human cognition.

People as Information-Processors

How can we understand these various kinds of cognitive activity? Cognitive psychologists face the enormous task of explaining phenomena such as these in systematic, scientific terms. The approach that seems to show the most promise of providing an explanation is based on the notion that human beings are systems for processing information. You should keep in mind that information-processing is not a theory. Rather, it is an evolving framework or domain of discourse that permits cognitive psychologists—and, it is hoped, readers of this book—to exchange cogent ideas regarding cognitive phenomenon. The framework is no fixed prescription either for explanation or for research. Rather, it provides us with certain conventions for talking about theoretical or research possibilities.

The way people behave is dependent on the information available and a set of processes for operating on that information. The information a person has to work with at any moment comes from at least three sources: (1) current circumstances, which usually include some focal source of stimulation; (2) memory, which is defined as information about past experiences and about functional skills; and (3) feedback contingent upon action, that is, information that derives from sensing one's own activity, and from the reactions of one's social and physical environment to that activity. Without attempting to provide a technical or definitive treatment at this point, we proceed next to a description of how information is processed so as to control behavior.

HOW INFORMATION IS PROCESSED

Information is processed over time. For the sake of organizing our discussion, it is convenient to think of information as passing through several stages, each with its own characteristics. A simplified representation of possible stages of information-processing is given in Figure 1-4.

If information is to have any effect at all, it must first be registered perceptually. That is to say, a person must see, hear, feel, or otherwise sense some energy change in the environment for there to be any information for further processing. To the extent that energy persists over time, processing can be done directly. But as we are all well aware from personal experience, sometimes an event occurs and is gone before we have an opportunity to make a complete or thorough examination. Under those circumstances, we are forced to rely on memory. Thus, memory becomes an important component in human information-processing.

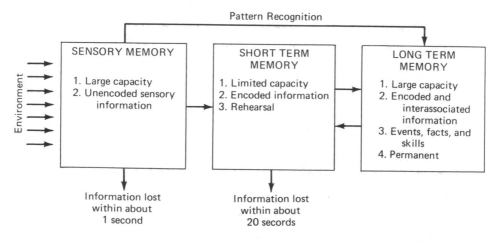

Figure 1-4.   A simplified representation of the human information processing system.

Sensory Memory.   Human memory appears to have several different forms. There is evidence to the effect that the impression left by a sensory experience may persist in all its complexity, either at the receptor level or in the brain, for a brief period of time. This persistence is called sensory memory. While quite primitive, it is nonetheless different from an after-image which follows typically only after prolonged or intense stimulation. Two major characteristics of sensory memory are its high capacity for information and its fast decay. That is, sensory memory will record for some period of time nearly an exact replica of the event that occurred in the environment. The period of time, however, is very short, possibly less than a second. Thus, if information in sensory memory is not converted to some more durable form, it will for all intents and purposes be forgotten.

Even at the level of sensory memory, complicated information processes can take place. For example, we see at this level the first evidence of *attention*. While the sensory system is capable of registering vast amounts of environmental information, those events which are at the focus of attention are registered with greatest clarity. What the focus of attention is can be determined either by environmental characteristics, such as the brightness or loudness or general saliency of events, or by cognitive factors, such as what we expect or want to see. In addition, a process which we refer to as *pattern recognition* can be initiated while information is in sensory memory. Environmental energy registered in sensory memory is in itself meaningless until identification or recognition is achieved. In order for an image in sensory memory to be identified or recognized, past experience or knowledge needs to be brought to bear. The process of coming to identify, name, or otherwise understand an image begins with perception but requires further processing. That is what we mean by converting information to a more durable form. For an event to have meaning and to be retained beyond simple sensory memory, it must be recognized and encoded as something recognizable. This brings us to another stage of information-processing.

Short-term Memory.   Pattern recognition and pattern encoding make for greater durability of information in memory. At the present time, there is no general agreement on how encoding is accomplished in detail or about the form that it takes. Some theorists have argued that encoding is a matter of converting sensory experience into words, at least in human beings. Others have suggested that encoding may be image-like or analogue-like in nature, containing many characteristics of the sensory experience itself. Still others assume an abstract representation which is neither verbal nor image-like. We shall discuss these issues later. For the time being, however, we merely assert that encoded information is more durable than pre-processed information and can be passed from sensory memory into short-term memory.

Short-term memory is a lot like *consciousness*. Short-term memory is what we are aware of at any given moment. It is an active form of memory, consisting of information that has just been encoded or of information which has been retrieved from our general storehouse of knowledge. There are two points about short-term memory that stand out. One is that its capacity is very limited. Evidence suggests that we can hold active in short-term memory only some small number of items of information at any given time. Thus, short-term memory is easily overtaxed and is generally thought to contain only those items to which we are attentive at the moment. Since the environment and our knowledge of the world provide us with a continual flow of information into short-term memory, items that might be contained there at one moment are subject to a good deal of competition and interference from other incoming items. Moreover, even if there were no significant interference, items tend to fade out of short-term memory in a relatively short period of time if they are not further processed. While not so brief as sensory memories, the limited duration of short-term memory is evident whenever we look up and dial a new telephone number. Unless we make a special effort to commit that number to a more durable form, we experience no lasting memory once dialing is complete.

To keep information alive in short-term memory, we must engage in further processing. One sort of process is *rehearsal,* the repetition of attended information in order to keep it active. Rehearsal has two primary functions. First is the *maintenance* of information over time, as we have noted. The second, which may require a somewhat different kind of rehearsal, is to convert or *elaborate* information in short-term memory into an even more stable form for storage as a part of our general knowledge about the world. Brenda Milner's work with HM indicates that the process required for converting short-term memories into more durable knowledge probably has a specific neurological base.

The second point to be made about short-term memory is that processes that are applied to items themselves take some of the capacity. Thus, if a person were required to add two multidigit numbers together, the number of digits involved would have to be small enough to allow some resources to be used for the calculation itself. The fact that processes other than simple item maintenance take the resources of short-term memory is one reason why we sometimes refer to this form of memory as *working memory*. It is also common to refer to the resources that apply to maintenance and calculation as *attentional resources,* because what is being maintained and what is being operated on are at the focus of attention.

Thus, we say that the capacity and the resources of short-term memory are limited. As a consequence, short-term memory serves as a bottleneck in the information-processing system. Only so much can get through or can be worked on at any particular point in time. As the work of Chase and Ericsson cited earlier suggests, there are ways to by-pass, overcome, or reduce the influence of this bottleneck by the skilled and strategic use of our general storehouse of knowledge. But there does not seem to be any way to change the basic fact that this part of the system, taken as a separate distinct entity, is severely limited.

Long-term Memory.   Information that is processed into long-term memory can pass from attention and from consciousness and still be remembered. Information encoded for long-term memory is information in its most lasting form. Some theorists have argued that information in long-term storage is never completely lost, though it may not be accessible for one reason or another. Whether that is the case or not, long-term memory is certainly more permanent than either of the other forms of memory that we have discussed. Moreover, its capacity seems to be virtually limitless. That is to say, individuals are capable of memories that last throughout a lifetime. Information in long-term memory constitutes our representation of the world. Often it is referred to as our knowledge of the world.

Knowledge, as we use the term, refers both to "knowing that" and "knowing how." That is to say, long-term memory contains both facts and procedures, both discriminations and abilities to act on those discriminations. One useful distinction that has been made is between *episodic, semantic,* and *procedural* memories. Episodic memory is memory of one's personal history. Facts of this sort have both a spatial and a temporal marking and are recalled less for their substance and more in terms of the context of their original occurrence. Semantic memory has to do with one's general factual knowledge—discriminations or concepts that a person knows without necessarily knowing how or when they were first encountered or acquired. This is one's repository for meanings in the world. Finally, procedural memory has to do with "knowing how" or with skills. Procedural memory is the storehouse of what one can do with facts, concepts, or episodes as opposed to what those entities are. It is a fast-acting form of memory, often appearing to be reflexive—as in playing a musical instrument or in typing. It is not built up out of reflexes, however, but rather out of extensive knowledge which has become automatized through prolonged practice. Note that the amnesia suffered by HM appears primarily as a deficiency in memory for facts and episodes; his procedural memory remains intact.

There is, of course, much more to be said about the content of long-term memory and its organization. We leave those fascinating questions for discussion in detail in a later chapter.

PUTTING INFORMATION TO USE

Out of all the information we experience, some is stored away for future use. Once memories begin to form, behavior will be a function of environmental and of internal sources of information. These sources become the data base on which we plan our actions and make decisions among alternatives. But it would be misleading to assert that behavior is a simple reaction to external and internal events and their interaction. There is considerably more. Human beings have an ability to go beyond information that is immediately available in any situation. We can react to hypotheticals as well as to particulars (realities?). Some of these possibilities are outlined serially in Figure 1–5.

Constructive Processes.   Either our memories play funny tricks on us or we play funny tricks with our memories. It is the rule, rather than the exception, that we tend to remember things not exactly as they originally were. How often does it happen that you agree in detail with someone who had the same experience, or watched the same movie, or read the same story as you? As an exercise, compare

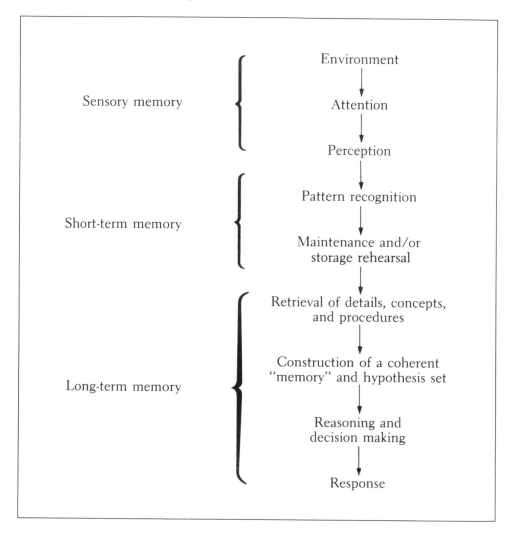

Figure 1-5. Flow of sequentially organized processes with corresponding theoretical structures leading from environmental input to response. As we will see in later discussions, the serial arrangement used here is a convenient fiction. These processes can run in parallel, interactively, and repeatedly. Later discussion will make these possibilities clear.

your memory of a movie to that of someone who sat through the same show with you. We guarantee that you will disagree on a number of important episodes.

Now, part of the difference may simply be a matter of forgetting certain details. The more interesting possibility, argued by some theorists, is that memory is reconstructive. Usually you remember some particulars of an experience, but these are merely fragments of what went on. Other people, having the same experience, will remember different particulars. No one is likely to remember everything that happened. Thus, we are left with the necessity of filling in gaps between particulars so as to make coherent connections between them. The connections are manufactured primarily on the basis of one's general knowledge of the world and on one's skills of inference. Thus, memories, as we describe them to others, are reconstructions of an experience from the few fragments we actually retain.

Thus, how we behave in any situation is a product of how the current situation is perceived, what recollections we have of previous related circumstances, and our ability to construct alternatives for behaving that are inferable from these informational inputs.

Abstraction. One kind of inference process that is typical of human beings is abstraction. That is, we are able to pick out or abstract from several or many different objects or events those aspects or features that are common. On the basis of abstracted common features we develop a classification scheme. That is, all objects with a certain set of features are classified together. For example, all objects that have feathers and wings and beaks and taloned feet are likely to be classified as birds. Any particular classification grouping is called a concept. Forming one of these groupings is called concept-formation. Concept-formation is an inductive process. That is to say, you learn a concept by observing a number of objects with features in common. You use these features to define a class or a concept that applies more broadly (in fact generally) than merely to the instances you have observed. Even as adults we would make no claim to have encountered every possible bird. Nonetheless, we have the concept of *bird* and we extend that concept to new examples every day, making the discrimination between new birds and all non-bird objects easily.

Our earliest concepts center around objects that are familiar and repeated from time to time in our environment. Thus, early on we form concepts about *mother, father, people, dogs* and *cats, toys.* Early concepts tend to be concrete, basic, and centered on familiar, repeated, and interesting examples. Later in life, concepts become more complex, often building up out of earlier primitive basic concepts. Thus, we learn that tables, chairs, and lamps can be further categorized together as objects of furniture. We learn more abstract groupings of people, say for example based on their profession; we learn about religion, forms of government, and the like.

Forming the full repertoire of adult concepts is a considerable intellectual undertaking that obviously takes many years. In the process we learn not only that certain items go together but also the reasons for their going together. The process of concept-formation affords considerable economy in cognition in the sense that, in most circumstances, instances of the same concept can be treated as if they were identical and need not be distinguished. In most theories of memory, especially semantic memory, concepts, not individual instances, are the basic content element, even though concepts themselves were initially built up from experience with individual instances.

Deductive Reasoning. But the mind is not an entirely inductive device. It also works in a deductive way. That is to say, we use informational input and our knowledge of the world for making decisions about what must logically be the case. If all A's are B's and if all B's are C's, then it logically (deductively) follows that all A's are C's. The conclusion drawn here does not extend beyond the given information. Rather, it is logically compelled by that information. No other conclusion could be true. While we will not claim that the mind is always deductively logical, we do possess deductive skills and we use these skills for drawing conclusions on which we can base our own actions or interpret the actions of others.

Comment. There are certainly other high-level cognitive processes of which the human mind is capable. We have not talked at any great length, for example, about problem-solving or judgment or about language or reading. We have covered enough, however, to illustrate the general point. The human mind can be described as a system for processing information. Human behavior can be described as a consequence of information-processing. The processing that occurs depends on, but is not wholly determined by, informational input from the environment and from memory. Information represents the elements on which our cognitive skills operate to calculate possible and inferable forms of behavior. This is the framework in which we will discuss cognitive processes. We use these general notions throughout the remainder of the book as a guide to studying and understanding the cognitively-based behavior of human beings.

A Brief History of Cognitive Psychology

Human beings have always been curious about themselves. The most frequent, if not the most intense, of these expressions of curiosity have been directed toward the mind and how it works. The mind has been most resistant to giving up its secrets—which may, in a perverse fashion, account for why we are so curious about it.

Written history provides a record of how various scholars over the centuries tried to answer questions about mental process and structure. Through the eighteenth century, attempts to study the mind used largely the methods of formal logic and argumentation as practiced by philosophers. At the same time, the methods of science were being used to produce revolutionary new insights into the mysteries of matter and energy. By the middle of the nineteenth century, a fairly substantial body of knowledge about the physical world had been developed through experiment and scientific reasoning. Even the physical characteristics of the human body were beginning to become understood and to provide a basis for the modern practice of medicine. But the mind remained recalcitrant.

It was only a matter of time before scholars would seize upon the possibility of applying the scientific method to mental processes. It is difficult to say who should be given credit for first seeing this possibility. As Boring (1950) has argued, the idea of a science of psychology was in the air, a part of the Zeitgeist, in the mid-nineteenth century.

CONSCIOUS CONTENT OF THE MIND

Wilhelm Wundt was certainly one of the prime movers toward a science of psychology. Wundt is credited with the founding of the first laboratory of psychology at the University of Leipzig in 1879. In retrospect we would probably call Wundt a cognitive psychologist. The problem he wished to deal with was human consciousness. His approach was analytic in a true scientific sense. That is, he wished to analyze consciousness into its component elements much as a chemical compound can be analyzed to its atomic constituents. His chief method was introspection, a technique practiced accurately only by highly trained observers who are capable of reporting on the content of their consciousness provoked by stimuli presented under carefully controlled conditions. The experiments of Wundt were quite modest. He dealt only with simple stimuli, such as colors, to which the mental reaction is also likely to be quite simple.

Trained introspectionists could be quite consistent in their reports about these basic stimuli. According to Wundt, this approach gave evidence of three primary mental elements: sensation, or the immediate conscious response to a stimulus; images, the mental counterpart of sensation; and feelings, an affective component. Wundt felt that these were the categories of irreducible elements of the mind and that all mental responses were composed of combinations of basic sensations, images, and feelings. The task of psychology, according to Wundt, was to describe the content of consciousness. The goal was to analyze the structure of this content. Thus, the theory that Wundt devised has often been called structuralism.

In the sense that it was concerned with the conscious content of the mind, structuralism was a form of cognitive psychology. But, although Wundt had no way of knowing it at the time, his version of cognitive psychology was self-defeating and doomed to fail. It is often said that structuralism failed because of its reliance on introspection as a method. Researchers outside of Wundt's laboratory who tried to use introspection were later to report the phenomenon of "imageless thought" or, as it might be more aptly called, "the blank mind phenomenon." Introspection on the activities that led to successful performance in simple word association tasks produced no mental content whatsoever; it appeared as though the mind could be at work without any supporting conscious content. The method of introspection seemed then, to be wholly inadequate to capture significant aspects of mental life. But history has shown that introspection, per se, was not entirely at fault. Indeed, introspection and retrospection—that is, looking back upon the events of a mental episode and reporting them—are heavily in use today as methods for exploring cognitive processes and structures, thanks to the efforts of Alan Newell, Herbert Simon, and their co-workers (Newell and Simon, 1972).

The problem with Wundt's psychology was not so much its method but rather its self-imposed limitations on the problems and issues it considered scientific. Research in Wundt's laboratory dealt almost exclusively with basic sensory and perceptual processes. The stimuli upon which subjects were asked to introspect were simple, for example, a tone or a color. Wundt himself ruled higher mental processes out of his laboratory because he felt them inaccessible to experimental introspection. Thought processes, according to Wundt, are complex and capricious. They lack the stability necessary for precise introspective observation. Being vague or ephemeral, thoughts were considered to achieve a constancy sufficient for recognition only when externalized and agreed to by consensus, as within a given society. Thinking was, for Wundt, a kind of social-psychological problem, best studied in natural, rather than experimental circumstances.

It is something of an enigma that a person so ingenious and productive as Wundt could found a new scientific psychology dedicated to the study of the conscious content of the mind, and at the same time rule out just about all interesting cognitive phenomena. Fortunately, not all of Wundt's contemporaries were similarly inclined. While Wundt struggled with the consciousness of simple stimuli, other investigators examined more complex problems using different experimental methodologies.

TIMING MENTAL EVENTS

From the notion of a personal equation employed by astronomers to correct for individual differences in the temporal recordings of star transits and other celestial events, F.C. Donders, a Dutch psychologist, working in the mid-nineteenth century, constructed a system for calibrating the time characteristics of the mind. The system is sometimes called mental chronometry. Donders's primary assumption was that the duration of a mental event can be computed from the difference between simple reaction time (RT) (one stimulus and one response) and the speed of reaction in more complex tasks which require an intervening process. For example, to measure the time to make a discrimination, Donders would determine both the speed of reaction to a single stimulus (simple reaction time) and the speed of reaction in a task that required the subject to respond to only one of two or more stimuli. In the second task, the subject has to discriminate between stimuli before responding. Only after such a discrimination can he or she respond properly. If the second task involves all of the first task plus discrimination, then it follows that the time for discrimination is the difference between the speed of reaction in the two tasks (see Figure 1–6). By similar reasoning, procedures can be designed for measuring mental events other than discrimination, such as choice, association, judgment, and the like.

This technique has been criticized on the grounds that adding components to simple reaction time might do more than introduce another step in the chain of mental events. The effect of an additional component might be to change the chain in substance. If so, then comparing tasks might be a little like comparing apples and oranges. Moreover, researchers have observed that, with practice, performance on complex tasks like those involving discrimination may actually become just as fast as performance in a simple task. If so, can this be taken to imply that discrimination time disappears with practice? Criticisms of this sort were so compelling that mental chronometry fell into disuse during the early part of the twentieth century. But, like introspection, mental chronometry has made a comeback in recent years, thanks largely to new measurement techniques developed by Saul Sternberg (1966) and others.

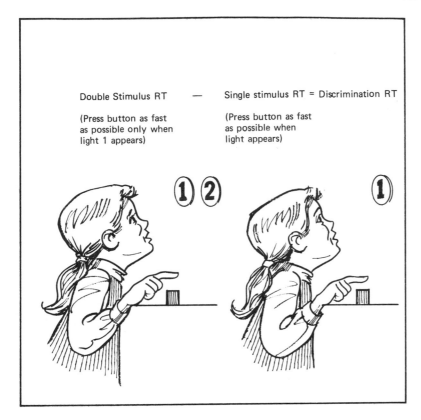

Figure 1-6. Timing mental events, here, discrimination, according to Donders.

FORMATION OF ASSOCIATIONS IN THE MIND

Herman Ebbinghaus was another nineteenth century experimental psychologist who ignored Wundt's dictum about complex mental events. Ebbinghaus set himself the task of studying how associations are formed between or among mental elements. He developed new measurement techniques, experimental procedures, and learning materials which dominated the study of human learning and memory during the first fifty years of this century.

Ebbinghaus wanted to study the formation of associations from scratch. Thus, he sought a set of materials for which any meaningful connection in the mind would be lacking at the outset. For this purpose, he invented a kind of quasi-verbal material. These nonsense syllables consist, for English-speaking people, of three letters: a consonant, a vowel, and a consonant (in that order). All known three-letter words, prefixes, or suffixes are ruled out of the list on the grounds of preexisting associations.

In addition to the material, Ebbinghaus invented a number of testing methods to track the formation of associations and their memory over time. With these techniques, he substantiated several important empirical laws including the effectiveness of repetition or frequency as a determiner of the strength of an association between two items and the reduction of associative strength over time (see Figure 1–7). He was also able to demonstrate that, in a list of nonsense items which an individual learns in serial order, not only direct associations between successive items in the list but also remote associations between non-adjacent items and backward associations between an item and its predecessors are formed. There is a great deal of content in Ebbinghaus' work, some of which will be encountered later in this book (see, for example, the discussion of forgetting in Chapter 4). For now, the important point to grasp is that Ebbinghaus was responsible for inaugurating an intensely active field of research in cognitive psychology, the study of human memory.

A BIOMODAL VIEW OF MEMORY

William James was the first significant American psychologist. Like Ebbinghaus, James studied memory. Unlike Ebbinghaus, whose work focussed on empirically based laws, James did few if any experiments. He was, rather, a theorist or systematizer. His ideas, set forth in his *Principles of Psychology* (1890), portray human consciousness as a dynamic stream of events and processes that assist the organism in its adaptation to an often hostile environment. Except for its greater intricacy, the mind, according to James, is no different from any organic structure, such as the heart or the lungs, which plays a vital role in the functioning of the whole organism. The human mind has evolved to a point where its functions are more versatile and pervasive than any other single system.

James was the first to offer a scientific theory of memory. To remember, according to James, is to think about something that was previously experienced but

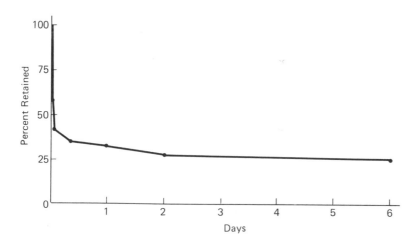

Figure 1-7. The forgetting function. An empirical law established by Ebbinghaus. These data show that the amount of previously learned material, in this case a list of nonsense syllables, still retrievable from memory decreases systematically over time since original learning.

was not being thought about in the immediately preceding unit of time. Primary memory is our current awareness of past experiences, the immediate focus of attention. Secondary memory is the vast storehouse of knowledge that we hold onto for a great duration at an unconscious level. James's distinction between primary and secondary memory is remarkably similar to contemporary concepts of short-term and long-term memory which we have already discussed, and is clearly anticipatory of contemporary work in cognitive psychology.

THE CASE AGAINST COGNITION AND CONSCIOUSNESS

Beginning with Wundt and extending into the twentieth century, the new science of psychology took it for granted that consciousness and the activities of the conscious mind were the primary matters to be explained. That assumption was disputed in 1913 by John B. Watson who argued that mind and other mentalistic notions had no place in science. To Watson, evidence accumulating at the time about the structure of the nervous system signified that the concept of the mind could be completely replaced by the concept of brain, nervous system, and in general by biological substructure. Moreover, the proper subject of the science of psychology, according to Watson, is that which can be observed, namely behavior or performance. Because the mind and consciousness cannot be observed, no suitable scientific data about them can be colleced. Watson's viewpoint has come to be called behaviorism. On this viewpoint, cognitive structures and processes are inaccessible, unimportant, irrelevant, or non-existent.

From today's perspective, it is difficult to resolve the extreme behavioristic position of Watson with what seems to be the obvious fact that much of animal and human behavior is symbolic and without gross motor accompaniments. But it is not so much that Watson denied the existence of cognition. Basically, he felt that rigorous data and more refined ideas were necessary to the development of psychology as a science. For the behaviorist, what we call thoughts and feelings are really covert behaviors which, if we knew when, where, and how to look for them, could be recorded and measured just as reliably as grosser forms of overt behavior.

According to Watson, much of what is considered mentalistic or cognitive is, in reality, miniaturized or internal motor activity. To be more specific, what we call thinking often comes down merely to talking to ourselves. Words are overt responses that we have learned to apply to objects and events in the everyday world. They are symbols in the sense that they stand for or represent things that they themselves are not. We can then "think" of these objects or events in terms of their verbal counterparts. When we "think to ourselves" about them, we are merely suppressing the overt verbal responses to a point where they become difficult or impossible for others to detect. But, with sensitive recording and measuring apparatus, we should find evidence of them in minute laryngeal movements or sub-audible speech.

Watson's position on this matter is sometimes called the motor theory of thinking and indeed, experimenters working with newly developed electromyographic techniques in the 1920s and early 1930s were able to show that thoughts (for example, imagining flexing the right forearm) are accompanied by electrical signs of muscular activity (voltage changes in the right arm but not elsewhere). When we think of reciting a poem without actually doing so, electrical activity can be detected by a sensitive recording apparatus from the voice mechanism.

No one would dispute that there are muscular (or sub-vocal) correlates of thinking. Indeed, it may be that mental activity, just as life itself, is dependent in some sense on a certain level of muscular tonus. But the evidence that thinking or cognition can be reduced to physiological underpinnings has not been sufficient to convince a majority of modern psychologists that thought and action are identical. It is possible that the muscular activity recorded in the early electrophysiological experiments is merely an overflow phenomenon. That is, as thinking occurs, its neurological correlates develop and send the muscles of the body weak signals to respond. Peripheral organs are thereby activated during thinking, but comprise no central part of it. Such a position represents the antithesis of behaviorism. In this book we adopt a more moderate view that allows for facilitative support of thinking provided by some (optimal) level or muscular tonus, but also admits to the important role of cognitive events in the ongoing behavioral stream.

COGNITIVE ORGANIZATION

While there are many substantive differences among the approaches to cognition we have reviewed thus far, they share one assumption. They all agree that the best way to approach the study of behavior is through analysis. Scientific psychology should seek the basic building blocks of mind or behavior, whether they be sensations, associations, or conditioned responses. There is an important contrasting historical perspective on psychology that emphasizes wholes rather than parts and processes rather than structures. This is a point of view adopted by Gestalt psychologists, the earliest among them being Max Wertheimer, Kurt Koffka, and Wolfgang Köhler, who worked together in Germany in the early part of the century, before immigrating to the USA.

Gestalt is a German word with no precise English equivalent. It is typically translated as "organized whole" or "configuration." The translations capture the essence of the Gestalt movement, pointing up the contrast with scientific analysis. Gestalt psychologists argue that psychological experience and behavior neither consist of nor are compounded from static, discrete, denumerable elements that come and go in time. Rather, psychological processes are dynamic and highly organized. They take place in an ever-changing field of events which mutually effect each other. When an organism experiences its environment, it does not perceive or react to individual elements but rather to the whole configuration of forces. The properties of the psychological field are different from the simple sum of its parts.

To illustrate the argument, Gestalt psychologists often cite the perceptual phenomenon of apparent movement. It is well known that, if two lights are properly spaced and blinked on and off with appropriate timing, one continuous light moving from side to side is seen. The experience of apparent movement, which is the principle underlying motion pictures, is certainly different from what one would expect from the simple perception of the two contributing parts alone.

From a Gestalt point of view, thinking can be described as follows. A problem exists when there are unresolved tensions or stresses created by an individual's environment. The correct behavior is not obvious. The person has a perspective on the environment which does not afford an immediate solution. Thinking occurs as these stresses work themselves out. Of course, stress resolution does not occur automatically or immediately. What is required is that the problem-solver restructure or reorganize the environment. The problem-solver typically will have to take different perspectives on the environment, looking at it from several different angles before the interactions of events force a clear picture through to the solution. When this happens it is called insight. Often, the problem-solver will require external direction in order to readjust his or her perspective. When the proper way of looking at the problem is achieved, however, a solution appears almost automatically and that solution will virtually force a certain activity on the part of the problem-solver.

Recall the sequence of events leading up to Otto Loewi's solution to the perplexing problem of neural transmission. This is a prime example of thinking and problem-solving from the Gestalt perspective. Over a period of time in which multiple perspectives on the problem were taken, Loewi experienced only continuing unresolved stress. Then, by some unknown process, he achieved the correct perspective. He had instantaneous insight into the problem, resulting in its solution.

Clearly there is a strong relationship in Gestalt theory between thinking and perception. Both processes are governed essentially by the same principles, the major difference being that thinking goes on at a more symbolic (or internal) level and is somewhat less under the control of external events than perception.

Probably the most influential Gestalt research on thinking was conducted by Köhler who, in the years just prior to and during World War I, studied the activities of captive apes in a variety of problem-solving situations. As an example, there were several problems in which the animal was required to use one or more sticks as tools to pull in food that was out of reach beyond the bars of its cage. Köhler observed considerable activity among his subjects that might be called overt trial and error. But, rather than acquiring some useful habit to secure food over a series of trials within a given problem, as Watson might expect, Köhler's subjects almost invariably undertook the proper behavior leading to solution after insight into the problem. Köhler reported that his subjects might hit upon a solution to a problem accidentally but, once having seen the problem in its proper perspective, could repeat the solution without hesitation on subsequent occasions.

Duncker (1945), a more recent Gestalt psychologist, also made significant contributions to the study of thinking. His most influential work dealt with a phenomenon called functional fixedness, a form of mental set that reduces one's tendency to use a given object in a necessary problem-solving way because of some prior function which the object has served. As we will discuss in a later chapter, this is a phenomenon which psychologists still do not completely understand and is the object of research even today.

Gestalt theory is not limited to perception and problem-solving. Another focus of research is memory. The memory trace we have of an event from the past assumes a unitary, highly configured form, possibly even more rigid than the original event. This tendency toward the unification of memories is the basis for certain predictions from Gestalt theory. For example, a picture, as remembered, should be a "better figure" than it was when originally seen. That is, it should become more symmetrical and freer from irregularities. Similarly, our memories of stories should come with time to be more coherent than the original recitation of the story. Gestalt theory also assumes that an event is never truly forgotten. What happens is that its trace changes and may merge with other remembered events. Its memory trace may no longer be clearly identifiable with the original experience.

Wulf's (1922) experiments on memory for pictures provide some evidence on these matters. Subjects were shown a series of somewhat irregular nonsense figures. Some time later they were asked to draw these figures from memory. The reproductions obviously were not exact copies of the original figures shown. The interesting result is that differences between the original figures and the reproductions fell into three distinct categories, according to Wulf. In one kind of change, which he called *leveling,* the reproduced figure lacked certain details contained in the original figure. In another, *sharpening,* some part or aspect of the original figure was accentuated. Finally, there were changes of *assimilation,* meaning that the figure was regularized or normalized or made to look like something familiar. Examples of these three kinds of changes are presented in Figure 1–8. All changes are consistent with the Gestalt theory that memory drifts in the direction of simplicity, prior knowledge, and better quality.

Early Gestalt theory left its mark on contemporary cognitive psychology in a number of ways. Its insistence on the fundamental importance of perception and

Original figures   Sample reproductions

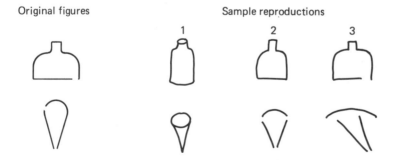

Figure 1–8. Examples of the forgetting processes observed by Wulf (1922). The subject first studies several original figures. Later he draws what he remembers having seen. Reproductions tend to be more normal (assimilated, Column 1), to be smoother and more symmetrical (leveled, Column 2), and sometimes to accent irregularities (sharpened, Column 3).

the original encoding of an event, on insight and understanding as a principle of learning and problem-solving, on mental set as a controlling factor in problem-solving, and on memory as a dynamic process involving qualitative changes over time all influence contemporary thinking. However, these principles lay more or less fallow through most of the first half of this century. Through 1950, the dominating influence in American psychology was behaviorism. Behaviorism portrayed the organism as a mechanism that reacts to its environment in an essentially automatic way, that is, without cognition. Behaviorism, as practiced by psychologists, stripped animal and human subjects alike of "higher mental processes." Gestalt psychology can be seen as a healthy antedote to that point of view. But, perhaps because Gestalt principles were never formally developed by their early practitioners, behaviorism dominated the field. Only after the limitations of a behavioristic analysis became clear was it possible for experimental psychology to rediscover the importance of Gestalt thinking.

COGNITION: PRODUCTIVE OR REPRODUCTIVE

In its efforts to emulate the more established sciences, psychology adopted the paradigm of the laboratory. Wundt argued that introspection would only work under highly controlled conditions with observers who were trained to know what to expect and how to report it. Ebbinghaus devised artificial verbal material so that he could study the process of association-formation devoid of any influence from real life experience. The behaviorists used animal subjects to study conditioning because their environment could be rigidly controlled from birth. Even the Gestalt psychologists, during their early history, studied relatively simple phenomena with well controlled stimuli under laboratory conditions.

There are good reasons for insisting on experimental control, using stimulus materials whose properties are well known and response procedures that delimit possibilities for action. All of these techniques help to establish conditions that can be replicated in different laboratories. If the results are replicable, then we are more certain that we have a useful fact or principle. But one can carry the insistence on rigorous procedures too far, to the extent of eliminating important psychological processes that might otherwise be observed. This was the argument of Sir Frederick Bartlett (1932) about the study of memory and cognition by psychologists in the early part of this century. In particular, Bartlett felt that Ebbinghaus and other early investigators of verbal memory had more or less excluded any possibility of important real life memory processes from occurring in their experiments by using highly artificial pseudoverbal material. The limitations imposed by this material so constrained what a learner might be able to demonstrate in the experiments that the basic phenomena of learning and memory could not thereby be studied.

Bartlett's theory was a lot like William James's. He felt that the mind is a constructive force—that when a person senses any new information, the mind constructs a representation. Bartlett was particularly interested in memory for verbal materials. Thus, he had subjects read stories and later studied their reproductions of those stories. The stories were purposefully somewhat ambiguous to allow maximal room for constructive processes to operate. Just as story comprehension is constructive, according to Bartlett, memory is largely reconstructive. That is, when a person tries to reproduce a story from memory, he or she works from the representation constructed during initial reading to reconstruct the story. The representation was described by Bartlett as a schema, a general outline of the original story with a few details attached. At the time of retention, the subject calls not only upon the scheme and those details that happen to be included, but also upon his or her general stock of ideas, knowledge, interests, and so forth to round out the reproduction into a consistent and coherent product. Thus, memory, in general, corresponds only in a rough and approximate way to the original event. What we tend to remember is the gist of what we have experienced rather than a verbatim copy.

THE RE-EMERGENCE OF COGNITION

Important as Bartlett's point about the dynamic properties of memory seems to be, it drew only modest attention from experimental psychologists in the USA. Indeed, from the early 1920s, when the behaviorists assumed dominance, through the 1950s, the study of cognition can be described in terms of a very few fragmentary and isolated efforts that were at most minor curiosities to behavioristically-oriented psychologists. There are reasons for this. Behaviorism made some real progress toward understanding basic issues in psychology over this period of time. The progress was both methodological and substantive and people were excited about this progress. The accomplishments were impressive. Students of the field were less concerned with the simplicity and artificiality of the problems studied than they were with being able to collect data that would stand up to close objective scrutiny and be reproducible. The methods for studying more complex cognitive processes were not well developed at the time nor were cognitive theories as clearly and precisely articulated as those provided by behaviorism. Thus, sorties into the study of thinking tended to be dismissed as crude and imprecise and as exercises in mentalism rather than science.

But the problems of cognition were too important to be ignored for long. Beginning in the late 1940s, psychologists, began to take a serious look once again at cognitive processes. The reasons for this redirection in the field and the re-emergence of interest in cognition are complex and not entirely clear. But we can point to certain factors that were certainly involved. First of all, weaknesses in the behavioristic approach to psychology were beginning to become more obvious. As investigators attempted to extend principles of conditioning, the fundamental learning process according to behaviorists, to complex human behaviors involving verbal learning, concept-formation, and problem-solving, the limitations of this approach began to show. Conditioning analyses of how it is that a person commits verbal material to memory or solves a problem in chess were in fact attempted but were essential failures. The theoretical accounts involved long strings of conditioned response connections that were simply too cumbersome to capture what seemed obvious even to an unsophisticated observer. Thus, because questions about memory and problem-solving were obviously important, researchers began to look for other theoretical and methodological ideas.

New ideas were becoming available at the time through allied fields of investigation. One such development came out of communications engineering, a field concerned with the design of electromechanical equipment for transmitting information. In the late 1940s, Shannon and Weaver (1949) developed what has come to be called information theory. The theory analyzes messages into bits of information which are basically binary or "go/no go" decisions. Messages are produced by a transmitter (for example, a speaker), are carried over channels (for example, a telephone line), and are accepted by a receiver (for example, a listener). Fragments of the original message may be lost at any point in the system, because of articulation problems on the part of the speaker, noise problems in the channel, or receptor problems in the listener. Information theory provides a way of measuring how much information is available at each point in the communications system. Moreover, it identifies conditions or variables which can either enhance the probability of information transmission (for example, putting repetition into the message) or reduce it (for example, providing a channel with limited capacity for carrying information). The importance of information theory for psychology is not so much as a natural cognitive theory but as a model for talking about complex levels of performance involving speaker and listener interactions.

Another development impacting on psychology in the 1950s was work in linguistics by Noam Chomsky (1957) and his students. At that period of time in psychology, the dominant theory claimed that verbal memory was based on the establishment of item associations. Linguists pointed out that if this was all there was to it, language could be nothing but mere repetition of what had already been heard or learned. But it is obvious that our use of language is creative in the sense that we are able to utter and to understand totally novel mesages. In fact, it is theoretically possible to show that a competent speaker of any language has the ability to create and to understand an infinity of different meaningful sentences. This and other observations led Chomsky to develop a linguistic theory based on the distinction between competence (or knowledge) and performance (or action). Competence is described of a set of abstract rules, some of which are part of our biological heritage, for interpreting and generating linguistic utterances. These rules have no concrete realizations. They do not appear in words or as a part of meaningful utterances. They nonetheless provide the basis on which we interpret and, in turn, generate messages. Such a theory is far removed from the simpler associative theory of language which predominated in psychology. It drew the attention of psychologists for its power to account for some aspects of language which, prior to that time, had not been given an adequate psychological interpretation.

Finally, and perhaps more than any other event, we can point to the modern electronic computer as an impetus to the re-emergence of interest in cognitive processes. A computer is a system for processing symbolic information. The information is fed into the system, operated upon, transformed, stored, and in other ways manipulated so as to produce a programmed output. If a machine can accomplish these cognitive tasks, often referred to by the behaviorists as mentalism, why not human beings? If we understand how a machine can be built to encode information maybe that would tell us something about how human beings encode information into their memories.

The computer has become the dominant metaphor for cognitive psychology. Computer programs, designed to simulate human behavior, provide the primary components of theory in psychology. Successful simulations of expert behavior have given rise to a new subfield called artificial intelligence. In general, we try to understand human cognitive processes in terms of what we know about their electronic counterparts. There is a danger of overextending this form of reasoning, of course, but that's part of another story. The point to be understood here is that developments in computer science were another impetus to the redirection of the field in psychology.

Conclusion

So, by the mid-1950s, the stage was set for a new brand of scientific psychology. The contribution of behaviorism had peaked and was on the wane, as the constraints of conventional psychological theory became increasingly more obvious and vulnerable. New developments in parallel fields became a welcome source of new ideas about human behavior. People like George Miller (1956) adopted the paradigm of information theory to provide a new approach to the study of speech, judgment, and decision. Herbert Simon, Alan Newell (see Newell & Simon, 1972) and their students developed a highly influential theory of problem-solving based on an analogy between human beings and electronic computers. Richard Atkinson and Richard Shiffrin (1968) developed a theory of human memory based on notions of information-processing and analogies with information storage mechanisms in the computer. Chomsky's transformational grammar was the impetus to a new sub-area of research within cognitive psychology called psycholinguistics, the study of how languages are learned, remembered, and used, and of how linguistic variables influence human behavior.

By the mid-1950s, cognitive psychology had experienced a rebirth. Cognition, cognitive processes, and cognitive structures are the dominant theoretical ideas in psychology today. They guide our empirical and theoretical work in almost all problem areas, from animal learning and motivation through psychopathology. The aim of the remainder of this book is to review what we have come to know as a consequence of research in cognition over the last twenty-five years.

TWO

Sensory Memory and Recognition

Outline

The most elementary memory processes are those that constitute our sensory memory. We use the term "sensory" here because the memory processes resemble sensation or perception. Sensory memory is a continuation or persistence of the processes involved in perceiving a stimulus when that stimulus is no longer physically present.

Although we no doubt have a sensory memory associated with each of our senses, psychologists have studied in depth only two types of sensory memory—those involving the auditory and visual senses. Auditory sensory memory is often called "echoic" memory because it resembles an echo. The auditory stimulus (a spoken word or noise) seems to keep ringing in our ears even when the sound has ceased. Visual sensory memory is typically called "iconic" memory. When we still seem to see a visual stimulus such as a slide even when it is no longer in view, we are actually experiencing that stimulus from iconic memory. Unlike an afterimage, which may have properties complementary to that of the original stimulus, the iconic image corresponds precisely to the original stimulation.

The sensory memory representation of a stimulus resembles our original perception of the stimulus. But that representation is much too detailed for us to keep very long. If we want to retain information about a stimulus for more than a second or so, we must represent the stimulus in a more compact form. It is easy for us to devise a simpler representation for stimuli that are familiar to us. If we recognize the stimulus, we can represent it with its name or another symbol that refers to it. If we do not recognize the stimulus as a whole, we may still be able to identify its component parts. (We shall address this process of stimulus pattern recognition at the end of this chapter.) Once we have identified the stimulus and formed a simpler representation of it, we no longer have to rely on our sensory memory. A more durable, though less veridical and complete, memory is available for retaining the coded information. However, this memory representation is still short lived compared to the relatively permanent storage we can accomplish by thinking about the stimulus and associating it with other events in our lives. As we learned in Chapter 1, the intermediate representation that is used after stimulus recognition is called short-term memory and it contrasts with the more persistent long-term memory. In Chapter 3 we will be concerned with the short-term memory processes, and long-term memory will be the focus of subsequent chapters.

Sensory Memory

ECHOIC MEMORY

Stimulus Suffix and Modality Effects.   Let us begin our discussion of echoic memory with a demonstration. We will make use of a technique made popular by Robert Crowder and John Morton (1969) called the "stimulus suffix effect." You will need to get together a group of your friends to conduct this demonstration, since the stimulus suffix effect, like many findings in cognitive psychology, requires the combined observations from a number of trials and subjects. In your job as experimenter you will read to your friends eight lists of nine digits, each list containing the digits 1 to 9 in a different arrangement. Your friends' task will be to recall the digits in the order specified on each list, writing them down from left to right. The eight lists of digits are divided into two blocks of four trials. The first four lists constitute the "control trials"; they will include only the nine to-be-remembered digits, and you should indicate when each list is complete by clapping your hands as a cue to your friends that they can begin their recall responses. The last four trials are "suffix" trials. On these trials the digit 0, which will never be included as a to-be-remembered digit, will follow each list and will be the cue to begin responding. Make sure that your friends understand that they are not to include the final 0 in their responses, that it, like the clap on the control trials, is merely a recall cue. In order to make certain that your friends respond with exactly nine digits on every trial, ask them to form a response grid with eight rows (one for each trial) and nine columns (one for each digit). The eight lists of digits are shown in Table 2–1. Read the digits at a rapid pace (about two per second) and an even tempo.

Table 2-1. *Eight lists of digits for demonstration of suffix effect*

TRIAL TYPE	DIGITS									
Control	6	9	4	2	7	3	1	5	8	
	7	6	2	3	9	4	5	1	8	
	1	3	6	5	2	4	7	9	8	
	8	4	5	9	1	6	7	3	2	
Suffix	6	3	7	2	5	4	1	8	9	0
	6	5	3	7	2	1	4	8	9	0
	2	7	4	5	1	3	9	8	6	0
	4	6	3	5	8	9	1	2	7	0

The findings from this demonstration can be summarized by computing for each condition a function known as a "serial position curve." In order to derive the serial position curve, each digit position (column in the response grid) must be examined in turn. Considering just the first four lists (control trials), add up the number of correct responses made by your friends to the first digit (in the first column); then do the same thing for the second digit; and so on. You should end up with nine numbers, one for each position in the list. These numbers can be plotted on a graph with the nine serial positions forming the horizontal axis and the numbers of correct responses forming the vertical axis. When the nine points on the graph are connected with straight lines, the result is the serial position curve for the control condition (see Figure 2-1 for an idealized curve). Doubtless the curve you found, like the idealized curve in Figure 2-1, has a bowed shape (like a bow used in archery), with a greater frequency of correct responses in the first and last serial positions than in the middle. The advantage for the few initial positions is known as the "primacy effect," whereas that for the final position is the "recency effect."

Now consider just the last four lists (the suffix trials) and form a serial position curve for them in the same manner. Most likely, as in Figure 2-1, you will find that the serial position curve for the suffix condition closely resembles the curve for the control condition at all positions but the last. The large recency advantage for the final position in the control trials is not evident in the suffix trials. The relative disruption of performance on the final digit in the list for the suffix trials constitutes the stimulus suffix effect.

Although a number of explanations have been put forth for this effect (see, for example, Kahneman & Henik, 1981; Spoehr & Corin, 1978; Nairne & Walters, 1983), the most popular explanation is that proposed by Crowder and Morton (1969). They argued that the suffix effect can be explained by postulating an auditory sensory memory. They did not call this memory "echoic" but rather gave it a new name, "precategorical acoustic store" or, for short, PAS. This storage mechanism is limited in capacity—holds only a limited number of digits at a given time, perhaps only one. It has a rapid decay rate—holds those digits for only a short interval of time.

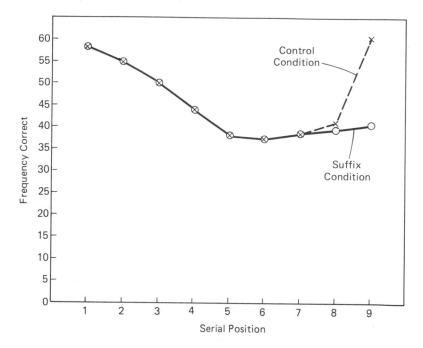

Figure 2-1.   Idealized serial position functions for the suffix and control conditions.

In the control condition the item at the end of the list is recalled better than the earlier items because it is retained in PAS. It is as though we can still hear the last digit ringing or echoing in our ears when we attempt to recall the digit string. Why is performance worse on the final item in the suffix condition? The suffix 0 is presumed to have its effect by substituting itself for the final item in PAS. Since PAS is strictly limited in capacity, the 0 takes up the slot in PAS that would otherwise be held by the terminal list item. Instead of the last digit resounding in our ears, the echo we hear contains the suffix digit 0. Thus, according to this theory, we have little or no control over what enters PAS; the redundant 0 enters PAS and takes up space there, even if we try to prevent it.

What kind of evidence did Crowder and Morton put forth for their PAS model? Perhaps the most important evidence derives from the parallel nature of the "modality effect" and the suffix effect. The modality effect in the digit span task is the difference in serial position functions between auditory and visual methods of presenting the digits (see, for example, Conrad & Hull, 1968). In other words, the modality effect is produced by comparing a condition like the control condition in our demonstration, in which the digit string is presented auditorily, to a new condition in which the digits are not heard but are rather presented visually, say on cards or slides. In both cases, only the digit string, no redundant suffix, is presented. Whereas digits presented auditorily yield the bow-shaped serial position curve exemplified by our control condition, digits presented visually yield a curve that has a smaller recency advantage and is remarkably similar to the suffix curve in our demonstration (see Figure 2–2 for the idealized curves).

These results make sense according to the PAS model. The final digits when they are presented auditorily, but not when they are presented visually, would have the advantage of being recallable from PAS. The modality effect has a straightforward practical implication: If you want to recall a telephone number, or some other short list of words, say it aloud to improve your memory for the end of the list.

One important property of the auditory sensory memory postulated by Crowder and Morton in their PAS model is that, as its name implies, the system is *precategorical*, occurring at a time prior to categorization or naming of the stimulus. This memory is thus affected by variables relating to the sound but not the name of the stimulus. A series of experiments by Morton, Crowder, and Prussin (1971) demonstrated this property of PAS by establishing that postcategorical properties of the suffix such as its meaning, frequency of occurrence in the language, and emotionality do not influence the magnitude of the suffix effect, whereas precategorical properties of the suffix such as its apparent spatial location, timbre, and pitch do determine the size of the suffix effect. As an example, let us review in detail one of the experiments in their series. This experiment included five different conditions, and in all of these conditions to-be-remembered digit strings were presented binaurally through earphones. The conditions differed in the presence or nature of the suffix which followed the digit string. In condition 1, the digit string on each trial was terminated by the binaural suffix "nought" (the experiment was conducted in England and this is the English word for "zero"). In condition 2 the suffix was

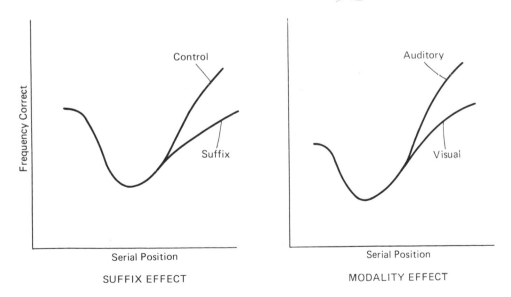

Figure 2-2.   Idealized serial position curves illustrating the suffix and modality effects.

the same except that it was presented monaurally (through earphones to only one ear) instead of binaurally. The binaural suffix "recall" was presented in condition 3, and condition 4 involved a binaural random word suffix which was not redundant but rather varied from trial to trial even though it was not to be recalled. Finally, no suffix at all was presented in condition 5, the control condition.

What do you think were the results? You might have expected that the binaural condition involving the suffix word "nought" would yield a larger effect (a greater reduction in the recency advantage) than would the binaural conditions with the suffix "recall" or the randomly chosen suffix word, since the word "nought" belongs to the same category (digits) as the to-be-remembered items. You might predict further that the random words would yield a more pronounced suffix effect than the word "recall" since that word was completely predictable. However, none of these predictions were verified: There were no differences among these conditions, which all showed the standard suffix effect when compared to the control condition. In contrast, the monaural suffix condition, although it was not different from the binaural suffix conditions at the early serial positions, did differ at the last serial position; it did not produce as much of a decrement in the recency advantage (see Figure 2–3). This finding makes sense in terms of the PAS model be-

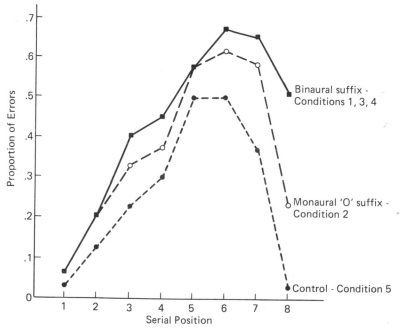

Figure 2-3. Results from the suffix experiment by Morton, Crowder, & Prussin (1971, Experiment II). (Source: Redrawn from Figure 2, in Morton, J., Crowder, R.G., & Prussin, H.A. [1971]. Experiments with the stimulus suffix effect. *Journal of Experimental Psychology Monograph, 91,* 169–190. Copyright 1971 by the American Psychological Association. Reprinted by permission of the author and the American Psychological Association.)

cause the digit string was presented binaurally so that it could be distinguished acoustically from the monaural suffix but not from any of the binaural suffixes. It thus seems that subjects can block out a suffix from PAS if it differs from the stimulus digit string in some precategorical acoustic features, but not if it differs along some features only recognizable after categorization.

Perhaps the most important acoustic variable shown to influence the suffix effect was elucidated in a later study by Crowder (1971). In this work Crowder showed that the suffix effect depends on the type of linguistic information being remembered by the subject. When the memory span strings consisted of syllables that differed only in their consonants (/ba, da, ga/), there was no suffix effect, but the typical suffix effect did result when the strings were composed of syllables that differed only in their vowels (/gæ, ga, gʌ/). Further, as would be expected on the basis of the relationship between the suffix and modality effects, there was no recency advantage for auditory presentation of the consonant lists nor a difference between auditory and visual presentations of consonants, but the typical modality effects did occur for the vowel lists. It thus appears that information about vowels, but not that about consonants, is stored in PAS.

Categorical Perception Effects.   How can we make sense of these differences between vowels and consonants? This pattern of results is consistent with the findings in the field of speech perception where a special mode of processing linguistic information has been identified and is called "categorical perception." Stimulus dimensions that are perceived categorically are processed in a manner that is qualitatively different from the way most stimulus dimensions are processed. For most dimensions, we can discriminate between many more stimuli than we can identify. For example, we can tell that two sounds differ in loudness even if we describe them with the same label, say "soft." Specifically, if we are given a long list of stimuli varying along a single dimension (such as loudness) and asked to identify each in turn by placing it in a particular category or giving it a specific name, we can perform accurately as long as we are limited to about seven categories (see Miller, 1957). We begin to make many errors on such an identification task if more than seven categories or names must be employed. In contrast, if we are given pairs of stimuli and asked to discriminate between the two members in a pair by judging whether they are the same or different, we can perform accurately even when we are given thousands of stimuli differing along a single dimension. In other words, we can easily judge that two stimuli sound different, say in loudness, even if we would give those two sounds the same name or place them into the same loudness category when asked to identify them.

The situation is quite different, however, when we are dealing with stimuli that are categorically perceived. For such stimuli discrimination is no better than identification. In the case of categorical perception, we can tell that two stimuli are different only when the two stimuli come from different categories or have different names. This special form of processing has been demonstrated only for linguistic stimuli (although there is some debate about this conclusion; see, for example, Cutting, 1982) and only for some types of linguistic sounds. It has been shown that consonant sounds, especially stop consonants (/b/, /d/, /g/, /p/, /t/, /k/) are categorically perceived, whereas vowel sounds are not. In order to reach this conclusion, an acoustical analysis of vowel and consonant sounds was necessary so that appropriate sets of speech stimuli could be generated. This important work was achieved at Haskins Laboratories by Alvin Liberman and his colleagues (Liberman, Cooper, Shankweiler, & Studdert-Kennedy, 1967).

These investigators analyzed speech sounds by means of a device known as a sound spectrograph, which reveals the frequency of the sound stimuli as a function of time. Spectrographic plots of naturally produced speech show that acoustic energy is concentrated within a small number of frequency regions which are called "formants." Formants are typically numbered in ascending order of frequency; the first formant is the lowest in frequency, the second formant is the next highest in frequency, and so on. Schematic spectrographic plots showing just the first two formants are given in Figure 2–4 for the syllables /be/, /de/ and /ge/. Note that each plot can be divided into two portions—one in which the formant levels are rapidly changing and one in which they remain constant for a relatively long period. The portion of rapid change is referred to as the "formant transition," and the constant portion as the "steady state" formant level. It has been found that consonant-vowel syllables that differ only in their consonant sounds, like the set /be/, /de/, /ge/, yield spectrographic plots that have the same steady-state formant levels but differ in the size and direction of the formant transitions, as shown in Figure 2–4. In contrast, variations in the vowel sound are accompanied by changes in the steady-state formant levels.

With this information about spectrographic plots of speech sounds and with the aid of a special device known as the "pattern playback," researchers have been able to construct the speech stimuli needed for an assessment of categorical perception. By means of the pattern playback, a spectrographic plot can be converted into a speech sound, so that the location and duration of the formants can be systematically manipulated. In this way a set of consonant-vowel syllables can be

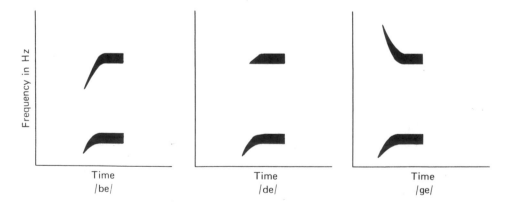

Figure 2-4. Schematic spectrographic plots of syllables /be/, /de/, /ge/.

generated that have identical acoustical properties except for their second formant transition, which is gradually shifted in its size and shape (see Figure 2–5 for spectrographic plots of the stimuli used by Liberman, Harris, Hoffman, & Griffith, 1957). The first three of these stimuli sound like /b/, the next six like /d/, and the last five like /g/. Although the stimuli in the /b/ set all are given the same name, it is clear from the spectrograpic plots that they differ in their acoustical properties.

In order to test for categorical perception, subjects must participate in two separate tasks, one involving identification or labeling of the stimuli and one involving the discrimination of pairs of stimuli. In the standard identification task, subjects hear the fourteen stimuli, one at a time, in a scrambled arrangement. Their task is simply to name each stimulus as /b/, /d/, or /g/. In the standard discrimination test, an "ABX" procedure is employed in which subjects listen to three stimuli, the first two of which (A and B) differ from each other and the third of which (X) is identical to either the first (A) or the second (B). The subjects' task is to indicate which of the first two stimuli matches the third. For consonant-vowel syllables like those shown in Figure 2–5, it has been found that subjects perform accurately on the ABX discrimination test only when the A and B stimuli are given different names on the identification test, not when they are given the same names. For example, subjects discriminate accurately when stimulus numbers 3 and 4 are used because stimulus number 3 is heard as /b/ whereas stimulus 4 is heard as /d/. On the other hand, subjects do not discriminate accurately when stimulus numbers 2 and 3 are

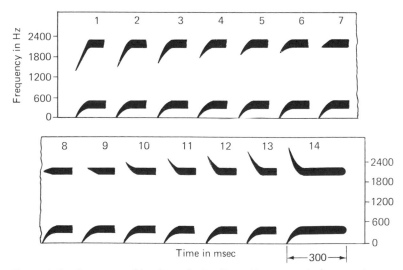

Figure 2-5. Spectrographic plots of stimuli used in categorical perception experiment by Liberman, Harris, Hoffman, & Griffith (1957). (Source: From Liberman, A.M., Harris, K.S., Hoffman, H.S. & Griffith, B.C. [1957]. The discrimination of speech sounds within and across phoneme boundaries. *Journal of Experimental Psychology, 54*, 358–368. Copyright 1957 by the American Psychological Association. Reprinted by permission of the author and American Psychological Association.)

used, since these are both given the same label, /b/. Note that in acoustical terms, the difference between stimuli 2 and 3 is as great as that between stimuli 3 and 4; however, stimuli 2 and 3 are in the same category whereas stimuli 3 and 4 are in different categories.

This pattern of results is the hallmark of categorical perception—discrimination is no better than identification. Whereas consonants have been shown to be categorically perceived with these procedures, vowel stimuli do not yield the same pattern of results. By systematically varying the steady-state levels of the formants, a set of vowel stimuli can be generated for use in identification and discrimination tasks like the consonant stimuli shown in Figure 2–5 (see, for example, Fry, Abramson, Eimas, & Liberman, 1962). In the case of vowels, however, subjects have been found to be able to discriminate accurately between two different stimuli even when they are given the same label; discrimination is better than identification (see Healy & Repp, 1982, for a more detailed discussion of the differences between vowels and consonants in this regard).

Thus, vowels and consonants differ in the way they are perceived—consonants but not vowels are perceived categorically—and in the way they are remembered—vowels but not consonants are stored in PAS. Can these two findings be related? Crowder (1975) and other investigators (for example, Darwin & Baddeley, 1974) claim that it is the memory result which is the more fundamental of the two. Crowder remarks that the evidence for categorical perception of consonants derives from experiments which may be considered minimal memory tests. Consider the ABX discrimination test. A list of two sounds, A and B, is presented and then a third sound X is presented for recognition as the first or the second. The recognition decision in the ABX task could be based on either or both of two types of memory—memory for the name of the stimuli (postcategorical short-term memory) or memory for the sound of the stimuli (precategorical sensory memory). If there is no PAS representation available for consonants, then the recognition decision about X would have to be based only on the names assigned to A and B, which would naturally yield a result indicating accurate discrimination of the A and B stimuli only when they are given different names.

ICONIC MEMORY

Have you ever tried to read and report the characters on a license plate of a car approaching you rapidly on the other side of the highway? If so, you might have found that you could not successfully report all of the letters and numbers but rather stopped after the first four or five. A similar situation occurs in the experimental laboratory when subjects are shown a display of characters flashed briefly on a screen with a device known as a tachistoscope, or t-scope. The t-scope, which is just a fancy slide projector, gives the investigator precise control over the duration of the display. When the display is very brief (up to about ½ second), it has been found that even if as many as twelve letters are displayed, subjects can report only about four or five of them. Why are the reports so severely limited? Is it that we only have a chance to store in memory four or five letters, or do we store more characters in memory initially but lose their memory representations very rapidly so that they are not available when we need them? The second alternative was given support by a set of elegant experiments conducted by George Sperling (1960) and described in his doctoral dissertation. Sperling's experiments pointed to the existence of a rapidly decaying memory system which has an impressive capacity to store visual information. This visual sensory memory, called "iconic" memory (Neisser, 1967), is the visual analog to echoic memory and has many of the same properties. However, the two memory systems differ in at least two important respects: Whereas echoic memory is severely limited in capacity and may contain only a single item, the capacity of iconic memory is much greater, and whereas echoic memory may last at least three seconds (see Cowan, 1984; Crowder, 1982), the duration of the iconic trace is much briefer.

Partial Report Results. Sperling was able to achieve his breakthrough in our understanding of this system by making use of a trick which is commonly used in the classroom. If we want to discover how much of the material in a given course a student has learned or stored in memory, we do not ask the student to tell us everything he or she knows. Rather, we ask the student a limited set of questions about the material and then reason that if the student answers, say, 75 percent of our questions, then he or she knows about 75 percent of the material in general. Of course, in order for this trick to work we must make sure that the student has no way of anticipating the questions we are going to ask. If the students could guess in advance what the questions would be, then they might decide to study only the material relevant to those questions and ignore the rest of the course material. Under such circumstances it would certainly not be reasonable to assume that a student who answers 75 percent of the questions accurately knows 75 percent of the course material.

With these considerations in mind, Sperling, like previous investigators, briefly presented to his subjects an array of letters, but instead of asking them to report all the letters they could from this array, he questioned them about only a subset of the letters shown. Specifically, Sperling displayed an array composed of three rows of four letters. After the display had been turned off, he sounded one of three tones, high, medium, or low, the particular tone selected indicating to the subject which of the three rows to report. Figure 2–6 illustrates this "partial report" technique. Sperling then reasoned that if the subject accurately reported say 75 percent of the letters in a given row, then the subject would have stored in memory 75 percent of the total array of letters. In fact Sperling found that if he presented the indicator tone immediately after the array was turned off, the subjects typically recalled three of the four letters in the prescribed row, thereby indicating that they had been able to register in memory about nine of the twelve letters in the entire array. However, if the indicator tone was delayed by as little as a second, subjects' performance in this partial report procedure was no better than in the case of the standard "whole report" task; only four or five of the letters in the entire array were

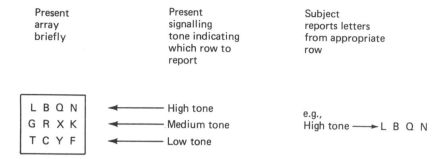

Figure 2-6. Sperling's (1960) partial report technique. (Source: Sperling, G. [1960]. The information available in brief visual presentations. *Psychological Monographs, 74,* 1-29. Copyright 1960 by the American Psychological Association. Adapted by permission of the publisher and author.)

available for report (see Figure 2-7). It is clear from these results that the critical variable in these experiments was the time when the indicator tone was presented. Sperling made sure to present the tone after the array was no longer visible, thereby assuring that the tone did not allow the subjects to concentrate their perceptual processes on the critical row. Since the tone occurred after the display was turned off, any concentration of effort must have been in terms of memory processes, not perceptual ones. The fact that the indicator tone was not useful if it was delayed by a second suggests that the relevant memory processes are very brief indeed. It seems as though for a short period of time the subjects can see the array in their

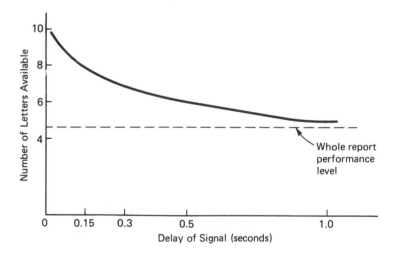

Figure 2-7. In a partial report situation, the number of letters available declines as the signal to report is delayed. (Source: Sperling, G. [1960]. The information available in brief visual presentations. *Psychological Monographs, 74,* 1-29. Copyright 1960 by the American Psychological Association. Adapted by permission of the publisher and author.)

mind's eye, after it is no longer physically present. If the indicator tone occurs during this period, they can read off from their image the letters in the designated row, ignoring the other letters in the display. However, if the tone occurs after the memory has faded or if no tone is given, the subjects may choose haphazardly the letters to be read from their image and they may only have time to recognize four or five of them altogether.

Interpretative Problems.   Quite a while after Sperling first published his work, a critical review by Dennis Holding (1975) appeared. Holding argued that the advantage Sperling found for the partial report procedure could be explained without any reference to iconic memory. Rather, two separate factors could account for the enhanced performance in the partial report task. The first factor has been called "output interference." It is a well-known finding in memory research (for example, Tulving & Arbuckle, 1963) that when recalling a list of items, the act of recalling one item can have harmful effects on the subsequent recall of the other items. For example, in trying to recall the items from a shopping list, you may have no trouble recalling one of them (say, orange juice) initially, but if you wait to recall that item after you have finished recalling the others, you may not be able to do so. The very act of recalling the other items on your list may interfere with your memory for the critical item, orange juice. Perhaps subjects did better in the partial report task than in the full report task merely because of the difference in output interference. Fewer items were recalled or output during partial report (the subjects reported approximately three of the four letters in a row) than in full report (the subjects reported four or five of the twelve letters in the display), so output interference should have been smaller in the partial report task. The second factor discussed by Holding is one mentioned earlier when considering school examinations—cue anticipation. Perhaps some aspect of the design of the experiment (say, for example, the constraint that all rows be cued equally often) allowed the subjects to anticipate correctly on at least some of the trials which row was going to be cued. Then the subjects could have focused their perceptual processes on that row before the display was turned off. Such anticipation would be analogous to learning in advance which questions would occur on an examination and concentrating study effort on these topics.

Although these concerns raised by Holding about output interference and cue anticipation are reasonable and serious, Coltheart (1975) has argued convincingly that these factors cannot, in fact, account for Sperling's findings. They leave unaccounted for the effects of the critical variable in these experiments—the time when the indicator tone is presented. Output interference and cue anticipation should be just as effective when the cue is delayed for a second as when it is presented immediately after the display has been turned off. Nevertheless, performance in the partial report procedure depends strongly on the time when the cue is presented. Since performance is no better under the partial report procedure than under the whole report procedure when the cue is delayed by a second, neither output interference nor cue anticipation could be playing a major role in this task.

An additional source of evidence that these factors are unlikely to be responsible for the partial report advantage comes from another experiment in the series by Sperling (1960; see also the later work by von Wright, 1972). In this case Sperling examined various stimulus attributes to determine which ones could serve as a basis for selecting part of the array to be reported. If the partial report superiority was due to the existence of iconic memory, and if iconic memory is precategorical as is the analogous auditory store, then only precategorical attributes should be effective in selection, not postcategorical attributes that refer to the name or category of the stimuli. Indeed Sperling found support for this hypothesis. In one condition he showed subjects an array containing both digits and letters, as in Figure 2-8. He then provided the subjects with a partial report cue that indicated they were to recall either just the digits or just the letters from the array. Unlike the cues based on spatial location, Sperling found no partial report superiority in this case. Presumably this postcategorical attribute was ineffective as a cue because the subjects could not use it to focus their processing on only the critical items in the iconic image. Subjects were not able to read off from their image only the letters or only the numbers, as they could read off only the items from a designated row, because they could determine if a given item was a letter or number only after they had processed it to the point of identification.

As further support for the precategorical nature of iconic storage, Sperling (1960) provided evidence that a physical attribute of the display had a major impact on performance. Specifically, he varied the luminosity of the visual field just after the stimulus array; the screen was either bright or dark. Sperling found that performance on the partial report task was greater with the dark field than with the bright field. This effect of brightness is consistent with the hypothesis that the partial report superiority is due to the existence of an iconic image that resembles the original sensation.

Information Flow Model.   In order to provide a coherent account for his findings, Sperling (1963, 1967) proposed a series of models that took the form of information flow diagrams of the type used in programming. The models are noteworthy because they anticipated many of the critical features of subsequent more complex models. The flow diagram for the final model in this series is shown in Figure 2-9. Note that it includes two separate memory stores—VIS (visual information store) and AIS (auditory information store). The VIS corresponds to what we have been calling iconic memory, but the AIS, which occurs subsequently in the course of processing visual information according to the model, does not correspond to echoic memory, as its name might suggest. Rather, Sperling's AIS is better identi-

Figure 2-8. A stimulus array composed of letters and numbers of the type used by Sperling (1960) in his partial report procedure in which the cue indicated which class of stimuli to report. (Source: Sperling, G. [1960]. The information available in brief visual presentations. *Psychological Monographs, 74,* 1-29. Copyright 1960 by the American Psychological Association. Reprinted by permission of the publisher and author.)

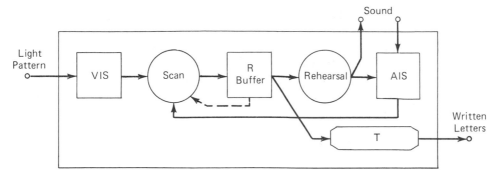

Figure 2-9. Information flow diagram from Sperling (1967). (Source: Sperling, G. [1967]. Successive approximations to a model for short term memory. *Acta Psychologica, 27,* 285–292. Reprinted by the permission of the author and North-Holland Publishing Co.)

fied with what we call short-term memory, the system that we shall discuss in greater detail in Chapter 3.

Why did Sperling label this system auditory information store? He found evidence in his experiments that the to-be-remembered digits or letters were translated into a representation based on the sound or articulation of their names. The evidence for this translation took two forms. First, Sperling noted that he often heard the subjects mumble the letters to themselves before recalling them. Second, he found a preponderance of "acoustic confusion" errors: When the subjects misrecalled a given letter they often replaced it with another letter that had a similar sounding name. For example, if subjects saw the letter *b*, they might report the letter *v* which is not visually confusable with *b* but has a name which sounds similar. We will discuss acoustic confusion errors at greater length in Chapter 3.

Between the two memory stores in Sperling's model is what he calls the "Recognition Memory Buffer," which is the location in this system where the stimulus is categorized or named. The model thus makes explicit the precategorical nature of iconic storage and the postcategorical nature of the subsequent short-term memory store. The process of stimulus pattern recognition that takes place in the recognition memory buffer is by no means a trivial one, and we will not be able to do justice to this process here (see Reed, 1973, or Getty & Howard, 1981, for fuller accounts). However, we will discuss in detail one of the crucial questions concerning this process: What are the units in which recognition is made?

Stimulus Pattern Recognition: Basic Units

Just as we can describe the physical world in terms of units of various sizes, ranging from subatomic particles to galaxies, we can analyze our psychological world in terms of processing units of different sizes. Take for example the following stimulus: *Mickey Mouse loves French pastry.* There are numerous ways in which we can break down this stimulus into units. For instance, we can describe it in terms of the many vertical, horizontal, curved, and straight line segments that it contains. Or we can list the numerous letters that comprise it. Alternatively, we can identify the five words that are included or the two phrases. Finally, we can describe it as a single unit—a sentence. There is no doubt that all of these levels of analysis are employed at different times and for different purposes. The question we are concerned with at this point is which level or levels are used initially when we are given the stimulus to recognize. Although cognitive psychologists are concerned with our ability to recognize stimuli of all types, we will restrict our discussion here to our recognition of linguistic stimuli, since they have been studied most intensively in the past. Further, as in our discussion of sensory memory, we shall separate our discussion into two sections, one involving auditory stimuli and one visual.

AUDITORY UNITS

The basic unit of speech recognition has been said by linguists to be the phoneme. Phonemes correspond roughly, but not precisely, to letters of the alphabet. There are, for example, separate phonemes corresponding to the letters *b, d,* and *g* as they are typically pronounced in such words as *bore, door,* and *gore.* However, some letters may stand for several different phonemes. For example, the letter *a* is pronounced differently in the words *act, able,* and *art.* Further, sometimes the same phoneme is represented by two different letters, as in the case of *c* and *k* in the words *cat* and *kite.* English, which makes use of 26 alphabetic characters, is composed of about 45 different phonemes. Although the phoneme is clearly a useful unit for analyzing speech, and perhaps a necessary one from the standpoint of linguistic analysis, psychological studies indicate that it may not be the basic unit in which we recognize speech. Rather, it seems that we initially process speech in terms of units larger than the phoneme, and then we recover the phoneme by way of a subsequent analytic process.

Analysis of Acoustic Signals.   We have already introduced the seminal work on speech perception conducted by Liberman, Cooper, Shankweiler, and Studdert-Kennedy (1967). As you may recall, these investigators analyzed acoustic signals by means of a sound spectrograph which plots the frequency of sound as a function of time. This analysis elucidates how complicated is the information-processing required in order for us to recognize a phoneme on the basis of the acoustic signal alone. In order to illustrate the nature of the very complex code that links phonemes to speech sounds, Liberman and his colleagues provided a schematic drawing of the first two formants of the syllables /di/ and /du/ (see Figure 2-10).

As we discussed earlier, the steady-state portions of these formants reflect vowel sounds, and the differences in the steady state levels for the syllables /di/ and /du/ are due to the fact that different vowel sounds are included in the two syllables. We also learned earlier that the formant transitions reflect consonant sounds and that, in particular, the direction and extent of the second formant transition is the acoustic cue that enables us to distinguish the phonemes /b/, /d/, and /g/. Thus, it is the second formant transition which tells us that in the case of both of the syllables depicted in Figure 2-10 we can identify the phoneme /d/. In fact, if those

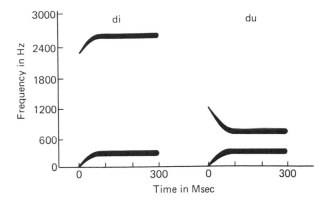

Figure 2-10. Spectrographic plots for syllables /di/ and /du/, from Liberman, Cooper, Shankweiler, & Stud-dert-Kennedy (1967). (Source: Liberman, A.M., Cooper, F.S., Shankweiler, D.P., & Studdert-Kennedy, M. [1967]. Perception of the speech code. *Psychological Review, 74,* 431–461. Copyright 1967 by the American Psychological Association. Reprinted by permission of the publisher and author.)

two spectrographic plots are reconverted to speech, using the pattern playback, the initial sounds of the two syllables seem indistinguishable; they both are recognized as the consonant sound /d/. What is interesting then is that the phoneme /d/ is the same perceptually in the two cases /di/ and /du/, but, as is clear from the figure, the phoneme is represented by two very different acoustic signals. The second formant transition informs us in each case that we are dealing with the phoneme /d/, rather than /b/ or /g/, but the second formant transition is markedly different for the two syllables. Specifically, in the case of /di/, the second formant transition rises from approximately 2200 hertz to 2600 hertz, whereas in /du/ it falls from about 1200 to 700 hertz.

To make clear just how different are these two acoustic signals, Liberman and his colleagues point out that when these formant transitions are removed from the rest of the signal and sounded in isolation by means of the pattern playback, they sound very different indeed. The transition from the /di/ pattern sounds like a rapidly rising whistle on high pitches, whereas the one from /du/ sounds like a rapidly falling whistle on low pitches.

This analysis of the syllables /di/ and /du/ reveals another related aspect of the speech code: The speech signal typically does not contain segments corresponding to discrete phonemes. In fact, Liberman and his colleagues found that they could not cut either the /di/ or the /du/ pattern so as to yield with the pattern playback some piece that sounded like /d/ alone. They found that when they cut more and more off from the last part of the syllable, they heard /d/ plus a vowel or a non-speech sound; they never heard only /d/. They explained this finding by proposing that the formant transition is at every instant providing information about both phonemes of the syllable, the initial consonant, and the following vowel; in other words, the two phonemes of each syllable are transmitted in parallel.

This analysis seems to provide convincing support for eliminating the phoneme as the basic unit of speech recognition, since it appears that phoneme recognition follows the recognition of the syllable containing the phoneme. However, in their authoritative textbook on psycholinguistics, Fodor, Bever, and Garrett (1974) argued that there are at least four problems with interpreting the sound spectrographic data in this way. First, the definition of a syllable is not undisputed. What, for instance, is the proper syllabification for the word *writing*? Does the *t* go with the first or second syllable? There is a debate among linguists about whether consonants that fall between two vowels should be assigned to the syllable containing the first or second vowel. Second, the internal structure of a syllable seems evident when hearing it. For example, the words *dog* and *date* are heard as beginning with the same sound and *den* and *mess* are heard as having the same intermediate sound. Thus an account of speech recognition will have to include a description of phonemes even if it does not include the phoneme as the first unit recognized. Third, some intersyllabic effects occur, although they are less dramatic than the interphonemic effects. That is, in some cases the acoustic form of a syllable depends to some extent on its neighboring syllables, just as, to a much larger degree, the acoustic form of a phoneme like /d/ depends on its neighboring phonemes including the subsequent vowel. Fourth, speech recognition would require a much greater information load if for every recognition decision we had to choose among about 5000 different English syllables instead of among 45 different phonemes.

Nevertheless, there is other evidence that syllables instead of phonemes are the basic units of pattern recognition in speech. Some influential evidence comes from a clever detection experiment conducted by Savin and Bever (1970). Although this study has been criticized because of experimental artifacts (see, for example, McNeill & Lindig, 1973; Healy & Cutting, 1976), it is worthy of our consideration because its elegant design clarifies what is the issue of concern. In this experiment, subjects listened through earphones to a sequence of nonsense syllables such as *bolf* and *reg*. The subjects' task was to respond by depressing a telegraph key as soon as they heard a particular preselected target. The target, given to the subjects in advance, was either a complete syllable like *bolf* or a phoneme from that syllable like /b/. The investigators made certain that there was only one instance of the target in the list so that subjects would respond to the same syllable in the list when given both types of targets. The surprising result of this study was that subjects responded more slowly to the phoneme targets than to the syllable targets even when the phoneme was the initial sound in the syllable as in the case of the targets /b/ and *bolf*. Savin and Bever argued that their results indicate that phoneme identification is subsequent to the recognition of larger phonological units like the syllable.

Analysis of Reading Problems.   Whether or not phonemes are the basic units of speech recognition, it is important to understand just how difficult is phoneme recognition. Further evidence for the complexity of phoneme recognition comes from an interesting study by Rozin, Poritsky, and Sotsky (1971), which deals with a problem found in teaching children to read. Rozin and his colleagues had noticed that many children with reading problems had particular difficulty in translating a series of visually presented letters into sounds. For example, when shown the rhyming words *cat, fat, mat,* and *sat,* these children were unable to read them reliably even after being told the pronunciation of the letters *at.* This observation suggested to Rozin and his colleagues that the child's difficulty in learning to read was not due to a memory defect or to a defect in visual perception but instead to the fact that the child was able to segment spoken utterances into syllables but unable to segment those syllables into phonemes. Clearly, in such a case, the child could be quite competent as a speaker and listener but would have difficulty with an alphabetic writing system in which the letters map roughly onto phonemes. On the other hand, such a child should have no trouble with a writing system in which symbols map onto syllables or words.

In order to test this hypothesis, Rozin and his colleagues conducted a study with nine children who had problems learning to read during their second semester of second grade in a Philadelphia school. These children were given a series of fourteen to twenty-five individual tutoring sessions, each of which lasted twenty minutes to an hour. A tutoring session typically consisted of four components: gaining rapport, tutorial in normal English reading (including the practice of letter-sound relationships and the reading of primer and preprimer material), intelligence testing, and Chinese tutoring. In this last and most important component, the students were taught to read a simplified version of Chinese with English interpretation. The point of using Chinese characters was that they map into language at the morphemic level, the level of the basic meaningful unit (roughly the word), rather than at the phonemic level. The students were taught thirty Chinese characters. These characters were read directly as English words; Chinese was never spoken. Also, the symbols were read from left to right, as is customary in English. The Chinese characters were chosen so that they could fit together to form a large number of English sentences. Typical sentences were "Good brother doesn't give man red car" and "Brother says mother uses white book."

The results of this study were dramatic. Rozin and his colleagues found that their tutoring resulted in little progress in reading words printed in the English alphabet. In contrast, tutoring with Chinese characters was extremely successful. Children who had failed to read English written in alphabetic characters after more than one-and-a-half years of schooling were taught, in a total of about four hours of tutoring, to read English represented by Chinese characters that were more complex visually than English letters. Why? The success with Chinese cannot be explained by the private nature of the tutoring session, since the children were also tutored privately in English. Further, the experiment demonstrated that the children's problems with reading English could not be attributed to difficulties in associating twenty-six arbitrary visual symbols with different sounds or in arranging these sounds so that they could be read in an orderly pattern. One factor that may account for the difference between Chinese and English is the novelty of the Chinese material, which may have given rise to an increased motivation. Another factor, as we discussed, is that Chinese characters do not map into speech at the level of phonemes, as do English letters, but instead map into speech at the level of meaningful units or words.

VISUAL UNITS

Just as phonemes are the most likely candidates for the basic units of speech recognition, letters, or "graphemes," are the most likely candidates for the basic units of visually presented linguistic material. However, experimental studies suggest that the grapheme, like the phoneme, may not be primary.

Word Superiority Paradigm.   An elegant study conducted by Reicher (1969) is relevant to this question. Reicher presented his subjects with brief displays shown in a t-scope. He used three different types of display, as illustrated in Figure 2–11: four-letter English words (*word*), four-letter anagrams (*rowd*), or single letters (*d*). Each display was preceded by a fixation point to prepare the subjects for the display and was followed by a masking field accompanied by two alternative letters that were displayed surrounding one of the positions that had been occupied by a letter in the display. The subject's task was to decide which one of the two alternative letters had been shown in the specified position of the display. Reicher's results were striking. He found that subjects were able to select the correct alternative letter more often when it had been shown in the context of a word than in a non-word. In addition, he found that subjects were more accurate in their choices when the letter was part of a word than when it was presented alone. For example, subjects were more often correct when choosing between *d* and *k* for the right-most letter

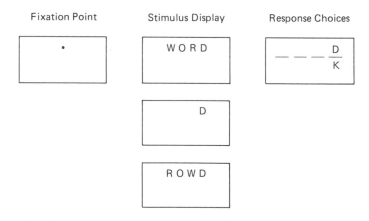

Figure 2-11.   Sample displays from experiment by Reicher (1969). (Source: Reicher, G.M. [1969]. Perceptual recognition as a function of meaningfulness of stimulus material. *Journal of Experimental psychology, 81,* 275–280. Copyright 1969 by the American Psychological Association. Adapted by permission of the publisher and author.)

position when the display contained the word *word* than when it contained the anagram *rowd* or the single letter *d*.

Normally, any advantage observed for words in such a task could be attributed to the redundancy or predictability of letters in English words—not all letter combinations occur in English words; some combinations are possible but not others (for example, *qu* is a possible combination but not *qa*). This "orthographic" redundancy may allow the subjects to infer or guess the identity of the critical letter if they have identified the other letters in the word. However, Reicher ingeniously eliminated such effects of redundancy in his experiments by making sure that both alternative letters formed an English word when combined with the remaining letters. For example, both alternatives *d* and *k* form words when preceded by the letter string *wor*. The three untested letters *wor* should contribute no information that would aid in the choice between *d* and *k*.

One explanation for these startling findings by Reicher is analogous to the explanations given for the various results in speech recognition: The basic unit of pattern recognition for visually presented text is not the letter but instead is the word, so it takes longer to recognize a letter than a word. A follow-up study by Johnston and McClelland (1974) provides dramatic support for the recognition unit explanation of this "word superiority" effect. All subjects in their study viewed four-letter words as stimuli and all subjects were to judge, in a forced-choice recognition test like Reicher's, which one of two words was shown in the display. As in Reicher's experiment, the two alternative words differed in only one letter. There were two conditions in this experiment, differing in terms of the instructions given to the subjects. In the "whole word" condition, the subjects were told to fixate the middle of the stimulus and attempt to see a whole word; at the start of each trial in the "letter" condition, the subjects were told the letter position that contained the critical letter, and were instructed to fixate this position and attempt to see only the letter that appeared there because the other letters in the word would not be relevant to their forced choice selection. The findings of this study were clear: Performance was significantly better with the whole word instructions than with the letter instructions.

These results are especially interesting because they are so novel. Johnston and McClelland claimed that their experiment was the only one known to them in which revealing which part of an array contained a stimulus made that stimulus more difficult to see. It is unlikely that this result is attributable to an experimental artifact because the investigators found the opposite pattern of results when they used four-letter non-words rather than words; in the case of non-words performance was better with the letter instructions than the whole word instructions. These findings imply that the word superiority effect is due to the fact that subjects normally recognize as units whole words rather than single letters.

Letter Detection Paradigm.   Another paradigm provides a different type of evidence that in reading, the basic units of recognition can be larger than single letters. This paradigm is illustrated in Figure 2–12. Read the instructions and perform the task described there. There are 40 *t*'s in the passage of Figure 2–12. In order to see how you performed, count the number of *t*'s you circled and subtract that number from 40 to obtain the total number of errors you made. Now count the number of *t*'s you circled that occurred in the word *the*. There are 11 *t*'s in *the* altogether, so subtract the number of *t*'s you circled in *the* from 11 to obtain the number of errors you made on *the*. Now form a ratio by dividing the number of errors you made on *the* by the total number of errors you made. By chance alone, if there was nothing special about the word *the*, this ratio should be 11/40 or .275. If the ratio was greater than .275 for you, you are among the great number of subjects who make disproportionately many errors on the word *the*.

INSTRUCTIONS:

Read the following passage at your *normal reading speed* but whenever you come to the letter *t* (typed as either t or T) encircle it with your pen or pencil. If you ever realize that you missed a *t* in a previous word, do *not* retrace your steps to encircle it. You are not expected to get every *t*, so do not slow down your reading speed in order to be overcautious about getting the *t*s.

PASSAGE:

Smoke was rising here and there among the creepers that festooned the dead or dying trees. As they watched, a spark of fire appeared at the root of one wisp, and then the smoke thickened. Small flames stirred at the base of a tree and crawled away through leaves and brushwood, dividing and increasing. One patch touched a tree trunk and raced up like a squirrel. The smoke increased, sifted, rolled outwards. The squirrel leapt on the wings of the wind and clung to another standing tree, eating downwards. The fire laid hold on the forest and began to gnaw.

Figure 2–12. Letter detection task from Healy (1976). (Source: Healy, A.F. [1976]. Detection errors on the word *the*: Evidence for reading units larger than letters. *Journal of Experimental Psychology: Human Perception and Performance, 2,* 235–242. Copyright 1976 by the American Psychological Association. Adapted by permission of the publisher and author.)

Why do subjects miss the *t* in *the* so frequently? In a series of experiments, Healy (1976) addressed this question by considering four alternative hypotheses. According to the *location* hypothesis, the position of *t* at the start of a three-letter word is critical. By the *pronunciation* hypothesis the atypical pronunciation of the *t* in *the* is what causes it to be missed so often. The predictability of the word *the* on the basis of the surrounding word context leads subjects to skip over the word *the*, according to the *redundancy* hypothesis (this hypothesis is concerned with syntactic and semantic redundancy, not orthographic redundancy). In terms of the *unitization* hypothesis, the high familiarity of the word *the* (it is by far the most frequent word in English) allows us to recognize the whole configuration as a single unit.

Healy ruled out the redundancy hypothesis by showing that the ratio of errors on *the* to total errors was just as great in a scrambled word passage as in a prose passage, even though the word *the* could not be predicted from the syntactic and semantic context in that case because the arrangement of the words was random. She also provided evidence against the location and pronunciation hypotheses by comparing the words *the* and *thy*, since the letter *t* occurs in the same location and is given the same pronunciation in the two words. In the letter detection task subjects missed many *t*'s in the very familiar word *the* but not in the rare word *thy*. Finally, Healy provided support for the unitization hypothesis by comparing detection errors in a set of common nouns (like *fact*) to those in a set of rare nouns (like *pact*) which were equated in length and the location of the *t*'s. Subjects made more errors on the common than on the rare words, presumably because the common words were read in terms of units larger than the letter whereas the rare words were read letter by letter.

Although this detection task, like the word superiority effect, provides evidence that a reading unit can be comprised of something larger than a single letter, there is a striking discrepancy between the two tasks. Whereas the familiar word configuration seems to aid letter recognition in the tachistoscopic task of Reicher, it hinders letter recognition in Healy's circling task. How can we account for this difference? In a recent study, Healy, Oliver, and McNamara (1982) provided evidence that the number of words in view at any instant is critical. Familiar word contexts sometimes aided in letter detection when only one word was seen at a time, but consistently disturbed letter detection when several words were seen at once. This effect was demonstrated in an experiment in which a passage of text was presented on a computer screen either one or four words at a time and the subjects' task was to press a response button whenever they detected the letter *t*. When subjects were shown four words at a time, they made more errors on *the* than on rare words or misspellings (*thd*), but when subjects viewed one word at a time, this pattern of results was eliminated or reversed.

These results can be understood if we make the assumption that readers move their attention to the next word in a passage once a given word has been identified, if there are other words in view. If only a single word is shown at once, however, subjects will continue processing that word and the letters it contains, even after they have recognized the word.

What are the reading units in which we process text? Clearly the units used depend on such properties as the familiarity of the words and the reading ability of the subjects (see, for example, Drewnowski, 1978). Therefore, we cannot give a single answer to the question. Perhaps the best way to view the recognition process is not in terms of the processing at any single level of analysis but rather in terms of an interaction among the many linguistic levels, as exemplified in a model proposed by Rumelhart (1977) and illustrated in Figure 2–13 (see McClelland & Rumelhart, 1981, for a more recent and quantitative version of this model).

In making our recognition decisions, we get help from our knowledge of the meaning of the text (semantic level) and its grammatical structure (syntactic level) as well as from our knowledge of the words in the language (lexical level). This "top-

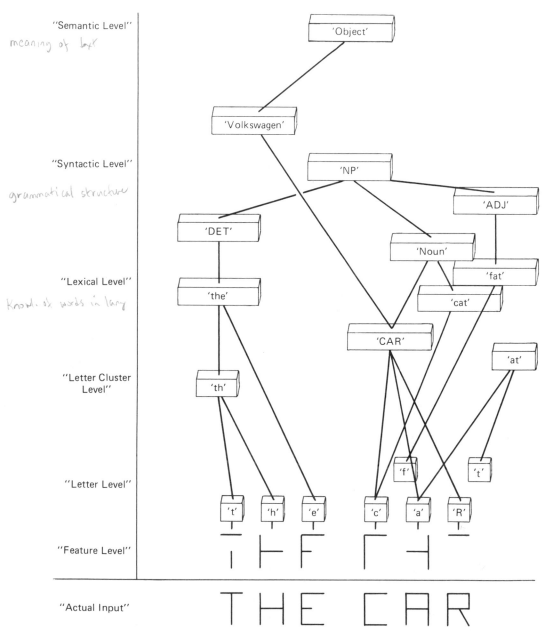

Figure 2–13. The linguistic levels used in reading printed text, according to the interactive model of reading proposed by Rumelhart (1977). (Source: From Rumelhart, D.E. [1977]. Toward an interactive model of reading. In S. Dornic [Ed.], *Attention and Performance* VI. Hillsdale, N.J.: Erlbaum. Copyright 1977 by Lawrence Erlbaum Association Inc. Reprinted by permission of the author and Lawrence Erlbaum Associates, Inc.)

down" processing enables us to decide, for example, that we have read *bat* and not *pat* in a story about flying animals. We are also aided in our decisions about which words occurred by our knowledge of the line segments (feature level) and letters that we can identify. This "bottom-up" processing allows us to determine, for instance, that the word *car* occurred instead of the word *auto* although both may be appropriate given the sentence's meaning and grammar. Our recognition decisions are not made by considering only a single linguistic level but rather by combining the information from all levels available.

Summary

For a brief time after perceiving a stimulus, we are able to retain a copy of that stimulus in our sensory memory. When the stimulus is presented auditorily, the sensory memory we use is called echoic memory or precategorical acoustic store (PAS). Only a small amount of information, perhaps only a single word, is held by PAS at once and that information persists for only a short time (at least three seconds). Not all linguistic information can be held in PAS; rather it seems we can retain information about vowels but not consonants. Evidence for PAS was derived by examining performance in a digit span test. A recency advantage is found for the last digit in a short list if the list is presented auditorily but not visually (modality effect) and if the list is not followed by another spoken word (suffix effect). The difference between vowels and consonants in PAS relates to a difference in perception. Consonants but not vowels are categorically perceived; for them, discrimination is no better than identification, whereas for most other stimuli we can discriminate between two different items even if we give them the same name.

The sensory memory we use for visually presented stimuli is called iconic memory. The partial report procedure of Sperling enabled us to discover that this storage system holds quite a lot of information (at least nine of twelve letters displayed in a tachistoscope) for a very short interval, less than a second. Like PAS, iconic memory holds information about the stimulus before pattern recognition and is sensitive to the physical attributes of the stimulus.

One fundamental question concerning the process of stimulus pattern recognition is what are the basic units in which we recognize linguistic material. Phomenes are the elementary units of speech, according to linguists, but phonemic recognition is complex and may be the basis for many problems children encounter in learning to read with our alphabet. It has been proposed instead that we recognize speech in terms of syllables and then recover phonemes only by way of a subsequent analytic process. Similarly, the basic units of reading may not be letters but rather larger units, especially in the case of familiar words. However, it seems most likely that our recognition decisions combine information from many linguistic levels, in both a "top-down" and "bottom-up" fashion.

Rocky had a little
cold c̄ a runny nose

Nov 16/1986

THREE

Attention and Short-Term Memory

We started our discussion of sensory memory in Chapter 2 by conducting a demonstration experiment in which you read lists of digits to your friends and asked them to write down each list. We found that your friends' ability to recall the last digit in a list depended strongly on the recall cue that followed the list. Performance was much better when recall was prompted by a clap than by the redundant suffix digit zero. We explained this difference by proposing that the last digit in the list was still available in auditory sensory memory, or PAS, after the clap but was displaced from PAS by the suffix digit. This explanation provides an account of how we remember the last digit in a short list, but it does not specify how the earlier digits are retained. We need to consider another memory store for that purpose, and that store has been called "short-term," or "primary," memory. What is short-term memory? Probably the clearest definition was provided nearly a hundred years ago by the eminent psychologist and philosopher William James (1890), who described short-term memory as that which is held in consciousness.

There are two fundamental questions we can ask about short-term memory. What information enters short-term memory and what information leaves short-term memory? Our discussion of short-term memory in this chapter will be focused on these two complementary issues. The first question, about entry into short-term memory, will lead us to consider issues surrounding selective attention and memory coding; the second question, about departure from short-term memory, will lead us to address the topics of forgetting, retrieval, and rehearsal.

What Information Enters Short-Term Memory?

ATTENTION

We cannot process too many things at one time. Have you ever been talking to someone on the telephone when someone else yells to you from another room? Or have you ever been watching television while someone asks you a series of questions? Experiences like these make it clear that it is difficult to carry on more than one conversation at a time. Psychologists describe such difficulty as a capacity limitation or an effect of attention. Once again a clear definition comes from William James:

> Everyone knows what attention is. It is the taking possession by the mind, in clear and vivid form, of one out of what seem several simultaneously possible objects or trains of thought. Focalization, concentration, and consciousness are of its essence. It implies withdrawal from some things in order to deal effectively with others. (1890, pp. 403–404).

Granted that we have such capacity limitations, the question arises when in the sequence of information-processing stages do these limitations operate. Does selective attention operate before Sperling's recognition memory buffer (see Chapter 2), or does it occur after stimulus pattern recognition has been completed? In other words, how much information enters short-term memory? Does selective attention operate before short-term memory to limit what enters that storage system or is the capacity limitation associated directly with the short-term memory store? These questions have been the topic of much debate among cognitive psychologists, and we can classify theories of attention into those that postulate an early limitation, at the stage of stimulus pattern recognition, and those that postulate a late limitation, at the stage of short-term memory.

Filter Theory.   In 1957 Donald Broadbent proposed a theory of attention which includes an early limitation. According to Broadbent, selection occurs on the basis of sensory channels. Such channels are defined in terms of the physical characteristics of the stimuli. For example, if different stimulation is presented to each of our two ears, the ears constitute two separate channels; if information from two different spatial locations is presented to a single ear, the spatial locations constitute two separate channels. A filter, or gate, allows information to be processed from only one sensory channel at a time. Broadbent described a mechanical model to illustrate his theory. This model, shown in Figure 3–1, consists of a Y-shaped tube which is employed in conjunction with a small set of balls. The Y tube has a narrow stem that can accommodate only one ball. A hinged flap at the junction of the stem and branches can be moved to one side or the other so that a ball dropped into one of the two branches will knock the flap aside and thereby enter into the stem while shutting out balls from the other branch. The balls in this mechanical model are meant to represent different pieces of stimulus information; the branches represent different sensory channels. The model specifies in effect that information from only one channel at a time is admitted to the recognition memory buffer.

In support of his model, Broadbent cited data from "dichotic listening" tasks in which subjects listen to two different messages which are presented simultaneously via earphones, one message to the right ear and the second message to the left. In one study of this type Broadbent (1954) required subjects to listen to lists of six digits presented in a conventional condition, each digit presented to both ears simultaneously, or to lists of six digits presented in a binaural condition, three digits to one ear and simultaneously three different digits to the other ear. For example, in the binaural condition the subjects might hear the digits 734 in the right ear and concurrently 215 in the left ear with the 7 and 2, then the 3 and 1, and then the 4 and 5 occurring at the same time. Subjects were to recall the digits in whatever order they chose. In the conventional condition, subjects' performance was very accurate, 93 percent correct, whereas in the binaural condition accuracy was depressed considerably, to about 65 percent correct. It is interesting to note

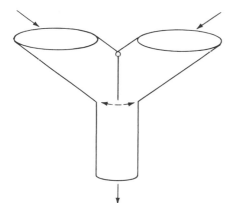

Figure 3-1.   Mechanical model used to illustrate filter theory of attention, from Broadbent (1957). (Source: From Broadbent, D.E. [1957]. A mechanical model for human attention and immediate memory. *Psychological Review, 64,* 205–215. Copyright 1957 by the American Psychological Association. Reprinted by permission of the author and the American Psychological Association.)

that subjects given the binaural lists almost always recalled all the digits presented to one ear before those presented to the other (they might respond "734215" to our sample trial), and, in fact, when subjects were specifically instructed to report the digits from the binaural lists in their order of presentation (for example, "723145" in our sample), they had great difficulty, with performance dropping to approximately 20 percent correct. How can the filter model account for this pattern of results? Subjects perform best when no attention-switching is required (so that the flap in the mechanical model stays pushed to the same side) but deteriorates as the required number of attention-switches increases. The conventional list requires no attention-switching; the binaural list with report from one ear at a time requires one switch; and the binaural list with report by temporal order requires at least three switches.

Attenuation Model. Broadbent's filter theory has been very influential among psychologists, but it has not stood up to continued experimental attack. One problem for the filter theory concerns the fact that whereas information from an unattended channel (such as one ear in a dichotic listening task) is usually inaccessible for report (see, for example, Cherry, 1953), sometimes information from the unattended channel seeps into consciousness. For example, Moray (1959) demonstrated that subjects in a dichotic listening task sometimes noticed that their own name occurred on the "unattended" channel (but see Loftus, 1974). Ann Treisman (1960) provided a vivid demonstration of this problem and resolved it by proposing a modification to the filter theory.

In Treisman's experiment, two messages were presented dichotically to subjects, one message to the right ear concurrently with a second message to the left ear. The subjects were instructed to "shadow" (repeat aloud) whatever came to one ear (for some subjects the right ear and for others the left), ignoring whatever was heard in the opposite ear. The messages to the two ears consisted of two different passages. At the start, one passage was sent to one ear and the other passage to the opposite ear, but somewhere in the middle of the recordings, the passages were switched, so that the passage originally heard in the right ear was continued in the left ear and vice versa, as illustrated in Table 3–1. Treisman found that despite the switching, subjects usually shadowed the material from the specified ear, as instructed. Three of her eighteen subjects never transferred to the other ear. However, the remaining fifteen subjects on at least one occasion did shadow one or two words from the unattended ear right after the passage switch and were especially likely to do so when the first passage shadowed was a meaningful narrative, as in the case of the passage to the right ear in Table 3–1. In order for this result to occur, the information from the unattended ear must have been processed by the recognition memory buffer. Whereas Broadbent's selective filter model cannot easily accommodate this finding, Treisman proposed instead that the filter is not an all-or-none barrier that blocks the information from the unattended channel but rather is an attenuation device that serves to raise the threshold of activation necessary for recognition, so that only stimuli that have a relatively low activation threshold

Table 3-1. *Excerpts from passages heard by subjects in a dichotic listening test, from Treisman (1960)*

Right ear	"While we were talking she would come and go with rapid glances at us
Left ear	"The camera shop and boyhood friend from fish and screamed loudly
	leaving on her passage an impression of grace and / is idiotic idea of
	singing men and then it was jumping in the tree / charm and a distinct
	almost there is cabbage a horse which was not always be the set
	suggestion of watchfulness. Her manner presented a curious combination
	works every evening is heaviest with bovine eyes looking sideways. . . ."
	of shyness and audacity. Every pretty smile was succeeded swiftly by a. . ."

(Source: Treisman, A.M. [1960]. Contextual cues in selective listening. *Quarterly Journal of Experimental Psychology, 12,* 242–248. Copyright 1960 by the Experimental Psychology Society. Reprinted by permission of the publisher and author.)

(such as one's own name or words that are expected on the basis of the preceding message context) could be recognized.

A subsequent experiment by Treisman and Geffen (1967) provided further evidence for this attenuation model of attention. In this experiment, as in the last, subjects were presented with two dichotic messages and were asked to shadow the message heard in one ear. In addition, subjects were given a secondary task which required them to tap whenever they heard a preselected target word in either ear. The investigators found that subjects were able to respond accurately to the targets on the unattended ear in some circumstances but that performance levels were much lower for the unattended ear (8.1 percent of the targets received a tapping response) than for the shadowed ear (86.5 percent of the targets received a tap). These results are consistent with the hypothesis that some but not all of the information from the unattended channel is processed to the point of recognition.

Unlimited Capacity Model. According to the attenuation model, only a limited amount of the information that impinges on our sense organs is recognized and then sent to short-term memory. Further, the model assumes that our processing of a given stimulus on one channel is disturbed by the requirement to process simultaneously stimulation from another channel. This attenuation model is consistent with results from the dichotic listening task, but it is inconsistent with findings from other paradigms, which have led to the conclusion that the attentional "bottleneck" does not occur prior to short-term memory but is rather a memory phenomenon. According to this viewpoint, proposed, for example, by Shiffrin and Geisler (1973), there is no limit on our capacity to recognize stimuli coming from different channels at the same time, and the process of recognizing a stimulus arriving on one channel does not disturb the process of recognizing a second stimulus arriving at the same time on another channel.

The most compelling evidence for the unlimited capacity model derives from the "detection" paradigm developed by Estes and Taylor (1964). In this paradigm, which was adapted by Reicher in his demonstration of the "word superiority effect" discussed in Chapter 2, subjects are shown a visual array of stimuli on a display screen. The array consists of a number of random "noise" letters along with one of two "critical" letters (say, T or F), the same pair of critical letters being used throughout the experiment. On each trial, the subject tries to determine which of the two critical letters (T or F) was present. The array is displayed for a very brief time using a t-scope, as in Sperling's (1960) studies of visual sensory memory reviewed in Chapter 2. Because of the brief viewing time, the error rate in this task is substantial so both the accuracy and latency (reaction time) of the reponses are treated as dependent variables. A principle finding in such experiments is that subjects' detection accuracy and speed decline as the number of noise letters in the array increases. For example, subjects may make more errors and respond more slowly to the stimulus AGTKP than to the stimulus GTK. Estes and Taylor interpreted this finding as evidence for a limited capacity model in which subjects scan or attend to the letters one at a time. However, in a later study Gardner (1973) argued that this finding is not incompatible with a model that provides for unlimited capacity in processing the stimulus letters so that processing of the letter in one channel (or spatial location in this case) is not disturbed by the concurrent processing of letters in other channels. Gardner showed that in order for an unlimited capacity model to account for these results it was necessary to add a decision component. If it is acknowledged that sometimes subjects mistake a noise letter for a critical letter (for example, they see the noise letter P and think that it is an F), then with more noise letters there are more opportunities for such mistaken identifications. Thus, the subjects may extract the same amount of information from the channel containing the critical letter when there are many noise letters as when there are few or none, but the subjects are more likely to make an error when there are many noise letters because their response is more likely to be mistakenly based on information from one of the channels containing a noise letter. For example, subjects may be just as certain that the central position contains the letter T in the array AGTKP as in the array GTK, but they may be more likely to make an error on the larger array because they may mistakenly base their response on the right-most position instead of the central one.

Whereas both limited and unlimited capacity models can handle the effects of array size reported by Estes and Taylor (1964), only the unlimited capacity model can handle some additional results found by Gardner (1973). In one experiment in his series, he required subjects to detect T's or F's in displays which included as noise characters items that were either maximally (7) or minimally (0) confusable with the critical letters. In the case of the confusable noise stimuli, Gardner found that detection accuracy decreased as usual. But there was no effect of array size for the nonconfusable stimuli (for example, subjects were no more accurate when they saw OTO than when they saw OOTOO).

An experiment by Shiffrin and Gardner (1972) provides even more compelling support for the unlimited capacity model because of its unintuitive results. Using the detection task, Shiffrin and Gardner compared two presentation conditions. In one condition, four items were presented together simultaneously for a fixed amount of time, say 40 msec. In the second condition, the four items were presented sequentially, one after another, with a brief interval separating adjacent items, and each item was exposed for the same amount of time as in the simultaneous condition. Thus, in the sequential condition, the total exposure time was four times greater than in the simultaneous condition. Clearly any limited capacity model would predict better performance in the sequential condition. In fact, though, for both confusable and nonconfusable displays, there was no significant difference in detection accuracy between the two presentation conditions. Whatever nonsignificant difference existed actually favored the simultaneous over the sequential condition. These results imply that the recognition of information from a given sensory channel is not affected by the concurrent processing of information from other channels.

The results from the studies by Treisman and Geffen (1967) and Shiffrin and Gardner (1972) seem contradictory. In the Treisman and Geffen task, stimulus recognition in one channel was disrupted by the requirement to process stimuli in another channel; tapping responses were less accurate to word targets occurring in the unattended ear than to those in the attended ear. In contrast, in the Shiffrin and Gardner study, stimulus recognition was just as accurate when only one channel was processed at a time as when several were processed concurrently; detection responses were no less accurate in the simultaneous than in the successive condition. How can we resolve this apparent discrepancy? Johnston and Heinz (1978) have taken an interesting step in that direction. They have proposed a "multimode" theory which is flexible and admits various modes of attention that depend on task requirements. By this theory, the shadowing task coupled with the requirement to identify word targets presumably leads to an earlier mode (the attentional bottleneck occurring earlier in the sequence of information processing stages) than does the letter detection task of Estes and Taylor.

CODING

Phonemic Coding.   How is information stored, in what format is it coded, in short-term memory? One means by which psychologists have tried to answer this question is by examining the kinds of errors subjects make in recall tasks that largely involve short-term memory. The classic study of this type was performed in 1964 by R. Conrad. On each trial of this experiment, subjects saw a list of six consonants, presented one after another on a display screen. The subjects were required to recall the consonants immediately after their presentation in the sequence they were shown. With the data from this experiment Conrad computed a *confusion matrix,* as illustrated in Figure 3–2. In this matrix, the columns stand for the letter actually presented in a given position and the rows represent the letter recalled by the subject at that position. The diagonal entries of the matrix are omitted because they reflect correct responses, as for example when the subject

MEMORY TEST

Stimulus Letter

	B	C	P	T	V	F	M	N	S	X
B	•	18	62	5	83	12	9	3	2	0
C	13	•	27	18	55	15	3	12	35	7
P	102	18	•	24	40	15	8	8	7	7
T	30	46	79	•	38	18	14	14	8	10
V	56	32	30	14	•	21	15	11	11	5
F	6	8	14	5	31	•	12	13	131	16
M	12	6	8	5	20	16	•	146	15	5
N	11	7	5	1	19	28	167	•	24	5
S	7	21	11	2	9	37	4	12	•	16
X	3	7	2	2	11	30	10	11	59	•

Response Letter (rows)

LISTENING TEST

Stimulus Letter

	B	C	P	T	V	F	M	N	S	X
B	•	171	75	84	168	2	11	10	2	2
C	32	•	35	42	20	4	4	5	2	5
P	162	350	•	505	91	11	31	23	5	5
T	143	232	281	•	50	14	12	11	8	5
V	122	61	34	22	•	1	8	11	1	0
F	6	4	2	4	3	•	13	8	336	238
M	10	14	2	3	4	22	•	334	21	9
N	13	21	6	9	2?	32	512	•	38	14
S	2	18	2	7	3	488	23	11	•	391
X	1	6	2	2	1	245	2	1	184	•

Response Letter (rows)

Figure 3-2. Confusion matrices from memory test (top panel) and listening test (bottom panel) of a study by Conrad (1964). (Source: From Conrad, R. [1964]. Acoustic confusions in immediate memory. *British Journal of Psychology, 55,* 75–84. Reprinted by permission of the author and the British Psychological Society.)

sees the letter *B* in the first position and also responds with *B* in that position. The off-diagonal entries, however, reflect confusions, or substitution errors, as for example when the subject sees *B* but responds with *C*. It is clear from looking at the matrix that the substitution errors were unequally distributed; some of the off-diagonal entries were much larger than others. Upon greater study of the matrix, a systematic pattern seemed to emerge from the error data and suggested to Conrad that subjects largely confused letters that sounded alike (for example, *B* and *V*), just as Sperling (1960) had found in his tachistoscopic studies summarized in Chapter 2. In order to test this hypothesis, Conrad compared this confusion matrix with another one which he obtained from a listening test, also shown in Figure

3–2. In the listening test, letters were heard in a background of white noise. Memory was not involved; subjects were simply to name each consonant as they heard it. Errors were made on this test, but these errors were caused by failures of perception, not memory. Nevertheless, the similarity between the error matrices from the memory experiment and from the listening test was remarkable. The relationship between the two confusion matrices was assessed by means of a rank correlation coefficient. A value of 0.64 was obtained, which is highly significant. Subjects in both tasks confused the correct letters with ones that were acoustically similar; in other words, they made "acoustic confusion errors."

This result suggests that information is coded in short-term memory in terms of phonemes, or auditory units, rather than visual properties, even when the information is presented visually and never spoken or heard, as in Conrad's memory experiment. Later work, with another technique, also indicates that short-term memory typically involves phonemic coding. In this technique the items presented in a recall task are all similar along a potential coding dimension; for instance, they may look alike, sound alike, or have similar meanings. If one type of similarity is found to disrupt recall performance, then it is concluded that items are represented in memory by the corresponding type of coding. Using this technique experimenters have found that in immediate recall tasks of the type used by Conrad and in our demonstration experiment, an ordered list of acoustically similar letters (like *B P V D C T G Z*) is more difficult to learn than a control list composed of letters that differ in their acoustical properties (see, for example, Conrad & Hull, 1964). On the other hand, lists of visually similar letters (such as *B C D G O Q R*) are no harder to learn than control lists composed of letters that are not visually similar (see, for example, Cimbalo & Laughery, 1967).

One pair of studies that employed this technique is particularly noteworthy because it illustrates clearly the difference between coding used to retain information in short-term memory and that used over longer time intervals. In one study of this pair, Baddeley (1966b) had subjects listen to a single ten-word list during four successive learning trials. Then, fifteen minutes later, after participating in an unrelated task consisting of copying digits, the subjects were tested on the list for serial recall (recall of the words in their order of presentation). Since there were fifteen minutes between list presentation and test, only long-term memory, not short-term memory, was assumed to be operating. Under these conditions, Baddeley found that lists of semantically similar adjectives—such as *big, long, broad, great, high*— were recalled much more poorly than control lists of adjectives of equal frequency of occurrence in English but with dissimilar meanings—such as *good, huge, hot, safe, thin*. In contrast, performance on lists of acoustically similar words—like *man, cab, can, cad, cap*—was no poorer than that on corresponding control lists of acoustically dissimilar words matched for frequency in the language—such as *pit, few, cow, pen, sup*. These results for long-term memory contrasted markedly to those from an earlier study by Baddeley (1966a), which was essentially the same except that testing proceeded immediately after list presentation so that short-term memory, not long-term memory, was relevant. Under these conditions, recall was poorer

for the acoustically similar lists than for their control lists, but there was no difference in recall accuracy between the semantically similar lists and their control. Thus,
phonemic coding seems to be preferred for short-term memory, whereas semantic
coding is preferred for long-term memory.

Memory Span. How many phonemes can we hold in short-term memory?
What is the capacity of the short-term memory store? Remember that the capacity
of PAS is quite limited; we may not be able to store more than one digit or letter
at a time in PAS. In contrast, we know that our long-term memory store is extremely large, essentially infinite. Just think of all the names, dates, facts, faces, words,
and episodes you can remember. The capacity of short-term memory is between
the two extremes defined by PAS and long-term memory but much closer to that
for PAS. In a classic study published in 1956, George Miller proposed that the capacity, or span, of short-term memory is equal to seven plus or minus two items. Thus,
for example, if we are given a list of digits to remember, as in our demonstration
experiment, we will be likely to recall the list perfectly if it contains only three or
four digits. We will do quite well for lists between five and nine digits long, sometimes remembering the entire sequence and sometimes not. But when the list contains more than nine digits, we will usually make at least one error. Since we know
that phonemic coding is used in short-term memory and that the memory store
holds seven items, does that mean that only seven phonemes can be remembered?
No. Miller showed that his "magical number seven plus or minus two" did not apply to phonemes, or to syllables, or to words, but rather to something more abstract
which he called "chunks." Even with considerable practice we cannot increase the
number of chunks we can hold in short-term memory, but we can increase the
amount of information contained in each chunk. For example, read the list of sixty
letters shown in Panel A of Table 3–2 to a friend at a rapid rate and then ask your
friend to recall the list immediately. Your friend may not take your request too seriously because sixty isolated items are many more than can be held together in short-
term memory. However, if the same letters are reordered in such a way that meaningful chunks can be identified, as in panel B, the same task becomes very easy.
This demonstration is reminiscent of the remarkable digit span performance exhibited by the subject SF studied by Ericsson, Chase, and Faloon (1980) and de-

Table 3–2. *Lists of 60 letters to be recalled*

PANEL A

ahiohssitsttnnesecerhuwoilshhcesvdeyberafyeeyorvornrltceaeol

PANEL B

thisisashortsentencewhichshouldbeveryeasyforeveryonetorecall

---

scribed in Chapter 1. Recall that SF after extensive practice was able to increase his digit span from 7 to 82 digits because he was able to increase his chunk size by relating strings of digits to familiar running times, just as we relate strings of letters to familiar words.

Order Information.   Now that we know the dimension along which items are coded in short-term memory and the number of items stored at one time, we can ask a more subtle question about coding: How do subjects store temporal sequence information? Subjects may very well know the identity of the letters on a list they studied (say, *B C D* and *G*) without knowing the order in which they occurred (was *B* first or second, was *D* before *G* or vice versa?). A paradigm was developed to study short-term memory that has been very helpful in throwing light on this question. The paradigm, known as the Brown-Peterson distractor task after the investigators (Brown, 1958; Peterson & Peterson, 1959) who originated it, is analogous to the following situation which should be familiar to all college students: Imagine yourself in a lecture in which you are taking notes, and imagine that in the middle of her talk the speaker defines an unfamiliar technical term, such as ACTH, and writes on the blackboard the letters forming its abbreviation. The speaker then immediately erases the letters and proceeds to describe some new and important facts. Some time later, when there is a momentary pause in the lecture, you attempt to recall the letters and transcribe them into your notes. But because of your concentration on the subsequent material you find that you have difficulty recalling the letters. Analogously, in the Brown-Peterson paradigm, a short list of items, usually safely within the memory span, is presented to the subject who is then required to participate in an interpolated task designed to prevent the subject from rehearsing the to-be-remembered items and thus cause them to be forgotten. At the end of the interpolated task the subject is required to recall the list of items.

In one experiment of this type conducted by Bjork and Healy (1974), the to-be-remembered items were four consonants, which were presented to the subjects, one after another, on a display screen. The intervening task consisted of shadowing, or reading aloud, digits which were presented, just like the consonants, successively on the display screen. The consonants and digits were presented at a very fast rate of more than two per second. This rapid presentation rate caused the recall task to be very difficult, since it allowed the subjects no time to rehearse the consonants and hence caused them to be forgotten. At the end of the intervening task subjects were to write down the four consonants they had seen in the order they had been shown. All subjects who participated in the experiment were tested for many consecutive trials. On some of these trials the subjects saw 3 digits, on some 8, and on some 18. The 3, 8, or 18 digits that comprised the interpolated task yielded three different retention intervals, 1.2, 3.2, and 7.2 seconds long, respectively. By noting and comparing the proportion of correct responses made by subjects at each of the three retention intervals, we can plot the time course of forgetting the consonants from short-term memory, as shown in Figure 3–3. Note that in this experiment, as is typical in the Brown-Peterson design, the time course is very steep;

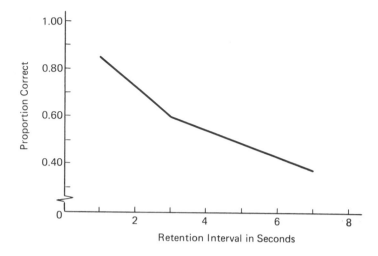

Figure 3-3. Time course of forgetting in Brown-Peterson distractor task in experiment by Bjork and Healy (1974). (Source: Bjork, E.L., & Healy, A.F. [1974]. Short-term order and item retention. *Journal of Verbal Learning and Verbal Behavior, 13*, 80–97. Adapted by permission of the author and Academic Press.)

forgetting was very rapid. This rapid forgetting is remarkable; after only a few seconds have elapsed the subjects could not correctly recall four letters just presented to them. This finding indicates clearly that the simple intervening task of reading digits aloud is effective in terms of preventing rehearsal and that information is lost from memory if it is not rehearsed.

In order to learn more about how temporal sequence information was coded in this experiment, Bjork and Healy examined one aspect of their data (which we also considered in the demonstration experiment described in Chapter 2), the serial position function, as shown in Figure 3–4 for each of the three retention intervals.

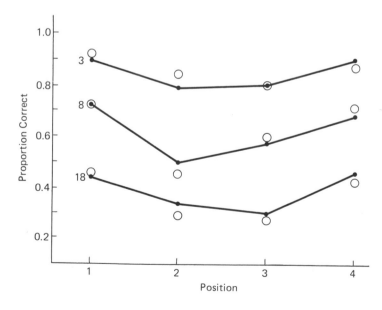

Figure 3-4. Serial position curves from Bjork and Healy (1974) study (connected points) compared with predictions (open circles) from perturbation model of Estes (1972). (Source: Estes, W.K. [1972]. An associative basis for coding and organization in memory. In A.W. Melton & E. Martin [Eds.], Coding processes in human memory [pp. 161–190]. Washington, D.C.: Winston. Reprinted by permission of the author and Hemisphere Publishing Corp.)

It is interesting to note that the curves in this case, as in the demonstration experiment, are bow-shaped; performance is better on the end items than on the ones in the middle. In addition, each of the three curves is nearly symmetrical; performance on the first and second positions is very comparable to that on the fourth and third, respectively. What caused these bow-shaped symmetrical functions? Are they in any way connected with the fact that the temporal sequence of the letters had to be remembered? In order to answer this question, Bjork and Healy analyzed their data still further by classifying each error the subjects made into one of two types: transposition or non-transposition. If the subject replaced the correct letter with another letter shown on the same trial but in a different serial position, then the subject has made a transposition error. In contrast, if the subject replaced the correct letter with one that had not occurred on that trial, then a non-transposition error occurred. For example, if the subject saw *BKPM* on one trial and responded *PKVM*, the subject would be scored as having made a transposition error in the first serial position and a non-transposition error in the third. The results of this analysis are summarized in Figure 3–5. It is clear from that figure that the bow-shaped serial position curves in Figure 3–4 were reflecting the pattern of transposition errors, which also showed a symmetrical bow-shaped function. Hence, it seems that subjects were best able to remember the position of the first and last letters they saw but often transposed the middle two letters. How can we account for this pattern of results?

In 1972, W.K. Estes proposed a simple and elegant mathematical model to account for the data we just examined (which had been collected earlier by Bjork and Healy and summarized in a preliminary technical report). More generally the model explains how we retain temporal order information in short-term memory. Estes' model is associative. However, rather than postulating associations, or bonds, linking successive items (or, more precisely, the memory representations of items), he postulates associative bonds between items and what he calls "control elements." In other words, given two items, say X and Y, rather than postulating bonds of the form X-Y, he postulates associations of the form X-C-Y, with C representing the control element. According to Estes, if the control element in such a representation is activated, as it might be given an instruction to recall, then the result would be the reactivation of all the items associated with the control element. Let us think of the control element as some aspect or feature of the current context or environment. We can then explain forgetting in part by assuming that the experimental context shifts with the passage of time so that subjects are sometimes not able to activate the appropriate control element for a given trial.

While forgetting can be explained in this general way, Estes also proposed a mechanism to explain the loss of order information per se. At the heart of this mechanism is a reverberatory loop connecting each item to its control element. Once a representation of the item has been established in memory and connected with a control element, a reverberatory loop linking the two produces a periodic recurrent reactivation of the item's representation. According to Estes, this reverberatory activity is the basis for short-term retention. Further, Estes assumes

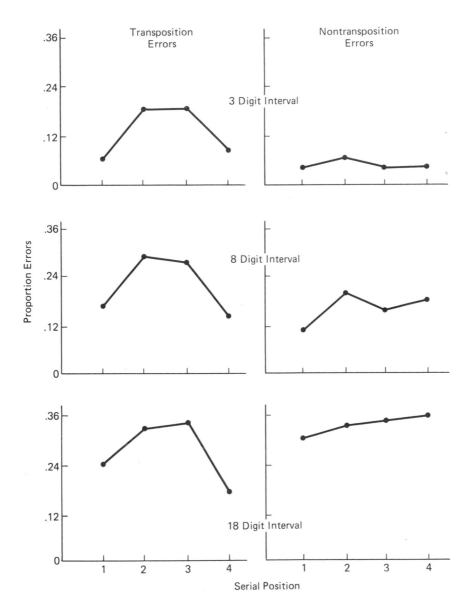

Figure 3–5. Serial position curves for transposition (left column) and non-transposition (right column) errors in experiment by Bjork and Healy (1974). (Source: From Estes, W.K. [1972]. An associative basis for coding and organization in memory. In A.W. Melton, & E. Martin [Eds.] *Coding processes in human memory.* [pp. 161–190]. Washington, D.C.: Winston. Reprinted by permission of the author and Hemisphere Publishing Corp.)

that if all the stimulus items in a sequence become associated with a single control element because the items are input together during the same context conditions, then a reverberatory loop is established for every item in the sequence with a difference in reactivation times that reflects the difference in input times. Upon activating the control element the items are reactivated in sequence, so that the timing of the reactivations provides for the primary representation in short-term memory of information about sequence or order.

How does forgetting of order occur? Estes assumes that there is some random error in the reactivations of the items in the reverberatory loops. These timing perturbations may arise from other activity in the nervous system, and as time progresses the perturbations may become so great that they lead to interchanges in the relative timing of two adjacent items connected to the same control element, and consequently to transposition errors in recall. Estes also points out that when the retention interval is filled with irrelevant distracting characters, as in the Bjork and Healy experiment which included digits, then the timing perturbations may further lead to interchanges in the ordering of the to-be-remembered items and the distracting items, thereby producing non-transposition errors at recall.

By making this model mathematically precise, Estes was able to compare its predictions to the data observed in the Bjork and Healy experiment. Specifically, he assumed that for any to-be-remembered item during any unit time interval after the string has been presented, there is a fixed probability Θ of a perturbation in timing great enough to span the interval separating adjacent items. By considering a range of values for the probability Θ, Estes was able to find a particular value which provided a good fit of his model's predictions to the serial position functions found by Bjork and Healy, as shown in Figure 3–4. The bow-shaped serial position functions occur because timing perturbations can lead to interchanges between two to-be-remembered items in either direction (forward or backward) for the middle items but in only one direction for each of the end items. Further, the functions are symmetrical, rather than showing an overall advantage for the late items, because the timing perturbations are not assumed to start until all of the to-be-remembered items in a sequence have been presented.

The perturbation model is not only able to account for the overall serial position functions but is also able to explain the separate functions for the transposition and non-transposition errors shown in Figure 3–5. According to the model, the bow-shaped functions are caused by interchanges among the to-be-remembered items resulting in transposition errors. Since non-transposition errors are assumed to be caused in part by interchanges in the ordering of to-be-remembered items and distractor items occurring during the retention interval, there should be more non-transposition errors among the most recently presented items, those presented closest in time to the intervening items. Indeed, the non-transposition errors yield a flat curve with a small primacy advantage coupled with a small disadvantage for the most recent items. In later work, the perturbation model has been extended to account for performance in more complicated task situations, and in each case it has been very successful (see, for example, Lee & Estes, 1981; Cunningham, Healy, & Williams, 1984).

What Information Leaves Short-Term Memory?

Information may leave short-term memory for different reasons and with different results. For example, it may depart from memory because it has been lost or forgotten. Or it may be retrieved from memory to be used for making a response on a memory test. Or, finally, it may be copied from short-term memory to the larger, more permanent long-term memory store. We will consider each of these departures in turn.

FORGETTING FROM SHORT-TERM MEMORY

How can we explain forgetting from short-term memory? Two primary theories have been proposed to account for loss of information from short-term memory—a *decay* theory and an *interference* theory. According to decay theory, when rehearsal is prevented so that the subjects are unable to say the to-be-remembered items to themselves, then the items will be lost from short-term memory purely as a matter of time. As more time elapses, more will be forgotten. In contrast, according to interference theory, the passage of time per se cannot cause forgetting. Instead, items are forgotten only when they are interfered with (that is, only when they become confused with or are displaced by) other similar items. The dispute between decay and interference theory has still not been resolved even though it began more than twenty-five years ago (see, for example, Shiffrin & Cook, 1978).

One of the original proponents of decay theory was John Brown (1958), who was also one of the originators of the Brown-Peterson distractor paradigm. Brown was impressed by the rapid forgetting that occurred in the distractor task with digit-reading as the task interpolated between presentation of to-be-remembered letters and their recall. Brown showed that the rapid forgetting was due to the intervening task. He compared conditions with a distracting task to those with an unfilled period in which subjects were free to rehearse the to-be-remembered items. When rehearsal was permitted, forgetting was minimal. The time course of forgetting during the distractor task then supports decay theory: Short-term memory representations decay rapidly unless they are continually reinstated through active rehearsal. Forgetting during the retention interval does not seem attributable to interference because the interpolated digits are easily distinguished from the consonants; digits and letters are not confusable because they belong to two different categories or semantic classes.

In a subsequent study, however, Reitman (1971) argued that any verbal material, whether or not of the same category, is potentially interfering with verbal material residing in short-term memory. Reitman, therefore, conducted an experiment with the Brown-Peterson distractor paradigm and with three nouns as the to-be-remembered items but with a nonverbal intervening task. Instead of working with numbers during the retention interval, the subjects were required to perform a difficult auditory signal detection task. Weak tones were sounded at random intervals through a continuous background of white noise, and the subjects were to press a key as soon as they heard a tone. This task was difficult enough to keep the subjects fully occupied during the retention interval so that they reported that they were unable to rehearse the to-be-remembered words. However, despite the fact that no rehearsal was permitted, forgetting was not evident; the function illustrating the time course of forgetting was not steep like that in Figure 3–3 but rather was completely flat. This dramatic finding—no forgetting when there was no interfering material as well as no rehearsal during the retention interval—refutes decay theory, since decay theory postulates that time alone will cause forgetting if rehearsal is prohibited. Instead, this finding supports the hypothesis that forgetting from short-term memory is caused by interference from items which are similar to the to-be-remembered items. Note that in this context similarity is not in terms of category or meaning but rather in terms of phonemic properties. Letters and digits are composed of similar phonemes even if they are not similar in meaning. This observation makes sense when we remember that typically only phonemic, not semantic, information is coded about items in short-term memory. Despite the clear-cut nature of these results, the controversy between decay and interference theories has not ended, because subsequent findings (see, for example, Reitman, 1974) have indicated complicating factors which must be considered. Perhaps at present the best way to view short-term forgetting is in terms of a combination of decay and interference.

RETRIEVAL FROM SHORT-TERM MEMORY

In order to make a response on a memory test, we must locate the to-be-remembered item in memory and then retrieve that item. Such searching and retrieving processes may not seem to be of much importance in short-term memory because of its very small capacity, especially in a task situation in which we are simply asked to recognize whether or not a given item was shown earlier. According to the popular two-process or generation-recognition model of memory (see for example, Kintsch, 1970), retrieval processes are minimal in recognition tasks. The generation-recognition model postulates that when presented with an item the subject has immediate and direct access to the item's location in memory with no need to search for it. However, it has been shown in a series of very elegant experiments by Saul Sternberg (1966, 1967, 1969) that search and retrieval processes play an important role in short-term recognition tasks. Sternberg's experiments not only give support to the existence of a searching mechanism but they also suggest that this mechanism is a particularly unintuitive one. This has made these experiments as controversial as they are important (see, for example, Sternberg, 1975, for a discussion of this controversy).

On a trial in Sternberg's experiments, subjects were given a short list of items (typically digits) to be remembered as the "positive stimulus set." A sample positive stimulus set is 5 8 4 2. During the test phase of the experiments, the subjects were given a single item to which they were to respond "yes" or "no" by selecting the appropriate one of two levers to indicate whether or not the test item was part of the positive set. To continue with our example, the digit 4 might be presented and should lead to the "yes" response (see Figure 3-6). After responding to the test item, the subjects were required to recall the positive set. The purpose of this recall test was to force the subjects to retain the positive set in its proper order and to work with the positive set, not its inverse, the negative set (the digits 0, 1, 3, 6, 7, 9 in our example). The primary dependent variable of concern was reaction time, or response latency, since errors were minimal; the primary independent variable was the number of items in the positive set. Sternberg found that reaction time (RT) increased as the size of the positive set increased; as more items were included in the positive set, it took longer for the subject to respond to a particular test item. This result is inconsistent with the hypothesis that retrieval from short-term memory is immediate or automatic, as would have been indicated if adding more items to the list did not lead to an increase in reaction times. Instead, this result suggests that the items in short-term memory must be scanned and implicates a specific scanning process which is *serial* rather than *parallel*. In a serial scan, not all items on the memory list are examined together at one time but rather the subjects examine only one item at a time.

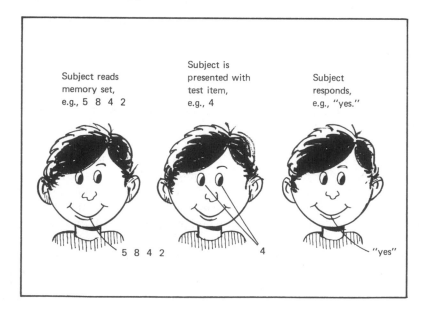

Subject reads memory set, e.g., 5 8 4 2

Subject is presented with test item, e.g., 4

Subject responds, e.g., "yes."

5 8 4 2   4   "yes"

Figure 3-6. Sternberg's (1966) paradigm for studying retrieval from short-term memory.

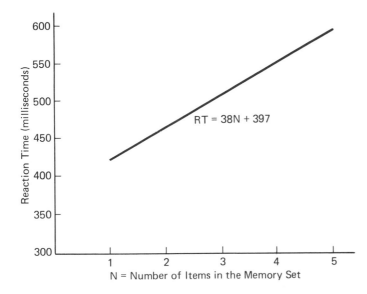

$$RT = 38N + 397$$

Figure 3-7. Results of the Sternberg (1966) experiment. (Adapted from Figure 1 in Sternberg, [1966]. Copyright by American Association for the Advancement of Science.)

The precise reaction time function found by Sternberg took the form of a straight line, as shown in Figure 3-7. This linear function suggests that a fixed amount of time is needed for scanning each additional item in the positive set. How long does it take a subject to consider one memory item and compare it to the test item? This scanning rate can be easily computed by examining the slope of the reaction time function. Sternberg found that scanning took place at an amazingly rapid rate—26 characters per second, or 38 msec per character. Whereas the slope of the reaction time function indicates the scanning rate, the intercept of the function reveals the time it takes the subject to complete those processes that occur only once, such as encoding the test stimulus and making a decision about the correct response after finding or failing to locate that item in the memory set. The intercept time was 397 msec in Sternberg's study.

A comparison of the reaction time functions for "yes" and "no" responses is also diagnostic. The functions for the "yes" responses are parallel to those for the "no" responses; the slopes are the same. In other words, the reaction times increase at the same rate for both types of responses. Sternberg argued that this result implies that the serial scanning process is *exhaustive* instead of *self-terminating*. It seems that subjects in scanning through the memory list do not stop when they find the correct item, but rather they continue scanning the list and respond only after they have reached the end, examining each member of the positive set in turn. This process is particularly unintuitive; hence, it has been especially vulnerable to attack by other investigators (see, for example, Theios, Smith, Haviland, Traupmann, & Moy, 1973).

What are Sternberg's arguments in favor of an exhaustive scan? He contends that in a self-terminating scan the subject would stop in the middle of the list, on the average, when making a "yes" response, but would stop only at the end of the list when making a "no" response. In a self-terminating scan, then, as list length increases the latency of the "yes" responses would increase at roughly half the rate of increase for the "no" responses, so the slope of the reaction time function for "yes" responses would be about half that for "no" responses. In contrast, in an exhaustive search, the subject would stop only at the end of the list when making "yes" responses as well as "no" responses so the slopes of the two reaction time functions would be equal, as was indeed found by Sternberg.

A second important independent variable in Sternberg's task, as in other tasks we have considered, is the serial position of the test item in the positive set. In Sternberg's experiments, reaction time for the "yes" responses was found to be a flat function of serial position. Flat functions like that found here are consistent either with an exhaustive scan or with a self-terminating scan in which the items are examined in a random order. Flat functions, however, are incompatible with a serial self-terminating scan in which the items are examined in a regular order, since there should be an advantage (faster reaction times) in that case for the positions scanned first.

Along with these general findings, Sternberg (1969) made a number of other interesting discoveries in some additional experiments he reviewed. For example, Sternberg compared the situation in which the positive stimulus set was held in short-term memory since it was varied from trial to trial ("varied set procedure") to a situation in which the positive set was stored in long-term memory since it was held constant across a sequence of trials ("fixed set procedure"). Surprisingly, the results in these two situations were essentially the same—the intercepts and the slopes of the reaction time functions in the fixed set procedure were the same as those in the varied set procedure, implicating a single comparison process. These results suggest that the same scanning process is employed whether the positive set is held in long-term memory or short-term memory. Sternberg explained this finding by proposing that the items stored in long-term memory during the fixed set procedure were entered into short-term memory for the test so that a scan of the contents of short-term memory was made in each case.

Another interesting observation is Sternberg's finding that when the information about the positive stimulus set resided exclusively in long-term memory, which was ensured by interposing a memory task before the critical test probe, the intercept and slope of the reaction time functions increased relative to those for the standard fixed-set procedure. Sternberg explained the increase in intercept as due to the time it took to search for the positive set in long-term memory and the increase in slope as due to the time it took to copy each item in the positive set from long-term memory to short-term memory for the scan.

Another set of experiments by Sternberg (1967) used a recall task instead of the usual recognition procedure. In the recall task subjects were given a positive stimulus set of digits; when presented with a test stimulus they were to respond with its immediate successor in the positive set. For example, given the ordered list 5842 as the positive set and 4 as the test stimulus, subjects should respond with

2. This task, unlike the standard procedure, implicated a serial self-terminating scanning process with a relatively long comparison time (248 msec per character) because there was a steep increase in reaction time both as a function of list length and as a function of serial position, as shown in Figure 3–8. Why did subjects use a self-terminating process instead of an exhaustive scan for this task? According to Sternberg, one of the prices of exhaustive scanning is that the subject loses information about the position of the test item within the list of items comprising the positive set. Presumably in an exhaustive scan, when the subjects scan through the list and find the test item, they change a mental switch or register. However, even after discovering the test item, the subjects continue to scan through the list, examining the remaining items, until they reach the end. At that point the subjects check the mental switch to determine whether it registered that the test item was found. The switch, however, does not reveal the position of the test item in the positive set list. Thus, for any task that requires information about the location of the test probe in the list, an exhaustive search will not suffice and a self-terminating process will be needed. The recall task employed by Sternberg does require such information.

While this line of thinking clarifies when a self-terminating search would be necessary, it also makes clear why exhaustive searches may be chosen under the standard recognition conditions. The exhaustive procedure allows for a very rapid scan because subjects do not have to check their register and decide on a response

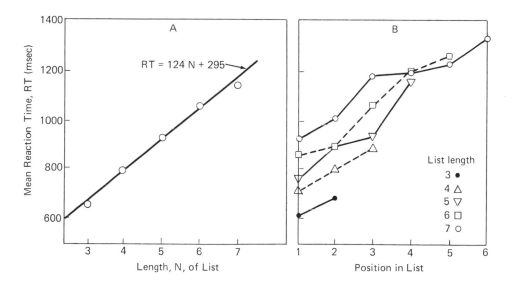

Figure 3-8. Mean correct reaction time as a function of size of positive set (panel A) and serial position (panel B) in probed recall task of Sternberg (1967). (Adapted from Sternberg, S. [1967]. Retrieval of contextual information from memory. *Psychonomic Science, 8,* 55–56. Reprinted by permission of the author and the Psychonomic Society.)

after every item but, instead, do so only once at the end of the list. The remarkable speed of the comparison process, indexed by the slope of the reaction time function, indicates just how efficient the exhaustive scan can be.

TRANSFER FROM SHORT-TERM MEMORY
TO LONG-TERM MEMORY

Free Recall Task. Information may leave short-term memory because it is lost or because it has been retrieved for use on a memory test. Alternatively, it may leave because it has been transferred to a more permanent memory store. This last possibility is best illustrated with a second demonstration, which makes use of a simple procedure known as the "free recall" task. Get together another group of friends and this time tell them that you will read aloud a list of words at a fairly rapid regular rate and that at the end of the list they are to write down as many of the words as they can in any order they wish. The list of words is presented in Table 3–3 (list 1) and is comprised of 24 common nouns. After your friends have completed that task, present them with a second list of the same type (Table 3–3, list 2). However, this time do not let them recall immediately after list presentation. Instead end the list by showing them the following set of 24 digits grouped into pairs. Tell them to multiply the two numbers in each pair and then add all the products: $5 \times 9 + 4 \times 7 + 3 \times 6 + 2 \times 8 + 4 \times 9 + 5 \times 6 + 7 \times 2 + 3 \times 8 + 6 \times 9 + 4 \times 5 + 8 \times 7 + 3 \times 2$. Allow your friends 30 seconds to complete the calculation after which they should write down the answer or, if they have not finished, the intermediate result they have calculated to that point. Next your friends should write down all the words they can remember from the second list, in any order they want.

When your friends have completed their recall responses you can begin to score their protocols. As an initial point of interest, notice that exactly half of the words on the first list are in italics and determine the number of correct responses

Table 3-3.   *Word lists for free recall demonstration experiment*

LIST 1

Mind, doctor, *idea,* paper, money, forest, *hope, hour,* seat, *cost, position,* letter, *answer,* house, *chance, moment, amount,* judge, *trouble,* animal, baby, *method,* sugar, fire.

LIST 2

Heaven, truth, car, tree, strength, blood, butter, form, grass, lip, silence, star, spirit, arm, mother, soul, dress, power, chair, pleasure, love, thought, shoes, interest.

---

your friends made on these words and then on the remaining words. You will doubt-less find that your friends scored higher on the words that are not in italics. Why? Both sets of words are common in the language, according to a trusted frequency count (Thorndike & Lorge, 1944), but whereas the words in italics are hard to pic-ture or image, it is easy to form a mental image of those words not italicized, ac-cording to a collection of subject ratings (see Paivio, Yuille, & Madigan, 1968). As we shall discuss in Chapter 4, imagery plays an important role in memory; it helps us to memorize words if we can easily form an image of them.

Another analysis of the data from this task will provide insights into the rela-tionship between short-term memory and long-term memory. This analysis, just like that for our earlier demonstration, involves computing the serial position function. Let your friends help you score their data by reading to them each list of words grouped into word pairs in accordance with the order of presentation and by ask-ing them to raise neither, one, or both of their hands depending on whether they got neither, one, or both of the words in a pair correct. Count the number of hands raised for each word pair and plot the results, as shown in Figure 3–9. Because we did not counterbalance words across positions (a given word was in a given serial position for all subjects), the serial position functions you obtain should be more irregular and jagged than the idealized curves shown in Figure 3–9. Nevertheless,

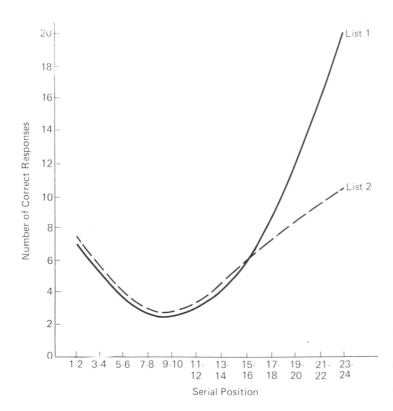

Figure 3-9. Idealized serial position functions for list 1 (solid line) and list 2 (broken line) in free recall demonstra-tion experiment.

even with the irregular functions, two important features of the serial position curves should be evident—primacy (an advantage for the initial positions) for both lists and recency (an advantage for the final positions) for the first list but not the second list, which was followed by mental arithmetic.

Two common subject strategies can explain these effects. To what extent did your friends use such strategies? The first strategy concerns the order in which subjects report the items. This order is not random, nor is it strictly serial, starting with the first item and finishing with the last. Rather subjects usually report first the items from the last part of the list, then typically return to the start or middle of the list. This *output order* strategy provides at least a partial explanation for the recency effect: The items in the last few positions of the list are recalled best because they are reported first. As time progresses, and the subjects report more items, they forget some of the items not yet reported. The first few items reported are thus not subject to the "output interference" that disturbs the subsequent items (see Chapter 2 and Tulving & Arbuckle, 1963, for further discussions of output interference).

While the output order strategy can account for the recency portion of the serial position curve, the rehearsal strategy explains the primacy portion. Although rehearsal is typically covert and thus not witnessed by the experimenter, Dewey Rundus (1971) cleverly circumvented this problem. He was able to witness rehearsing using a very straightforward technique: He told his subjects to study the items in a list by repeating them aloud during presentation. He allowed five seconds between adjacent items so that the subjects had the opportunity to repeat each several times before the free recall test. Rundus placed no restrictions on which items were to be rehearsed or the rate of rehearsal. With this procedure, Rundus found that the initial few items in the list were rehearsed, or repeated aloud, more frequently than the subsequent items. He explained this result by proposing that at the start of list presentation there are fewer items competing for rehearsal than there are as presentation of the list progresses. The primacy effect in the serial position function can then be explained simply by the fact that the initial list items are given more rehearsals than the later items.

Buffer Model.   Let us now consider one of the most popular memory models to determine how it accounts for these findings from the free recall task. This model, called the "buffer" model and proposed by Richard Atkinson and Richard Shiffrin in 1968, provided the basis for our initial discussion of memory in Chapter 1. Atkinson and Shiffrin characterize their memory model as having two dimensions. The first dimension contains the permanent or structural features of the model, like the hardware of a computer. The second dimension contains "control processes," which are operations performed by subjects and under their control, such as the rehearsal and output order strategies just discussed. Returning to the computer analogy, we can view these control processes as similar to the programs or software used with a computer.

In addressing the structural features of their model, Atkinson and Shiffrin divide memory into three distinct components: the sensory registers (their term for sensory memories, including iconic and echoic memories), the short-term store (STS), and the long-term store (LTS). As in many current information-processing models, the relationships among the components can be best illustrated by means of an information flow diagram (see Figure 3–10). According to this diagram, information is processed by and held in the sensory registers and then entered into STS. The information remains temporarily in STS, with the length of stay a function of control processes. While information resides in STS, other information associated with it in LTS may be activated and brought into STS to accompany it. (Note that this is another means, not considered in our earlier review, by which information can be entered into short-term memory.) Furthermore, during the period when information is held in STS, it may be copied or transferred into LTS. Atkinson and Shiffrin emphasize that this transfer process to LTS is not necessarily accompanied by removal of the information from STS; a particular piece of information can reside in both STS and LTS at the same time.

The buffer, from which the model derives its name, is considered part of STS. The buffer is intimately concerned with the subject strategy of rehearsal. If the subject employs a strategy different from one of repetition of the to-be-remembered items (such as an imagery strategy), then the buffer will *not* be the dominant part of STS. However, Atkinson and Shiffrin demonstrate that in many tasks the buffer plays an essential role. The buffer is a small capacity store holding a fixed number of items to be rehearsed. As each new study item is presented, it may enter the buffer for rehearsal and if it does, one of the current inhabitants of the buffer will

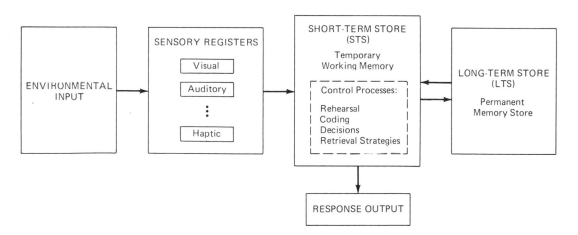

Figure 3-10.   Information flow diagram illustrating Atkinson and Shiffrin's buffer model. (From Atkinson, R.C., & Shiffrin, R.M. [1971]. The control of short-term memory. *Scientific American, 225,* 82–90. Copyright 1971 by Scientific American, Inc. All rights reserved. Reprinted by permission of the author and Scientific American, Inc.)

be removed, since the capacity of the buffer cannot exceed a certain limit. As an analogy, the rehearsal buffer can be thought of as a storage bin which contains a fixed number of compartments; each new item that enters the buffer removes an item already there.

Atkinson and Shiffrin have applied a more specific form of the buffer model to the free recall situation. According to this particular version, every item on the free recall list enters the subject's rehearsal buffer, which has a capacity left as a free parameter of the model, r, a variable which is expected to depend on the specific subjects tested and the particular testing situation. One by one, the initial items fill up the compartments of the buffer, and thereafter each succeeding item removes from the buffer a randomly chosen inhabitant. The model assumes that mental arithmetic, like that performed by your friends as part of their task with the second list, operates in the same way as further item presentations, so that arithmetic operations remove items from the buffer, or displace them, at the same rate as do new incoming items. The model postulates further that information about an item is copied into LTS during the period of time that it remains in the buffer; in fact, the amount of information transferred is a linear function of the amount of time the item spends in the buffer. If an item remains in the buffer for j seconds, the amount of information transferred to LTS about it is equal to Θ times j, where Θ is another free parameter of the model. Finally, the model includes the assumption that when the subjects scan through LTS during recall to find the items they wish to remember, they make precisely R searches with replacement (which means that they may find the same item on more than one search), and then they terminate their search. For each of the R searches of LTS, the probability that information about one of the items will be found is equal to the ratio of the amount of information in LTS about that item to the total amount of information in LTS about all the items in the list. Thus, items with more information in LTS will be more likely to be found during the LTS scan.

To summarize, there are three free parameters in the buffer model: r, the buffer size; Θ, the rate at which information concerning a given item is copied into LTS while the item is contained in the rehearsal buffer; and R, the number of LTS searches made.

The buffer model is able to yield close fits to the data from free recall experiments. How can the model explain the primacy advantage? According to the model, the initial items are not removed from the buffer until it is filled so that, on the average, these items stay in the buffer longer than the subsequent items in the list. The recency advantage is also explained by the model, because the final items in a list tend to remain in the buffer at the time of test. Likewise, the buffer model can explain the loss of recency when the list is followed by mental arithmetic, like that seen in the demonstration experiment, since arithmetic operations are assumed to remove items from the buffer just as do new entering items. Thus, following mental arithmetic, the items from the end of the list are not in the buffer when the test starts; rather, they have been displaced by the numbers in the arithmetic calculations. Along these same lines, the buffer model provides reasonable explanations for the subject strategies we discussed earlier: Subjects report the final items in the list first because they are still in the buffer at the time of recall. Also, subjects rehearse the initial items more than the others because they are not removed from the buffer until it is filled.

What happens when we vary the length of the to-be-remembered list in the free recall task? It has been found (for example, Murdock, 1962) that increases in list length lead to decreases in the proportion of correct responses for each serial position in the list except for the final positions; see the idealized serial position functions in Figure 3–11. The changes in the results evident as list length changes are explained by the model in terms of retrieval difficulty associated with parameter R. Since R is fixed, the probability of finding or retrieving a particular item decreases as list length increases. As list length increases, the number of items in LTS increases; the more items there are, the smaller is the probability of retrieving a particular item in R searches. Atkinson and Shiffrin point out that the effect of list length could also be explained by interference assumptions. According to these assumptions, items in the list before or after any given item interfere with the memory for that item.

An ingenious experiment reported by Atkinson and Shiffrin (1971) was able to resolve the question of whether the list length effect was due primarily to interference or retrieval difficulty. In this experiment subjects were presented with a series of lists. The lists were of different lengths; they were either five or twenty words long. After each list the subjects recalled *not* the list just studied, as in the typical free recall test, but rather the list just before the last list studied. In this procedure, the length of the test list being recalled did not necessarily correspond to the number of potentially interfering items. A long (twenty-item) or short (five-item) test list was followed by either a long or short interpolated list. The buffer model predicts that the probability of correctly recalling an item will depend only on the length of the test list, assuming that the subjects can limit their search and retrieval to the items on that list. The interference model, on the other hand, predicts that performance will be determined largely by the number of words in the interpolated list. The results were quite clear: Words in test lists of length five were

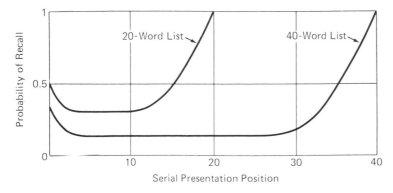

Figure 3-11. Idealized serial position functions for short (20-word) list and long (40-word) list in a free recall task. (From Atkinson, R.C. & Shiffrin, R.M. [1971]. The control of short-term memory. *Scientific American, 225,* 82–90. Copyright 1971 by Scientific American, Inc. All rights reserved. Reprinted by permission of the author and Scientific American, Inc.)

recalled much better than those in test lists of length twenty, but the length of the interpolated lists had essentially no influence on performance (see Figure 3–12). Clearly then the buffer model, but not the interference model, can account for these findings.

Similarly, it has been shown (for example by Glanzer & Cunitz, 1966) that changing the rate of list presentation affects performance on the prerecency items (all those before the end of the list) but not the most recent items, as illustrated in the idealized serial position functions of Figure 3–13. Atkinson and Shiffrin remark that perhaps the most impressive feature of their model is its ability to explain the effects of varying presentation rate. Their simple assumption seems to be well founded that the amount of information transferred to LTS is a linear function of the time spent in the buffer. Θ is the amount of information transferred per second, so that according to the model, for an item that stays in the buffer during 2 subsequent item presentations, 2Θ will be the amount of information in LTS about it if the presentation rate is 1 item per second and 4Θ if the rate is 1 item per 2 seconds. However, if presentation rates are too fast or too slow, the buffer model will probably break down. In particular, as presentation rate decreases sufficiently,

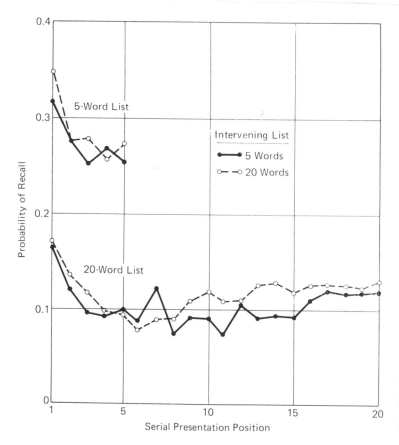

Figure 3-12. Serial position functions in free recall experiment that varied the length of the to-be-remembered list and the length of the intervening list. (From Atkinson, R.C. & Shiffrin, R.M. [1971]. The control of short-term memory. *Scientific American, 225*, 82–90. Copright 1971 by Scientific American, Inc. All rights reserved.

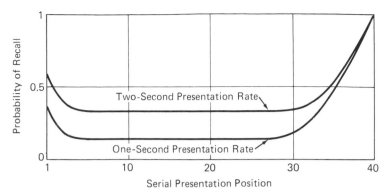

subjects will have time to make use of imagery and other coding strategies more effective than the rote rehearsal used in the buffer.

Dual Process.   One of the most important attributes of the buffer model is its postulation of two distinct memory stores, LTS and STS. Such a "dual process" notion has been widely, but by no means universally, accepted by memory theorists. Let us briefly consider some of the evidence for this notion.

Perhaps the most impressive evidence supporting the distinction between STS and LTS comes from outside the experimental psychology laboratory. It is clinical evidence deriving from patients who have damage in that area of the brain known as the hippocampus. Such patients, like the patient HM studied by Milner (1967) and discussed in Chapter 1, seem to have relatively normal verbal short-term memory processes along with an almost complete inability to construct new verbal long-term memory representations. In the terms of the buffer model, such patients cannot transfer information from STS to LTS. If you hold a conversation with a patient who has this disorder, everything seems normal initially. The patient can remember both events that occurred to him or her before the brain damage and new information provided during the conversation. However, the patient's memory problem will become evident to you if, for example, you break off the conversation temporarily by leaving the room. Returning after such a break, you will probably find that the patient has totally forgotten the conversation and the information provided during it. Milner's patient HM was also studied at length by Wickelgren (1968) and subjected to a standard laboratory task that is used to measure short-term retention. Wickelgren reported an unusual problem he had to overcome when working with this particular subject. Since HM had difficulty transferring information from STS to LTS, Wickelgren had to make sure that HM did not forget the instructions for the laboratory task in the middle of the task. Thus, the experimenter reminded HM continually concerning what he was to do.

The most frequently cited experimental evidence supporting the distinction between STS and LTS involves free recall tasks like the one in our demonstration. As we noted, the serial position curves in these tasks typically show a large recency effect, a small primacy effect, and a flat function in the middle. It has been argued to explain these curves, that the middle and primacy portions of the curve reflect retrieval of information from LTS, whereas the recency portion reflects largely retrieval from STS. Such an explanation clearly implies that manipulations which differentially influence STS and LTS should differentially influence the recency and prerecency portions of the serial position function. In fact, we have already reviewed a number of such manipulations. For example, mental arithmetic interposed between list presentation and recall is a manipulation that should influence the contents of STS but not LTS. Indeed, Glanzer and Cunitz (1966) found, just as we observed in our demonstration, that mental arithmetic (in their case counting out loud from a given number) immediately after presentation of the list decreased the recency portion of the serial position curve but left the prerecency portion unchanged. Conversely, they found, as we noted earlier, that manipulations of list length and rate of presentation, which should affect LTS but not STS, left the recency portions of the serial position curves intact but changed the prerecency portions significantly—longer list lengths and faster presentation rates decreased the proportion of correctly recalled items at the beginning and middle serial positions of the list.

Another type of experimental evidence which suggests that there are two different memory stores involves the format in which information is represented in memory. As we discussed earlier, short-term memory representations are based on phonemic codes, whereas those in long-term memory involve semantic coding.

Levels of Processing.   An important attack against the distinction between STS and LTS was initiated by Craik and Lockhart (1972), who also proposed an alternative conceptual framework in which memory phenomena can be understood. Craik and Lockhart raised three arguments against the dual process approach; arguments involving capacity, coding, and the time course of forgetting. The first argument concerns the fixed limited capacity that most dual process models, like the buffer model, attribute to STS. The problem is that empirical estimates of the STS capacity have varied considerably. Whereas measures of memory span vary between five and nine items (recall Miller's magical number seven plus or minus two), estimates of the buffer size by Atkinson and Shiffrin (1968) are much lower (r = 2–4 in the fits of the buffer model). The second argument concerns the coding distinction just mentioned. Although STS was originally thought to be restricted to phonemic coding, later evidence (see Kroll, Parks, Parkinson, Bieber, & Johnson, 1970) suggested that coding in STS is more flexible so that STS and LTS cannot be sharply distinguished on the basis of coding (see also Shulman, 1971). Finally, Craik and Lockhart argued that if the memory stores are distinguishable in terms of their forgetting functions (forgetting from STS much more rapid than that from LTS), then it would seem crucial that the time courses of forgetting be invariant across different experimental paradigms. However, such invariance is not found; different methods of testing lead to different pictures of the time courses of forgetting.

As an alternative to the dual-process notion, Craik and Lockhart proposed the notion "levels of processing." Basically, they suggested that stimuli may be processed in different ways and to different extents, and the level of analysis determines the rate of forgetting. For stimuli that are analyzed only to a superficial level such as that involving visual or phonemic attributes, the memory traces are transient, whereas for stimuli that are analyzed to more deep, meaningful levels the traces are more permanent. The depth to which an item is processed is a function of the nature of the stimulus and the specific requirements of the task. Craik and Lockhart view the different levels not as distinct stages but rather as a continuum of analysis. Further, they postulate a limited-capacity central processor which may be used to maintain information at one level of analysis. The capacity of the processor is a function of the particular level at which it is operating, thereby accounting for the variation in the estimates for STS capacity. As soon as an item leaves the central processor, it will be lost at the rate determined by its level of processing (slower rates for deeper levels), thereby accounting for the variation in forgetting rates. The central processor may work to keep information at one level of analysis, which is known as Type I processing or maintenance rehearsal. Alternatively, it may work towards deeper analysis of the information, which is called Type II processing or elaborative rehearsal (see Chapter 1). In other words, Craik and Lockhart postulate two distinct types of rehearsal processes, not just the single process included in the buffer model.

To support their hypotheses concerning levels of processing, Craik and Lockhart review studies which show that incidental learning can be as good as intentional learning when the subjects are required to process the items to a deep level of analysis. For example, in a study by Hyde and Jenkins (1969), a free recall test followed after standard intentional learning instructions or after various incidental learning tasks in which the subjects were given no warning in advance that their memory would be tested later. One task required the subjects to judge whether or not each word contained the letter *e*, and another task required them to rate the pleasantness of each word. Free recall after the pleasantness rating task, which involved deep semantic processing, was equivalent to that after the intentional learning instructions (in which subjects were explicitly told to study the words for a subsequent memory test), and was superior to that after the *e*-judging task, which involved low-level processing of the words.

Support has also been provided for Craik and Lockhart's distinction between Type I and Type II processing. At the core of this distinction is the notion that Type I processing, or maintenance rehearsal, does not lead to an improvement in long-term retention or learning. One clever experiment that gave evidence for this hypothesis was performed by Craik and Watkins (1973). They presented subjects with lists of words and told them to report for each list only the most recent word that began with a particular target letter. The number of distractor words interpolated between one test word (a word containing the target letter) and the next test word in the list was the independent variable of concern. For example, for the target *B* and the list *candy, bean, rooster, roach, button, goat, bottle, moon, table, pig,* there are two distractor words between *bean* and *button* and one between *button* and *bottle.* Since the Atkinson and Shiffrin buffer model clearly postulates that the amount of information transferred to LTS about an item is a function of the length of time that item is held in the STS buffer (as reflected in the parameter Θ), and since the number of distractors following a test word should determine how long that word resides in the buffer, one might expect to find a clear relationship between the number of subsequent distractors (preceding the next test word) and the recall level of the test word. However, on a subsequent surprise recall test of the words presented in all the lists, Craik and Watkins did not find such a relationship. Instead the number of subsequent distractors had essentially no effect on the recall of the preceding test word, suggesting that only Type I processing was used to keep these words in memory.

When Do We Use Short-Term Memory?

Since short-term memory has neither a large capacity nor a long duration, you might think that it is not very useful. To the contrary, short-term memory is essential for many cognitive activities, including, for example, comprehending spoken and written sentences. We usually have no need to retain the precise wording of sentences in long-term memory, but in order to avoid problems of understanding, we need to retain a verbatim record of the initial part of the sentence while we are attending to the latter part. Consider, for example, the following sentence: "Mary, who is the daughter of the woman I met yesterday on the plane when I was going from New York to Denver, is opening a new shop in town." We must hold Mary's name in memory while we are reading or listening to the long relative phrase in order to identify her as the person who is opening the new store. When words have more than one meaning, it is even more critical that they be retained verbatim in memory until the presentation of the sentence is complete. The following sentence illustrates this principle: "The bat seemed to come flying down from the sky and hit the catcher on his head." When first reading or listening to this sentence, we might assume that the "bat" in question was an animal, but when we get to the word "catcher" we are able to correct our interpretation if we still remember the precise word that was presented. The memory system that is used for this purpose is short-term memory.

We may be surprised to find that short-term memory is used for some activities that do not at first seem to require that resource, and we may be able to understand errors in performing such activities if we take into account the limitations of short-term memory. A recent study by Nairne and Healy (1983) illustrates that the simple activity of counting backwards involves short-term memory processes and that counting errors can be best understood to be a consequence of memory failures. Nairne and Healy found that subjects rapidly counting backwards systematically made errors of two types: They missed repeated digits (when the decade prefix and second digit of a number match, for example, 77) and decade numbers (when the decade prefix exists alone, for example, 70). Nairne and Healy explained these two types of errors by proposing that when subjects count backwards they keep track of where they are in the sequence by checking the contents of short-term memory to determine whether the next number generated has already been said. When the decade prefix and the next second digit sound similar, as with the repeated digits, the subjects may mistakenly conclude that they have already said the next second digit since the similar decade prefix is found in short-term memory from the immediately preceding number. Likewise, when the next correct response is a decade number, the subjects may mistakenly conclude that they have already said that number because the decade prefix is in memory from the previous number said.

In order to test these proposals, Nairne and Healy compared the standard counting backwards task to a new task in which the subjects said only the digits making up each number (for example, "two two" instead of "twenty-two"). As expected, they found an increase in errors on the repeated digits in this new task (because the decade prefixes and second digits now sound exactly the same) along with a decrease in the percentage of errors on the decade numbers (because the decade prefix is now coupled with the second digit zero). Although the explanation for these changing error patterns is by no means certain, it seems likely that short-term memory processes play a major role in counting behavior. More generally, as should be clear from this example, short-term memory is used not only to hold information but also to process it (see the workbench analogy of Klatzky, 1975).

Summary

Short-term memory is that system which allows us to remember items presented in a short list for immediate recall. Although not as limited in capacity as precategorical acoustic store, short-term memory is restricted to about seven chunks of information. Some argue that it is this capacity limitation which accounts for our inability to attend to many things at the same time, but others have argued that our attentional limitation is caused by processes occurring before information enters short-term memory.

Typically information is coded in short-term memory in terms of phonemic attributes, even when the information is presented visually. The retention of temporal sequence information in short-term memory seems best captured by Estes's notion of reverberatory loops connecting item representations in memory to control elements that represent the experimental context. Loss of order information can then be understood as resulting from perturbations in the timing of the reactivation cycles that link different items to a single control element.

Information leaves short-term memory for different reasons. One reason is simply that is is lost or forgotten. Although the time course of forgetting is known to be rapid, it is not known whether the forgetting is due to decay with the passage of time without rehearsal or whether interference from similar items is necessary to promote forgetting. A second reason why information may leave short-term memory is that it may be retrieved for use (as on a memory test). Sternberg has found evidence for a very rapid short-term memory retrieval or scanning mechanism, which occurs exhaustively rather than terminating as soon as the test probe is discovered on the memory list. A final reason for leaving short-term memory is transfer to the more permanent long-term memory. (In this case, as with retrieval but not forgetting, information may be extracted from short-term memory for use in another way but may still remain available in short-term memory for future extraction.) The buffer model of Atkinson and Shiffrin includes distinct short- and long-term memory stores with the extent of transfer of information from short-term store to long-term store dependent on the amount of rehearsal that an item receives in the short-term memory buffer. In contrast, Craik and Lockhart have postulated a continuum of processing levels along with two distinct rehearsal mechanisms—Type II processing, which leads to long-term retention, and Type I processing, which merely maintains information over a short time interval.

Short-term memory may be transient and limited in capacity but it is very useful nonetheless. For example, it seems necessary for doing problems "in your head," such as the common activities of comprehending sentences and counting.

FOUR

Learning
and Remembering

Outline

Most of our life we are engaged in learning. We learn how to walk and talk when we are very young. Later in school we learn arithmetic, then geometry, then, sometimes, advanced calculus. We learn the names of new friends when we move to a new location. In fact there are almost no activities that do not involve learning in some way.

The process of learning is essentially one of transferring information from our environment into our long-term memories. Long-term memory is a (more or less) permanent repository of general knowledge about the world and past memories and our own lives. Like the other components of the cognitive system, it has a number of important features. First of all, it is virtually unlimited in its capacity. Although you may sometimes think that you are totally incapable of stuffing another piece of information into your memory, especially if you have just been studying for an exam, you are wrong. No-one has ever discovered any absolute limit on long-term memory capacity. If you work at it diligently enough, you are capable of learning new things—that is, of storing new information in your long-term memory—for as long as you live.

In this chapter, we first discuss the methods for getting information into long-term memory. As we shall see, rehearsing the information is one method, although it may not necessarily be the best. Imagery plays an important role in the storage of information in long-term memory, and so it will be discussed in some detail. We follow this with a discussion of forgetting from long-term memory. As we shall see, information in long-term memory is capable of being forgotten, although such forgetting is a relatively slow process. We conclude with a discussion of the all-important "constructive processes"—mental processes that may be responsible for much of what appears to be forgetting. In the next chapter, we will discuss more fully the general knowledge that is part of our long-term memories, the types of information we possess, and how this knowledge is retrieved when we need it.

Learning New Things

Imagine you have just looked up a phone number and are now walking to a pay phone to dial it. If you are like most people, you rehearse that number to yourself. Rehearsal serves two purposes. It keeps the information in our immediate consciousness, but it also serves to transfer it to our long-term memories. That is, we learn the number as we rehearse it.

The idea that rehearsal is a mechanism for learning new information received empirical support in the work of Rundus (Rundus & Atkinson, 1970; Rundus, 1971). Rundus presented his subjects with a list of words for later recall. The subjects were told to rehearse out loud any word they wished during the presentation of the list, while a tape recorder kept track of what they said. So, the first word in the list might be "hoof" and the subjects might say out loud "hoof, hoof, hoof. . . ." The second word might be "kindness" and the subjects might then rehearse "hoof, kindness, hoof, kindness . . ." and so on. Obviously as the list length increases, it becomes impossible to rehearse all of the items in the short time between the presentation of words. Rundus then asked the subjects to recall all of the words they could remember in any order they wished. The results are very clear: The more times a word was rehearsed, the more likely it was to be recalled later on.

Subsequent experiments indicated that there may be more than one way to rehearse new information. Craik and Lockhart (1972) for example, suggested that there are at least two major types of rehearsal. They called the first type "maintenance rehearsal," by which they meant merely repeating the material without thinking about it. Maintenance rehearsal may allow indefinite maintenance of the material in short-term memory, but it may not cause any of the material to be transferred to long-term memory. The second type of rehearsal has been termed "elaborative rehearsal" and is thought to involve taking the new information and doing something with it. That something might include creating an elaboration of some sort, for example, associating to it, trying to imagine it, trying to relate it to other things that are known. In this way information is transferred to long-term memory.

The two types of rehearsal are quite distinct; in fact subjects find it easy to switch between the two types if they are instructed to do so (Bjork, 1975). Further, there is other evidence to support the distinction. Consider an experiment by Craik and Watkins (1973). Presented with a long list of words, subjects were instructed that when the list ended they were to report the last word in the list that began with some particular letter, say *p*. Because the subjects do not know how many *p*-words will be in the list, they must maintain in short-term memory any given *p*-word that occurs until it is replaced with another *p*-word. Thus, suppose the subject hears, "Table, pen, horse, kind, pit, apple, pond. . . ." The subject must maintain "pen" until it is replaced with "pit," which is maintained until it is replaced with "pond." In this way the amount of time a subject maintains any given word in short-term memory can be manipulated. At some point the subject will be asked to report the last *p*-word in the list, and for the above example the subject would respond "pond."

To the subject's surprise, after receiving several such lists, an unexpected final free recall test is given. Figure 4–1 shows the probability of correctly recalling a given word as a function of the length of time the word has been maintained in short-term memory. The curve is nearly flat. Thus a word that was maintained for a considerable length of time is not recalled any better than a word that was only briefly maintained. How do we reconcile this result with Rundus's postulate of a

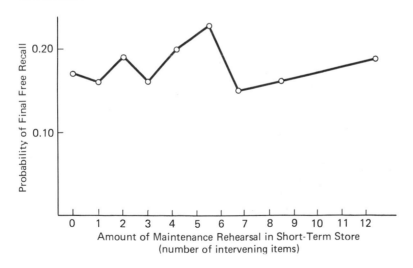

Figure 4–1. Results of the Craik and Watkins (1973) experiment: Probability of final recall as a function of maintenance time. (Adapted from Craik & Watkins, [1973]. Courtesy of Academic Press, Inc.)

relationship between rehearsal and probability of correct recall? The answer is that rehearsal does not automatically lead to transfer of information into long-term memory. If the rehearsal is of the shallow variety—like the type we perform to keep a new telephone number in mind from the time we get it until it can be dialed—little may be transferred to long-term memory. If the rehearsal is of the deep, elaborative type, as when we try to set up meaningful connections among the items we are trying to remember, much can be transferred. When we deliberately try to learn new material, we often engage in these deeper activities, and one consequence is that we succeed in committing the material to memory.

Some early observations that learning is influenced by what a person does with material being presented led to the notion of "depth of processing" as a key determiner of memory. The idea is that the durability of a memory trace is determined by the "depth" to which it is processed. The deeper the material is processed, the stronger the trace that is stored in long-term memory. The basic experimental paradigm for studying depth of processing involves a deception of sorts. For example, in Craik and Tulving (1975) subjects made judgments about individual words that were presented to them. In the "shallow" processing condition, subjects simply judged whether the word was printed in capitals or lower-case letters. In the deep processing condition, subjects judged whether the word fit into a particular sentence frame. Later, subjects were given a surprise recall test. Performance on this test was superior for those subjects who had processed the words deeply.

Numerous variations on this basic experimental paradigm have now been conducted. In the shallow conditions, subjects typically judge whether the words contain a particular letter, or how many syllables they have. In the deeper condition, subjects might decide whether the word is pleasant, or whether it names an object that can be held in the hand. The findings are the same: as the depth of processing increases, so does the likelihood of transfer into long-memory (see for example, Bellezza, Cheesman & Reddy, 1977; Cermak & Reale, 1978; McDowall, 1979).

Recently the depth-of-processing notion has been criticized on several grounds. Some investigators have alleged that it is scientifically empty because of problems it encountered in identifying particular encoding activities with theoretical levels of processing (Baddeley, 1978; Nelson, 1977, Postman, 1975). The theory is circular, some say. If you find an activity that leads to good memory, you call it deep. If you find an activity that leads to poor memory, you call it shallow. Despite the difficulties with the depth notion, however, one thing is clear: Different kinds of processing yield different memory performance. It is important to uncover some of the strategies people can pursue that will enhance the learning and remembering of new information. One important strategy involves the use of imagery.

Imagery

Imagine going to your refrigerator for a drink; imagine opening the door; imagine reaching for a bottle of soda; now go to the freezer compartment for an ice cube.

Is the freezer compartment at the top or at the bottom? Are the ice trays on the left or on the right? Imagining these things is relatively easy for most people. When we construct mental images such as these, we are experiencing a sensation in the absence of an external stimulus. Although the mental images can be tactile, auditory, or involve some other modality, cognitive psychologists have generally confined their studies to visual imagery. As we shall see, such imagery is extremely useful for learning new things.

MENTAL ROTATION

We know from examining our own personal experience that it is possible to conjure up new images in our minds. We can imagine a professor walking around with a copy of this book on her head even though we have never actually seen this combination. To study how mental images are generated and manipulated is extremely difficult, however, because images are simply not accessible to direct observation. But a series of ingenious experiments by Shepard and his co-workers clearly demonstrated that such studies are possible.

In one of the first experiments (Shepard & Metzler, 1971), subjects looked at pairs of figures constructed to possess several special properties. The A pairs were identical except one had been rotated on the plane defined by the surface of the page. The B pairs were identical except one had been rotated on the plane perpendicular to the surface of the page (that is, rotated in the third dimension, back into the page). The C pairs were not identical. The two figures looked similar, but one could be rotated so that it exactly corresponded to the other (see Figure 4–2). A, B, and C type pairs were presented to the subject at various angles; the task was to indicate whether the two members were the same (identical, as in A and B) or different (as in C). Reaction time was recorded. Imagine an A pair in which one member was rotated only slightly from the other. These would look very similar. However, if one member were rotated 180 degrees from the other, that member would appear to be upside down. The angle of rotation was one of the major vari-

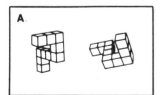

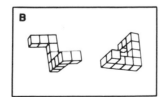

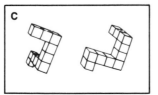

Figure 4-2. Determining whether one of a pair of figures can be rotated into the other. The A pair: A rotation on the plane of the page. The B pair: A rotation in the third dimension. The C pair: The task cannot be completed. (Adapted from Figure 1 in Shepard & Metzler, [1971]. Copyright by American Association for the Advancement of Science.)

ables of interest in this experiment. The reasoning was that if a subject must actually "mentally rotate" one figure into the other in order to respond that they are identical, it ought to take longer to respond when the angle of rotation is large. As we can observe in Figure 4-3, when the angle was very small (close to 0 degrees),

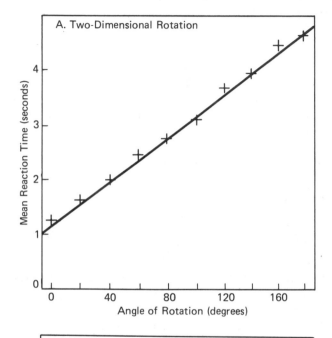

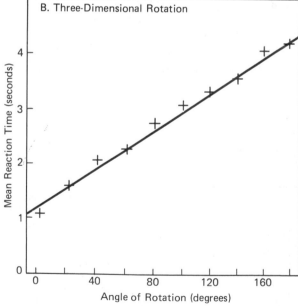

Figure 4-3. Subjects take longer to respond to pairs of stimuli (such as those shown in Figure 4-2) when the angle of rotation is large rather than small. (Adapted from Shepard & Metzler, [1971]. Copyright by American Association for the Advancement of Science.)

subjects took an average of one second to respond; however, for 180-degree rotations they took more than four seconds.

Two points are worth mentioning. The relationship between mean reaction time and angle of rotation is a linear one, which means that mental rotation proceeds at a fairly constant rate. That rate is about 60 degrees per second. Second, the data are almost identical for both the A (two-dimensional) and the B (three-dimensional) rotations. In other words, subjects perform equally fast and accurately on both of these types. We might have thought that rotating back into the third dimension would be more difficult, but these data contradict that supposition. The experiment as a whole provides rather impressive evidence for a remarkable ability to rotate objects in the mind's eye.

More details of mental rotation were provided by Cooper and Shepard (1973), who presented subjects with letters or digits, such as R or P, and instructed them to press one button if the stimulus was normal and another button if it was a mirror image. As in the study with complex block figures, the stimuli could differ from the usual upright position by a rotation. Figure 4–4 shows some of the orientations for a normal letter R and for its mirror image. Notice the symmetry in the stimuli. The 60-degree normal R is tilted slightly clockwise from the 0-degree normal R, whereas the 300-degree normal R is tilted slightly counterclockwise. It turned out that subjects sometimes rotated clockwise and sometimes counterclockwise, depending on the particular stimulus.

In earlier experiments, subjects' response time had varied directly with the magnitude of an object's deviation from the normal vertical, upright position. As shown in Figure 4–5, however, the longest reaction times were obtained when the stimulus was upside down (180 degrees from vertical). Apparently, then, subjects do not simply rotate the representation in a clockwise fashion until it reaches the upright position and then decide if the character is normal or a mirror image. Rather,

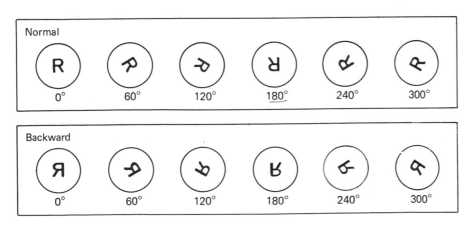

Figure 4-4. Subjects had to decide whether a given stimulus was normal or a mirror image of normal. (After Cooper & Shepard, [1973]. Courtesy of Academic Press, Inc.)

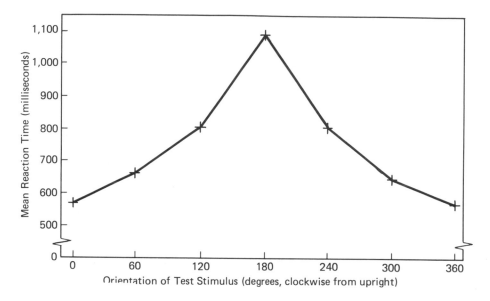

Figure 4-5. The orientation of a character, such as R, influenced the time it took a subject to respond whether the character was normal or a mirror image of normal. (After Cooper & Shepard, [1973]. Courtesy of Academic Press, Inc.)

they decide whether to rotate clockwise or counterclockwise, complete the rotation, and then make their decision.

These results provide compelling evidence that people can rotate mental representations in their minds. The techniques allow us to measure approximately how quickly people can perform these rotations and further indicate that people have some control over the direction of their rotations.

Because of the importance of the work on mental rotation, and because of its elegance, it has become a fascination for cognitive psychologists. A collection of the most important articles, and some of the latest views on the work, have been assembled in a recent book (Shepard & Cooper, 1982).

IMAGERY AND MNEMONICS

The word "mnemonics" is derived from *mnemosyne,* the name of the ancient Greek goddess of memory (Higbee, 1977). The word itself can be defined as "aiding the memory" and the use of such aids is hardly new. In fact, one key method (the method of loci) can be traced back to about 500 B.C. and was used by Greek orators to remember long speeches.

One of the most powerful mnemonic devices is the use of imagery. In one study designed to look at imagery as a mnemonic, Bower (1973) found significant improvements in recall. In this study, subjects had to learn noun pairs, such as "piano-cigar," and later were tested. At the time of the test, the left-hand word was presented as a cue and the subjects had to recall the right-hand word. Half the subjects were instructed to study the pairs by imagining a visual scene or mental picture in which these two objects were interacting in some way. Some sample images are shown in Figure 4–6. For example, when presented with "piano-cigar," the subject might conjure up a mental image of a piano smoking a big black cigar. Subjects who used imagery remembered over twice as many items as control subjects who were simply told to rehearse the pairs over and over.

Imagery mnemonics have been successful both in helping people to remember foreign language vocabulary and in helping people remember name-face associations. Consider foreign language learning. In Step 1 you form an association between the spoken foreign word and an English word that sounds approximately like it. The English word is called the keyword, and it must be a word that has an easily imagable, concrete meaning. In Step 2 you create a mental image in which the keyword and the English translation are interacting in some fashion. So suppose you had to learn the Spanish word *caballo* (pronounced "cob-eye-yo") which means horse. The key word might be "eye" which is contained in the sound of *caballo*. Imagine a horse kicking a giant eye, and you have easily linked eye to horse. The Russian word *zvonok* ("zvahn-oak") means bell. You might form a mental image of a large oak tree with little tiny bells for acorns. Later you would use this image to help you retrieve the meaning of *zvonok*. Investigators have found enormous improvements in learning when imagery is used in this way. In one study (Atkinson & Raugh, 1975) imagery subjects scored over 70 percent correct while control subjects scored a mere 46 percent correct. In other words, the imagery technique has been shown to improve recall by as much as 100 to 150 percent over ordinary learning methods.

The mnemonic technique to have received the most detailed analysis is the method of loci (Bower, 1970). Using this technique to memorize a series of items, you follow three steps. 1) Memorize a list of familiar locations. 2) Make up a vivid image symbolizing each item to be remembered. 3) Take the items in the sequence they must be learned and associate them one by one with the corresponding imaginery locations in memory. Here you actually mentally visualize an image of the item placed into the imaginary location. To illustrate, the locations might be your

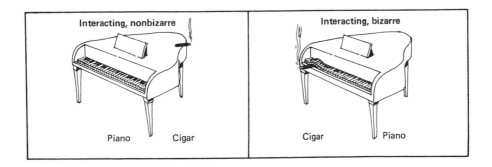

Figure 4-6. Examples of two kinds of drawings that accompanied the word pairs presented in the Wollen et al. experiment. (After Wollen, Weber, & Lowry, [1972]. Courtesy of Academic Press, Inc.)

driveway, your mailbox, your front door knob, your front hall, your living room couch—in that order. The list is easy to remember because the places and their order should be familiar to you. Suppose now that you wish to remember a grocery shopping list—bananas, paper towels, lettuce, wine, and so on. You would try to imagine bananas lying in your driveway, paper towels sticking out of your mailbox, a head of lettuce dangling from your front door knob. . . . Then later, when you wish to remember the shopping list, you need only walk mentally through the list of locations, asking yourself "What's in the driveway?" "What's in the mailbox?" and so on. Recalling the scenes that you constructed enables you to recall the object you mentally placed there.

The method of loci is extremely effective. In one study (Ross & Lawrence, 1968) subjects studied lists of 40 items. Subjects who used the method of loci (using 40 locations around a college campus) could recall about 38 out of 40 items on the list when tested immediately, and a day later their recall averaged 34 out of 40 items. In comparison, those who used rote memorization strategies remembered very little. These data tell us something of the staggering magnitude of the imagery/mnemonic effect.

A careful analysis of the components of any given mnemonic device reveals something of the overall method and shows which components are essential and which are inconsequential. The method of loci has a number of distinct components, many of which are also common to other mnemonics.

1. A list of cues is involved—in this case memory images of geographic locations.
2. These cues are associated with a list of items during the learning of the items.
3. The associations are effected through visual imagery.
4. The person cues recall by thinking of the geographic locations; each one triggers a memory.

Most mnemonic devices involve adding something to the material to be learned. In many cases, this addition may make the mnemonic seem awkward to use, especially to a naive user. Experienced users of mnemonic techniques have practiced with the additional material (for example, memorization of the locations in the method of loci), and using it requires little in the way of processing resources. For the less experienced, the added material uses up substantial processing capacity and the value of mnemonics is diminished. Memory performance for these individuals may be no greater than the performance of subjects who engage in rote memorization.

This problem was shown recently in a test of the effectiveness of a phonetic mnemonic system (Bruce & Clemons, 1982). The phonetic mnemonic system studied was one originally invented in 1634 by a French mathematician, Pietro Herigon, and thought to be an extremely powerful technique for learning and remembering numbers. Briefly, the system involves substituting consonants for particular numbers and then using the consonants to create words (see also Baddeley, 1982). Part of the code used in the present study was: 1 = t, d, th; 2 = n; 3 = m;

4 = r; 5 = l; . . . 9 = n,p. With this code, one can translate words into numbers and numbers into words. To turn a number sequence into a word involves selecting one of the appropriate consonants, and inserting vowels between the consonants when needed. Thus 91 = "pit" and 32 = "men," for example. The system is thought to work on the principle that words are more meaningful and thus easier to remember than numbers. So a person ought to find it relatively easy to store the word and correspondence rules in memory and then decode the word at the time the numerical information is needed.

Bruce and Clemons used this system to teach students the conversions between the metric system and the present system of measurement in the United States (the cousumary system)—1 in. = 2.54 cm and 1 kg = 2.2 lb, for example. The subjects were students at Florida State University, half of whom were assigned to the mnemonics condition and half to the no-mnemonics condition. Both groups learned a number of metric conversions. Mnemonics subjects were also taught the phonetic number = consonant system. Finally they were tested several times, and motivated to do well by a promise of bonus points added to their final grade for correct responses. Whether the subjects used the mnemonic technique or not did not affect their test performance.

Bruce and Clemons point out a number of problems that students may have experienced in using the mnemonic system. They may have had trouble remembering which mnemonic keyword went with which conversion, or with remembering the keywords and then remembering how to translate from keywords to numbers. Analyses of errors indicated that many subjects forgot which keywords went with which conversions rather than forgetting the keywords themselves.

The failure of the mnemonic to work in this case should remind people that care needs to be taken in applying mnemonics to the learning of new information. The system used by Bruce and Clemons is a complex one and probably needs to be learned thoroughly in order to be effective. Also, the system might not be useful for all sorts of material. It might be helpful in remembering detached numerical facts. So, for example, Bruce and Clemons effectively used a word ("Edsel") to remember a computer account number (2105). But the phonetic system may not work with an extensive set of numerical relationships as was the case in the present study.

In sum, mnemonic devices clearly can be used effectively by normal rememberers. Moreover, they can be used to advantage by special rememberers, such as Luria's subject discussed in Chapter 1. However one cannot assume that they will always work even when the to-be-remembered information seems perfectly suited to a particular mnemonic device.

Forgetting From Long-Term Memory

Forgetting is a common experience for all of us. After learning some new information, it often seems as if we have forgotten more of it than we can remember. When asked "What did you eat for breakfast?" most people could probably come up with a fairly accurate response. But "What did you have for breakfast a week ago Tuesday?" or "What did you have for breakfast on the first day of last month?" for most people are difficult, if not impossible, questions. Of more consequence might be the forgetting we experience when we forget the name of someone we run into at a social event. This can often be quite embarrassing. And it is just this sort of embarrassing occurrence that probably accounts for the stupendous success of memory improvement books, such as *The Memory Book* (Lorayne & Lucas, 1975). This is a practical book filled with techniques to help you remember speeches, playing-cards, grocery lists, and other types of things that you do not want to forget. It maintains that "you can remember all the things that make the vital difference in your everyday existence, eliminating the unnecessary loss of so much knowledge and information that should be yours to keep and use forever" (p. 1). The techniques work for some people, largely by helping to organize and elaborate upon material in the same way that mnemonic devices do. But why are they needed in the first place? What causes forgetting?

Before tackling that question, let us examine the classic demonstration of forgetting, that of Ebbinghaus (1885/1964). This work is probably the most frequently cited study dealing with forgetting over the course of time. Ebbinghaus used only a single subject in his experiments—himself. Typically, he learned a list of nonsense syllables, put them away for a certain length of time, and then relearned them. He recorded the saving in time or the saving in number of readings necessary for relearning, assuming that the better his memory, the less time it would take to relearn the material. His results (which can be plotted in the now-famous forgetting curve shown in Figure 4–7) showed that we forget very rapidly immediately after an event, but that forgetting becomes more and more gradual as time passes.

In discussing the subject of forgetting, most modern textbooks include the

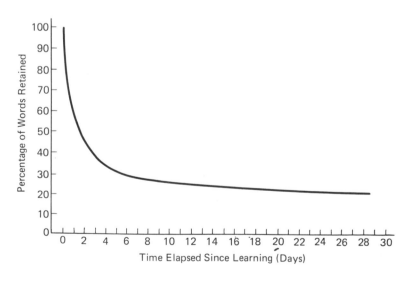

Figure 4-7. The classic forgetting curve. (After Ebbinghaus, [1964].)

original Ebbinghaus curve, along with a remark about its typical shape. One recent example is this: "Many kinds of forgetting curves drop rapidly at first and then level off, as Ebbinghaus demonstrated a century ago. . . ." (Houston, Bee, Hatfield, & Rimm, 1979). But the truth of the matter is that many forgetting curves, while showing an overall decline, have a distinctly different shape. Consider, for example, memory for important personal experiences such as automobile accidents. Some time ago, the National Center for Health Statistics conducted a motor vehicle injury evaluation study that consisted of interviews with a sample of persons known to have been in injury-producing accidents at some time during the twelve-month period preceding the interview. Information obtained from the respondent during the interview was compared with data on the official report form filed at the time of the accident. Of primary interest was the relationship between the respondent's ability to report motor vehicle injuries and the length of time between the occurrence of the accident and the date of the interview (Cash & Moss, 1972). Interviews were conducted with 590 persons who were involved in an accident in which one or more persons were injured, and of these approximately 14 percent did not report the accident at all.

Figure 4–8 presents the percentage of individuals who reported the accident, as a function of the time between the accident and the interview. As can be seen, the percentage declines as the retention interval increases. Put another way, the nonreporting of accidents increases over the retention interval. In the words of the investigators:

> The nonreporting of accidents increases . . . from 3.4 percent for less than 3 months to a maximum of 27.3 percent for the interval of 9–12 months. The obvious reason for this trend is a decreased ability to recall the occurrence of a motor vehicle accident as the time between the date of the accident and the date of the interview increases.

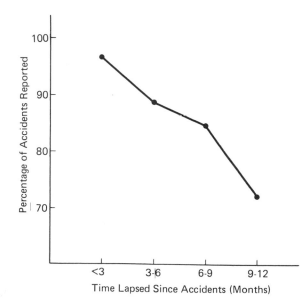

Figure 4-8. The percentage of accidents reported as a function of time elapsed since the accident. (From Loftus, Elizabeth F. [1982]. Memory and its distortions. In Kraut, A.G. [Ed.] *The Stanley Hall Lecture Series.* Washington: American Psychological Association, p. 128.)

What is interesting for the present discussion is that, despite the demonstration of forgetting, the nature of the curve is quite a bit different from that observed by Ebbinghaus in his experiments with nonsense syllables.

Another demonstration of forgetting, but with a different-shaped forgetting curve, can be found in a study by Linton (1982). Like Ebbinghaus, Linton served as her own subject. Every day, for a six-year period from 1972 to 1977, she recorded at least two events from her own life. Every month she tested her ability to remember, to order, and to date a sample of the events she had previously recorded. She originally expected a rapid loss of memory that would resemble Ebbinghaus's classic negatively accelerated forgetting curve. But that is not what she found. Rather, the items were lost from her memory at a linear rate. Her analyses revealed that by the end of any one year, she had forgotten 1 percent of the items written during that year. By the time those items were about two years old, she had forgotten about 5 percent more. Forgetting continued so that by the time the study ended, she had forgotten over 400 items of the 1350 she wrote down for 1972, or about 30 percent. In general she seemed to forget things at a low, fairly steady rate, with the number of forgotten items usually increasing slightly from year to year.

These studies document the decline of memory over time, but further indicate that the precise nature of the forgetting curve may vary from one type of material to another. Whatever the precise nature of the curve, the pervasiveness of forgetting compels researchers to wonder "Why?" Does forgetting occur because of the spontaneous erosion of our memories over time, or because of interference from other experiences which occur during this passage of time?

SPONTANEOUS DECAY

One possible reason for forgetting is that there are processes which cause memories to deteriorate passively over time unless they are rehearsed. According to this view, memories gradually fade, just as the print of a newspaper fades when the pages are left in the sun. Most psychologists do not believe this to be a very satisfying explanation for forgetting. The idea that time per se accounts for anything has essentially been rejected in favor of a view that something going on in time must be responsible for the memory loss.

INTERFERENCE THEORY

A major alternative theory is that forgetting occurs because other events interfere. Since most people are fairly active, both physically and mentally, they are likely to encounter numerous events that potentially interfere with others they may wish to remember.

If this position is correct, then we ought to be able to eliminate forgetting by eliminating interfering events. One way to accomplish this might be to have people go to sleep immediately after learning some new material. This is exactly what was done in a classic experiment performed over fifty years ago (Jenkins & Dallenbach, 1924). Only two subjects were used, each of whom had to learn lists of nonsense syllables under various conditions. In some cases they learned the lists and immediately afterwards went to sleep. In other cases, they learned the lists and then carried on with their normal activities of eating, studying, swimming, or whatever. After either one, two, four or eight hours, the subjects were asked to recall the material they had learned. (In the sleep conditions, the subjects were awakened at the appropriate times.) The resulting forgetting curves are shown in Figure 4-9. For all retention intervals, recall was better after sleeping than after being awake. After eight hours of being awake, subjects could remember only about one nonsense syllable, whereas after eight hours of sleep they recalled nearly six. Jenkins and Dallenbach said of their results, "... forgetting is not so much a matter of the decay of old impressions and associations as it is a matter of the interference, inhibition, or obliteration of the old by the new" (p. 612). Since the original experiments, many investigators have replicated the basic superiority of the sleep over the awake condition for remembering (for example, Ekstrand, 1972).

While on the subject of sleep, we should note that some portions of the sleep cycle can be sources of interference with memory. One example is REM sleep. In adults REM sleep occurs periodically throughout the night, beginning about 90 minutes or so after the onset of sleep. For a normal night's sleep about 22 percent of it is spent in the REM state. This is thought to be the period during which dreaming occurs, (Cohen, 1979), and when dreaming occurs dreams can cause interfering information to intrude into memory. Despite the fact that dreams can produce some interference and can influence memory, it is still the case that subjects who sleep during the retention interval do not experience as much forgetting as those who are awake during the retention interval.

If we stop to examine the interference theory of forgetting, we find that it actually consists of two subtheories. One, proactive interference (sometimes called

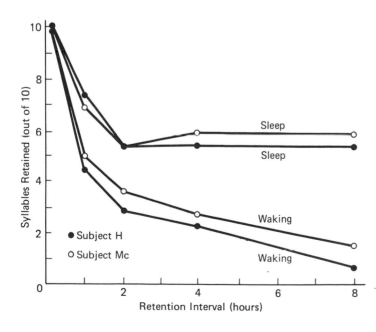

Figure 4-9. Amount of material remembered after sleep and waking conditions. When subjects sleep after learning some new material their retention is superior. (After Jenkins & Dallenbach.)

proactive inhibition, and denoted PI), refers to forgetting that is caused by interference from material learned previously. The other, retroactive interference (sometimes retroactive inhibition, denoted RI), refers to forgetting caused by information learned afterward. These two types of interference are illustrated in Figure 4–10.

RETROACTIVE INTERFERENCE

After we have learned something, other things presented to us during the retention interval produce forgetting of that original learning. Experiments that have been conducted on RI have used this basic paradigm:

EXPERIMENTAL GROUP	Learns information A	Learns information B	Recalls information A
CONTROL GROUP	Learns information A	No new Learning	Recalls information A

Both the experimental and the control group learn some new information, A, and later attempt to recall that information. The experimental group learns some additional information, B, during the retention interval, while the control group does not. Usually B is related to A in some way. As you might expect, the experimental group has a much harder time recalling information A. This is as interference theory would have it; the finding indicates that B serves to disrupt or interfere with the retention of A.

Representative data pertaining to retroactive interference were reported by Briggs (1957). Briggs demonstrated a basic fact about RI: The amount of interference depends upon the number of trials with an interfering list of material. In his study, subjects learned two lists comprised of adjective pairs. In the language of our basic paradigm, we can consider the first list to be information A and the second to be information B. Experimental subjects were given either two, four, ten, or twenty trials on the interfering list. The control subjects either were not given an interfering list or received no trials on the interfering list. Briggs measured the amount of RI for each condition by a formula called relative retroactive interfer-

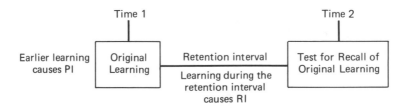

Figure 4–10. Interference theory. At time one, some material is learned. After a retention interval, the material is tested for recall at time two. Material learned before time one produces proactive interference (PI), whereas learning occurring during the retention interval produces retroactive interference (RI).

ence. The measure takes percentage correct for the control group, minus percentage correct for the experimental group, all divided by percentage correct for the control group. In other words:

Relative RI = $\dfrac{\textit{control group percentage} - \textit{experimental group percentage}}{\text{control group percentage}}$

This formula expresses interference as a percentage of control group learning. By so doing, the formula takes into account the difficulty of the original information and allows relative RI in one situation to be compared to relative RI in another situation.

To see how this formula is actually used, we apply it to the data from one of Briggs's conditions. In this particular condition, experimental subjects who received extensive interfering material (twenty trials) correctly recalled only 43.8 percent of the original material, whereas control subjects who received no interfering material correctly recalled 94.4 percent of the original material. Applying the formula for relative RI,

$$\dfrac{\textit{Control \%} - \textit{Experimental \%}}{\text{Control \%}} = \dfrac{94.4\% - 43.8\%}{94.4\%} = 54\%$$

Figure 4–11 shows a relative RI function for subjects who learned the original material extremely well. After no intervening material, subjects showed no retroactive interferences. After ten trials of intervening material, they showed about 60 percent retroactive interference. Finally, after twenty trials, they showed over 70 percent retroactive interference. Briggs also measured relative RI for subjects who had not learned the material as well. His results are qualitatively similar: Interference is positively related to the amount of practice on an interfering list.

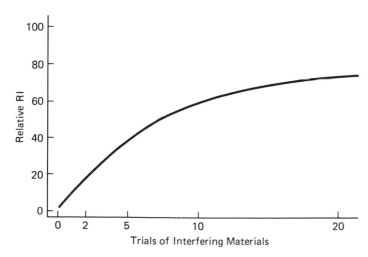

Figure 4-11. Relative retroactive interference as a function of the amount of interfering material. (Source: Briggs, G.E. [1959]. Retroactive inhibition as a function of the degree of original and interpolated learnings. *Journal of Experimental Psychology, 53,* 60–67. Copyright 1959 by the American Psychological Association. Reprinted by permission of the publisher and author.)

PROACTIVE INTERFERENCE

When we learn some new material, things that we have learned previously can also produce forgetting of that new material. Experiments that have been conducted on proactive interference, or PI, have used this basic paradigm:

EXPERIMENTAL GROUP	Learns information B	Learns information A	Recalls information A
CONTROL GROUP	No prior learning	Learns information A	Recalls information A

Both groups learn information A and then recall that information. However, prior to that learning, the experimental group has learned some other material, whereas the control group has not. As may be expected from interference theory, the experimental group has more difficulty recalling information A than does the control group.

An experiment reported by Underwood (1957), but conducted by Archer, nicely shows the effects of amount of prior learning on the learning of new material. The subjects learned lists of adjectives, and then attempted to recall them one day later. Then they learned a new list and recalled it one day later. This procedure continued until nine lists had been learned and recalled. As Figure 4-12 shows, performance was initially fairly good (71 percent of the adjectives from List 1 were recalled correctly); but it declined steadily so that subjects were recalling only 27 percent from List 9.

By the systematic investigation of proactive interference, Underwood was able to provide a key that would unlock an interesting mystery. The mystery was this: The great psychologist Ebbinghaus, inventor of the nonsense syllable, taught himself syllables and then attempted to recall them. He did this with hundreds of lists, and usually found that he was able to recall only 35 percent of what he had initially

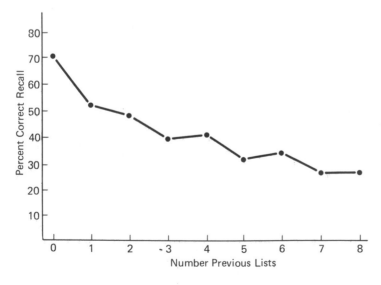

Figure 4-12. As the number of prior lists learned and recalled increases, performance declines. Thus proactive interference, due to prior lists, increases. (Source: Underwood, B.J. [1957]. Interference and forgetting. *Psychological Review, 64,* 49–60. Copyright 1957 by the American Psychological Association. Reprinted by permission of the publisher and author.)

learned. On the other hand, the typical college student of the 1940s who learned a list of nonsense syllables and was tested one day later, could recall 80 percent of the items (Underwood, 1948a, 1948b, 1949). How could the performance of a college student who had learned only a single list so far outweigh the performance of the great memorizer Ebbinghaus? Reflecting upon this question, Underwood noted that a key difference between Ebbinghaus and the college students was that the former had learned hundreds of lists while the latter had learned only a single list. Thus, when Ebbinghaus tested himself, his recall was preceded by the learning and recall of many, many prior lists. It was these prior lists that produced the decrement in his performance. Thus, Underwood had unraveled this mystery, and had accounted for the seemingly disparate performances of Ebbinghaus and the college students. By demonstrating that students' recall drops from 80 percent on the first list to 20 percent on the twentieth list, he vindicated what had seemed to be Ebbinghaus's rather modest performance of 35 percent after exposure to hundreds of lists. The point should be clear: How much new material we can remember strongly depends on the activities we have engaged in before that new learning took place. Prior learning can interfere extensively with current learning.

A more modern-day experiment demonstrating the importance of interference was conducted by John Anderson (1976). Subjects first learned a set of sentences all of the general form: "A (person) is in the (location.)" So, subjects may have learned a list that included these items:

1. A hippie is in the park.
2. A hippie is in the school.
3. A debutante is in the bank.
4. A debutante is in the park.
5. A debutante is in the store.
6. A lawyer is in the church.

After subjects had stored all the facts into their memory, they were tested. A test item consisted of a sentence, to which the subject responded true or false. So, "A hippie is in the park" and "A lawyer is in the church" are true items; "A hippie is in the church" and "A lawyer is in the church" are false items.

Subjects responded to the test sentence by releasing a "true" or a "false" button and reaction times were measured. Of major interest to Anderson was the effect on reaction time of the number of propositions in which each concept occurred. For example, in the sample sentences studied above, lawyer occurs once, hippie occurs twice, and debutante occurs three times. When should subjects be faster? When a concept occurs only once or when it occurs often? Anderson's results were clear. Whether the sentence was true or false, subjects responded more quickly when the concept occurred relatively few times. Test sentences involving the lawyer were responded to faster than test sentences involving the debutante. Put another way, the larger the "propositional fan"—as Anderson called it—the slower the reaction time.

This result can easily be discussed in terms of interference theory. Learning additional facts about a concept produced interference when subjects had to search for one particular proposition.

Anderson has discussed his propositional fan effect in terms of a theory called ACT, which is described in a book entitled *Language, Memory and Thought* (1976). The goal of this theory is to explain the structures and processes of long-term memory that allow us to engage in complex mental activities such as comprehending language, reasoning, and problem-solving. (We discuss the theory more fully in Chapter 6.) Anderson's goals were far more ambitious than simply to explain RI and PI. However, the understanding of RI and PI occupied the interest of many of Anderson's predecessors.

THEORETICAL BASIS FOR INTERFERENCE THEORY

Several hypotheses have been proposed to account for RI and PI. One of the most prevalent views proposes that these types of interference are due to extinction and unlearning, while two other views rest heavily on the notion of competition.

Extinction and Unlearning.   The well-known work of Pavlov (1927) and his followers on classical conditioning forms the basis of one of the major hypotheses about interference. As most students learn in introductory psychology, Pavlov used a paradigm in which he paired a conditioned stimulus (for example, a bell) with an unconditioned stimulus (for example, food). After the two had been paired a number of times, the conditioned stimulus came to elicit the conditioned response of salivation. As long as the bell was usually followed by food, salivation occurred at the time the bell rang.

Suppose the bell were presented without the food. If this happened continually, the conditioned response, salivation, would gradually decline, and soon it would not appear at all. This phenomenon is called extinction. We can also observe another phenomenon within this paradigm, called spontaneous recovery. If a response has been extinguished over a period of time and we once again present the conditioned stimulus (bell), the conditioned response (salivation) will spontaneously reappear. The longer the interval between the last extinction trial and the new presentation of the conditioned stimulus, the stronger the conditioned response. We say that the response has spontaneously recovered.

With this background material, we can better understand the extinction or unlearning explanation of RI and PI. Consider a typical RI with a paired associate experiment. The term A-B will be used to refer to a paired associate list in which stimulus terms are taken from set A and response terms from a different set, B. Thus the A terms might be adjectives and the B terms might be a set of digits, so that "happy-3" might be a typical member of the AB list. An A-C list would be constructed by using as stimuli the same A terms as were used in the A-B list, but the responses would now be taken from set C. If C consisted of a different set of digits, "happy-8" might be in the A-C list.

Suppose a subject first learns an A-B list. Next he or she learns an A-C list. Finally, the subject is required to respond to an A term with a B term, for example, to respond to the word "happy" with the digit "3." As we already know, it is likely that a subject who has had the A-C interpolated learning will perform worse on this final test than a control subject who has not. Further, the more time and effort the subject expends on the A-C list, the poorer his or her performance on the final (A-B) test. This situation is directly analogous to Pavlovian theory: During the learning of the A-C list, the B responses to A stimuli are extinguished because they are elicited but not reinforced.

Similarly, the proactive interference experiment is explicable within a Pavlovian framework. In the PI experiment a subject first learns an A-B list, then an A-C list. Finally, he or she must recall the C terms in the presence of the A terms. As we know, a subject performs worse on the final A-C test than a control subject who has not learned the original A-B list. Furthermore, as the period of time between the initial A-C learning and the final A-C test is increased, the subject becomes progressively worse at giving correct C responses and occasionally recalls some of the earlier learned B responses. In the language of Pavlovian conditioning, we assume that between the initial A-C learning and the final A-C test, some of the original B responses undergo spontaneous recovery and interfere with the recall of the C terms.

The extinction or unlearning hypothesis has perhaps one overriding weakness (Adams, 1976). Its principles have been taken from the area of animal learning and may have very little to do with the way human beings process and retain verbal material. Future research will show the extent to which concepts derived from animal work can be extended to human verbal behavior. Perhaps we have overextended them.

Response Competition.   Another explanation of interference effects is in terms of response competition (McGeoch, 1942). It holds that if two or more interfering responses compete at the time a subject is attempting to recall one of them, the strongest wins out. Thus, if a subject learned an A-B list containing the pair "happy-3" and subsequently learned the A-C pair "happy-8," both responses would be "connected" to the adjective "happy," but the digit "8" might be stronger since it was learned more recently. If sufficient time passed between the learning of "happy-8" and the final test, the other response ("3") might increase in relative strength. Thus the actual response a subject makes might come from either the to-be recalled list or from the interfering list, depending on which was stronger at the time. One problem with this explanation for interference is that it predicts that when a subject makes an error, the error will come from the interfering list. In the previous example, if the subject were supposed to remember "3" and erred, the erroneous response would be "8." Unfortunately for the survival of the response competition theory, research showed that errors did not take on this predicted form (Melton & Irwin, 1940); errors often did not come from the interfering list.

Response-Set Interference. A somewhat different "competition" theory has been called response-set interference (Postman, Stark, & Fraser, 1968). Rather than postulating that individual responses compete with each other, this view proposes that whole sets of responses compete with each other. If a subject learns an A-B list, all of the B terms would compete with all of the C terms to which the subject was subsequently exposed. More specifically, when a subject learns an A-B list, all of the B terms are readily available or activated. During A-C learning, the C terms become activated and the B terms are temporarily inhibited. If we test on A-B immediately after A-C learning, retroactive interference will be observed since the C terms will still be more strongly activated. As time passes between A-C learning and A-B recall, it will become harder and harder for subjects to differentiate between the B and the C terms. Note that unlike the relearning hypothesis, this hypothesis does not assume that A-C learning causes a weakening of the A-B responses. It assumes that the B responses become harder to generate and eventually harder to distinguish from C responses.

A further assumption of this view is that under special conditions there will be no RI. One such special condition is when subjects are asked not to recall the B terms, but merely to recognize which ones match the A terms. Since the subject in this situation are not asked to differentiate the B from the C terms, they should experience no retroactive interference. This prediction was empirically supported by results of Postman and Stark (1969), which indicated that subjects have difficulty generating or retrieving B terms (after A–C) learning, but experience no difficulty associating those terms with their proper A terms.

Interference Theory: A Final Note. To wrap up our discussion of interference theory, it is fair to say that we now understand a great deal about the interference paradigms. We even have some tentative hypothesis to explain behavior observed in these paradigms. The theory has been useful in explaining forgetting of many different kinds of material, ranging from syllables and single words to meaningful sentences (Bower, 1978). However, resolving the inconsistencies in experimental findings and uncovering the actual mechanism of interference will require much more work. Gilani and Ceraso (1982) have tried to do this. They have tried to specify more precisely the situations in which interference will and will not occur. For example, they have found that interference occurs when new information entering the system refers to a different entity. Their work shows that the interest in interference theory continues today. But, as we see in the section on reconstructive processes, interference theory cannot be the whole story.

FAILURE TO STORE

When assessing the reasons for forgetting, we must not overlook the possibility that some items of information that appear to have been forgotten may never have really been stored in the first place. We know that it takes some time for information to get into long-term memory, and it is customary to talk of this time as the time needed for the "consolidation" of memory (Deutsch & Deutsch, 1966; Miller & Marlin, 1979). Certain events, such as head injuries, electroconvulsive stimulation, and the administration of a variety of drugs, can interfere with the process of consolidation (Stern, 1981). But even in the absence of these critical events, new information which a person seemingly sees, hears, feels or touches, does not always get stored in long-term memory. Even information to which we are exposed repeatedly, sometimes hundreds of times, can fail to be stored in long-term memory, and thus will not be recalled. In one study, investigators examined people's ability to recall the visual details of a common object, a United States penny (Nickerson & Adams, 1979). Most people would be willing to say that they know what a penny looks like or at least that they would have no trouble recognizing one when they saw it. We have seen and handled thousands of pennies in our lifetimes. But, surprisingly, Nickerson and Adams found that people cannot reproduce a penny very accurately, cannot recall what is on it, and cannot recognize the difference between a real penny and a fake one that has been altered in simple ways.

This study began by asking people to draw from memory what is on each side of a U.S. penny. Subjects were asked to include all details that they could. In general, the subjects performed remarkably poorly. There are eight critical features that people could have included—on the top side, a head, "In God we trust," "Liberty," a date; on the bottom side, a building, "United States of America," "E Pluribus Unum," "One Cent."

Of the eight critical features, people recalled and correctly located an average of three. Only one person, an active penny collector, accurately remembered all eight.

In another study, subjects were given fifteen different drawings of the head of a U.S. penny, as shown in Figure 4–13. The subjects had to look at all of them and decide which was the accurate reproduction. Fewer than half of the subjects choose penny Λ, which is correct. A significant number of people thought that G or M were the correct pennies, even though these were in fact inaccurate renditions.

Why were people so poor at retrieving this information from memory? One reason is that while a penny is certainly a meaningful object, the particular details that appear on it are not. We do not learn the details of a penny because there is no need for us to know them. All we need in life is to be able to distinguish a penny from other coins, which means learning its color and size. Even when we have to tell it apart from a foreign coin of a similar color and size, a gross comparison of their features will generally be sufficient.

Nickerson and Adams drew some other conclusions:

> ... the results from these experiments demonstrate that frequent exposure to an object and ability to "recognize" that object for practical purposes do not guarantee that the object is represented accurately in memory in any great detail. To the contrary, they raise the question of whether visual long-term memory is much less rich and elaborate than has often been supposed. (1979)

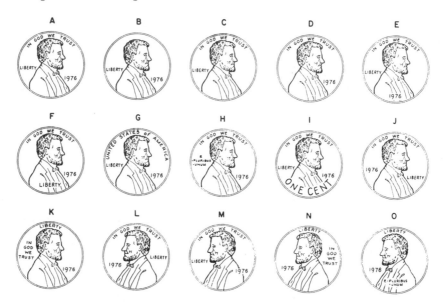

Figure 4-13. Which is the "honest" penny? (After Nickerson & Adams, [1979]. Courtesy of Academic Press, Inc.)

Reconstructive Processes in Memory

During the Senate Watergate hearings in 1973, John Dean testified regarding a meeting with Herbert Kalmbach. He claimed that he had met Kalmbach in the coffee shop of the Mayflower Hotel in Washington, D.C., and that they had both gone directly upstairs to Kalmbach's room. Dean had no motive to lie. Yet he was pressed repeatedly in a way that suggested he might be lying. Each time, Dean vehemently reaffirmed his testimony—the meeting had taken place, it began in the Mayflower Hotel coffee shop and it ended in Kalmbach's room in the same hotel. At one point, one of Dean's questioners revealed that the register of the Mayflower Hotel did not show Kalmbach to have been registered at the time in question. Dean still confidently stuck to his story and explained the apparent inconsistency by suggesting that Kalmbach might have been using a false name. Eventually, the difficulty was cleared up. It was pointed out that the Statler Hilton Hotel in Washington has a coffee shop called the Mayflower Doughnut Coffee Shop. Kalmbach had been registered at the Statler Hilton at the time in question. (See Neisser, 1981, for a more detailed analysis of this incident.)

Dean's testimony illustrates something fundamental about human memory, namely that it can be reconstructive in nature, and often the reconstructions lead to errors. Reconstructions often lead to errors because they involve inferences that may or may not be correct. Consider an example provided by computer scientist Roger Schank (1982), concerning a trip he took to Palo Alto, a place he had traveled to many times, and where he had also lived for a year. During the trip he could answer many questions about what his hotel room number was, what kind of car he rented, and so on. One year later, a few particularly interesting details remained in his memory, but the majority were gone. Some of the details could be reconstructed, however. For example, although he could not readily retrieve the name of the hotel or rental car company, he could "calculate" such answers in the following way:

> a) I always stay at the Holiday Inn, so that's where I would have stayed. b) There are only two rent-a-car agencies that I ever used and I had received my Hertz discount card around that time, so it would have been Hertz. c) I can't recall the room number but I remember where it was. . . . (p. 13)

Such answers are instances of what is commonly called reconstructive memory. Recall from Chapter 1 our discussion of constructive comprehension and reconstructive memory.

The reconstructions of Roger Schank and John Dean remind us of the classic work of the English psychologist, Frederick C. Bartlett (1932). In Bartlett's studies, subjects were presented with a story or drawing and later were asked to repeat or reproduce this information several times. This was called the method of "repeated reproduction." In other cases, a complex story was read by one subject, who told it to another, who in turn told it to another, and so on. This was the method of "serial reproduction." The most famous of his stories was a legend called "The War of the Ghosts," a story about a tribe of North American Indians. The story is given in Figure 4–14.

Printed below the story is a sample subject reproduction which illustrates many of the things that Bartlett observed. Subjects' reproductions tended to be shorter, more concrete, and more modern in phraseology than the original. Subjects distorted the story so that it fit into their own cultural conceptions of what is logical and conventional. Unfamiliar terms dropped out in their recall. For example, the name of the town, Egulac, does not appear in the subject reproduction. In discussing his results, Bartlett offered the notion that subjects form abstract representations, or mental "schemas," of stories they read. These schemas are assimilated into the subject's existing knowledge, beliefs, and emotions. The process of assimilation itself results in the kinds of changes that Bartlett observed. Put differently, when subjects hear a story for the first time, they usually do not remember portions of it which do not fit in with their existing long-term memory structures. Further, they change certain items to become more familiar and coherent. Without substantial modification, a straightforward interference theory would have difficulty explaining these "constructive" changes.

Another classic study on constructive processes that is worth mentioning briefly is the one by Allport and Postman (1958). In their study, subjects saw the illustration in Figure 4–15. As can be seen, the drawing shows several people on a subway car, including a black man and a white man with a razor in his hand. Using the method of serial reproduction, where one subject describes the picture to another, who repeats the description (to the best of memory) to another, and so on, these in-

THE WAR OF THE GHOSTS

One night two young men from Egulac went down to the river to hunt seals, and while they were there it became foggy and calm. Then they heard war-cries, and they thought: "Maybe this is a war party." They escaped to the shore, and hid behind a log. Now canoes came up, and they heard the noise of paddles, and saw one canoe coming up to them. There were five in the canoe, and they said:

"What do you think? We wish to take you along. We are going up the river to make war on the people."

One of the young men said: "I have no arrows."

"Arrows are in the canoe," they said.

"I will not go along. I might be killed. My relatives do not know where I have gone. But you," he said, turning to the other, "may go with them."

So one of the young men went, but the other returned home.

And the warriors went on up the river to a town on the other side of Kalama. The people came down to the water, and they began to fight, and many were killed. But presently the young man heard one of the warriors say: "Quick, let us go home: that Indian has been hit." Now he thought: "Oh, they are ghosts." He did not feel sick, but they said he had been shot.

So the canoes went back to Egulac, and the young man went ashore to his house, and made a fire. And he told everybody and said: "Behold I accompanied the ghosts, and we went to fight. Many of our fellows were killed, and many of those who attacked us were killed. They said I was hit, and I did not feel sick."

He told it all, and then he became quiet. When the sun rose he fell down. Something black came out of his mouth. His face became contorted. The people jumped up and cried.

He was dead.

SUBJECT'S REPRODUCTION

Two youths were standing by a river about to start seal-catching, when a boat appeared with five men in it. They were all armed for war.

The youths were at first frightened, but they were asked by the men to come and help them fight some enemies on the other bank. One youth said he could not come as his relations would be anxious about him; the other said he would go, and entered the boat.

In the evening he returned to his hut, and told his friends that he had been in a battle. A great many had been slain, and he had been wounded by an arrow; he had not felt any pain, he said. They told him that he must have been fighting in a battle of ghosts. Then he remembered that it had been queer and he became very excited.

In the morning, however, he became ill, and his friends gathered round; he fell down and his face became very pale. Then he writhed and shrieked and his friends were filled with terror. At last he became calm. Something hard and black came out of his mouth, and he lay contorted and dead.

Figure 4–14. (From Bartlett's War of Ghosts, [1932]. Courtesy of Cambridge University Press.)

Figure 4-15. Original figure in Allport and Postman (1958).

vestigators found that the razor tended to migrate from the white man to the black man. One subject reported, "This is a subway train in New York headed for Portland Street. There is a Jewish woman and a Negro who has a razor in his hand. The woman has a baby or a dog. The train is going to Deyer Street, and nothing much happened" (1958, p. 57). Something more than simple interference is at work here. In this case, we see that subjects' stereotpes (for example, "blacks are more violent") are affecting what they perceive and recall.

More recent experiments on the constructive nature of memory have shown that the prior knowledge a person has will interact with new material and lead the person to construct new information—to create inferences—that then become a part of memory. This is illustrated by experiments showing that people tend to confuse inferences constructed from new material with that new material. For example, in one study, subjects were presented with written passages. One was about a ruthless dictator: "Gerald Martin strove to undermine the existing government to satisfy his political ambitions. Many of the people of his country supported his efforts. Current political problems made it relatively easy for Martin to take over. Certain groups remained loyal to the old government and caused Martin trouble. He confronted these groups directly and so silenced them. He became a ruthless, uncontrollable dictator. The ultimate effect of his rule was the downfall of his country."

Subjects in one group believed that the dictator was the ficticious Gerald Martin. Subjects in another group were told after reading the passage that the main character was really Adolph Hitler; these subjects could then understand the passage with respect to their prior knowledge about Hitler. In the final test given to all subjects, seven sentences from the passage were randomly mixed together with seven false sentences. Of special interest was the subjects' performance on critical false sentences such as, "He hated the Jews particularly and so persecuted them." This sentence did not occur in the original passage and thus would not apply to the fictitious Gerald Martin but would be true of Hitler. When the test was delayed for one week, subjects in the group which had been told that the passage was about Hitler were much more likely than the other group to answer that they had read this critical sentence. This study suggests that items of prior knowledge were integrated with the passage, and that both were used in making the final recognition decisions. (See Dooling & Christiansen, 1977, for a review of their work.)

Other researchers have similarly shown that memory appears to change to accommodate new information added after the original experience (Spiro, 1977, 1980). In Spiro's studies, subjects were presented with a very detailed story about an engaged couple named Bill and Margie. In the story, Bill is having doubts about discussing a very important issue—that he does not ever want to have children. He anxiously hesitates about bringing the subject up with Margie for he fears that it will jeopardize their relationship. Finally, the matter is discussed. In one version of the story (given to one group of subjects) Margie becomes very upset, indicating that she wants very much to have children. They have a fight, and the story ends. In one condition subjects are told that the experiment is concerned with the way people react to stories involving interpersonal relations. They are asked to think about and react to the story, are casually told that the story was true, and that in fact Bill and Margie did marry and are living happily together. Some time later, the subjects return and are asked to recall the story. Note that in the version given above, there is a conflict between the information presented in the story (the fight) and the contrary information presented after the story (that is, that the two actually did marry). Subjects resolved this conflict by making a substantial number of erros in recalling the story. They "recalled" that Margie decided she really did not want to have children, or that Margie was a bit upset at first but then she calmed down, or that Bill decided that he would like to have children after all. (Other subjects who did not get this "conflicting ending" did not make these same errors in recalling the story.) It is interesting to note that the subjects were as certain that the inferred events occurred in the original story as they were that the actual events of the story occurred. Both Spiro, and Rumelhart (1977) have suggested that these results indicate that subjects use previously acquired schemata in their recall of complex events. After a period of time, subjects apparently cannot distinguish between events that were actually reported and those required by the schema.

Reconstructive processes have also been demonstrated in situations that are analogous to those facing eyewitnesses to crimes, accidents, and other important events. Imagine yourself in this situation. It is New Year's Eve and you are rushing home to get ready to go to a party. Just as you turn into your driveway you see a man trying to cross the street a couple of houses down the road. A pickup truck runs right into him. You have witnessed a serious auto accident, and it is likely that you will be questioned about it. Research on people's ability to answer questions regarding such events has shown that subsequent information introduced by another witness, or by the police officer asking the questions, could alter your recollection of what you yourself had seen.

In one study, subjects viewed a brief videotape of an automobile accident and then answered some questions (See Loftus, 1979, for a review of this research). For half the subjects, one of the questions was "How fast was the white sports car going while traveling along the country road?" For the the other half, a similar question was "How fast was the white sports car going when it passed the barn while traveling along the country road?" In fact, there was no barn in the film. Yet when questioned again a week later, more than 17 percent of those exposed to the false information about a barn answered "yes" to the question "Did you see a barn?" In contrast, only about 3 percent of the remaining subjects answered "yes" to the same question. Apparently, the assumption of a barn during the initial questioning caused many subjects to incorporate the nonexistent barn into their recollections of the event.

In this case, it appears that the initial memory of the accident is being supplemented with additional (false) information. On a previously empty country landscape, subjects now imagine a barn. A question arises as to whether the memory could actually be altered, not simply supplemented. The answer to this appears to be yes. In one set of studies, subjects saw thirty color slides depicting successive stages of an automobile accident involving a red Datsun (Loftus, Miller & Burns, 1978). The critical slide was of the Datsun stopped at an intersection before it eventually turned right and hit a pedestrian. Half the subjects saw a slide with a stop sign at the corner; half saw a slide with a yield sign. (Figure 4–16 shows these two almost identical pictures.)

Immediately after viewing the slides, the subjects answered a number of questions about them. One of the questions presupposed the existence of either a stop sign or a yield sign. For half the subjects the presupposed sign was consistent with what they had actually seen; for half it was inconsistent. The subjects then performed a distracting task for minutes, after which a final recognition test began. Subjects looked at pairs of slides and had to chose the one slide out of each pair that they had seen before. On the critical stop/yield pair, when subjects had been questioned with correct information, 75 percent chose the correct slide. In contrast, when the earlier question presupposed an inconsistent traffic sign, the subjects chose the correct slide only 41 percent of the time. Thus, presuppositions do indeed seem capable of transforming a witness's memory. The rate at which such transformation occurs, moreover, can be substantially increased by changing the timing of misinformation. If exposed to inaccurate information a week after an accident, when the true details have begun to fade, subjects are susceptible to the misinformation 80 percent of the time (Loftus, Miller & Burns, 1978).

These experiments, and others that have used variations of this procedure (for example, Greene, Flynn & Loftus, 1982; Weinberg, Wadsworth & Baron, 1983) show that people will pick up information, whether it is true or false, and integrate

Figure 4-16. These photographs were used in an experiment designed to test the accuracy of recollection of two groups of subjects. The only difference between the two photos is that there is a stop sign in one and a yield sign in the other. (From Loftus, Miller & Burns, [1978].)

it into their memory, thereby supplementing or even altering their recollection. Once the alteration has occurred, it appears to be very difficult although not impossible to retrieve the original memory (Bekerian & Bowers, 1983).

Still a question remains about why people's recollections are so easily altered by exposure to new information. Why is the new information remembered instead of what was originally experienced? A further question concerns the fate of the underlying memory traces. Have they truly been updated or altered by the new information so that the original traces could not be recovered in the future? This is the "alteration" hypothesis, and it suggests that the original memory representations are altered when new information is encoded that differs from what was originally experienced. The alternative position is the "coexistence" hypothesis, which assumes that the original and post-event information coexist in memory (Loftus, 1983). The introduction of new information, under this position, is thought to make the original memories less accessible, but still potentially recoverable at some future time.

— The coexistence-alteration issue is important from both a theoretical and a practical standpoint. Speaking practically, the dichotomy bears on attempts that one might make to correct a memory after it has been biased by new information. Under the coexistence view, but perhaps not the alteration view, it makes sense to vigorously pursue retrieval techniques (such as hypnosis, reinstatement of context) that might make the original information accessible. Under the alteration view, one's efforts would be placed elsewhere because it is likely that the only way to return to the original information is by a "re-alteration" of memory.

Theoretically speaking, the dichotomy bears on one of the most fundamental questions about memory; the permanence of memory traces. The coexistence view is consistent with the idea that all information, once stored in memory, remains there more or less permanently. The alteration view implies a true loss of information from memory due to the updating, substitution, or blending in of new inputs.

Many people hold the view that memories, once stored in the human mind, last forever. Canadian neurosurgeon Wilder Penfield, for example, believed that the brain holds a record of past experience that contains virtually all past details, a sort of tape recorder in the mind. Penfield arrived at his belief on the basis of descriptions given by patients while their brains were being electrically stimulated during surgery. A few patients reported astonishingly detailed memories: "I hear voices. It is late at night, around the carnival somewhere—some sort of traveling circus. I just saw lots of big wagons that they use to haul animals in." Yet Penfield never verified these so-called "memories," and never seemed to consider the possibility that they might have been pure fantasy. To base such strong conclusions on the dubious protocols of a handful of patients was clearly unwarranted. And yet Penfield was sure that he had found evidence for a permanent record in the brain (Penfield & Roberts, 1959; Penfield & Perot, 1963).

Penfield is only one of many people who believe in the permanence of memory. In a recent survey of psychologists and lay people, over two-thirds of respondents indicated a belief that nothing is really ever lost from memory (Loftus & Loftus, 1980). Neisser, in an article entitled "On the trail of the tape-recorder fallacy" (1982), has offered an intriguing explanation for why people have clung so uncritically to this view. He claims that wide acceptance of any interpretation of human nature depends on the cultural availability of the concepts involved. People easily believe in mental tape recorders because they are familiar with physical tape recorders. Models of the mind in general—and views about the working of memory specifically—seem to follow the latest advances in gadgetry. At one time, scientists based their theories on hydraulics because this technology came into vogue. Later they based theories on the telephone switchboard. Currently, they base their theories on the computer. Commonplace notions of memory, it seems, are heavily influenced by technology. Neisser hopes that understanding this influence may help us become free of it.

The view that all memories are potentially recoverable and that faulty recall is a problem of accessibility has become a part of many recent theories of memory (Morton, Hammersley & Bekerian, 1983; Shaughnessy & Mand, 1982). For example, Morton and co-workers have proposed a "headed-records framework" which assumes that when an event is seen, a record is laid down in memory. Each time the event is subsequently brought to mind, a new record is established, each with its own individualized heading. Later headed-records can interfere with the retrieval of earlier ones, but if the proper cue is provided, the original headed record will be accessed. A major assumption of this framework is that once a headed-record has been formed, it cannot be deleted, changed or updated. The only changes permitted to the memory structures are the addition of new headed-records. We will have more to say about memory structures in Chapter 6.

Before leaving the topic of memory permanence, however, we should note the contrasting position that some memories may undergo destructive transformation due to new inputs. This position has been strengthened (although by no means proved) by the failure of numerous empirical attempts to recover original memories. Even the mysterious technique of hyponosis has failed to lead to original memories once they have been altered (Sheehan & Tilden, 1983; Sanders & Simmons, 1983). Of course, such failures do not prove that the original memories do not exist, because it can always be argued that the original memory does exist but the appropriate retrieval method was not used, or that the method used was not sufficiently powerful. We return to the topic of retrieval methods in the next chapter.

As we mentioned, Bartlett recognized over fifty years ago the fact that distortions are characteristic of memory. Alba and Hasher (1983) have noted that present-day adherents of Bartlett's views also share his rejection of the notion that memory contains accurate traces that are stable over long durations waiting to plucked out when needed. The commonness with which distortions are observed has provided fuel for those who advocate "schema" theories of memory. Briefly, schema theorists propose that what is stored in memory is heavily influenced by guiding knowledge frames (schema) that select and actively modify experience in order to arrive at a coherent, unified representation of an experience (Alba & Hasher, 1983). Such theories tend to emphasize the inaccuracy and incompleteness of memory, rather than its successes. Schema theories and the closely related frame theory (Minsky, 1975) and script theory (Schank & Abelson, 1977), have in common the general idea that the knowledge a person possesses about the world can influence what is stored and remembered. These ideas account for a considerable portion of current research in memory.

Besides helping reveal something about the reconstructive nature of memory, research on memory for complex events is important for another reason. In criminal and civil trials, jurors tend to believe the testimony of eyewitnesses, and yet such testimony can be faulty. This sometimes leads to a mistaken identification. No-one is immune from the possibility of being mistakenly identified—whether he is a criminal or a priest. In fact, in August 1979, a Catholic priest stood trial for a series of armed robberies in Delaware. He had been identified by seven witnesses as the "gentleman bandit," so called because of the polite manners of the well-dressed robber. At the trial, this parade of witnesses positively identified the accused priest. Then, in a move that could have come from a television melodrama, the trial was abruptly halted as another man confessed to the robberies. Police became convinced

Father Pagano. (Courtesy
of UPI/Bettmann Archive.)

William Jackson.
(Courtesy of UPI/Bett-
mann Archive.)

that this man had committed the crimes when he told them details that only the
robber himself could have known. The prosecutor dropped charges against the priest,
whose ordeal was finally over. Father Pagano was lucky in one respect; others who
have been convicted of crimes on the basis of misidentification have not been released until they have spent many years in prison. For example, William Jackson
of Columbus, Ohio, was convicted for raping two women (Loftus, 1984). Two women
had positively identified Jackson as the man who had raped them in September
and October of 1977. The October victim said she had absolutely no doubt about
her identification. Yet Jackson had an alibi; he was at home when the rapes occurred. But the jury believed the eyewitnesses and Jackson spent five years in prison
for crimes he did not commit. We return to the topic of eyewitness testimony later
in Chapter 11.

Summary

In this chapter, we have discussed how we learn new things, and how we remember
these things at a later time. The process of learning involves the storage of information into what is commonly called long-term memory. Many strategies can be
called upon to aid us in our attempt to store information in long-term memory.
Rehearsal strategies, and the use of imagery and other mnemomic techniques are
some examples.

Imagery mnemonics have been successful in helping people to remember
foreign language vocabulary and in helping people remember name-face associations. The method of loci has been successful in helping people to remember lists
of objects. The phonetic mnemonic system was successful in helping people learn
conversions between the metric system and the present system of measurement
in the United States.

Once we manage to get new information into long-term memory, we still may not be able to retrieve it. Difficulty in retrieval seems to be due in part to interference produced by other sources of information. Both retroactive and proactive interference can substantially reduce our ability to remember things. Retroactive interference refers to the fact that after we have learned something, other things presented to us during the retention interval can produce forgetting of the original learning. Proactive interference refers to the fact that when we learn some new material, things that we have learned previously can also produce forgetting of that new material. Both types of interference can substantially reduce our ability to remember.

Another source of error is the reconstructive aspect of memory. When we try to remember things, we often use information from other sources and make inferences from what we know. These activities typically serve us well, but occasionally lead to errors. The reconstructive aspect of memory was shown in the classic work of the English psychologist, Frederick Bartlett, who proposed that people form abstract representations, or mental schemas, when they are presented with new information. These schemas are assimilated into the person's existing knowledge structures, and the assimilation process produces some of the distortions that are observed in recollection. Modern day cognitive psychologists have similarly used the idea of schemas in their theories of how information is represented in long-term memory.

FIVE

Concepts and Concept Formation

At a cognitive level, we deal in abstractions. We do not store objects or events as such in memory, but rather their representations. Moreover, these representations are, in some sense general, encompassing a number of independent experiences. Thus, what we carry around as knowledge seems to come in the form of concepts or categories rather than specific independent events.

We have made reference in preceding chapters to the concepts and the conceptual knowledge that people have. We have talked about how concepts are embedded in memory and how they are retrieved and used when required by the situation at hand. We discussed these matters as if everyone knew what concepts are. But we have said little or nothing about how concepts get in the mind in the first place and become the object of cognitive processes. Concepts come from somewhere—they are not just there when you need them. The formation of concepts has been the focus of active research in psychology for the last thirty years.

We will review in this chapter some of the recent factual and theoretical developments concerning this question.

Our knowledge of the world is comprised of concepts and relationships among concepts. Consider the concept *bird*. This real-world concept applies to all objects meeting certain criteria. Concepts are neither true nor false—they just are. However, relationships between concepts ("all robins are birds"), between concepts and properties ("all birds have wings"), and between concepts and the real world ("this object is a bird") do have truth value. Concepts become part of our factual or semantic knowledge of the world by entering into observable relationships.

In another sense, concepts represent discriminations that can be acted upon. That is, your knowledge of the concept *bird* allows you to sort out birdlike objects from non-birdlike objects, or to fire a shotgun at the appropriate time during duck-hunting season. Thus, concepts form an important component of our procedural as well as our declarative knowledge about the world.

How Are Concepts Formed?

A variety of ideas has been proposed about how people form concepts. We will talk about three classes of theories that in one way or another capture these ideas. We will call the classes (1) concepts learned by association, (2) concepts learned by hypothesis-testing, (3) concepts learned by instance memory (exemplar theory). One should note at the outset that none of these theories provides a totally accurate picture of concept-formation and concept use. They are perhaps best thought of as pretheoretical principles that fit some but not all of the empirical evidence on conceptual behavior.

CONCEPTS BY ASSOCIATION

Stimulus Response (S-R) Associations.   One of the earliest definitions of the term "concept" in psychology was based on the sharing of common elements or stimulus features by concept instances. An early advocate of this idea was the behaviorist, Clark L. Hull (1920), who described concept-formation as the attachment of a single (common) response, the concept response, to a set of stimuli with one or more common elements. A novel stimulus, having a collection of features that has never before been seen by a person, would nonetheless elicit the concept response if it contained the right common elements. Indeed, novel stimuli that are similar (though not identical) to instances of a known concept would tend to elicit the concept response on the basis of stimulus generalization.

Hull demonstrated the feasibility of his theory of concept-learning by having adult subjects learn several lists of stimulus-response paired associates. The stimulus in each pair was a Chinese character and the response a nonsense syllable. Each list was twelve pairs in length. The stimuli changed from list to list but the same twelve responses applied in each list. Unknown to the subject, each Chinese character in a particular list had its own unique radical embedded within it. While the overall characters changed from list to list, the same twelve radicals appeared in each list and the same twelve nonsense syllable responses were associated with them (see Figure 5–1).

Subjects learned how to respond correctly to each character in each list. The important finding was that performance improved from list to list. The ability of a person to give the correct nonsense syllable to each character after a single study trial increased from less than 30 percent on the first list to approximately 60 percent on the sixth list. This signified to Hull that his subjects were abstracting the radical common to a given class of characters. He also concluded that the abstraction process must have been relatively unconscious, for most subjects were unable to verbalize the basis for their reaction to new characters. Hull's conclusion was probably premature; he did not probe his subjects in depth. More recent evidence reveals that subjects are quite conscious of the processes involved in at least some of their efforts at concept-learning (Ericsson & Simon, 1980).

Association and Adaptation. Instances of a particular concept differ from one another in a variety of inconsequential ways—for example, instances of *bird* differ in their size and their flight characteristics. The associative basis of concept-learning was further elaborated by Bourne and Restle (1959) to take account of these irrelevant variations. Bourne and Restle proposed that, in addition to abstracting the relevant elements of stimuli and associating them with the proper category response, concept-learners also become adapted to (or learn to ignore) the irrelevant or non-common features of stimuli. During learning, the subject performs a perceptual analysis on each stimulus, associating the conceptual response to common features and adapting out the irrelevant features. Thus, once a concept has been learned, irrelevant stimulus features exert no control over responses. Asso-

Name	Radical (concept)	List 1	List 2	List 3	List 4	List 5	List 6
oo							
yer							
li							
ta							
deg							
ling							

Figure 5-1. Some of the stimulus materials used by Hull (1920). Each of the six different radicals is embedded in a unique character in each list. Each radical is associated with a nonsense name, which is the response to be given to that radical regardless of the character in which it occurs. (Source: Hull, C.L. [1920]. Quantitative aspects of the evolution of concepts. *Psychological Monographs* [Whole No. 123]. Copyright 1920 by the American Psychological Association. Reprinted by permission of the publisher and author.)

ciative and adaptation processes were described mathematically in this theory, which gives fairly accurate quantitative accounts of a variety of experiments manipulating the number of relevant and irrelevant features in concept instances (see Figure 5–2).

Mediational Processes.   Still another variation on learning concepts by association was introduced by Tracy and Howard Kendler (1962). Capitalizing on the notion of a preliminary perceptual analysis, these investigators proposed that any stimulus triggers off within the learner a set of (nonobservable) mediational responses, corresponding to the dimensions of the stimuli. Consider a concrete example. Suppose, in a concept-learning problem using geometrical designs, the subject is presented with a large, red square that is said to be an instance of an unknown concept. The subject undertakes a covert perceptual analysis of the stimulus, identifying independently its dimensions (size, color, and form) and the value exhibited on each dimension (large, red, and square respectively). Because the stimulus is an instance of the concept, the overt category response is associated independently with all identified stimulus values. Over a series of trials, each with a different stimulus, however, the category response is consistently associated only with those stimulus values that are characteristic of concept instances. As the subject gradually learns the concepts, mediational responses that correspond to the relevant dimensions of the stimuli are strengthened as are their associations to the category response. Eventually, when the subject knows the concept, only relevant mediators control overt behavior. If the concept, for example, is known to be *all red stimuli are positive*, then each new stimulus triggers off first, and perhaps only, a mediational reaction to color. If the color of a stimulus is determined to be red, then the

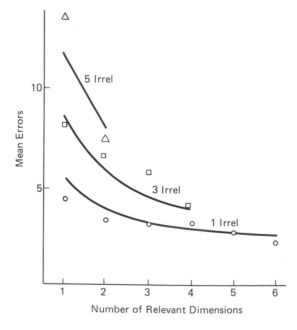

Figure 5-2. Mean number of errors made by subjects solving a simple concept problem as a function of the numbers of relevant and irrelevant stimulus dimensions. Obtained data are shown as points. Lines are predicted by the theory of Bourne & Restle (1959). (Source: Bourne, L.E., Jr., & Restle, F. [1959]. A mathematical theory of concept identification. *Psychological Review, 66,* 278–296. Copyright 1959 by the American Psychological Association. Reprinted by permission of the publisher and author.)

appropriate category response is given. If the stimulus is determined to be some other color, then a negative response is elicited.

Mediational processes are conceived to be primarily, though not exclusively, verbal in nature. In some sense, they represent the subject talking to himself or herself about the stimulus at hand and how to respond to it. The Kendlers used this analysis to account for some striking performance transitions revealed in developmental studies. While these studies will be discussed in detail elsewhere, one kind of evidence, coming from studies where solution shifts are introduced into a concept problem, might be mentioned here. After the subject has learned one way of categorizing stimuli, an unannounced change in the rule is made by the experimenter and a new way becomes appropriate. Two kinds of solution shifts are examined. For an intradimensional shift, the solution changes from one value to another on the same dimension, for example, from *all red figures are positive* to *all green figures*. For an extradimensional shift, the relevant dimension is changed, for example, *all red figures are positive* to *all square figures*. In the case of an intradimensional shift, the subject has established the appropriate mediational activity for postshift performance during preshift learning, according to mediational theory. That is, the subject is already attending to the dimension that is relevant after the shift. An extradimensional shift requires the subject to learn to ignore the former relevant dimension and refocus attention on a new relevant dimension. Therefore, mediational theory predicts that the extradimensional shift will be more difficult for a subject than the intradimensional shift. In fact, this turns out to be the case, at least for adult subjects.

There is, however, an interesting and important developmental process to be contended with. Children younger than five or six years of age actually show the opposite result; extradimensional shifts are easier for them than intradimensional shifts (Kendler & Kendler, 1961). This suggested to the Kendlers that younger children might be premediational. That is, younger children do not engage in the same internal processing of information as adults, responding to the stimuli presented directly, non-mediationally and as whole units. Because of the marked change in a person's ability to use language around age four to six, this developmental shift is highly consistent with the idea that mediators are, at least in some important way, verbal in nature.

CONCEPTS BY HYPOTHESIS-TESTING

Another idea, with a history as long and extensive as associationism, asserts that people solve problems, including concept problems, by forming and testing hypotheses. This idea is fundamental to the landmark research of Bruner, Goodnow, and Austin (1956). Bruner and his co-workers concluded that a person is never really at a loss for how to respond in problematic situations. Rather, a problem arises because a variety of behaviors are possible and it is not clear which one will produce the solution. Bruner's goal was to discover what kind of procedures people use to sort through these possibilities. The general theoretical idea behind this work is that concepts are formed by an active, cognitive, strategic, logic-driven hypothesis-testing process, rather than passively through the detection and association of common elements in exemplars with a category response.

Strategies for Hypothesis-Testing.   The following experiment illustrates the approach of Bruner, Goodnow, and Austin. An array of stimulus materials is laid out before the subject. The stimuli have four physical dimensions—size, color, form, and number of objects—each with three values. Some stimulus within the array, say, *one large, red triangle,* is designated as a positive instance of an unknown concept, to be discovered by the subject. On the basis of this single example, the subject is asked to formulate his or her best guess—that is, hypothesis—about the unknown concept. Subsequently, the subject is allowed to select any other instance from the array and to ask the experimenter whether it is a positive or a negative instance of the concept. The experimenter responds and then asks the subject for a new or revised best guess. Each successive stimulus selected by the subject provides information to help improve the current hypothesis. The procedure repeats itself until the subject knows what the concept is.

Bruner and his co-workers observed that subjects go about formulating hypotheses and selecting stimuli for testing them in a fairly systematic way. Many subjects were observed to perform as follows, for example. After the first positive instance has been identified by the experimenter, the subject proceeds to formulate a hypothesis that takes into account all the features of that stimulus. Thus, if *one, large, red triangle* is called a positive stimulus, then one, large, red, and triangle are all potentially relevant features of the unknown concept. None of them can be ruled out. On the other hand, small and medium stimuli, green and blue stimuli, circular and square stimuli, and stimuli with two or three objects on them can be ruled out as possibilities. The subject then proceeds to select a new stimulus that differs in one and only one way from the first. The subject might, for example, select next, *two, large, red triangles.* Such a selection is guaranteed to pay off in new information. If the selection is positive, the subject can immediately determine that the number attribute is not important. If both single and double patterns are examples of the concept, then number does not distinguish examples from nonexamples. Under these conditions, the subject can formulate a revised hypothesis, "large, red triangles are positive." If, on the other hand, the newly selected instance is negative, the subject has a different kind of information. Such an outcome implies that number *is* an important attribute and that positive instances must be singular. Therefore, the subject should state, as the next hypothesis, the same features contained in the first hypothesis. The third selection (and all subsequent selections) change one other attribute from the initial positive instance, for example, *one, small, red triangle.* Once again depending on the outcome of the selection, the subject can determine whether the changed attribute, in this case size, is relevant to the concept.

This procedure for formulating and testing hypotheses is called the *conservative focusing strategy* and is illustrated in Table 5–1. At least in certain problems, subjects tend to gravitate toward this strategy, even if they do not use it initially.

Moreover, the emphasis in this strategy on disconformation of the current hypothesis is characteristic, as we will see in Chapters 8 and 9, of much of human reasoning. Conservative focusing is not necessarily the best strategy from a logical standpoint but it is workable, at least for certain types of problems. Its main advantage is the small demand it makes on the subject's memory. Rather than having to remember each stimulus selected and its category, positive or negative, the subject merely needs to remember the current hypothesis, for the current hypothesis contains within it all features that are still plausibly relevant. Using this strategy, the subject cycles systematically through all variable attributes of the stimuli, identifying them as relevant or irrelevant. When the cycle is completed, the subject has enough information to state the correct concept.

Of course, not all subjects follow the exact same strategy. Bruner and his coworkers identified a number of other possibilities that were used in the same experimental problem. Some of them had a less conservative character. Subjects might, for example, decide to check on more than one attribute with each selection. This decision introduces something of a gamble, for such a selection could either rule out several attributes at once or provide no information whatsoever. Alternatively, rather than formulating composite hypotheses, subjects sometimes take a flier on a pet hypothesis involving certain, but not all possible, features of the stimuli. Strategies of this sort, called hypothesis *scanning* strategies by Bruner and his colleagues, put a heavy toll on the subject's memory for hypotheses that have been tested in the past and been proved to be incorrect. Nonetheless, whatever the reasons, scanning strategies are fairly commonly employed in concept problems.

Table 5-1. *An example of conservative focusing*

	STIMULUS PATTERNS	CATEGORY	HYPOTHESIS
Focal stimulus	1LR △	+	"1LR △"
Subject's selections			
1.	2LR △	∣	"LR △"
2.	1SR △	−	"LR △"
3.	1LG △	+	"L △"
4.	1LR □	−	"L △"
	Concept: L △		

Levine's Hypothesis-Testing Theory.   The pioneering research of Bruner, Goodnow, and Austin touched off a flurry of empirical and theoretical work designed to expand psychological knowledge about what variables influence hypothesis-testing behavior. Over the course of the ensuing twenty years, from the 1950s to the mid-1970s, hypothesis-testing became the dominant theoretical idiom in concept-learning. Concept-learners were conceived to be active formulators and testers of possible solutions, discovering the concept when the correct hypothesis is somehow uncovered and used. The culmination of this work was realized in the systematic efforts of Marvin Levine, spanning primarily the last ten years of this period (1965–1975). Levine's efforts are summarized in an important book that not only reviews the literature of the field but contains a resumé of his own major publications (Levine, 1975).

The development of Levine's theory is a classical illustration in science of the interplay between methodological, empirical, and theoretical factors. Levine's early work revolved around the development of an experimental procedure that would provide a more detailed measure of the subject's hypothesis-testing behaviors than the techniques used by Bruner and others. As the methodology became more precise, he produced new kinds of data not available elsewhere. These data, and the insights they allowed, in turn permitted clearer, more explicit, and more exact theoretical statements. As his theory evolved, it not only suggested refinements in methodology but also exposed questions that only further experiments could answer. Thus, over a period of approximately ten years, through continual interaction of method, results, and theory, Levine developed the dominant theoretical position on concept-formation for the 1970s.

Method. Levine used what has come to be known as the Blank Trials Procedure for studying hypotheses in concept tasks. In simplest form, the Blank Trials Procedure requires the learner to respond to a series of stimuli in the absence of any corrective feedback. If the subject responds systematically to the stimuli, it is possible to determine the unique hypothesis underlying that series of responses. To be more specific, in a typical experiment, the subject responds to stimuli that differ on four dimensions. First, the stimulus may either be the letter X or the letter T. Either letter can be large or small, black or white, and, in a given stimulus pair, appear either on the left or the right side. Thus, the dimensions are letter, letter size, letter color, and letter position, each dimension with two values. The stimuli are presented to the subject in pairs and the two letters in each pair differ on all four characteristics. For example, if the stimulus on the left is a large, white T, the figure on the right is a small, black X. The subject is instructed that one of the figures is an example of some unknown concept while the other figure is not. Only one attribute, for example, black versus white, determines the positive-negative distinction. In each pair, the subject is asked to pick the figure that he or she thinks is positive.

Because only one attribute defines the concept, there are only eight possible hypotheses. Positive stimuli could be large, small, on the left, on the right, black, white, Xs, or Ts. Levine assumes that one such hypothesis governs the subject's response selection on any trial. Suppose that, in the example given, the subject chooses the left hand stimulus, that is, the large, white T. This illustrates that the subject's hypothesis is one of the following: left, large, white, or T. It would not be clear at his point, however, which of these hypotheses really did govern the subject's response selection. Suppose that the subject is told that the response is correct. This should confirm whatever hypothesis the subject has in mind, giving no basis for changing that hypothesis. The uniqueness of Levine's method derives from the next step. The subject is presented with a series of four trials, each constructed more or less like the trial described above, on which a selection between two stimuli is required. On these trials, however, the subject is given no feedback; these are the so-called blank trials. Levine assumes that subjects do not change their minds over a series of blank (no feedback) trials.

A sequence of blank trials is shown in Figure 5–3. The four pairs of stimuli are selected so that each possible hypothesis, black, white, X, etc., yields the unique sequence of four responses. The four response patterns corresponding to each of the eight possible hypotheses is shown by the position of the dots in the columns of Figure 5–3. For example, if the subject chose the left member of stimulus 1, the right member of stimulus 2, the left number of stimulus 3, and the right member of stimulus 4, the controlling hypothesis must be black. Notice that the response sequences listed in Figure 5–3 are not the only ones possible. The subject might, for example, pick the left-hand stimulus for the first three pairs and then switch to the right-hand stimulus. Such a pattern corresponds to no simple hypothesis. Just as there is one response sequence for each of the eight possible hypotheses, there are eight response sequences that do not correspond to any hypothesis. If a subject does not follow or test hypotheses, we would expect 50 percent of each type of sequence to occur, by chance, in the course of a problem. If a subject does test hypotheses, we expect a predominance of hypothesis sequences.

Characteristically, in Levine's experiments, the subject is presented with several blank trial sequences, each following a feedback or outcome trial. This procedure allows the experimenter to track the sequence of hypotheses used.

Theory. According to Levine, hypothesis-formulation and -testing proceeds in the following fashion. The subject begins with a pool of possible hypotheses, including but not necessarily limited to the eight simple hypotheses discussed above. When the first stimulus pair is presented, the subject chooses one (for example,

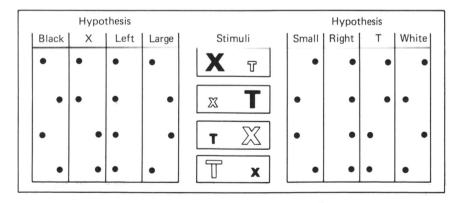

Figure 5–3.   Eight patterns of responses corresponding to each of the eight hypotheses which a subject might test one of M. Levine's experiments. (Source: Levine, M. [1966]. Hypothesis behavior in humans during discrimination learning. *Journal of Experimental Psychology, 71,* 331–338. Copyright 1966 by the American Psychological Association. Reprinted by permission of the publisher and author.)

large, black, T, on the left), possibly at random, calls it positive and verbally encodes its features. If he or she has chosen correctly, the encoded feature set (large,
black, T, left) becomes the hypothesis pool for the forthcoming series of blank trials.
The subject chooses one hypothesis (for example, black) from that pool as a focal
or working hypothesis and responds accordingly on the blank trials. The subject
attempts to keep the remaining three hypotheses (large, T, left) in short-term
memory, however, for possible use on the next feedback trial. If the subject chooses
incorrectly, then the encoded hypothesis set must be altered. Because the two stimuli
on any given trial differ in all their features, this alteration involves taking the complement of the encoded feature (in this case, small, white, X, right). Because the process must be done in short-term memory, in the absence of the two stimuli, it will
take some time and opens up the possibility of error. In any case, the recoded set
now becomes the hypothesis pool for the blank trial series. Once again, the subject
chooses one hypothesis (for example, small) to work with, and monitors the remainder (white, X, right).

This set of theoretical ideas applies to all blocks of five trials, consisting of
one feedback trial plus four blank trials. The major sources of difficulty for the subject are first, monitoring hypotheses that are still viable but not currently in use,
and second, taking the complement of an encoded hypothesis set when an error
trial dictates. If we assume that the subject can do both of these tasks perfectly,
then a certain set of expectations follows, including the fact that the subject should
solve every problem with a logically minimal amount of information. We can compare actual performance against this theoretically perfect model, and determine
where, if at all, the subject deviates and what sort of errors are made.

There are several ways in which Levine's theory differs from earlier versions
of hypothesis theory. For one thing, a subject learns something about problem solution on every trial, regardless of whether the stimulus selection is correct or incorrect.
That is, each trial provides the subject with an opportunity to narrow the hypothesis pool, regardless of whether the positive instance is correctly chosen. Whereas
some earlier theories suggested that subjects only learn on error trials (for example,
Trabasso & Bower, 1968), Levine's theory actually implies that it may be harder
to learn on error trials than on correct response trials because of the necessity to
recode the hypothesis set after an error has been made. Secondly, Levine's theory
takes into account the subject's use of memory. Mechanisms are provided for retaining information from preceding trials and assumptions are made about the kind
of processes that must take place in short-term memory to permit successful problem solution. Levine's theory is the most complete of all the efforts to capture concept-formation within the hypothesis-testing idiom.

Empirical Data. It has been repeatedly and consistently found (Levine, 1975)
that subjects use a single hypothesis on blank trial sequences (approximately 98 percent of the time). The percentage of non-hypothesis sequences is small enough that
it can be attributed simply to inattentiveness on the part of the subject. As Levine's
theory implies, subjects typically exhibit a "win-stay, lose-shift" strategy with respect
to their hypotheses. That is, if the hypothesis used by the subject on a given series

of blank trials is confirmed on the succeeding feedback trial, then the subject employs the same hypothesis (95 percent of the time) on the next blank trial sequence. If the hypothesis is disconfirmed on the feedback trial, the subject switches to a different hypothesis (98 percent of the time). It should be noted that, once disconfirmed, the probability of the hypothesis being repeated is far below what would be expected if the subject were simply sampling the hypotheses in a random way. Because there are eight possible hypotheses, each hypothesis would have a probability of 1/8, or .125, of being repeated by random sampling, even though disconfirmed by feedback. The observed probability of repeating an hypothesis (.02) is well below expectation based on random sampling, indicating that subjects sample in a way consistent with the feedback they have been given.

When an hypothesis is disconfirmed by feedback, the new hypothesis used on the next blank trial series tends to be chosen from the hypothesis set currently being monitored by the subject. In other words, the subject's new hypothesis is consistent (approximately 90 percent of the time) with previously given information. This observation suggests that subjects go through a narrowing-down process on the original hypothesis pool as information on the relevancy of certain hypotheses is accumulated.

Levine's method is set up so the subject who is able to process optimally the information provided by the experimenter can systematically decrease the hypothesis pool by half on each feedback trial. A subject who does this is said to use a *global focusing* strategy. Of course, a subject who has problems monitoring all the available hypotheses or recoding hypotheses when an error is made will deviate from this optimal, global focusing function. If the subject were merely testing hypotheses at random, and did not remember which hypotheses he or she had tested in the past, there would be no change whatsoever in the hypothesis pool from one trial to the next. The performance of most subjects falls somewhere in between random hypothesis-testing and optimal information-processing, usually closer to optimal processing. Figure 5–4 shows some data collected by Levine (1966) which are fairly representative of the level of performance of most adult subjects.

Global focusing requires not only optimal information-processing, but also complete memory either for rejected hypotheses or for hypotheses still viable as solutions. The importance of these memory effects has been demonstrated by Dyer and Meyer (1976) who showed that the performance of relatively naive subjects can be improved by giving instructions in the use of visual imagery as a mnemonic device for remembering positive instances. The effects of imagery were especially noticeable when subjects were required to solve two concurrent concept problems, a task that places heavy demands on both information-processing and memory.

Whether or not imagery can be used to assist memory in a concept task depends on the "imagability" of the stimulus material. Dyer and Meyer used pictorial stimuli that were highly imagable. But what if the stimulus were verbal? As we know, some words are concrete and readily suggest a visual image. However, other words are abstract and provoke little or no imagery. Katz and Paivio (1975) found that concepts vary widely in their imagery-arousing capacity. Futhermore, they observed

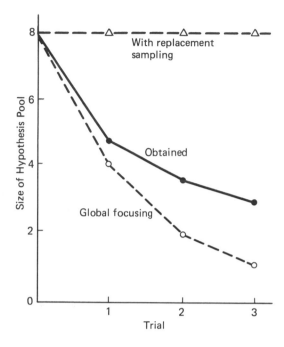

Figure 5-4. The estimated size of the hypothesis pool from which the subject samples immediately following a wrong response. (Source: Levine, M. [1966]. Hypothesis behavior in humans during discrimination learning. *Journal of Experimental Psychology, 71,* 331–338. Copyright 1966 by the American Psychological Association. Reprinted by permission of the publisher and author.)

that concept labels rated easy-to-image were attained or identified more readily than concept labels that were difficult to image. Finally, these experimenters demonstrated that only the attainment of easy-to-image concepts is facilitated by instructing subjects to use imagery as a means of remembering concept instances.

SOME EVIDENCE AGAINST HYPOTHESIS THEORY

Hypothesis Memory. In its general form, hypothesis theory portrays the process of concept-formation in terms of complex information-processing activities on each trial that result in the formation of an hypothesis or hypothesis set to be used on the next trial. Information provided by the stimulus and its associated feedback is the grist on which the hypothesis mill operates. Once an hypothesis or hypothesis set has been formulated on any trial, the stimulus presented, the response made, and the feedback given on that trial can be purged from memory, leaving only hypothesis information to be carried forward to the next trial. This line of reasoning suggests that, if one were to probe memory for the events of a previous trial, performance should be near perfect for the preceding hypothesis and possibly near chance for any other kind of information. At the very least, hypothesis memory should be better than memory for the stimulus, the response or the feedback of an earlier trial.

Kellogg, Robbins, and Bourne (1978, 1983; Kellogg, 1980a) tested directly subjects' short-term memory for trial events during a simple concept problem. In these studies, subjects were occasionally asked to respond to a recognition probe for an event of the immediately preceding trial. These probes tested short-term recognition of stimulus, hypothesis, response, and feedback, each type equally often, but on some randomly sequenced basis and only on half of the trials. The primary task for the subject was to identify the concept in as few trials as possible, though subjects were warned about the possibility of memory probes.

The results obtained were unexpected and difficult to reconcile with hypothesis theory. First, subjects showed almost perfect recognition memory for the response made and the feedback received on the preceding trial. Second, memory for the hypothesis formulated on the preceding trial and presumably carried forward to the next was no better than memory for the stimulus (both were relatively poor). Most unusual was the fact that there was no difference in memory for winning versus losing hypotheses. Neither was remembered any better than features of the preceding stimulus.

Kellogg and co-workers interpret their results in terms of a feature frequency principle. The general idea is that subjects attend primarily to the features of positive instances of the concept. When subjects are required to state an hypothesis, they generally select the most frequently occurring features among the positive instances (Kellogg, 1980). Feature frequencies are compiled automatically and unconsciously (Hasher & Zacks, 1979) as a consequence of the mere perception of stimulus-feedback information. These authors suggest that, in fact, what may be required for concept-formation is a two-process theory. Under some circumstances people do appear to solve concept problems by testing hypotheses. It would be inappropriate to conclude that concept-learning is never mediated by hypotheses. But, when hypotheses-testing is not made a central part of the task, as in the experiments reported by Kellogg and co-workers, many subjects appear to behave differently, relying on the potential automatic compilation of frequencies to distinguish relevant from irrelevant features of the stimuli. Similar dual-process notions have been suggested by Anderson, Kline, and Beasley (1979), Elio and Anderson (1981), Fried and Holyoak (1980) and Kellogg (1982).

Implicit Learning.   The research presented above suggests that hypothesis-testing may not be the primary activity that people normally engage in while attempting to solve a concept problem. On some occasions, subjects appeared to adopt a different analytic approach based on the frequency with which certain features of stimuli occur within the positive (and/or the negative) category. There is some evidence, however, that when subjects are forced to use hypotheses, they perform better than otherwise (Dominowski, 1974). Thus, it might be that hypothesis behavior is a high-efficiency approach to concept-learning, even though subjects do not normally adopt it, especially while they are still naive to the task.

This would be a reasonable general conclusion from the literature if it were not for a series of studies conducted by Reber and Allen (1978) and Brooks (1978). Reber and Allen (1978) showed that giving adult subjects instructions to search for rules that underlie the classification of certain stimuli can have a *detrimental* impact on their ability to learn to categorize those stimuli. Reber used strings of letters ("words") generated by the word-forming rules of what Reber refers to as a "synthetic language." Subjects who were given explicit instructions to try "to discover the rules for word-letter order" took more trials on a word memorizing task and came up with more incorrect rules than did subjects who were given no instructions other than to "try to memorize the letter strings." In other words, subjects who were given no biasing instructions about rule structure learned more about the rules of the synthetic language than did those who consciously tried to decipher the rules. None of the subjects was able to verbalize accurately what he or she had learned.

Reber's results run contrary not only to hypothesis-testing but to any analytic theory of concept-learning. The results suggest that, where the stimulus structure is highly complex, the learning process proceeds most effectively in a relatively passive non-analytic fashion. Reber's idea is that complex structures such as those involved in language and abstract concepts are acquired implicitly and perhaps unconsciously.

A similar conclusion was reached by Kellogg (1980b) on the basis of results collected in a divided attention experiment. Subjects were asked to perform relatively complex mental multiplication, designed to require full conscious attention, as a primary task, while schematic faces were presented visually as secondary stimuli. After 50 mental multiplication problems and 30 faces had been presented, subjects were given a surprise recognition test for the faces. Subjects were able to discriminate presented from unpresented faces on this recognition test at a level significantly higher than chance. Thus, Kellogg argues that face-encoding for long-term memory does not require attentional resources. However, subjects were not able to discriminate presented faces from previously unseen faces bearing a family resemblance to the presented faces. In other words, subjects had little specific memory for the faces presented but rather formed a category for those faces. Like Reber's results, these data suggest that even fairly complex categories can be formed on the basis of superficial or incidental processing. As others have argued, category-formation is the cognitive activity that we have evolved to handle informational overload (Rosch et al., 1976). Kellogg's results suggest that, in addition, the process of category-formation itself may proceed automatically when there are other tasks that demand our immediate and full attention.

Allen and Reber (1980; see also Reber, Kassin, Lewis, and Cantor, 1980) report that the material learned by their subjects is remarkably resistant to forgetting. Two years after subjects initially learned about the underlying grammatical structure of an artificial language, they were re-tested for their ability to discriminate grammatical from nongrammatical letter strings. Performance was exceptionally good and only slightly worse than that on tests given two years earlier. Even after two years, all subjects in the experiment were significantly above chance at assigning grammatical status to the correct test items.

The data, overall, suggest that the complex categories defined by syntactic rules can be learned by procedures other than those prescribed by hypothesis-testing theory. Once learned, these rules are well retained in useable form for long periods of time. Finally, whatever is learned cannot be verbalized by the subject and therefore, in that sense, is unlikely to develop through a conscious, hypothesis-testing process.

Structure of Concepts

Neither the associative theory nor the hypothesis-testing theory of concept-learning gives an adequate or a complete description of how concepts are formed. Under some circumstances, concept-formations seem to rely on memory for stimuli or stimulus features. Under other circumstances, the process appears to be an active, analytic, logic-driven kind of hypothesis-testing. This has suggested to some theorists that a dual-process theory, combining both associative and hypothesis-testing ideas, may be necessary to give a general account of concept-learning (for example, Kellogg, 1982).

But there is another kind of problem inherent in these theories and the research designed to test them. The problem was first explicitly identified by Eleanor Rosch (1973), and led her to formulate an entirely different approach to concept-learning. The basis of Rosch's criticism is the overriding concern of cognitive psychologists, through the early 1970s, with the *process of concept acquisition*. Neither research nor theory evidenced any concern about the *structure of concepts*, especially natural concepts, and how they were represented in memory. As a consequence, or understanding of concept-formation was limited to evidence about how relatively simple, well-defined logical concepts are learned in the laboratory. Rosch argued that this research, while adequate on scientific grounds, gave a wholly distorted picture about how we learn and use natural concepts in our everyday commerce with the environment.

EXEMPLAR THEORY

Rosch proposed an alternative theoretical approach that has come to be known, in general, as exemplar theory. Exemplar theory contends that concepts are represented in memory by their examples rather than by some abstract rule or a listing of relevant features. The critical claim is that a concept exists in memory as a set of separate descriptions of (some of) its previously encountered examples. Thus the concept *bird* is represented in terms of previously seen or imagined robins, sparrows, eagles, and so on.

To develop this idea further, it is important to examine in detail Rosch's criticisms of earlier work. First of all, Rosch pointed out that laboratory studies of the process of concept-formation typically used problems whose solution was an artificial, deterministic, and already familiar concept. The stimuli used in these experiments were simple, based on two or at most a few discrete values on a small number of completely independent stimulus dimensions, such as color (red or green) or shape (square or triangle).

Concepts were commonly defined on a single arbitrarily selected value (for example, red) or some artificial combination of a few values (red triangle). The concepts studied were completely deterministic in the sense that each stimulus either was or was not a member of the concept. Any one instance was as good as any other instance. If, for example, the concept was *red triangle* then any stimulus that had both those features was positive and was just as representative of the concept as any other positive instance.

According to Rosch, this arrangement is not typical of concepts we encounter in everyday life. Natural concept, such as *table* or *bird* are not easily described as arbitrary combinations of discrete values taken from some number of independent stimulus dimensions. Moreover, the dimensions of natural concepts are often hard to specify and may themselves be made up of combinations of underlying dimensions. The dimensions are typically continuous rather than discrete and may not be entirely independent of one another.

Rosch went further to point out that all tables or birds are not equally good examples of their respective categories. Most people agree that robin is, in some intuitive sense, a better example of *bird* than penguin or ostrich. For any category, there are more typical and less typical examples. Often, there is a most typical example called the prototype. Thus, one's understanding of a natural concept must include both the notion of prototype and a dimension of typicality or category membership. In Rosch's view, natural concepts are almost always fuzzy. Some stimuli are clearly classifiable under the concept, others are borderline and are classifiable as members only hesitantly or with some low probability. For most people, a tomato is a borderline *fruit* at best.

Rosch's criticisms are well taken. There is reason to be concerned about the arbitrariness of simple laboratory studies of concept-learning and the theory based on them. It became apparent in the mid-1970s that there is much more to the structure of concepts than earlier theories, which emphasized logical concepts and the process concept-learning, had taken into account. Rosch's proposal to deal with these deficiencies was her notion of an exemplar theory, utilizing heavily the notions of prototypical stimuli, degree of category membership, and the fuzziness of categories.

Perceptual Concepts.   In Rosch's view, even rudimentary dimensions like color are structured into nonarbitrary fuzzy categories centering around perceptually salient natural prototypes. Particular categories of color, for example red, include some wavelengths of light which seem purest or best. Relative to other nearby wavelengths, these best examples tend to attract the viewer's attention. They are, in a sense, easier to "see" and serve as the foci for organizing the range of different values that we ordinarily classify together as red (or any other basic color).

In the case of perceptual dimensions like color, Rosch (1973) hypothesized that what is typical may be determined by a fundamental neurological process. The best red may be best because, among all red wavelengths, the human visual system is most sensitive to that one. If this is the case, then it seems likely that people of different cultures, to the extent that they have the same biological sensory systems, would pick up the same focal points or prototypes for that dimension. Rosch was able to demonstrate this fact in a study of a Stone Age people in New Guinea known as the Dani. Despite the fact that, in the Dani language, there exist only two "color" terms that apply to bright and dark, the Dani showed more attention and better learning and memory for the same color prototypes found in Western culture. Thus, Rosch concluded that even the most basic of natural concepts have a universal internal structure, centering on a prototype but ranging over certain allowable variations.

It should perhaps be noted that other interpretations of these results are possible. Lucy and Shweder (1979) suggested that Rosch's data may have been biased by factors of stimulus discriminability favoring prototypical colors. When perceptual discriminability is controlled for, they argue, ease of verbal encoding provides a better predictor of which stimuli are easiest to learn and remember.

Ill-Defined Categories. Long before there was an experimental psychology, philosophers debated the process of abstraction and what type of "ideal" forms it yielded. Some argued that abstraction leads to an analog-like representation of a category, having all the basic features of category instances, though it may differ from any particular instance encountered in the real world. Others found it impossible to imagine what such a composite might be. Where, even in your wildest imagination, can you find the abstraction of a triangle that is neither equilateral, isosceles, scalene, nor any other you might have seen, but is equally representative of them all? Yet, there is some experimental evidence to the effect that, when learning a category, people do abstract a schematic kind of representation that may be different from any particular previously encountered instance.

This conclusion is demonstrated in a series of studies by Michael Posner and his colleagues (Posner, Goldsmith, & Welton, 1967; Posner & Keele, 1968). Briefly, Posner constructed certain well-known forms, such as a triangle or a block letter F, from patterns of dots placed on a 30 × 30 matrix. Each form was comprised of nine dots as shown in Figure 5–5. Subjects were allowed to study distortions of several different prototypes (but never the prototypes themselves). They were required to learn which of several categories each stimulus belonged to. Actually, each category contained only the distortions of a single prototype. Different groups of subjects saw distortions of low or of moderate degree. After subjects had learned to classify distortions consistently into their proper categories, a test was given. In the test, a mixture of old distortions and new distortions (never seen before) were presented to the subject for classification.

Distorted stimuli that the subject had in fact learned to classify in training were more easily classified on the transfer test than were new distortions at the same level, indicating some specific memory for the acquisition stimuli. But new distortions of the same prototypical stimulus were classfied quite accurately and well above chance. One remarkable outcome of the experiment was that the prototype, which the subject had not seen during the original learning, was classified into its correct category more readily than even the originally learned distorted

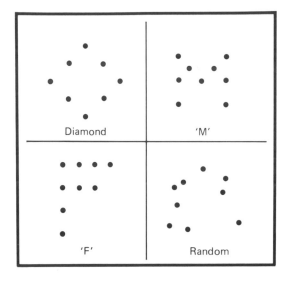

Figure 5-5. Basic dot patterns defining four categories. (Source: Posner, M.I., Goldsmith, R. & Welton, K.E., Jr. [1967]. Perceived distance and classification of distorted patterns. *Journal of Experimental Psychology, 73,* 353–363. Copyright 1967 by the American Psychological Association. Reprinted by permission of the publisher and author.)

stimuli. These results suggest that, during learning, the subjects acquired information not only about the particular stimuli presented but also about an ideal form for that category and about the tolerable variability among instances of that category.

Indeed, Omohundro (1981) has collected evidence in a similar task to suggest that the relative amount of category-level information to instance-level information retained from an original learning experience is a function of how many different examples are presented during original learning. The more examples, the greater the prominence of category-level information. There appears to be a trade-off in Omohundro's data. Classification of new examples is mediated by category-level information while recognition of the examples used in original learning requires retention of instance-level information. These data have been used to argue that ill-defined categories are represented in memory in terms of some schema that captures the central tendency of exemplars that have been presented plus an underlying similarity dimension. Supporting evidence has been reported by Elio and Anderson (1981) and by Homa, Sterling, and Trepel (1981). The greater the variety of instances presented during original learning, the more general knowledge this subject has, leading to greater accuracy in classifying previously unseen patterns properly.

Prototype and Transformation. The stimulus distortions used by Posner were generated by abitrary probabilistic rules for moving component dots. These rules are difficult if not impossible for any person to identify from the distortions themselves. Thus, subjects in these experiments were forced to rely upon some non-analytic judgment of similarity as a basis for category response. But under different circumstances, it might be possible for a person actually to learn something more precise about the allowable variations within a conceptual category. This possibility was addressed by Franks and Bransford (1971) in a series of studies that led them to formulate a theory of category representation in terms of transformational rules. First of all, Franks and Bransford used an arbitrary arrangement of four discrete, discriminable attributes as their prototype. An example of the material used is presented in Figure 5–6. Then they defined a set of simple transformational rules to produce distortions. The degree of distortion in their studies depended upon how many transformational rules were applied.

The experiment begins, as in Posner's studies, by showing the subjects a set of stimuli, one at a time, representing all possible transformations on the prototype. Any particular stimulus in this set of materials was the result of one, a combination of two, or a combination of three of the allowable transformations on the chosen prototype. To illustrate, the prototypical pattern might consist of a small, red triangle on the left bottom, a large, blue square on the left top, a large, yellow diamond on the right bottom, and a large, green heart on the right top of the stimulus card. The subject is never shown this prototype. Rather, the set of stimuli presented to the subject consists entirely of distortions of the prototype, just as in Posner's experiment. The allowable transformations might be: (1) a switch in the right-left position of pairs of figures, (2) an exchange in the up-down positions within a pair, (3) deletion of a figure, or (4) substitution of a new figure of an old one, such as a hexagon for a square.

After the initial set of stimuli was presented, the subjects were asked to decide whether each of a series of recognition stimuli had been present in the original set and to rate their confidence in that decision on a five-point scale. Results indicated

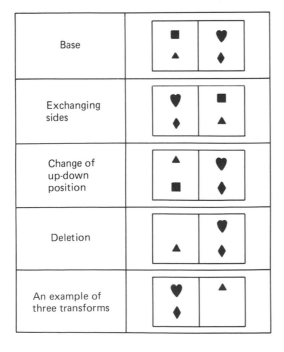

Figure 5-6. Examples of a base pattern and transformations on it used by Franks & Bransford (1971). (Source: Franks, J.J., & Bransford, J.D. [1971]. Abstraction of visual patterns. *Journal of Experimental Psychology, 90,* 65–74. Copyright 1971 by the American Psychological Association. Reprinted by permission of the publisher and author.)

that the prototype (which, remember, was not included in the original study set) received the highest positive recognition rating, followed by patterns in order of increasing transformational distance. The experimenters included some patterns in this recognition set that could not be produced by the allowable transformational rules. These stimuli tended to receive negative (nonrecognition) ratings. The results are portrayed in Figure 5-7.

Franks and Bransford concluded that subjects can abstract, out of a welter of stimuli belonging to one category, the single best example and some sense of how category members vary. This is true abstraction because the single best example is never presented to the subject. They argue that the category is represented in memory as a schema, consisting of two components. One component anchors the set of examples to the best possible or middle-most example. The second component is a set of rules that one can perform on the best example and still remain within the category. During the presentation of the original set of stimuli, subjects apparently learned something in addition to the particular configurations that had been presented. They acquired general information about the whole set of stimuli. This information allowed them to recognize novel configurations and to rank order these configurations in terms of their transformational distance from the abstracted prototype.

Semantic Concepts.   The research we have just discussed may be criticized in much the same way as Rosch criticized traditional laboratory work. That is, the stimulus material on which conceptual problems were structured is relatively simple, highly dimensionalized, and arbitrary. There is a need for experiments to move beyond this kind of material and into the domain of natural concepts. But we also

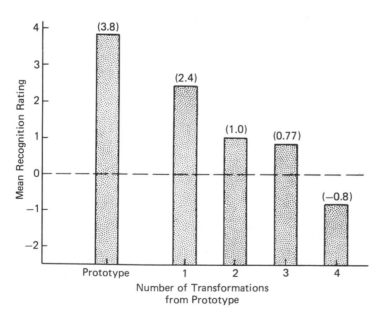

Figure 5-7. Recognition performance of subjects on stimulus patterns at varying transformational distances from a prototype. (Data from Experiment II, Franks [Bransford, [1971].)

note that Rosch's characterization of natural concepts is fundamentally very similar to the concepts studied by Posner and Franks and Bransford. That is, natural categories are composed of a core meaning (prototype or best example) and a distance dimension defined by the decreasing similarity of other instances to the prototype. Rosch argues that this is the way concepts are coded in memory. The coding holds not only for simple perceptual concepts based on color or form, according to Rosch, but also on semantic categories that have no obvious perceptual basis.

There has been a tendency in psychology to treat the world as essentially un-organized and meaningless—a booming, buzzing confusion. Each of us has to learn and apply to the world a kind of semantic matrix that serves to distinguish a large number of separate categories, each with its own label. Rosch takes a position con-trary to this viewpoint. She argues that the world is meaningfully prepackaged, pri-marily because of their attributes things are not independent of one another (see also Garner, 1974). Creatures with feathers are more likely to have wings, fly, lay eggs, and so on, than are creatures with fur. Objects with the visual attributes of tables are more likely to have functional "put-on-able-ness" than objects with the visual features of birds.

Rosch carries this argument one step further. Of the many possible levels of abstraction on which objects can be classified—for example, the object you are sit-ting on might be said to be a chair, an article of furniture, a household object, an inanimate thing, and so on,—there is one level that is psychologically the most basic. Categorization occurs to reduce the infinite differences among stimuli to psycho-logically manageable proportions. It is to the organism's advantage both to have each classification as rich in information as possible and simultaneously to have as few classifications as possible. The basic level of classification is a compromise between these two antagonistic principles. The basic level is one at which the organism can obtain the most information with the least cognitive effort.

Studies designed to examine this idea have the following characteristics. First, an intuitive guess is made by the experimenter about what constitutes a basic level object, for example, chair. Then, two other levels of abstraction are defined, super-ordinate and subordinate. Chair, for example, has a superordinate category furniture and a subordinate category deck chair. Several superordinate through subordinate arrangements are chosen.

Maximizing Information. In one experiment (Rosch, Mervis, Gray, Johnson, & Boyes-Braem, 1976), subjects were asked to list all the common features they could think of for items at each of the three levels, superordinate, basic, and sub-ordinate. Relatively few features were listed for superordinate categories (for exam-ple, furniture, clothing, vehicles, fruit). A much greater number were listed for the basic level item (for example, chair, pants, automobile, apple). The subordinate level (for example, deck chair, jogging pants, sports car, macintosh apple) did not receive significantly more features than those at the basic level. If you take the number of common features as a measure of information conveyed by a name, then it is clear that basic level objects are informationally richer than the superordinate category to which they belong and that little additional information is added by moving to the subordinate level. Because there are fewer basic categories than subordinate categories, the findings are consistent with Rosch's notion of maximizing information while minimizing cognitive effort at the basic level of natural categories.

Common Actions.   In a subsequent experiment, (Rosch, et al., 1976), the same words were presented to subjects with the instruction to describe, in as much detail as possible, the sequence of muscle movements they would make when using or interacting with the object. How does one interact, for example, with a living-room chair, with a sports car, with a tree, or with an apple? The results were that virtually no movements or activities occurred in common for superordinate categories. There were, in contrast, a large number of movements common to basic level objects. Few additional movement patterns were elicited by subordinate objects. To illustrate, there are a few motor patterns we carry out on all articles of furniture. What is in common among our interactions with chair, table, and lamp? On the other hand, specific motor programs are carried out in regards to all chairs, namely sitting. Moveover, we sit on kitchen chairs and on deck chairs and on living-room chairs using essentially the same motor programs. Thus, the communality of interactions is maximal at the level of basic object.

Imagable Prototypes.   Consider one final experiment (Rosch, et al., 1976). Four superordinate categories were used for which it was possible to obtain a large sample of pictures. A number of pictures of four different basic level objects in each superordinate category were chosen, such that each object was roughly the same in size and orientation. Similarity and shape were measured by the amount of overlap of object outlines when placed on top of one another. The results indicated that the ratio of overlapping to non-overlapping area when two objects from the same basic level category, for example, two chairs, were superimposed was far greater than when two objects from the same superordinate category, for example, chair and bed, were superimposed. In contrast, there was relatively little gain in this overlap ratio when members of subordinate level categories were superimposed. The point of this exercise is to demonstrate that objects in a basic level category are at the highest level at which a generalized, common image can be formed.

Overall, the experiments establish three parameters that can be used to identify basic level categories. First, basic level categories maximize attribute information while keeping number of categories at a minimum. Second, basic level categories maximize the communality of interactional motor programs. Basic level categories are the most inclusive categories at which identical or similar motor programs are employed for all objects within the category. Finally, basic level is the most inclusive level at which shape similarities occur and at which an average shape of two objects is recognizable as "that kind of object." The basic level is the most inclusive level at which it is possible to form an image of the "average" member of the class or the most abstract level at which it is possible to have a relatively concrete image as the prototype.

Categories Based on Family Resemblance.   How do you decide whether a novel stimulus belongs to a particular category? According to some theories, you decide on the basis of a rule that you have learned more or less as a definition of the category. But rules tend to be difficult to apply in cases that are not particularly clear-cut. Rosch and Mervis (1975) offered a different hypothesis based on family resemblance: An instance will be accepted as a member of a category to the extent that it bears a family resemblance to other members of the same category. Family resemblance is defined as the degree to which a stimulus possesses attributes that overlap with the attributes of known category members. In fact, this principle provides the basis for the dimension of typicality among category members. That is, an instance is accepted as typical to the extent that it bears a family resemblance to other members of the same category. A corollary to this hypothesis is that items typical of one category are unlikely to have a family resemblance to members of other categories.

Rosch and Mervis reported several experiments to test the family resemblance hypothesis. They began by determining the distribution of attributes of members of a number of superordinate natural categories. Subjects were given the name of a common object and were asked to write down all of the attributes of that object that they could think of in 90 seconds. A total of 120 items, 20 from each of 6 different superordinate categories, were rated. Each attribute was given a score, 1 to 20, representing the number of items in the category which had been credited with that attribute.

Figure 5-8 shows how attributes were used by subjects to describe various numbers of items within a given category. Few attributes were applied to all or even

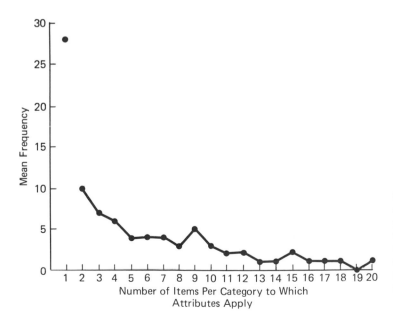

Figure 5-8. Frequency distribution showing the number of attributes which were applied by subjects to various numbers of items within a given category. (Data from Rosch & Mervis, [1975]. Courtesy of Academic Press, Inc.)

the majority of members of any category. In other words, there were practically no common attributes on which the category, as a whole, could be defined. Indeed, only a relatively few items shared any substantial number of attributes. Thus, the salient attribute structure of these categories tended to reside not in defining features in common to all members of the category but in the large number of attributes true of some but not all category members.

A major hypothesis of this experiment was that the family resemblance structure and rated typicality of an item are highly correlated. The larger the number of shared attributes a stimulus has, the greater is its typicality with respect to the category. The measure of typicality was the mean rating, on a seven-point scale, of the extent to which an item fit the subject's idea of the meaning of the category name. That is, how well does chair or lamp fit the meaning of the category name furniture? The measure of family resemblance for an item was the number of attributes of that item shared by it and other items in the same category. In other words, how many attributes of chair are shared with lamp or table? Over six different superordinate categories, correlations between typicality and family resemblance ranged from .84 to .94 (the highest possible correlation being 1.0). Thus, the results strongly confirm the hypothesis that the more an item has attributes in common with other members of a given category, the more it will be considered a representative member of that category.

Rosch and Mervis observed that, while category members as a whole may not share many attributes, the five most typical items in each category tended to have a number of attributes in common, and many more than the five least typical members. Thus, if the subject thinks of the best example of a category when hearing the category name, the illusion of common defining attributes is likely to arise, making the definition of categories in terms of defining features seem reasonable. In fact, however, such a definition will leave out many qualifying but peripheral examples. Rosch and Mervis also demonstrated that the family resemblance among exemplars within basic level categories is significantly higher than at the superordinate level. This observation is, again, consistent with their earlier finding that basic level categories are the most inclusive at which a concrete, imagable exemplar can serve as prototype.

Prominence of Basic Level Concepts.   Rosch and her co-workers (1976) have produced a convincing amount of empirical evidence on the prominence of basic level categories among all natural semantic categories. For example, they found that an object or a picture of an object can be categorized faster at the basic level (as an apple) than at either a subordinate (as a Macintosh Apple) or at a superordinate level (as a fruit). They attribute this result to the relative informational richness of basic level categories as reflected in the tendency to have the maximal number of distinctive common features. Murphy and Smith (1982), however, have pointed out that many factors other than the number of distinctive attributes might have produced these results. For example, basic categories typically have shorter and more common names than do subordinates. Thus, Murphy and Smith undertook a series of experiments using an artificial conceptual hierarchy in which name character-istics, frequency, category size, and the like could be controlled. The results of these studies support the findings of Rosch and her co-workers. Objects can be categorized fastest at the basic level, even within a contrived hierarchy. The studies strongly support the claim that informational richness and distinctive common features are major factors defining the basic level within hierarchies of natural concepts.

One potential implication of the prominence of basic level concepts concerns the order in which concepts are acquired developmentally. Mervis and Crisafi (1982) asked children in the age range from two to six years to indicate which of two stimuli was the "same kind of thing" as a standard for sets of stimuli at the basic, subordi-nate, and superordinate levels. Children performed best at the basic level, next best on superordinate categories and worst on subordinate categories. Again, the evi-dence suggested that attribute differentiation is the major factor underlying the prominence of basic level categories and determining the order in which natural semantic categories are acquired by young children.

Category Prototypes: How General?   The concepts studied by Rosch, while considerably more natural than those used in the process-oriented research of Le-vine and others, still represent a fairly concrete level of abstraction. Perhaps more abstract concepts are not structured in the same way. Several researchers have ex-amined this possibility. Hock and Schmelzkopf (1980) studied the process of ab-stracting schematic representations of real-life street scenes from a sample of still photographs. They demonstrated that subjects form a three dimensional prototypical representation of the street scene from these two-dimensional stimulus inputs. Hampton (1982) analyzed the internal structure of eight abstract concepts including a work of art, a leaf, a crime, a just decision, an instinct, a rule, a science, and a kind of work. Five of the eight abstract concepts evidenced a prototypical struc-ture. Hartley and Homa (1981) showed that undergraduates are able to abstract the artistic style of a painter from observation of a number of works by that painter. Welker (1982) demonstrated the abstraction of a musical theme from listening to set of variations on that theme. Finally, Cantor, Mischel, and Schwartz (1982) dem-onstrated that common situations in which people find themselves have a proto-typical structure. This latter result is reminiscent of the notion of frames or scripts used commonly in contemporary discussions of memory to represent our stereo-typed notion of routine knowledge of the world. There are other examples that might be cited. These are sufficient, however, to illustrate the generality of prototypical structure. Our knowledge of the world, no matter how concrete or abstract, might very well have the kind of representation claimed in Rosch's version of exemplar theory.

INSTANCE MEMORY OR FEATURE LIST

What does a person know when he or she learns a concept? According to ex-emplar theory, the person knows primarily about concept examples. In Rosch's ver-sion, the person knows especially about the best example and about limitations on category membership in the form of a principle of family resemblance. But other versions of exemplar theory assert that the person will have at least a partial representation of all previously encountered instances (Reed, 1972; Medin & Schaffer, 1978) and that knowledge of the concept is distributed throughout these instances. In contrast, associative and hypothesis-testing theories emphasize a person's knowledge of a rule or definition of the concept, usually including a list of critical or defining features (Levine, 1975). Formally,

$$C = R(x, y, \ldots)$$

where C is a concept, x, y, . . ., are its relevant features, and R is a rule that ties those features together (Bourne, 1970, 1974).

Rosch has criticized rule-based or feature list theories because they appear to be too rigid or deterministic to account for the fuzziness of natural categories. But this criticism is not universally accepted. While it is true that many experiments have studied concept-learning with features that are perfect predictors of category membership, such an arrangement is not necessarily entailed by feature list theory. Indeed, the notion of cue validity was introduced in the context of feature list theory (Bourne & Restle, 1959) and first studied experimentally with arbitrary concepts (Haygood & Bourne, 1960). In many ways, prototype or instance memory and feature list theories might not be so far apart as Rosch's criticism implies.

Paul Neumann (1974, 1977) has shown that prototype and category membership principles can be derived from feature list considerations. By analysis of existing data (Franks & Bransford, 1971) and data specifically collected for his purpose, Neumann was able to demonstrate that the number of appearances of each separately identifiable property or feature shared between previously seen category members and a newly encountered stimulus is the best predictor of how the new stimulus will be categorized. Neumann's claim is that subjects automatically encode frequency counts on the attributes of instances within a particular category (see Hasher & Zachs, 1979 for a similar claim). The features of a new stimulus are compared to those frequency counts. If the new stimulus has a sufficient number of high-frequency features, it is placed into the same category. The greater the sharing of high-frequency features, the higher the confidence a subject will have in the categorization.

In feature list theories, such as those of Neumann (1974), Fried and Holyoak (1980), and Bourne (1982), a concept is defined in terms of some relation among a set of relevant features. Not all members of the category need to have all relevant features. Indeed, features occur with differing probabilities among members of most natural categories. Some features are highly likely; others are relatively unlikely. Each dimension of an unknown concept can be represented by an underlying frequency distribution, built up as the person encounters more and more examples of the concept. Some one or more values on each dimension will have maximal or modal frequency (or probability) over all instances and will become the "relevant features." The stimuli belonging to any particular category may differ from one another on many dimensions not considered critical. These irrelevant dimensions have a flat (or rectangular) frequency distribution. No particular feature or value on those dimensions stands out as occurring more frequently in instances of the concept in question.

From this point of view, a concept is defined by a set of features, their probability (or frequency) values, and the relationship among the features. The prototype would be predicted to be the stimulus that contains all (or a maximal number of) modal features. The stimuli rank order themselves in terms of the degree of category membership on the basis of how many modal features they have, which ones, or how similar the features are to the modal ones. In such a theory, the prototype has no special status. It does not serve as the focus for organizing the category. Neither is degree of category membership a special or primitive characteristic of categories. Rather, these phenomena are derived from a more basic process, namely the emergence of probability distributions associated with stimulus dimensions (see Fried & Holyoak [1980] for a more complete development of these ideas).

Bourne (1982) was able to reproduce many of the phenomena of natural categories, including the selection of a prototype and the evaluation of category membership, with a completely logical, deterministic concept, using probability of feature occurrence within the concept category as the only predictor. Results such as these suggest that the characteristics of natural and artificial categories are not as different as Rosch's research would imply. Natural and logical categories may be acquired and represented in the same way, leading to similar empirical outcomes. Osherson and Smith (1981) have argued that people probably retain both instance-specific and category-specific information in memory. Instance-specific information is used when the task calls for a rapid judgment of category membership for any stimulus. Where logical operations are required, the subject relies on category-level information, primarily in terms of the definition of the category in terms of critical features and their relationship.

Martin and Caramazza (1980) have also collected evidence on the common processing strategies used by subjects in forming logical and ill-defined categories. They suggest that in both cases the primary mode of category-formation is for mulating and testing deterministic rules of hypotheses for exemplar classification. In their tasks, the evidence suggests that all subjects use systematic and deterministic rules for classification. These rules differ, however, from subject to subject. Some are more efficient than others. Typicality and probablistic differences among stimuli result from averaging across different subjects using different sets of rules.

Research into the distinction between instance and category-level knowledge is very active at the present time. Furthermore, there is a good deal of controversy about whether instance memory, category level information, or some combination of the two is necessary for a complete theory of concepts. All we can say with certainty at the present time is that we may eventually discover, as has so often been the case in the past, that seemingly antagonistic theories actually come down to very much the same interpretation once we look at them in proper perspective. (For an in-depth discussion of this and related issues, see Smith and Medin [1981]).

CONCEPTUAL RULES

Thus far, our discussion has focused on the features of stimuli, how they are identified as relevant to some concept, and the role that they play in the structure of that concept. At various points, however, we have alluded to the fact that more than stimulus features are involved in the definition of a concept. A complete description must include not only relevant features but also a rule that ties those features together (Bourne, 1974). For example, the concept of *canary* can be defined in terms of a collection of features such as yellow *and* song *and* household pet *and*. . . The concept of a *strike* (in baseball) is a pitched ball passing through a prescribed imaginary rectangle over home plate *and/or* a pitched ball that the batter swings at and misses. These are simplified examples but serve to illustrate how both features and rules enter into the definition of a concept. Note that the rule for integrating features is not the same in the two examples. In the case of *canary*, the rule requires that all attributes be present before a given instance can be classified as a canary. For *strike*, an instance need have only one of the defining characteristics to qualify.

In the laboratory, we can make even a clearer distinction between rules and features. We select any two features of a well-defined stimulus population, say redtriangle. The category red *and* triangle is distinctly different from the category red *and/or* triangle. In the first case, the stimulus must have both relevant features in order to be a positive instance. In the second case, it need have only one. The difference between these categories is a matter of which rule is applied to the two relevant features. Learning or identifying the rule is as much a part of concept-formation as is learning or identifying the relevant features.

The preponderance of research on concept-formation has used simple concepts in which the rule is trivial. For example, from Levine (1975), the concept *all large letters are positive* is based on the simple affirmation of the feature, large. As a consequence of using simple problems, researchers have directed little attention to the rule-learning component of the task. Nonetheless, there are circumstances in which the rule-learning component takes on awesome proportions.

Isolating the Rule-Learning Component.   The modest amount of research on rule-learning that has been reported to date has used, exclusively, logical concepts defined by rules from set theory or the calculus propositions. The rules that we have used above for the sake of illustration—the "and" rule or conjunction and the "and/or" rule or disjunction—are only two of several possible logical relationships that can hold between two stimulus features. Indeed, there are sixteen possible ways of assigning a set of stimulus patterns to positive and negative response categories based on the presence or absence of (at most) two relevant features. These sixteen different possibilities are presented in Table 5–2. Two of these rules, A and P in Table 5–2, are trivial because they assign all stimulus patterns either to the positive or to the negative category. Four other partitions, F, G, I, and K, make assignments on the basis of either the presence or absence of a single feature. The remaining ten partitions depend on the presence or absence of both defining features, and can be shown to collapse to four types and their mirror images. All partitions involving the two relevant attributes belong to one of these four pairings, called the four primary bidimensional rules and their complements. The primary rules are labelled conjunctive ("and"), disjunctive ("and/or"). conditional ("if, then") and biconditional ("if and only if"). The relationship of this analysis to the full calculus of sixteen possibilities is shown in Table 5–3. All published research on rule-learning has focused on the four primary bidimensional rules.

Table 5-2. *Sixteen unique partitions of a stimulus population.*

STIMULUS TYPES (TRUTH TABLE SUBSETS)		PARTITION																
		A	B	C	D	E	F	G	H	I	J	K	L	M	N	O	P
Both features present	(TT)	+	+	+	+	−	+	+	+	−	−	−	+	−	−	−	−
First present, second absent	(TF)	+	+	+	−	+	+	−	−	−	+	+	−	+	−	−	−
First absent, second present	(FT)	+	+	−	+	+	−	+	−	+	+	−	−	−	+	−	−
Both absent	(FF)	+	−	+	+	+	−	−	+	+	−	+	−	−	−	+	−

Imagine a person learning a new concept from scratch. The person knows neither the relevant features of the concept nor the rule integrating them. Consequently, if there is a real distinction to be made between rule and features, any difficulty the person has with the problem could be attributed either to feature- or to rule-learning. Because the types of concepts illustrated in Table 5–3 differ from one another rather markedly in difficulty (Neisser & Weene, 1962), it is important to find an experimental paradigm in which rule- and feature-learning can be examined separately.

Such a paradigm was developed by Haygood and Bourne (1965). Subjects solved problems wherein the rule or the relevant features, but not both, were unknowns to be discovered. To study feature identification, the experimenter must be sure that the subject understands, at the outset, the general form of solution required by the task. This information is usually imparted through preliminary instructions and examples of the rule to be used. If a subject thoroughly understands the rule, the only task remaining is to find the unknown feature or features. By contrast, in a rule problem, the subject is provided, at the outset, with the name or names of the features that are relevant. The task that remains, then, is to discover how these features are combined in the unknown concept.

Suppose the concept to be learned is *red and/or triangle*. In a feature problem, the subject would be told that the concept is based on a disjunctive rule, that there are two attributes of the concept combined by the and/or rule. The subject's task is to determine the unknown features, X and/or Y. In a rule problem, the two relevant features, for example, red-triangle, are named at the outset. The subject is instructed that redness and triangularity are somehow combined by an unknown rule

Table 5-3. *Conceptual rules describing partitions of a population with two focal attributes (Bourne, 1970).*

	BASIC RULE				COMPLEMENTARY RULE		
Partition	Name	Symbolic description*	Verbal description	Partition	Name	Symbolic description*	Verbal description
F	Affirmation	R	All red patterns are examples of the concept.	I	Negation	$\bar{R}$	All patterns which are *not* red are examples of the concept.
L	Conjunction	$R \cap S$	All red and square patterns are examples.	E	Alternative Denial	$R\|S$	All patterns which are *either not red or not square* are examples.
B	Inclusive Disjunction	$R \cup S$	All patterns which are *red or square or both* are examples.	O	Joint Denial	$R \downarrow S$ $[\bar{R} \cap \bar{S}]$	All patterns which are *neither red nor square* are examples.
D	Conditional	$R \rightarrow S$ $[\bar{R} \cup S]$	*If a pattern is red then must be square* to be an example.	M	Exclusion	$R \cap \bar{S}$	All patterns which are red *and not square* are examples.
H	Biconditional	$R \rightleftarrows S$	Red patterns are examples *if and only if they are square.*	J	Exclusive Disjunction	$R \bar{\cup} S$	All patterns which are red or square *but not both* are examples.

(Reprinted by permission of author and American Psychological Association.)

to form the concept. The concept is *red ? triangle* and the subject's task is to find the rule that connects the two known relevant features.

Haygood and Bourne (1965) established the relative difficulty of various rules. Subjects solved problems in which the relevant features were known and one of the four primary bidimensional rules was an unknown. A variation of the reception procedure used by Levine (1975) was adopted. Stimuli were presented to the subject one at a time for classification as positive or negative instances. After each response, immediate corrective feedback was provided and the series of instances continued until the subject could either state the rule or had made a certain number of correct category responses in a row. The order of difficulty observed in this and in subsequent experiments is quite regular; for the inexperienced subject, conjunctive is the earliest, followed by disjunctive, conditional, and biconditional, in that order.

Rule difficulty changes with practice. That is, initial differences in difficulty disappear with familiarity. Typically, in these experiments, each of a group of subjects solves a series of problems based on the same conceptual rule. The difference from one problem to the next is merely in terms of the particular pair of features designated to be relevant. The results of one such experiment (Bourne, 1970) are portrayed in Figure 5–9. As you can see, after six problems, all subjects were essentially perfect on the rule to which they were assigned. The subject knows the pair of relevant attributes from preliminary instructions and comes to know the rule through practice. Thus, on the sixth or later problem the subject can sort stimuli with no errors whatsoever.

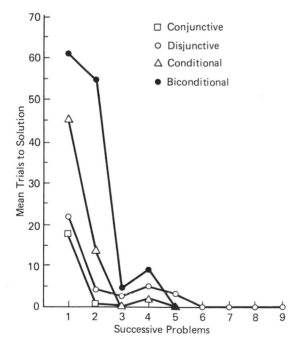

Figure 5-9.   Mean trials to solution of nine successive rule learning problems based on the four primary bidimensional rules. (Source: Bourne, L.E., Jr. [1970]. Knowing and using concepts. *Psychological Review, 77,* 546–556. Copyright 1970 by the American Psychological Association. Reprinted by permission of the publisher and author.)

Concept Hierarchy.   Any particular concept has both abstract and concrete components. The concrete components are the specific perceptible features of the stimuli to be categorized. The abstract component is the rule. There is no concrete or physical realization of a rule. Rather, it is defined as the relationship between or among concrete entities. The acquisition of a rule, then, as distinct from identifying relevant stimulus features or learning any particular concept, is an abstract process. It is an essentially-different level of performance from that required by feature identification.

✓ Once learned, a conceptual rule covers an indefinite number of individual concepts. For example, the disjunctive rule can be used as an operator on any pair of features from any stimulus population to form a unique category. Whereas any particular concept covers an indefinitely large population of concrete stimuli, a rule covers an indefinitely large number of distinct categories and represents thereby a more abstract level of knowledge.

Bourne (1970) and Hiew (1977) observed the emergence of another, even more abstract level of rules in the hierarchy of logical concepts. The general aim of these studies was to assess the degree of transfer between one rule and others within the set of primary bidimensional rules. These experiments were arranged such that subjects solved three successive problems based on each of the four primary bidimensional rules, for a total of twelve training problems. The order in which problems were administered was counterbalanced across subjects. In one study (Bourne, 1970), the subject was given a final rule identification task. Instructions to the subject were that this final problem was based on one of the four previously practiced rules from the same system of rules (see Table 5–3).

As in previous experiments, subjects improved—that is, they demonstrated interrule transfer or rule-learning—over three problems within a set based on the same rule. When the rule changed from one block of three problems to the next, performance deteriorated. On the whole, however, there was significant positive transfer from training on one rule to performance on the next. The results are shown in Figure 5–10. At the end of the twelve training problems, most subjects approached perfect performance, even though they were given only three practice problems on any particular rule.

Now consider the final problem. In Bourne's study, subjects were instructed that the solution to this problem was based on one of the four "previously practiced" rules. As a theoretical minimum, the subject will need to see four stimuli, one representing each of the four truth table subsets (see Table 5–2) to discover the unknown rule. That is, the subject will need to find out the positive/negative status of stimuli containing both relevant attributes (TT), neither relevant attribute (FF), and one but not the other relevant attribute (TF and FT). Once the assignment of one stimulus from each of these four classes has been determined, the remaining stimuli can be categorized without error. Eighty-three percent of the subjects in this experiment solved the problem after seeing one example of each of the four stimulus subsets. In the experiment by Hiew (1977) in which the final pro-

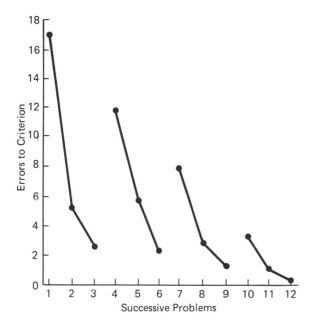

Figure 5-10. Mean errors to solution of 12 successive rule-learning problems. Problems were blocked into sets of three, each block being based on one of the four primary bidimensional rules. (Source: Bourne, L.E., Jr. [1970]. Knowing and using concepts. *Psychological Review, 77,* 546–556. Copyright 1970 by the American Psychological Association. Reprinted by permission of the publisher and author.)

blem was based on an unfamiliar and previously unpracticed rule, 58 percent of the subjects performed perfectly.

These results suggest that, after sufficient practice with some rules within a given system, the subject comes to know or to understand the system as a whole. Knowledge of the system allows high-level performance on any rule within the system, whether the subject has previously been exposed to it or not. The subjects' familiarity with the structure of the rule system allows them to induce new rules that are consistent within that system. Reasonable practice with the four primary rules seems to be sufficient for complete transfer to the entire system for a majority of subjects. The system—in this case the set of categories defined by the calculus of propositions—subsumes a variety (a total of sixteen, see Table 5–2) of different rules. It is, thus, superordinate to the rules themselves. The subjects' acquisition of the system reveals the highest level of comprehension of concepts and their relationships that we have discussed.

The basis for interrule transfer within the calculus of propositions actually reduces to a quite simple strategy, called the truth table strategy because of its obvious relationship to the logical bidimensional truth table of formal logic. The four subsets of stimuli described above correspond to the logicians' TT, TF, FT, and FF combinations, where T is true and F is false for any premise. The translation required is merely to allow the presence of an attribute to be called T and its absence F. Knowing the truth value of these four combinations fully determines the truth function for any combination of arguments in logic or response assignments of stimulus patterns in a bidimensional rule-learning task. In a sense, then, subjects in the foregoing experiments may, on some intuitive level, have discovered the truth table, an algorithm recognized to have considerable power within formal logic.

Processes in Rule-Learning. What accounts for initial differences in difficulty among conceptual rules? The idea that seems most consistent with the results is based on response biases (Bourne, 1974). That is, subjects have certain pre-established tendencies at the outset of any problem. One of these tendencies is to place stimuli with both relevant features (TTs) in the positive category. Another is the tendency to place stimuli with neither relevant feature (FFs) in the negative category. Somewhat weaker is the subjects' tendency to place stimuli with one but not both relevant features (TFs) and (FTs) into the negative category. These tendencies are to be thought of as productions in a person's procedural knowledge. They will change over time in the light of disconfirming feedback from the experimenter. But, while these tendencies are dominant, the subject will make errors, especially on nonconjunctive problems. It can be shown that rule difficulty aligns rather well with the number of changes in these initial tendencies required by the unknown rule.

Over a series of problems based on a variety of different rules, response biases are lessened. As a subject gains familiarity with a variety of rules within the system, he or she learns to adopt a neutral orientation toward initial stimuli. That is, the subject observes the placement of an instance belonging to a particular class before invoking a procedure for assigning other instances of the same class to response categories. At this point, the subject operates on the problem with a truth table strategy.

The truth table strategy is deceptively difficult. Its use depends upon a variety of cognitive operations. To employ it, the subject must attend only to those dimensions of the stimuli that have been confirmed (by instruction) as relevant and ignore all others. Further, the subject must be able to focus upon the relevant values or features within those dimensions. Beyond attending selectively, the subject must mentally form all possible combinations of relevant features—TT, TF, FT, and FF. In addition, the subject must understand what it means to negate or to take the complement of an attribute because some of the stimulus sets that must be dealt with are defined in terms of characteristics that the stimulus *does not have*. Finally, the subject must be able to work mentally and simultaneously with four unique coded classes of stimuli.

All of these skills are present in the performance of well-trained adult subjects. The majority of these subjects do attain the truth table level of performance. However, for the naive adult subject, this is not a natural way to organize information and to perform such tasks. Achieving facility with a system of rules is something that takes considerable time, effort, and ability.

Perceptual Factors in Rule-Learning. Rule-learning has generally been treated as an abstract process, related to the acquisition of a general principle that applies in any context and to any stimulus object. Recent evidence (Bourne, 1979; Reznick & Richman, 1976) raised some questions about this matter. In particular, these experimenters observed that, contrary to the usual results, the disjunctive rule problem is easier for naive subjects to solve than a conjunctive problem when certain pairs of stimulus features are involved. Some pairs of features seem to coalesce and unitize naturally, corresponding to Garner's (1978) notion of integral dimensions. Such combinations lead naturally (or perceptually) to a conjunctive organization of the stimulus population, because the positive instances of the concept are by definition a conjunction based on the joint presence of the critical features. Logical operations are required only if the features must be artificially separated in order to sort the stimuli according to some other nonconjunctive rule. Other pairs of features might be naturally disparate, corresponding to Garner's notion of separable dimensions. The perceptual nature of these features leads directly to sorting the stimuli disjunctively, based on the independent appearance of either feature in a stimulus. In this case, the conjunction, which requires the joint presence of features, necessitates additional mental activity for solution and is therefore more difficult. Thus, in a population of geometrical designs, Bourne found, for example, that color-form feature pairs produced disjunctive problems that were easier to solve than conjunctive problems. In contrast, noncolor-form pairs generated easier conjunctive problems.

Thus, it is not entirely correct to treat rule-learning as a stimulus-independent process, proceeding on an abstract level and applying equally readily in all stimulus contexts. The knowledge required by rule-learning is a set of procedures which should be useful for any stimulus materials. But the data of recent experiments imply that there is something more concrete and stimulus-determined about rule-learning, particularly for the naive subject. Obviously, some modifications of the model of rule-learning described earlier are required by these data. The modifications are straightforward. Indeed, they are essentially an extension of the principles already inherent in that model. Assume that there are only two major subsets of feature pairs, conjunctively-oriented (integral) and disjunctively-oriented (separate) pairs. The present assumptions of the model are consistent with a conjunctive relationship. To make those assumptions consistent with a disjunctive relationship, we need only one procedural change relating to the bias regarding assignments of stimuli with one but not the other relevant feature (TF and FT stimuli). This modification is neither arbitrary or capricious, if we have independent means for determining the integrality or separability of dimensions. Techniques for specifying these characteristics have been worked out by Garner (1976).

Summary

A concept is an abstraction in the sense that it refers to no particular object or event but rather to a collection of such concrete entities. Concepts are learned through experience with their exemplars. Most of the research and theoretical work in this area has dealt with how the features of a concept are learned or identified. A variety of theoretical ideas for concept-learning and concept-utilization has been proposed. According to one theory, concepts are learned by forming associations between concept examples and the concept label; sometimes these associations are mediated by internal or implicit activities. An alternative characterizes the learning process as a matter of hypothesis-testing generated by some overall strategy. The most complete version of hypothesis-testing theory was developed by Levine. His theory includes an assumption that subjects monitor more than one hypothesis at a time and that learning or problem-solving can take place both on correct response and on error trials. Still a third, and more recent, possibility puts more emphasis on the structure of a concept than on the process by which it is formed. Exemplar theory claims that concept-learning is accomplished by memorizing specific instances and by using some measure of instance similarity.

Laboratory studies of concept-formation have traditionally used arbitrary tasks in which the concepts bear little resemblance to ordinary natural concepts. This approach has been criticized for its failure to tell us much about how natural concepts are acquired or about their memorial representation once they are known. Research on natural concepts suggests that their representation may take the form of a prototype or best instance and that members of a natural category can be evaluated in terms of their goodness of category membership. This structure seems characteristic of a wide variety of concepts, ranging from simple perceptual ones, like colors, through complex semantic ones, like animals.

Natural concepts align themselves hierarchically. In the hierarchy, there is a basic level with certain characteristics that make it unique. Categorization occurs to reduce the infinity of differences among stimuli to manageable proportions. The basic level of classification preserves a great deal of information about items while at the same time reducing real-world variation to as few classifications as possible. Moreover, it is the highest level in the classification hierarchy at which a person can interact with exemplars using consistent movement patterns. Finally, the basic level is the highest at which a recognizable "average" object can be identified by shape. The basis for forming categories, particularly basic level categories, seems to be shared attributes defining a family resemblance relationship.

The definition of any concept involves both relevant features and a rule or relationship among those features. Differences among rules is a factor to consider in concept-formation. Research has shown that rules taken from the calculus of propositions vary widely in difficulty. A number of explanations has been offered for these differences. The most successful explanation at the present time is couched in terms of a person's initial response biases. The difficulty of a given rule is a function of how many pre-existing response tendencies are appropriate and how many have to be changed. In any case, rules can be learned. Moreover, when the rules in question are chosen from the same system, for example, the calculus of propositions, there is interrule transfer. Experience with a subset of rules is sufficient for complete transfer for all rules within the system. Under these circumstances, a person can learn something that goes beyond a specific concept or even a specific rule. Learning a system of rules represents the most abstract level in the conceptual hierarchy.

SIX

General Knowledge and Its Retrieval

Outline

Introduction

Think of times you have called somebody on the phone, using a phone number that you called several times before. How often do you find that you must look the number up again because you don't remember it?

How often do you find, at the end of a conversation that you forgot to bring up some point or some question that you had intended to mention?

When you want to remember an experience, a joke or a story, how often do you find that you cannot do so?

When you are in a restaurant and want to speak to your waiter or waitress, how often do you forget what he or she looked like (so you don't know which waiter or waitress to call)?

These questions, and many others, were asked of college students by Herrmann and Neisser (1978) as a way of examining people's everyday memory experiences. In answering each of these questions, the students made use of their long-term memories. Herrmann and Neisser were particularly interested in subjects' self reports about their own memories. But equally important to the understanding of long-term memory are the issues of how information is retrieved from memory and how it is stored. It is these issues to which this chapter is addressed.

In previous chapters, we outlined some crucial distinctions about memory, and discussed briefly how information gets into long-term memory and some of the mechanisms by which it is forgotten. In this chapter we will consider the general knowledge that is part of our long-term memories, and how this knowledge is retrieved when we need to use it.

Retrieval: Some Observations

Suppose you were asked for the name of the person who fired a shot at President Ford as he stepped out of a downtown San Francisco hotel on September 22, 1975. If you cannot recall the name immediately, let us offer a hint. Ford's attempted assassin was a woman, and a forty-five-year-old activist at the time of this incident. Who was she? Need another hint? Her initials were SJM. A final hint? Her first name was Sara. At this point, if not earlier, you have probably realized that the woman was Sara Jane Moore. Even if you did not retrieve her name initially, the name may have been in your memory all the time. If you were able to retrieve it later with the proper hints, it must have been stored.

Retrieving information from long-term memory is a remarkable ability that most of us take for granted. The retrieval schemes we possess are crucial for efficient memory. Imagine being in a library full of books, but not a single one of them contained an index. If you wanted to read something about President Ford, you might have to skim through entire books, page by page, before you came across some desired information. That might take weeks. But by using an index, you can find useful information very quickly.

Analogously, long-term memory is accessible through an indexlike mechanism that permits efficient retrieval. Ask a person the name of his children, or his telephone number, or the name of the first President of the United States, and the answer comes easily and effortlessly. This means that we must have fairly direct access to a great deal of information in long-term memory.

RETRIEVAL CUES

When we try to retrieve something from memory, we often rely on cues. Cues help us check different parts of long-term memory to see if any of them contain the fact we are looking for. If you want to remember the name of the husband of the mayor of your city, you might begin thinking about the mayor herself. If you could not recall the name, you might think about men's names in general, essentially trying a few out for size. Eventually you might stumble across the correct name.

In a legal court, retrieval cues play an important role even if they are not called precisely by that name. Witnesses who cannot remember important details are occasionally asked a question that prompts their memory, or are handed a document that refreshes their recollection. In theory, anything that actually refreshes a witness's memory may be used. As one Court noted, the refresher could be "a song, or a face, or a newspaper item" (Jewitt *v.* United States, 1926), or "the creaking of a hinge, the whistling of a tune, the smell of seaweed, the sight of an old photograph, the taste of nutmeg, the touch of a piece of canvas" (Fanelli *v.* U.S. Gypsum Co, 1944).

Throughout literary history, writers have been fascinated by the idea of things that spur recollection. The feelings that often accompany successful cue-prompted recall of the past have been eloquently captured by Marcel Proust in his great novel *Remembrance of Things Past:*

> And once I had recognized the taste of the crumb of Madeleine soaked in her concoction of lime flowers, which my aunt used to give me . . . immediately the old grey house upon the street, where the room was, rose up like the scenery of a theatre to attach itself to the little pavilion, opening on to the garden . . . ; and with the house the town, from morning to night and in all weathers, the Square where I was sent before luncheon, the streets along which I used to run errands, the country roads we took when it was fine.

According to Tulving (1983), retrieval cues can be thought of as the especially salient or significant "aspects of the individual's physical and cognitive environment that initiate and influence the process of retrieval" (p. 171). In real life, retrieval cues are presented to us in our ongoing interaction with our world, as when we bump into a friend whom we have not seen for years and a flood of memories is brought back. In laboratory experiments, retrieval cues are presented by the experimenter. Such cues are excellent as a means of plucking recalcitrant information from long-term memory (for example, Tulving & Pearlstone, 1966; Raaijmakers & Shiffrin, 1981).

One impressive experimental demonstration of the power of retrieval cues was provided by Tulving and Thomson (1971, 1973). These investigators showed that there are circumstances in which a person can even fail to recognize a word he or she has recently learned, but, with the right retrieval cue, can recall it. A typical experiment is illustrated in Figure 6–1. Subjects saw a list of word pairs, such as pretty-BLUE, in which the left-hand, lower-case word was the cue and the right-hand, capitalized word was to be remembered later. After the capitalized words were studied, subjects performed a free association test in which they were given a different list of stimulus words, and had to write down a number of words that they thought of as associated with the stimulus words. If the subject wished to include

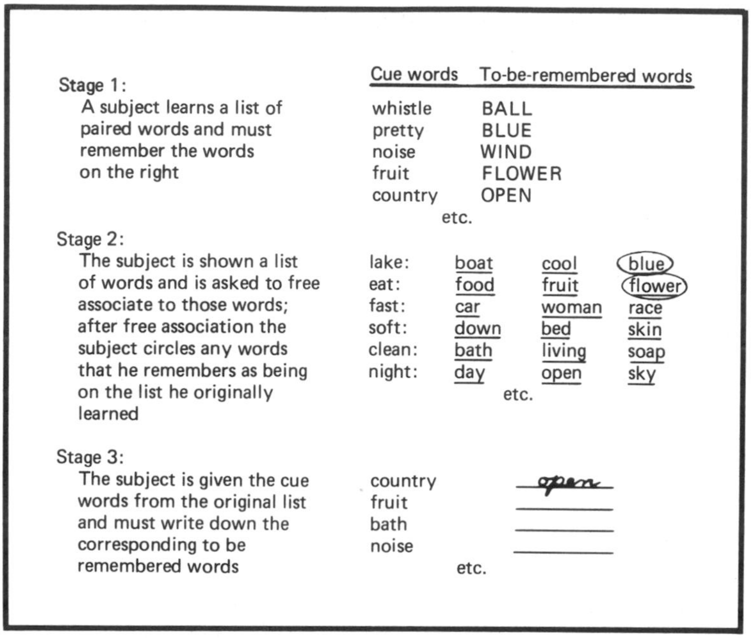

```
Stage 1:                              Cue words   To-be-remembered words
    A subject learns a list of
    paired words and must             whistle     BALL
    remember the words                pretty      BLUE
    on the right                      noise       WIND
                                      fruit       FLOWER
                                      country     OPEN
                                                etc.
Stage 2:
    The subject is shown a list       lake:   boat    cool    (blue)
    of words and is asked to free     eat:    food    fruit   (flower)
    associate to those words;         fast:   car     woman   race
    after free association the        soft:   down    bed     skin
    subject circles any words         clean:  bath    living  soap
    that he remembers as being        night:  day     open    sky
    on the list he originally                       etc.
    learned

Stage 3:
    The subject is given the cue      country        open
    words from the original list      fruit       _____
    and must write down the           bath        _____
    corresponding to be               noise       _____
    remembered words                            etc.
```

Figure 6-1. A three-stage experiment by Tulving & Thomson (1973). (Source: Tulving, E. & Thomson, D.M. [1973]. Encoding specificity and retrieval processes in episodic memory. *Psychological Review, 80,* 352–373. Copyright 1973 by the American Psychological Association. Reprinted by permission of the publisher and author.)

in their free associations any recently seen words, they were allowed to do so. To give an example, suppose a subject had been given the italicized words on the left as stimuli, and responded with the words on the right in the free association:

eat   food, fruit, flower, picnic, lunch
lake   boat, fish, swim, water, cold, blue
clean   bath, living, soap, mister, dirty

When the free association test was finished, the subject was asked to circle those words in the free association that he or she recognized as being on the list of previously memorized words. So if the subject recognized *blue* on the free association responses to *lake* as having been a word memorized earlier, this would be so indicated. Many previously memorized words were included in the free associations, but only about 25 percent of them were recognized as having been previously memorized. Thus, subjects performed poorly on the recognition task. However, when the subjects were subsequently shown the cue words from the original list and asked to recall the memorized words, over 60 percent of the memorized words were recalled. In other words, subjects *recalled* many words that they had failed to *recog-*

nize moments earlier. Once again, retrieval cues are instrumental in eliciting a desired word from a subject. Here we have the unusual case in which a retrieval cue for a word is more effective than seeing the entire word itself spelled out.

Of course there are different types of retrieval cues, and they vary in their effectiveness. When we were searching for the name of the person who shot President Ford, some hints were more helpful than others. If we had been told that the person was an adult, this would have been of very little help, since it is likely a priori that the person would have been an adult. But when told that it was a woman, and that her first name was Sara, retrieving the name became easier or at least more probable.

One type of retrieval cue is called a copy cue or identity cue (see, for example Tulving, 1983; Watkins, 1979). A copy cue is one that is physically identical with what the person is trying to remember. Recognizing your umbrella among a set of strange umbrellas, is an example. Generally (but not always) these are excellent cues. If the effectiveness of a cue depends on its similarity to what the person is trying to remember, the copy cues represent one extreme on the continuum of similarity and thus should be very effective. When I gave you the cue "Sara Jane Moore" many of you may have then recalled that you once knew it was she who attempted to assassinate President Ford. A name is a copy cue in that it is physically identical with what you are trying to recall.

When one moves away from copy cues to consider other types of cues, the situation becomes more complex. Should the letter H be considered an effective cue for eliciting recall of the previous-learned word *house*? After all, the retrieval cue and the word itself always occurred together, and thus the letter H might be expected to be an effective cue. As it turns out, H might or might not be a good cue depending upon the person's mental activity at the time of initial storage and at the time of attempted retrieval.

In an unpublished study, Tulving examined the effectiveness of various retrieval cues (Tulving, 1983, p. 208). His experiment was unique in that all of its eighteen subjects possessed a Ph.D. degree in psychology and were professors in a number of illustrious universities in the United States and Canada. Moreover, Tulving himself ran the subjects in this two-stage experiment. In the first stage, the subjects had to say the months of the year as quickly as possible. Subjects invariably named the months in their natural order, requiring about five seconds to do this. In the second stage, subjects had to say the months of the year in alphabetical order. The fastest of these accomplished subjects took 55 seconds to get from April to September, and the mean time was about two minutes. Although the subjects were producing well-learned items from memory, not a single one could recall the twelve names in alphabetical order without making any mistakes.

This simple demonstration shows, as have numerous full-fledged laboratory studies, that some ways of retrieving stored information are more effective than others. Moreover, for a given retrieval cue to be effective it must have a special relation to the target item which it is supposed to cue.

Based upon this work, Tulving proposed an important idea, namely the idea of "encoding specificity." The idea is that a retrieval cue will be effective to the extent that the cue was present when a particular event originally occurred. Put another way, a cue will be effective if it was specifically encoded with the original event.

TIP-OF-THE-TONGUE PHENOMENON

When you attempted to recall the name of the woman who shot President Ford, perhaps there was a moment in which the name was almost there. You almost had it, but not quite. We say it is on the "tip of the tongue." Suddenly the name, Sara Jane Moore, rises to your consciousness. What sort of search and evaluation processes go on in the mind when this happens?

The question motivated Brown and McNeill (1966) to develop a technique for producing the tip-of-the-tongue (TOT) state. They presented subjects with definitions for uncommon English words and instructed them to attempt to produce the proper word to fit the definition. For example, subjects might be given the definition "a navigational instrument used for measuring angular distances" in an attempt to get them to produce the word *sextant*. The definitions for other difficult words, such as *nepotism, ambergris, caduceus,* and *sampan,* were also used. Some definitions which may produce a tip-of-the-tongue state are presented in Table 6–1. (You might take a look at these definitions, first to give yourself a first-hand feeling for the TOT state and, second, just on the off chance that one of these definitions will appear on your Graduate Record Examination!)

Subjects indicated by raising their hands that a tip-of-the-tongue state had been produced. A graphic description of this mentally painful state has been provided by Brown and McNeill:

> ... the signs of it were unmistakable; he would appear to be in mild torment, something like the brink of a sneeze, and if he found the word his relief was considerable. While searching for the target, the subject told us all the words that came to his mind. He volunteered the information that some of them resembled the target in sound but not in meaning; others he was sure were similar in meaning but not in sound. The experimenter intruded on the subject's agony with two questions (a) How many syllables has the target word? (b) What is its first letter? ... (1966, p. 326)

Over 200 tip-of-the-tongue states were produced in the experiment. During the state, other words came to mind. Most often these words were similar in sound to the correct word (*secant* instead of *sextant, saipan* instead of *sampan*), but many were similar in meaning. Perhaps the reason that words tended to be similar in sound is because the subjects' task required that the word be pronounced. With both similar sound and similar meaning guesses, the subjects knew that these were not quite correct, but felt they were close. There were other patterns observed in the type of incorrect guesses that subjects produced; similar sounding words contained the same number of syllables as the correct word over 60 percent of the time, and the initial letter sound was guessed correctly over half of the time.

TABLE 6-1. *Some definitions used to produce a tip-of-the-tongue state. (The correct words are given below.)*

---

1. A fanatical partisan; one who is carried away in his pursuit of a cause or object.

2. Lying on one's back, with the face upward.

3. Selecting, choosing doctrines or methods from various sources, systems, etc.

4. A conciliatory bribe, gift, advance, etc.

5. An instrument having 30 to 40 strings over a shallow, horizontal sounding box and played with picks and fingers.

6. A hiding place used by explorers for concealing or preserving provisions or implements.

7. To clear from alleged fault or guilt; to absolve, vindicate, acquit, or exonerate.

Words corresponding to definitions.

1.	Zealot	5.	Zither
2.	Supine	6.	Cache
3.	Eclectic	7.	Exculpate
4.	Sop		

The TOT data show that partial information about both the sound and the meaning can be retrieved before complete access to the word is possible. (This, of course, runs counter to the alternative view that assumes that once a person locates an item in memory, the entire item becomes accessible—see Kintsch, 1970, for example.) When a person is in the TOT state, he or she can apparently retrieve bits of the sought-for item, but cannot gain access to all of it.

How must long-term memory be organized to permit TOT behavior? Brown and McNeill suggested first that a word is located somewhere, and further that its location contains information both about its sound and about its meaning. For this reason, most words can be retrieved from long-term memory either by sound or by meaning. For example, I can give you the word *umbrella* and ask you for its meaning, or I can give you the meaning "a screen of cloth on a folding frame, carried for protection against the rain" and ask you to give me the word. Stored with each word were thought to be associations, or marked pathways, to other words also located in long-term memory. Thus, when given a particular definition, a subject might come up with the target word or might produce a word that meant something similar. For Brown and McNeill, then, long-term memory consisted of a large set of associated storage locations, with each location containing information related to a single word or a single fact.

Later work on the TOT state involved asking subjects to look at photographs of famous people, such as Elizabeth Taylor or Winston Churchill, and try to recall their names (Yarmey, 1973). In these studies, subjects generally demonstrated that they had some knowledge of the first letters of the sought-after name, and a reasonably good idea of the number of syllables in the name. In searching for the name, subjects often tried to think of something about the person, such as his or her profession, and to use this information to aid in retrieving the full name.

In real life, people often resolve their TOT states successfully, which means that the sought-after item is successfully retrieved. Lucas (cited in Reason and Mycielska, 1982) wondered how this resolution came about. She persuaded thirty-five people to keep a diary of their resolved TOT states during a one-month period. A mean of 2.3 resolved TOT states were recorded, producing 75 TOT's in all. Lucas identified four types of pathway to the final solution, some examples of which are given here. The intermediate solutions are given in the order they were spoken, with the sought-after item in capital letters.

Mostly Phonological Pathways

Margaret, Muriel, MARY
Roydell, Royston, ROYSELL
Andrea, Angela, Anthea, ALISON

Mostly Semantic Pathways

Retaliate, Immunity, RESISTANCE
Alone, Unaided, INITIATIVE
Picasso, Correrra, GUERNICA

Multiple-Name Strategies

Ice-pick, Ice-axe, Ice-bolt, ICE-SCREW
Holt's Brewery, Ansell's Brewery, MARSTON'S BREWERY

Mixed Strategies

Jimmy Reid, Reid, NEIL
Rombart, Mille, MELITA
Embellish, Ripieno, CONTINUO

These examples illustrate how the mind focuses on items that are related in sound or meaning to the sought-after target. In some cases (the mixed strategy) both items related in sound and items related in meaning are produced. Moreover, the examples illustrate one commonly used strategy, namely to "try out on the mental ear" (1982, p. 125) a string of names linked either by a common part name (such as ice-pick, ice-axe) or by their inclusion in a particular category, for example breweries.

In roughly half of the TOT states produced by Lucas's subjects, there was persistent interference by a wrong word or name. These "interference" TOT's appear to be qualitatively different from non-interference TOT's. For example, interference TOT's are much more likely to be resolved by resorting to some external strategy, like asking someone else or looking up the item in a dictionary. The non-interference TOT states are more likely to be resolved by use of an internal strategy like alphabetic search, recall of contextual information, or an attempt to form a mental image of the target item.

Reason and Mycielska (1982) have identified some of the principal findings of studies involving the TOT state:

1. Retrieval from memory is a matter of degree, rather than being an all-or-nothing affair.
2. Intermediate solutions that people produce while in the TOT state often share similar sounds with the sought-after item. Occasionally they share similar meanings.
3. The "feeling of knowing", which is the extent to which a person is sure that the item is in memory, is a good indicator of whether the person will ultimately be successful in retrieving the item from memory.

The TOT studies give us insights into how our general knowledge is structured in memory and retrieved. Since the initial investigations of the TOT, numerous studies have been performed, using a variety of methodologies, to illuminate us about general knowledge—its structure and retrieval. Many major theories have been proposed. Befor turning to these theories, which will constitute one of the principle topics in this chapter, consider briefly a very difficult approach to and analysis of the tip-of-the-tongue phenomenon.

FREUD'S ANALYSIS OF TOT

Sigmund Freud once told a story of how he strove to recall the name of the master artist who painted the imposing frescoes of the "Last Judgment" in the dome of Orvieto. Two names—Botticelli and Boltrafio, both well-known artists in their own right—continued to intrude on his thoughts. But, as Freud well recognized, neither was the creator of the "Last Judgment." The situation Freud describes thus fits well into what we have been discussing as the tip-of-the-tongue phenomenon.

Freud's tip-of-the-tongue state occurred while he was riding with a stranger in a carriage bound for Herzegovina, a region south of Bosnia in central Yugoslavia. The story goes as follows. Freud told the stranger that he knew of a doctor in whom Turkish patients placed a great deal of confidence. Whenever this particular doctor admitted that he could not save a patient, it was common for relatives of the patient to say, "Sir (Herr Doktor, in Freud's native German), what can I say. I know that if he could be saved, you would save him." During the conversation, Freud remembered that his doctor friend had also told him that Turks value sexual pleasure highly and appear to be more concerned about losing their sexual potency than about dying. Freud felt, however, that he could not express this thought in polite conversation with a stranger, which is perhaps understandable given the Victorian times. In addition, he felt uncomfortable thinking about the theme of death and sex, for he had recently heard, while visiting the town of Trafoi, that one of his former patients had committed suicide because of a prolonged, incurable sexual problem. So Freud switched the topic to traveling in Italy and it was at that time that he found himself unable to recall the creator of the "Last Judgment"—Signorelli.

Freud's own analysis of his tip-of-the-tongue state relied heavily on the concept of repression, or the conscious pushing out of awareness of uncomfortable thoughts. Freud wanted to forget about death and sexuality, thoughts which were connected with the words Trafoi and Herr Doctor. Thus he repressed those words. By association, he also repressed Signor, the Italian word for Herr or Sir. In attempting to recall the name of the artist, then, he picked up pieces from the conversation with his companion—*Bo* from the region, Bosnia, *elli* from the artist's name, and *traffio* from the town Trafoi. This combination of parts led to the compromise responses, Botticelli and Boltraffio, both of which were, of course, incorrect.

Comparing the approaches of Freud and of Brown and McNeill, an important distinction emerges. Freud was interested in studying individual people, and from these case histories he hoped to establish general principles. Brown and McNeill, on the other hand, utilized statistics in order to establish those general principles of behavior. Many of Freud's ideas are compatible with the principles established in the laboratory, but Freud's emphasis was different. Freud was much more interested in the motives and needs, the experiences and fantasies of each individual whom he observed (including himself).

Sometimes we can learn a great deal by examining an individual case. For example, consider the case off a fifty-four-year-old patient who had aphasia, a general language impairment, and was trying desperately to name a picture of an anchor. The patient's injury was due to brain damage suffered during a wartime injury. Although he was generally healthy, and could function reasonably well intellectually, he had great difficulty naming objects (Wingfield, 1979; Wingfield & Byrnes, 1981). When shown a picture he could recognize it easily, but to name it was a struggle. His responses, in the order given, are displayed in Figure 6–2, along with an attempt to classify each response according to the search strategy that was being attempted. Notice how his initial approach was to try to think of the object's use ("belongs to a boat"). This got him nowhere. Next he tried a phonetic approach by thinking of a word of a similar sound ("hanger"). He returned to thinking about the object's use (" . . . throw it on a boat").

The extreme difficulty encountered by this aphasic patient is of interest not only to clinicians who work with such patients, but to students of human memory. It resembles, albeit in more extreme form, the TOT state so commonly experienced by normal subjects. Although it is a far more dramatic illustration, it helps to establish general principles of search and retrieval. Even in these extreme cases, patients search for information by using related phonological and semantic information.

Most experimental psychologists have not been concerned with the individual. Rather, data are collected from large numbers of subjects, and theories are constructed that are meant to encompass almost all human beings. Despite this tendency, the case histories are appreciated for their ability to offer occasional insights to the development of those theories.

Semantic Memory

EPISODIC AND SEMANTIC MEMORY

As noted in Chapter 1, information in long-term memory takes a variety of forms. It includes general knowledge about the world, such as the fact that a yacht

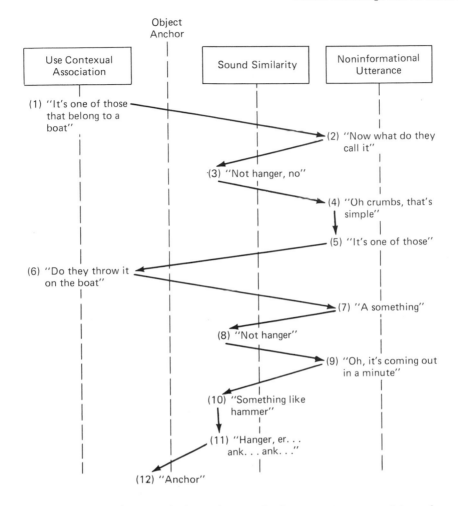

Figure 6-2. Complete record of an aphasic patient's attempt to name a picture of an anchor. Responses are categorized by the search strategies employed. (Source: Wingfield, A. [1979]. Human learning and memory: An introduction. New York: Harper & Row.)

is a type of boat, or that bananas are usually yellow. But is also includes our own personal experiences. Tulving (1972) coined a useful distinction between these two classes of memories—he labeled the former kind "semantic memories" and the latter "episodic memories." In his own words:

> Episodic memory receives and stores information about temporally dated episodes or events, and temporal-spatial relations among these events . . . Semantic memory is the memory necessary for the use of language. It is a mental thesaurus, organized knowledge a person possesses about words and other verbal symbols, their meaning and referents, about relations among them, and about rules, formulas, and algorithms for the manipulation of these symbols, concepts, and relations. (pp. 385–386)

In other words, episodic memory contains information about life experiences—information that is associated with a particular time or place. The information that you were in California for Christmas is episodic, as is the information that you participated in a psychology experiment in which you saw a film of a crime. Semantic memory contains information that is not associated with a particular time or place, such as the fact that a yacht is a type of boat.

Tulving conceived of episodic and semantic memory as two information-processing systems that (1) selectively receive information from perceptual and cognitive systems, (2) retain various aspects of that information, and (3) transmit that information when it is needed. The two systems are thought to differ in terms of the type of information that is stored, the conditions and consequences of retrieval, and possibly their vulnerability to interference. In his recent formulation, Tulving (1983) presents a much-expanded set of features that distinguish episodic and semantic memory. Tulving divides these features into three broad categories. One has to do with the kind of information, or knowledge, handled by the two systems; the second concerns the operations of the systems; the third pertains to what Tulving has referred to as "applications." For example, semantic memory seems especially relevant to education, whereas episodic memory is less so. The great relevance of semantic memory to education was also noted recently by Bahrick (1984). Bahrick commented that the organization and acquisition of semantic knowledge has been an important focus of psychological research, and that acquisition of such knowledge is in fact the objective of education. He lamented the fact, however, that questions concerned with the permanence of knowledge have been neglected in research. (We return to this topic later in this chapter.)

Episodic and semantic memory systems have a lot in common, especially when it comes to the type of information that is stored. Both systems, for example, clearly contain visual information. We can imagine the visual image of a banana, which is part of semantic memory. We can also visualize the face of a person whom we met at a party last week—something that is in episodic memory.

As Tulving (1983) notes, much of the information and knowledge that is registered is both episodic and semantic memory comes from the external environment through the senses. An important question arises as to how the information in long-term memory, whether semantic or episodic, is represented. If the input is visual in nature, is it represented in memory as a visual image? Or is it recoded as a set of descriptive statements? The new friend's face could be stored as an image, or it could be recoded into a set of statements like "Round face, dark curly hair, bushy eyebrows. . . ."

Cognitive psychologists have debated the issue of whether long-term memory contains picture-like codes or whether all information gets transformed into a more abstract format. Some of the most extensive work on this subject has been done by Paivio (1971) who assumes that long-term memory uses both verbal and image codes to represent information. His view has come to be known as the "dual-coding theory." Paivio has stated quite explicitly that verbal information and nonverbal information are represented and processed in functionally independent cognitive systems. One system, the imagery system, is specialized for processing information concerning concrete objects and events. The other system, the verbal system, is specialized for dealing with information involving language (Paivio, 1975).

Paivio conducted a number of experiments to try to support the dual-coding view. Most of these were directed toward demonstrating that pictures and concrete words are learned better than are abstract words (Paivio, 1971), or that when both the verbal and the image codes are used, retention is better than when only one is involved (Paivio, 1978). One interesting experiment utilized pictures and printed names (see Figure 6–3). Cards such as these were shown to subjects, who were asked to judge which member of the pair was conceptually larger. The time it took the subject to respond was recorded. Paivio reasoned as follows: If long-term memory contained only information stored in the semantic (or verbal) mode, then subjects should take longer to respond to pictures than words, since pictures would have to be translated into words before the judgment could be made. If, on the other hand, long-term memory contained a visual code then pictures would take no longer since they could be accessed directly from memory. Paivio also varied whether the pairs were congruent or incongruent, that it, whether relative sizes of the objects pictured corresponded to their actual sizes (compare the two cards in Figure 6.3). Paivio reasoned that if long-term memory contained a visual code, a conflict would

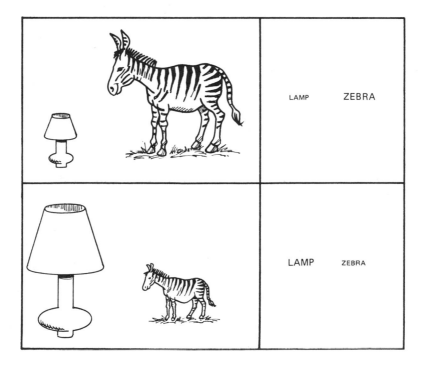

Figure 6-3. The pairs on the top are congruent while those on the bottom are not. (After Paivio, 1975. Courtesy of Psychonomic Society.)

be created by the incongruent pairs that would slow the subjects down. Incongruence in the verbal pairs, however, should not create a problem, since they would first be translated into their verbal equivalents. The results supported the existence of visual codes by showing that subjects responded to incongruent pictures more slowly than congruent ones, whereas word pairs were responded to equally quickly whether they were incongruent or not.

Despite the extensive work that Paivio and other have done, not everyone agrees with the dual-coding idea. One who holds a view contrary to Paivio's is Pylyshyn (1973). According to this view, when we have a visual experience, it does not get stored as a picture in the mind. Rather, we store pictures into more abstract representations, representations that resemble neither pictures nor words. Pylyshyn's theory is that both verbal and image material gets stored in the same format, and this view has come to be known as a propositional theory (see Anderson, 1978, for a fuller discussion). Pylyshyn came to this idea because it seemed inconceivable to him that the brain could store all of the images it receives through the senses. This, he felt, would place an impossible burden on the system. It would be impossible, for example, to retrieve a particular image when one needed to.

Other researchers have similarly suggested that pictures and other visualizable material are stored in an abstract representation (for example, Nelson, Reed & Walling, 1976; Potter, 1976; Intraub, 1979). In one study designed to shed light on the debate, subjects were shown pictures that they later had to recognize (Intraub, 1979). Some of the pictures could be named quite easily, while for others some time was required for the subject to come up with a name. The pictures were presented at a variety of rates, sometimes very quickly so that naming was not possible for many of them, and sometimes very slowly so that naming was possible for virtually all of them. The dual-coding view would seemingly predict that pictures that could be named would be better remembered because of the availability of two codes. However, the study showed no effect of the presumed ability of subjects to name the pictures on later recognition performance. The debate between the dual-coding and the propositional camps is not one that is easily settled. For one thing, both sides can usually come up with some interpretation to account for any particular experimental result.

Theorizing about long-term memory has generally neglected other kinds of information that are certainly a part of memory. If you have had the experience of picking up the phone, and recognizing the voice of a friend you have not spoken to for over five years, you would be convinced that long-term memory must contain auditory codes that can be long-lasting. Furthermore, it apparently contains codes that correspond to taste, to olfaction, and to motor knowledge. We must have these, for how else could we recognize the taste of an orange, the smell of fresh coffee? How else could we remember how to ride a bicycle or play the piano? Examples such as these attest to the wide variety of types of information that can be stored in long-term memory. Those who subscribe to the propositional view of memory would conclude that all of these types of information are represented in a similar format. Are they? This is a difficult question, and one that cannot easily be answered by experimentation.

We have previously concentrated heavily on episodic memory; the rest of this chapter concerns semantic memory. It focuses on the structure of the information contained in our semantic memory and on the way in which we retrieve and use that information.

Models of Semantic Memory

As Smith (1976) has noted, the phrase semantic memory has been used to denote several views about meaning and memory that vary in how inclusive they are. At the broadest level, semantic memory refers to our store of meaningful material. This includes our permanent knowledge of the meanings of words, as well as our tran- sient memory of a particular sentence. Under this broad definition, theories of semantic memory would encompass the large-scale memory models developed by Anderson and Bower (1973), Anderson (1976, 1983), Kintsch (1974) and Norman and Rumelhart (1975). However, a more restrictive definition of semantic memory is to view it as a system that contains word meanings and rules for operating on them. The system includes general world knowledge, but not our transient memory of a particular sentence.

Any theory of semantic memory, within the more restrictive definition, typical- ly aspires to one or more goals. The first goal is to describe the representation of word meanings in the mind. A second goal is to describe how information is retrieved from that representation. Many such models have appeared over the last several decades. What they have in common is their attempt to describe the representa- tion and utilization of word meanings.

In this section we describe a variety of models of semantic memory. Taken together, these models illustrate well the kind of assumptions that theorists have made about semantic memory. Some of the assumptions concern the retrieval of information from memory. But in order to theorize about a retrieval process, we need to know something about the structure from which we are retrieving, or the representation of the underlying knowledge in the mind. As Mandler (1983) has noted, the concept of "representation," at least in one of its major senses, refers simply to knowledge and the way in which it is organized. The concept of "representation" is a complex one since it refers both to what is stored and how it is stored. All models of semantic memory make assumptions about representation.

THE COLLINS AND QUILLIAN NETWORK MODEL

One of the most common models of semantic memory is the network model that assumes that memory can be represented as a network of associations between words and their underlying concepts. Retrieval is accomplished by winding one's way through this maze of pathways, or associations, that are formed as a result of past experience. A widely cited network theory is that of Collins and Quillian (1969). In their system, concepts are thought to be hierarchically organized into logically nested subordinate-superordinate relations. Thus, the superordinate of *canary* is *bird*, and the superordinate of *bird* is *animal.* The system is thought to be economical in the sense that a property characterizing a particular class of objects is assumed to be stored only at the place in the hierarchy that corresponds to that class. This assumption has been called, not surprisingly, the assumption of "cognitive economy." To illustrate, a property that characterizes all birds, such as the fact that they have wings, is stored only at *bird.* It is not stored with each of the different types of birds, even though they all typically possess wings.

How is information retrieved from the assumed hierarchical structure? To answer this question, Collins and Quillian presented subjects with simple statements, such as "A canary can sing," "A canary is a bird," "A canary is pink," or "A canary is a fish." The subjects had to decide whether the statement was true or false, and their reaction time (*RT*) was measured. The subject in each statement was always a concrete noun from the lowest level of a hierarchy similar to the one depicted in Figure 6-4.

All statements presented to the subjects were classified according to the semantic level at which the information needed to answer the item is stored. For example, for "A canary eats," the information "eats" is stored with *animal,* two levels from *canary.* Similarly, the information "has wings" is stored one level away, while "can sing" is stored zero levels away. Collins and Quillian predicted that subjects would take longer to answer questions when the information needed was located two levels away than when it was located only one or zero levels away. The prediction is borne out, as can be seen in Figure 6-5. Why do subjects take longer to retrieve information that is several levels away? Collins and Quillian's explanation was simple. In order to verify "A canary is yellow," the subject must first enter the level in memory that corresponds to *canary* and here is stored some information, such as the fact that canaries are yellow. Thus, the question can be answered relatively quickly. To verify "A canary can fly," the subject still enters memory at *canary* but

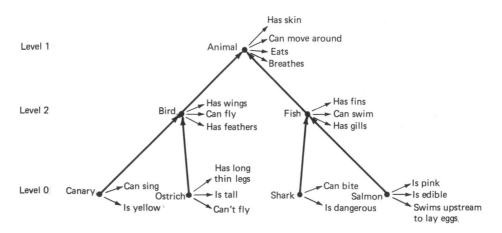

Figure 6-4. A portion of a hierarchically organized structure. (After Collins & Quillian, 1969. Courtesy of Academic Press, Inc.)

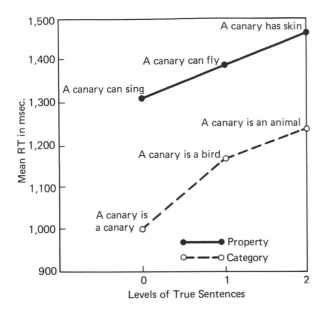

Figure 6-5. Reaction time taken to answer questions about various nouns and their properties and category membership. (After Collins & Quillian, 1969. Courtesy of Academic Press, Inc.)

does not find any information there concerning whether canaries can fly or not. Because a canary is a bird, however, the subject moves up a level to *birds* where the needed information is stored. Thus, since a canary is a bird and birds can fly, the question can now be answered in the affirmative. Of course, the extra step of moving up the hierarchy to the *bird* level takes time, and thus the question takes somewhat longer to answer. A similar analysis explains why it takes people even longer to determine that a canary eats. This statement requires that the subject move up an additional level in the hierarchy to *animal* in order to find the needed information. Because a canary is a bird, and a bird is an animal, and animals eat, it can be concluded that a canary eats.

A closer inspection of Figure 6–5 reveals that it takes on average somewhere between 75 and 90 msec longer to respond to a level 1 statement than to a level 0 statement, and an additional 75 to 90 msec to respond to a level 2 statement. This may represent the time to travel from one level of the hierarchy to the next level. Another inference from the data is that it takes about 200 milliseconds to search through the properties stored with a particular concept. This inference is based on the approximately 200 msec difference in times between those statements which ask about properties (for example, "a canary can fly") and those which ask about category membership (for example, "a canary is a bird").

Evaluation of the Collins and Quillian Model. The original Collins and Quillian paper stimulated a plethora of investigations on semantic memory. The modified Collins and Quillian model (1972b) provided the first detailed description of how information is represented and retrieved. As Smith (1976) points out, it was sufficiently attractive to be adopted by other semantic-memory researchers (among them, Freedman & Loftus, 1971) and even incorporated wholesale into a more general theory of language comprehension (Rumelhart, Lindsay & Norman, 1972).

However, evidence against its core assumptions soon began to mount. The assumption that noun concepts are organized hierarchically was crushed by studies in which statements involving immediate superordinate concepts sometimes took longer to verify than those involving distant superordinates (see Rips, Shoben, & Smith, 1973). According to the original model, a person should verify the statement "A collie is a mammal" faster than "A collie is an animal," since in a logical network *mammal* would be closer to *collie* than *animal*. Yet people do not. Similarly, people take longer to verify that "a cantaloupe is a melon" than to verify that "a cantaloupe is a fruit," even though *melon* is logically closer to *cantaloupe* in a semantic hierarchy.

The cognitive economy assumption also fell on hard times with the experimental results of Conrad (1972). Collins and Quillian's assumption was:

> Information true of birds in general (e.g., can fly, have wings and have feathers) need not be stored with the memory node for each separate kind of bird. Instead, the fact that "A canary can fly" can be inferred by finding that a canary is a bird and that birds can fly. By storing generalizations in this way, the amount of space required for storage is minimized. (1972a, p. 118)

Conrad tested this assumption by choosing level 3 properties and varying the level of the subject of the statement. (Recall that Collins and Quillian used level 0 subjects, and varied the level of the property.) For example, she used "A shark can move," "A fish can move" and "An animal can move," which use increasingly higher-level subjects. If "can move" is stored only with *animal,* it should take subjects longer to verify "A fish can move" than "An animal can move" and longer still to verify that "A shark can move." Conrad failed to find a difference in reaction times that corresponded to the number of levels separating a subject and a property.

In another study, Conrad asked subjects to describe a canary, a bird, an animal, and other concepts to be used later on. She then tabulated the frequency with which various properties were mentioned. She found that the properties frequently associated with canary (such as its being yellow) were those presumed to be stored directly with *canary.* She thus hypothesized that property frequency rather than hierarchical distance is what determines retrieval time, and she conducted an experiment to test this hypothesis. In her experiment both noun-property association (or frequency) and hierarchical distance were manipulated. She found that verification time decreased as the associative relation between the noun and property became stronger, but it did not vary consistently with the hierarchical distance (in terms of number of levels) between the noun and the property. Figure 6–6 illustrates her results. Note that strong associates, such as in "An orange is edible" are verified quickly even though orange and edible were presumed by Collins and Quillian to be separated by two levels.

Another problem with Collins and Quillian's model is that it does not differen-

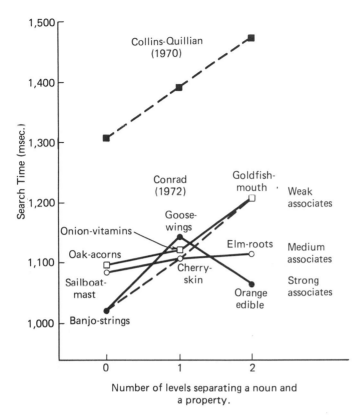

Figure 6-6. Search time depends on the strength of association between a noun and a property, and not on the number of levels separating the noun and property. (Source: Conrad, C. [1972]. Cognitive economy in semantic memory. *Journal of Experimental Psychology, 92,* 49–54.

tiate between the various members of a category. Yet, it is clear that not all members of a category have equivalent status, that is, they vary in the degree to which they are representative of the category. So, *apple* is generally considered to be more representative of the category *fruits* than *grapefruit* is. These differences in the "goodness" of a category member can affect reading comprehension, learning, reasoning and performance in other cognitive tasks (see, for example, Hupp & Mervis, 1982; Roth & Shoben, 1983). Even "ad hoc categories" (categories created spontaneously for use in specialized contexts), such as *things to sell at a garage sale* or *possible costumes to wear to a Halloween party*, possess exemplars that are more or less representative (Barsalou, 1983).

In addition to category members differing in terms of how representative they are, a further problem arises with the fact that a particular category member can be representative of a large natural category, but not particularly representative of a smaller subset of that large category. Take the large category *metals* and the smaller subset *elements*. Most people would say that the exemplar *mercury* is more representative of the category *element* than of the category *metal*. Yet there are other exemplars of *metal*, such as *gold*, that are thought to be more representative of the category *metal* than of the category *elements* (Roth & Mervis, 1983). Roth and Mervis found many similar instances in which the ordering of the two exemplars in a large category was the reverse of their ordering in the smaller subset. A *Cadillac* is a better example of *car* than of *vehicle*, whereas a *jeep* is a better example of *vehicle*. *Chablis* is a better example of *wine* than *drink*, but *champagne* is a better example of *drink* than *wine*. These results imply that the order of representativeness of exemplars in a category is not necessarily the same at all levels in a taxonomy.

Another problem with Collins and Quillian's model is that it does not readily explain how statements are disconfirmed. How does a person decide that an anteater does not have pages? In their 1972a paper, Collins and Quillian introduced the *extraneous-path hypothesis* to account for disconfirmations. It states that when a subject finds a promising clue, he or she will check that clue out, which, of course, will consume time. If asked whether a canary is blue the subject might note that some birds are blue, and be slowed by this extraneous path. The statement "a collie is blue" would not produce the same problem since there are no dogs which are blue. The extraneous-path hypothesis was tested in an experiment in which subjects were timed while they responded to plausible false statements such as "A tiger has a mane" or "A St. Bernard is a cat" and implausible false statements such as "A leopard is a snail" or "An elephant has a bill." The plausible statements are the ones which might cause the subject to trace out an extraneous path to check out a promising lead. For example, the response to "A tiger has a mane" might be slowed by the clue that lions have manes and tigers are similar to lions. Collins and Quillian's results are shown in Figure 6–7. Note that overall implausible statements are disconfirmed much more quickly than plausible ones. Furthermore, the

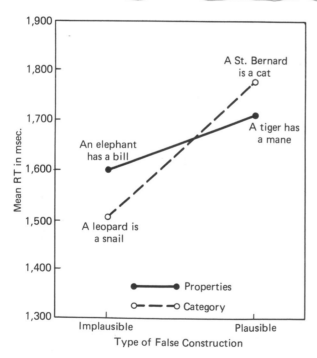

Figure 6-7. • Subjects are faster to disconfirm both category and property statements that are implausible than to disconfirm plausible statements. (After Collins & Quillian, 1972a. Courtesy of John Wiley & Sons, Inc.)

implausible category statements were rejected about 300 msec faster than the plausible ones, whereas the property statements were rejected about 100 msec faster. This experiment constituted at least a first step toward understanding how false statements are disconfirmed, but much work remained to be done. The fact that Collins and Quillian did not have a tidy theory to account for disconfirmation is not as serious a criticism as the fact, discussed previously, that ample counter-evidence to the specific assumptions of the model was accumulating.

Some of the charges were responded to in a paper by Collins and Loftus (1975). For example, these investigators noted that a minor methodological change introduced in the original Collins and Quillian procedure by Conrad may have accounted for her results. Conrad gave the object concept to the subject a full second before the property concept (for example, "lobster . . . has a mouth?") This extra second may have enabled the subject to call to mind the superordinates of lobster (for example animal), which would in term activate their properties, including the property "having a mouth." One consequence would be the elimination of any reaction time differences between superordinate levels.

More recently, several other weaknesses of the Collins and Quillian approach have been identified by Wingfield and Byrnes (1981). Briefly, these researchers were troubled by the following:

1. The Collins and Quillian network model overlooks important interactions between episodic and semantic memory. We know not only that PacMan is the name of a videogame, but our memory of the first time we played the game may be very much a part of this concept.
2. The Collins and Quillian network model is based too closely on logical relations and a priori intuitions. The structure of memory may contain many more idiosyncracies. For one player, PacMan may be the most dominant videogame, whereas for another that particular game is thought to be silly. The structure of the videogame category will be very different for these two players.
3. The Collins and Quillian network model overemphasizes the structure of the memory store, and gives too little attention to possible retrieval strategies.
4. The Collins and Quillian network model emphasizes the task of verifying specific propositions, but neglects the important role of inferences that are routinely drawn from potential relationships in the network.

OTHER NETWORK MODELS

The hierarchical network model proposed by Collins and Quillian is perhaps the best known model of semantic memory. Since its initial publication, other, far more ambitious efforts in this domain have appeared. These are actually large-scale theories of meaning and memory, and fit into Smith's first, and broader, definition of semantic memory. They include more detail, and encompass far more data than the original network model of Collins and Quillian. For example, in the model developed by Anderson and Bower (1973), called HAM for Human Associative Memory, long-term memory is viewed as a vast collection of locations and associations among them. However, the basic component of the model is a "proposition," an entity which is akin to a simple declarative sentence but much more abstract. Propositions are envisioned as representing not only linguistic information, but also visual scenes and other sorts of non-linguistic information. (We return to the topic of propositions in a later chapter.) Like the model of Collins and Quillian, HAM is hierarchical in structure.

Also like the Collins and Quillian model, HAM has been criticized on the grounds that people store more than a simple representation of input. We make inferences and deductions, and store these along with the original input (for example, Potts, 1974). We are exposed to new inputs that can influence our earlier storage (for example, Pezdek, 1977). Pezdek exposed students to sequences of slides showing either short descriptive sentences or line drawings of scenes. Subsequently, they were required to distinguish the original slides they had seen from foil slides that they had not seen. In the interval between study and test, subjects saw material designed to produce interference with the original memory. Thus, subjects who had seen a picture of a bird beside a tree on the study trial might later read a sentence referring to an eagle. Later, subjects were required to discriminate between a slide depicting the original bird or one that looked more like an eagle. Strong interference effects of picture on sentences, and vice versa, were shown. Later studies (Pezdek & Miceli, 1982) confirmed the influence of new inputs on previously acquired information.

Large-scale network theories of meaning continue to be developed by cognitive psychologists. Many of them take advantage of computer technology to simulate cognition. The act of writing and testing a computer program that includes analogous structures and processes can help a researcher determine if a proposed model of cognition is reasonable. HAM was such a simulation model. An elaboration of HAM called ACT, created by Anderson (1976), is also a simulation model. It too used a network conception of semantic memory, combined with a few additional processes, and together constituting a comprehensive view of cognitive functioning. One interesting aspect of ACT is that it proposed a basic distinction between two kinds of knowledge. The first, declarative knowledge, refers to facts, concepts, and the beliefs we have about our environment. (The fact that Carter was President before Reagan, or that Einstein was a smart person, are examples.) The second kind of knowledge is called procedural knowledge, and it refers to things that we know how to do, such as riding a bicycle.

The ACT theory comprises three sets of principles: principles concerning initial encoding of information, principles concerning storage, and principles concerning retrieval. The various memory processes proposed in the ACT theory operate on "cognitive units." A cognitive unit is similar to the idea of a chunk of information, a term originally coined by Miller (1956) (see Chapter 3). Usually no more than five elements make up a cognitive unit.

According to ACT, when a cognitive unit is created, either to record some external event or because some internal calculation has taken place, a copy of the unit is placed in working memory, and with some probability it turns into a long-term memory trace. Once formed, the strength of a trace can decay. Retrieving information from long-term memory is thought to involve a "spreading activation" process. The basic idea is that as concepts become activated in memory, this activation spreads out along the network. As soon as attention shifts, the activation of the concept begins to decay. Information from activated concepts is relatively readily accessible. As Anderson (1984) has noted, there are a number of reasons for believing in some sort of spreading activation mechanism. One stems from our knowledge of neurophysiology: the neurons and their connections exist in a network, and the rate at which a neuron fires is analogous to its level of activation. To carry this further, it is believed that neurons encode information by changes in how quickly they fire (see Hinton & Anderson, 1981). The intellectual origins of the idea of spreading activation probably go back to the time of Aristotle, and are very much alive today.

According to Anderson (1984) there are three basic premises behind the spreading activation construct. These are the representational, the state, and the process premises.

1. The representational premise. This premise asserts that knowledge can be represented as a network of nodes and links. Nodes correspond to concepts and links to associations among these concepts.
2. The state premise. The nodes in the network can vary in terms of their state. The states correspond to various levels of activation. The more active a node, the better it is processed.
3. The process premise. Activation can spread along the various network paths; when this happens one node causes its neighboring nodes to become active.

The concept of spreading activation is a major part of Anderson's (1983) latest large-scale theory, a version thought to be far more powerful than its predecessors. It can predict, for example, interference results in memory, the impact of extensive practice on memory, the difference between recognition and recall, and the effects of reconstructive recall, among many other phenomena. A good review of the theory can be found in Howard (1983).

SET THEORY MODELS

One alternative to the network models of semantic memory has been termed the set theoretic model, because it treats semantic memory as if it consisted of a huge number of sets of elements. One set may include all instances of dogs; thus collie, boxer, and sheepdog would all be members of this set. Sets can also include attributes of a concept, for example, the information that dogs bite, bark, wag their tails, and occasionally fetch sticks. Similarly another set might include exemplars of the *bird* category, such as robins, sparrows and parrots; while another set includes the attributes of birds, such as the fact that they have wings and feathers. In short, concepts are represented in semantic memory as sets of information.

A two-stage model of Meyer (1970), called the predicate intersections model, is an example of a set-theoretic model. Here Meyer assumes that memory consists of sets of attributes. Thus, *collie* is represented by a set of the defining attributes of a collie and *dog* by the defining attributes of dogs. To decide whether a collie is a dog, a person must decide whether every attribute included in *dog* is also an attribute included in *collie*. Of course, the process for this example would be very rapid indeed, for we are hardly aware of making a great number of decisions when we verify a simple statement such as "A collie is a dog."

Before elaborating on the role of these sets of attributes in Meyer's model, consider the task faced by his experimental subjects. The subject sits in front of a display screen where he is shown sentence frames such as "All _____ are _____" or "Some _____ are _____," depending on which experimental condition he is in. A few moments later the blank spaces are filled in with the names of two semantic categories, which we will refer to as S and P (for subject and predicate). For example, S might be collies and P might be dogs, resulting in "All collies are dogs" for some subjects and "Some collies are dogs" for others. The subject responds to these sentences by pressing one of two buttons to indicate whether they are true or false. Before reading further, can you predict whether "All" statements or "Some" statements would be faster, and why?

If you predicted that "Some" statements would lead to faster responses than statements using "All," you correctly predicted Meyer's result. What model can account for this finding? Meyer's predicate intersections model, involving two stages, does a reasonable job of explaining the Some-All difference as well as other more complex observed results. The model is shown in Figure 6–8. For statements of the form "All collies are dogs," the subject first looks through the names of all the categories that overlap, or intersect, or have some members in common with the P category (*dog*, in this case). In doing so the subject might find boxers and collies, but also animals and living things, among other possibilities. All of these have some members that are also dogs. If the search through these names produces an instance which is also a member of the S category, the two categories are said to intersect, and the first stage of the process ends with a "match." The search might not produce a match for the S category, however, and the subject would produce a negative response. "All S are P" would be disconfirmed at the end of the first stage.

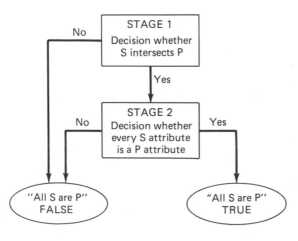

Figure 6-8. Meyer's two-stage model for verifying or disconfirming "All" statements. (After Meyer, 1970. Courtesy of Academic Press, Inc.)

Given that some member of S intersects P, the second stage of the process is then executed. At this stage the subject must decide whether every attribute of the P category is also an attribute of the S category. In our example, to verify "All collies are dogs," a subject must determine that the two categories intersect and then determine that every attribute of *dog* is also an attribute of *collie*.

Turning now to Figure 6–9, we can see what the model predicts will happen with "Some" statements. These involve only the decision as to whether the S category intersects the P category, that is, whether collies and dogs have at least one member in common. If so, the subject can respond *true*, for some collies (at least one) are indeed dogs. If not, the subject responds *false*. It should be clear why the model predicts that "All" statements take longer to verify than "Some" statements: "Some" statements require only one stage to be executed for verification whereas "All" statements usually require two.

Meyer's model makes another prediction having to do with disjoint statements, where the subject and predicate concepts denote mutually exclusive sets. "Some collies are gems" and "Some collies are stones" are examples of disjoint statements. The two examples we have cited share a subject term but differ in their predicate terms; further, *stones* is a larger category than *gems*. According to Meyer's model, both statements will be disconfirmed in the first stage; by extension of the theory, however, the search for the "stone" sentence should take longer than that for the "gem" sentence—since there are more intersecting categories to be searched when the predicate category is large rather than small. The reasoning is that with "stones" one must search through everything required by "gems" (for example, rubies, diamonds, emeralds) plus all the non-gem stones. Meyer (1970) performed an experiment to test what he termed the category-size effect. In the experiment, the category

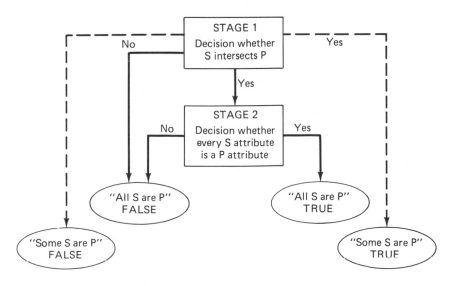

Figure 6-9. Meyer's two-stage model for verifying and confirming "Some" statements and "All" statements. (After Meyer, 1970. Courtesy of Academic Press, Inc.)

size of the predicate, P, was manipulated. Although it is usually difficult to measure the exact size of a category, Meyer got around the problem by using relative category size. That is, if one category is contained in another, then the latter must be larger than the former. This is the case with dogs and animals, with gems and stones, and so on. Meyer found the time to respond either *true* or *false* increased with the category size of P. Of course, Collins and Quillian (1969) also observed a category-size effect ("A collie is a dog" is verified faster than "A collie is an animal"), but they explained their results in terms of differential search times through a semantic network. For all investigators, the category-size effect became an accepted fact of life, an effect to be explained by anyone building a model of semantic memory.

Evaluation of the Predicate Intersections Model.   One the positive side of the coin, the predicate intersections model had an edge over the Collins and Quillian network model in that the former more easily dealt with disconfirmations. In Meyer's model, "Some" statements are disconfirmed after a single stage whereas "All" statements may require that both stages be executed. For Collins and Quillian the category-size effects for false statements posed a much greater problem. A second plus for Meyer's model is that it was subsequently successfully extended to account for the verification of statements containing negatives, such as "Some collies are not stones" (see Meyer, 1975).

A serious problem for the model, however, is presented by later findings that run counter to its critical predictions. We have seen an example of one such prediction, namely, that "Some collies are dogs" will be confirmed faster than "All collies are dogs." In Meyer's experiment, the "Some" statements were presented in one block of trials and the "All" statements in a different block of trials. When Rips (1975) randomly intermixed "Some" and "All" statements rather than presenting them in separate blocks, the advantage of "Some" over "All" statements, in terms of reaction time, disappeared. The fact that Meyer's model cannot explain the disappearance of this critical effect seriously discredits it.

Another difficulty with the model is that like the original Collins and Quillian model it has no easy way of explaining why some instances of a category can be verified faster than others. That is to say, why are people faster to verify that "a robin is a bird" than to verify that "a chicken is a bird"? This result has been observed often enough to know it is reliable (among others, Rips, Shoben & Smith, 1973; Rosch, 1971). Any model which follows the logic of set relations and which makes no differentiation among members of a category will certainly have difficulty with this observation.

One final difficulty with the model arises from our natural language use of "hedges." Hedges are linguistic modifiers that are used to qualify statements that we make about things we encounter in the world. "Strictly speaking" and "technically speaking" are hedges. "Technically speaking, a chicken is a bird" illustrates the use of a hedge in a sentence. It means something like "A chicken isn't a very good example of a bird, but it actually is a bird." "Loosely speaking, a bat is a bird," is another hedge, which means something akin to "A bat is a little like a bird, but it is not really a bird." How can the set-theoretic model explain our easy use of such hedges? The *bat* category and the *bird* category have no members in common, no overlap, no intersection; if Meyer's model is correct, how could anyone verify a hedged statement such as "Loosely speaking, a bat is a bird"? Some of these considerations led to the proposal of the feature-comparison model to which we now turn.

THE FEATURE-COMPARISON MODEL

Like the set-theoretic model, the feature-comparison model proposed by Smith Shoben, and Rips (1974) assumes that the meaning of any item in semantic memory can be represented as a set of semantic features. These are thought to vary continuously in the degree to which they define category membership. At one extreme there are features which are essential to the meaning of the item, and these are known as *defining features*. At the other extreme, there are features that are not essential, but are descriptive of the item. These are referred to as *characteristic features*. Although the features are thought to vary continuously in their degree of "definingness," we can select an arbitrary cutoff point to separate the defining features from the less important characteristic features. As we shall see, the feature-comparison model gives greater emphasis to the defining features.

Using the word *robin* to illustrate these two kinds of features, we single out the defining features that robins are living, they have feathers and wings, and they also have red breasts, since these characteristics must be present. Of course, robins are also undomesticated and harmless, and they like to perch in trees. These features are associated with robins, but they are not necessary to define the concept. When a subject is asked to decide whether an instance is a member of a category (for example, whether a robin is a bird), the feature-comparison model assumes that the sets of features corresponding to the instance and the category are partitioned into two subsets corresponding to the defining and characteristic features. Figure 6–10 gives an example of this partitioning for *robin* and *bird*. Note the difference in

	Concepts	
	Robin	Bird
Defining features	Is living Has feathers Has a red breast — — —	Is living Has features — — — —
Characteristic features	Flys Perches in trees Is undomesticated Is smallish — —	Flys — — — — —

Figure 6-10. The meaning of a concept is defined in terms of semantic features. The higher on the list a feature is, the more essential it is for defining the concept. (Source: Smith, E.E., Shoben, E.J., & Rips, L.J. [1974]. Structure and process in semantic memory: A featural model for semantic decisions *Psychological Review, 81,* 214–241. Copyright 1974 by the American Psychological Association. Reprinted by permission of the publisher and author.)

features between a category name such as *robin* and its superordinate, *bird*. Since the superordinate is more abstract and general, it will have fewer defining features; or, conversely, in addition to all the defining features of *bird*, *robin* will have some of its own unique ones. Thus, the more general the category, the fewer defining features it will have.

In an attempt to provide experimental evidence for the notion of semantic features, Rips, Shoben, and Smith (1973) collected subjects' ratings of how closely related each of several instances was to its category name. For example, subjects rated how closely related *chicken, duck*, and *robin* were to each other and to their superordinate, *bird*. If two items are closely related, it can be said that there is a small distance between them. Very sophisticated computer programs (for example, a "multidimensional scaling program") exist which can transform subjects' ratings into actual distances. These distances can then be plotted in a two-dimensional graph format which represents a subject's "cognitive" space.

Consider the two-dimensional spaces derived from subjects' ratings of items in the *bird* and *mammal* categories (see Figure 6–11.) It is assumed that when subjects initially rated the closeness of various concepts, they used the semantic features of the concepts that were contained in memory. The more features that two concepts had in common, the greater the judged relatedness. This being the case, an examination of the two-dimensional spaces should reveal the semantic features that subjects used in making their relatedness judgments. When Rips and co-workers examined the *bird* space in Figure 6–11, they noted that such large birds as hawks and eagles were at one end of the horizontal axis whereas the small birds were at the other end. Similarly in the *mammal* space, deer and bear and other large mam-

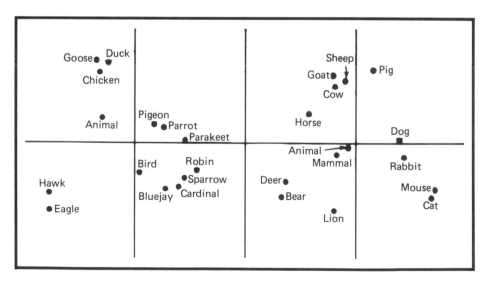

Figure 6–11.   Two-dimensional spaces derived from subjects' ratings of the relatedness of members of the categories birds (left) and mammals (right). (From Rips, Shoben, & Smith, 1973. Courtesy of Academic Press, Inc.)

mals were at one end while small animals such as mice and rabbits appeared at the other. The vertical dimension in both the *bird* and *mammal* spaces seems to reflect the extent to which the animals preyed upon others. It was thus termed the "predacity' dimension. Wild mammals were at the bottom whereas farm animals were at the top. Similarly, predatory birds like hawks were separated from tame birds such as ducks and chickens. The consistency of the dimensions in the *bird* and *mammal* spaces has been used to support the notion that these dimensions indicate something about semantic features that subjects are using in their relatedness judgments. It appears that the relatedness judgments were based on semantic features dealing with the size and predacity of the creatures being compared.

Using the Feature Model.   How does a person decide whether a robin is a bird? The process of verifying whether an instance is a member of some particular category is shown in Figure 6-12. Like Meyer's predicate intersections model, this is a two-stage model. The first stage involves a comparison of both the defining and characteristic features of the instance and the category to determine the degree to which the two sets of features are similar. If the two sets are highly similar, the subject responds *true*. If the two sets of features have very little correspondence

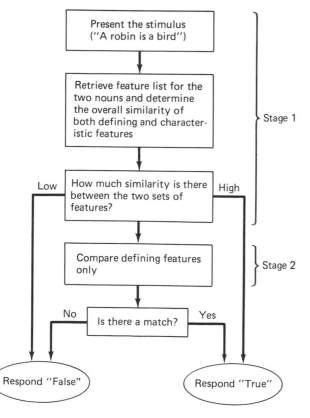

Figure 6-12. The feature-comparison model for the verification of such statements as "A robin is a bird." (Source: Smith, E.E., Shoben, E.J., & Rips, L.J. [1974]. Structure and process in semantic memory: A featural model for semantic decisions. *Psychological Review, 81,* 214–241. Copyright 1974 by the American Psychological Association. Reprinted by permission of the publisher and author.)

or very low similarity, the subject can respond *false* immediately. But if there is an intermediate level of similarity between the two sets of features, a second stage must be executed. In this second stage, the subject compares only the defining features of the instance and the category. If all of the defining features of the category are also defining features of the instance, then a *true* response can be made. If all of the features do not match, the statement is false.

It must still be determined how well the feature-comparison model accounts for the findings in the semantic memory literature. We consider several major findings. First, it has been shown that some instances of a category are verified faster than others. More typical instances (of, say, *birds*) such as robins are responded to faster than less typical ones, such as chickens, a phenomenon which has been termed the *typicality effect*. The feature-comparison model explains this effect by assuming that if the instance to be verified is highly typical of the category, then the two will share a large number of both defining and characteristic features. During Stage 1 it will be discovered that the instance and the category have a great number of overlapping features, and thus the subject can make an immediate response without executing Stage 2. Instances which are atypical, on the other hand, will not have much overlap with the category in terms of characteristic features. For these instances, Stage 2 will need to be executed, and the time to respond will accordingly be longer. In short, typical instances are verified faster because they may require only Stage 1 processing, whereas atypical instances require the execution of two stages.

The feature-comparison model can also explain the category-size effect, or the finding that subjects can verify "A canary is a bird" faster than they can verify "A canary is an animal." If one simply assumes that the features of *canary* overlap more with those of its immediate superordinate *bird* than with those of its less immediate superordinate, *animal*, the category-size effect reduces to a relatedness effect. In the *bird* case, Stage 2 processing is more likely to be omitted, and this causes reaction time to be quicker. According to this reasoning, if one could find a large category that was more related to *canary* than a smaller one, subjects would be faster with the larger category. This appears to be the case when we compare reaction times to "A dog is a mammal" and "A dog is an animal." From the two-dimensional *mammal* space in Figure 6–11 we see that *dog* is more related to *animal*, and, as we have shown, subjects are quicker to verify that a dog is an animal. In other words, it may be relatedness and not category size that counts. In fact, the effects of both typicality and category size are thought to result from the same mechanism—overall number of features in common between the instance and the category.

The model can also account for some of the more perplexing results that have been observed with false statements. "A table is a bird" can also be disconfirmed more quickly than "A bat is a bird." In general, it takes less time to disconfirm a statement if the instance and category are completely unrelated than if they have some relation to each other (Rips, 1975; Smith et al., 1974). The feature-comparison model handles this finding with the simple idea that unrelated statements can be disconfirmed by the first stage whereas the related statement needs two stages for disconfirmations.

In addition to doing a reasonably good job at accounting for both the category-size and typicality effects, and for false statements, the feature-comparison model can also handle the fact that we might agree with the hedged statement. "Loosely speaking, a bat is a bird," whereas we would not want to agree flatly that "A bat is a bird." The phrase "loosely speaking" indicates that the instance which follows possesses many of the characteristic features of the category. Bats possess many characteristic features of birds. But, when it comes to defining features, this similarity disappears. The defining features of the instance are not equivalent to those of the category. A person who hears "Loosely speaking, a bat is a bird" and is asked whether he or she would agree with this statement, executes a two-stage retrieval process, in the first stage determining that bats and birds do possess many features in common, and in the second stage that bats do not possess all the defining features of birds. Consequently, the person should find it reasonable to agree that "Loosely speaking, a bat is a bird," because many of the characteristic features are held in common. He or she would not be likely to agree with the flat statement, "A bat is a bird," because the defining features of the two concepts do not completely match. In a typical reaction time experiment, subjects are under a good deal of time pressure and will occasionally agree with the statement "A bat is a bird." Why does this happen? The explanation is that when pressured, subjects will occasionally omit Stage 2 and make a fast *true* response on the basis of Stage 1 processing. This is expected since Stage 1 processing indicated a large overall number of overlapping features between bats and birds.

"Technically speaking, a chicken is a bird." This statement illustrates another hedge in use, and is one most people would confirm. The hedge is handled by the model by assuming that "technically speaking" is used when an instance has the defining features of the category but not very many of the characteristic features of that category. A chicken is certainly a bird, since it possesses the defining features of birds. It has wings, it has a beak, etc. However, it does not have the characteristic features of a bird (that is, it doesn't fly or sing; it's much larger than average). Thus, it is a bird, technically speaking. Another example that has been bandied about is this: "Ralph Sampson is a regular giraffe." Can you explain how the feature-comparison model would handle this hedged statement?

Evaluation of the Feature-Comparison Model.   Perhaps this model's greatest strength is its ability to account for many of the major findings in the semantic memory literature by means of a single principle, namely, that similarity of features will aid in the case of a confirmation and hinder in the case of a disconfirmation. That is, a statement such as "A robin is a bird" will be verified quickly because of the higher featural similarity between the instance and category; on the other hand, a statement such as "A bat is a bird" will be disconfirmed slowly for the same reason. Further, it escapes the problems of a model that follows the logic of class relations, since it allows for degrees of category membership. Some members of the category are "better" members than others (Rosch, 1974), and these stereotypic members will be dealt with more easily.

The feature-comparison model is not without problems, however. For one thing, the distinction between defining and characteristic features has the inherent difficulty that there is virtually no feature that is absolutely necessary to define some concept. To illustrate, if a bird loses its wings, does it cease to be a bird? If the feathers are plucked from a peacock, does it stop being a peacock? Can a chair still be a chair with only three legs? Most people would answer these questions in the affirmative. Further, most people have difficulty deciding whether any particular feature you can name is a defining or a characteristic feature of some concept. Is "having a cover" a defining feature of books? What if a friend ripped the cover from this book, would you still call it a book? While Smith and his colleagues postulated the existence of degrees of definingness, assuming that features are more or less defining, the distinction between defining and characteristic features has been said to be somewhat artificial.

Perhaps a more serious problem for the model is that it cannot explain a result observed by Glass and Holyoak (1975) on disconfirmation times. They found cases in which false statements containing similar nouns were disconfirmed *more* quickly than false statements containing less similar nouns. For example, people can disconfirm the statement "Some chairs are tables" faster than the statement "Some chairs are rocks," even though chairs and tables are more similar to each other than chairs and rocks. According to the feature-comparison model, this should not happen; the nouns *chairs* and *rocks* have almost zero features in common and the subject should disconfirm quickly. The nouns *chairs* and *tables* do have features in common (both are pieces of furniture) and therefore it should take somewhat longer to disconfirm a statement about these two nouns, since Stage 2 must be executed. Thus, the feature-comparison model predicts a result the opposite of which has been observed experimentally.

These examples of models of semantic memory make clear the fact that several different views exist about the structure of semantic memory and the retrieval of that memory. Unfortunately the empirical evidence to date cannot provide us with a definitive choice among these views.

Moreover, most of these models fail to take into account some important individual differences in the way people use semantic memory. Such individual differences were shown, for example, in the recent work of Newstead and Griggs (1983). These investigators were interested in how people use quantified statements such as "All A's are B's" or "Some A's are B's." They were particularly interested in the statement by Revlin and Leirer (1980) that universally quantified statements such as "All A's are B's" are incorrectly interpreted by people as implying the converse, "All B's are A's." Revlin and Leirer went so far as to say that the converted interpretation is actually the preferred one, and that people actually reason with all statements in a converted form.

Another commonly discussed error is the error of inference that people make when they hear the quantifier "some." "Some" invites listeners to assume that not all the instances are positive, or, put another way, that "somenot" is also the case. This inference, while invalid, is certainly plausible. Newstead and Griggs (1983) found evidence for errors in interpretation of quantified statements. About one-third of their subjects made errors when it came to "some" statements. However, as these investigators note, only a certain proportion of subjects make such errors consistently, attesting to the vast individual differences in the interpretation of quantified statements. Most theories of semantic memory have tended to overlook such individual differences, in hope that future theories will not.

Forgetting from Semantic Memory

Tulving (1983) stated that information stored in the episodic system is more vulnerable—that is, changed, modified, and lost more readily—than is the information in the semantic system. He believed this to be true for two reasons. First, much of the information in the semantic system is overlearned. We review it numerous times, in contrast to the single occurrences that make up much of the episodic system. Second, information in the episodic system is organized more loosely than is information in the semantic system, and this may contribute to its greater vulnerability. Finally, information in the episodic system is characterized by a rich and varied combination of elements. In contrast, information in the semantic system is more streamlined and more abstract. Taken together, these features contribute to the ease with which information in the episodic system is modified, recoded, and erased.

This is not to say that there is no loss of semantic information. Although most of us will probably retain a good deal of semantic knowledge until the day we die, it is also true that much of the knowledge acquired in school—also semantic knowledge—appears to be eventually lost. Yet very little has been done to investigate these losses systematically. Bahrick (1984) sought to remedy this deficiency with a massive study of semantic memory for Spanish learned in high school or college.

Of the nearly 800 subjects who participated, approximately 150 were students who were enrolled in a Spanish course or who had recently completed such a course. About 600 subjects were people who had taken one or more Spanish courses during their attendance at high school or college, one to fifty years previously. Forty subjects had never taken Spanish but were included in the study in order to establish a baseline for performance based on sources other than coursework.

All subjects completed a questionnaire designed to provide information about Spanish instruction, grades obtained in courses, and various opportunities to read or speak Spanish since the courses were taken. All subjects took a Spanish test which measured reading comprehension, vocabulary, grammar, idioms, and so on. For example, subjects had to write the Spanish meaning of the English words time, to hear, to read, and the correct English meaning of the Spanish idioms *hace mal tiempo, hasta la vista,* and *en vez de.*

Bahrick plotted performance as a function of the years since Spanish course-

work had been completed. He observed forgetting curves which declined expo-
nentially for the first three to six years of the retention interval. After that, retention
remained unchanged for periods of up to thirty years before showing a final decline.
An example is seen in Figure 6–13.

From this observation, Bahrick concluded that large portions of the originally
acquired Spanish information remain accessible for over fifty years, in spite of the
fact that information is not used or rehearsed. The portion of the information that
remains in what he calls "permastore" state is a function of the original training,
the grades received in Spanish courses, and whether testing is by recall or recognition, but it appears to be unaffected by ordinary conditions of interference.

While some may agree that Bahrick's work on Spanish implicates a permastore (Cofer, 1984), others do not. For example, Neisser (1984) suggests that the
apparent permanence of memory for Spanish may be due simply to the survival
of an overall schema for Spanish from which a few correct responses can still be
generated. This debate resembles the debate about the permanence of episodic
memory that was described in the previous chapter.

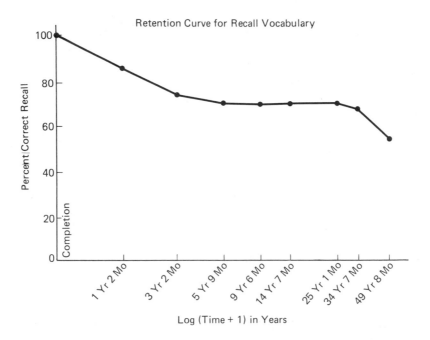

Figure 6–13. Frequency distribution for the life span of responses corresponding to the retention of Spanish-English recall vocabulary. (Source: Bahrick, H.P.
[1984]. Semantic memory content in permastore: Fifty years of memory for
Spanish learned in school. *Journal of Experimental Psychology: General, 113,*
1–29. Copyright 1984 by the American Psychological Association. Reprinted by
permission of the publisher and author.)

Summary

In the early 1970s a distinction was made between episodic and semantic memory, and this distinction has remained important today. Episodic memory is memory for temporally dated episodes or events and the temporal-spatial relations among those events. Semantic memory is the organized knowledge that a person possesses about words and other verbal symbols, their meaning and references, about relations among them, and about rules for the manipulation of these symbols, concepts and relations. Semantic memory is part of the general knowledge that we have about the world. Episodic and semantic memory differ in a number of ways. One difference is in terms of how vulnerable the information each contains is to interfering inputs. Semantic memory is a more resiliant system of information.

Most of this chapter concerns a general knowledge stored in long-term memory. From studies in which people have been asked to retrieve information from semantic memory, investigators have learned a great deal about semantic memory. For example, studies showing the important role played by retrieval cues suggest that some ways of retrieving stored information are more effective than others. Studies of the "tip of the tongue" phenomenon, in which a to-be-remembered item is almost, but not quite retrievable, give researchers insights into how our general knowledge is structured in memory and retrieved.

Many models have been proposed to account for the structure and retrieval of semantic memory. Some of these are network models that assume memory can be represented as a network of associations between words and their underlying concepts. Other models are set theory models that treat semantic memory as if it consisted of a huge number of sets of elements. One goal of all the models is to describe the representation of such information, and to account for how the information is retrieved.

SEVEN

Language

Language is hierarchical. There are many different levels of language and corresponding linguistic analysis. In Chapter 2 we examined the lowest levels in the hierarchy, and asked the question, What are the basic units of language? In this chapter we will examine several different levels in the language hierarchy, generally working our way through the hierarchy from lower levels to higher ones. First, let us get a general overview of the language system. At the lowest level of analysis are the phonemes (for spoken language) and letters (for written language) that we discussed earlier. These units are combined to form larger items at the next level of linguistic analysis—syllables (like *lev* and *el*). Syllables, in turn, are combined to form units one level higher—words (like *level*). Just as letters are grouped into syllables and syllables are grouped into words, words are grouped into units called phrases, phrases are grouped to form sentences, sentences are grouped into paragraphs, and paragraphs are grouped into stories or texts. As we go up the hierarchy, the units become increasingly larger and more meaningful.

Syntax: Phrases and Phrase Structure

SURFACE STRUCTURE

We will begin our ascent through the language hierarchy by examining in detail phrase units and the grouping of phrases into sentences. The description of a sentence in terms of its constituent phrases is called the "phrase structure" of the sentence and is often represented by means of a "tree diagram," which resembles a real tree in that it has a trunk and branches but differs from a real tree in that the trunk is at the top with the branches below it. The tree diagram not only indicates how the component phrases are arranged to form the sentence but also how the words in each phrase are related to each other and what function every word plays in its phrase. Consider, for example, the tree diagram in Figure 7-1 for the sentence "The student read the book." Not only does the phrase structure determine the functions of the words and phrases in the sentence and their relationships, it also specifies the location of pauses when the sentence is spoken. For instance, in reading aloud the sample sentence, we would say "The student . . . read . . . the book", pausing briefly between the words *student* and *read* and between *read* and *the*, rather than between *the* and *student* or between *the* and *book*. In other words, we would pause at the boundaries separating phrases but not in the middle of a phrase.

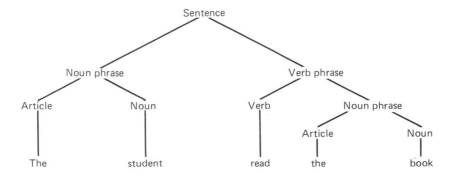

Figure 7-1. Tree diagram specifying the phrase structure for the sentence, "The student read the book."

Although we will all agree that the sentence "sounds best" when the pauses are made in accordance with the phrase structure, we do not always make pauses when we should. Most of us when engaged in normal conversation will pause in the middle of a phrase, even hesitate after an article like *the*, when we are groping for just the right word to express our thoughts. There is evidence from the psychology laboratory, however, that even when the speaker fumbles, the listener hears the pauses at the correct locations according to the phrase structure. This evidence derives from a series of experiments initiated by Fodor and Bever (1965). In these experiments, a sentence was tape-recorded; superimposed onto the recording was a brief clicking sound. The subjects' task in the experiments was to indicate as closely as possible the location in the sentence at which the click was heard. Fodor and Bever found that the subjects tended to "hear" the clicks at the major clause or phrase boundaries (for example, between *student* and *read* in our sample sentence) rather than when they actually occurred on the tape. Fodor and Bever concluded from this finding that listeners hear interruptions like clicks, coughs, or pauses at the points that they should occur according to the phrase structure. Thus, the major phrase units are kept intact.

Although clear-cut, the finding from this first study was not as decisive as it may seem because it allowed for the possibility that the phrase structure itself had nothing to do with the apparent "migration" of the click. Perhaps the click was heard at the phrase boundary because the speaker made some distinctive sound at that location (maybe just paused longer there, as is specified) and the distinctive sound, rather than the phrase boundary, acted as a cue or marker of the click's location. In a clever follow-up experiment, Garrett, Bever, and Fodor (1966) controlled for this possibility. In this study, pairs of sentences were recorded. The initial words of the two sentences in a pair were different, but the final words were identical. To make certain that the final words in the first sentence were spoken in precisely the same manner as those in the second sentence, a single tape recording of that section was made and then copied and spliced onto the different sentence openings. For example, one pair of sentences was the following:

A. (As a direct result of their new invention's influence) (the company was given an award)
B. (The retiring chairman whose methods still greatly influence the company) (was given an award)

The final section of these sentences ("influence the company was given an award") was recorded only once and then copied and spliced so that it was preceded by the two different openings. Note that although the two sentences overlap in meaning and have identical endings, the phrase structure boundaries are not in the same location. The major clause boundary (as indicated by the parentheses) falls between *influence* and *the* in sentence A and between *company* and *was* in sentence B. The investigators found that when they superimposed a click so that it actually occurred at the same time as the first syllable in the word *company*, the click was perceived by the listeners much earlier in sentence A than in sentence B, closer to the grammatical boundary in each sentence, despite the fact that any distinctive sounds made by the speaker were necessarily the same in the two sentences. A similar pattern of results was obtained for the other sentence pairs tested. This finding demonstrates that the phrase structure alone can determine when interruptions are heard. There need not be any marking sound or pause in the sentence itself to enable the listener to hear an interruption at the appropriate location.

The phrase structure of a sentence not only helps us decide when to make or hear pauses in the sentence, it also helps us decide on the meaning of the sentence. Consider, for instance, the "ambiguous" sentence "They are baking potatoes." This sentence can mean either (A) that some people are baking some potatoes, or (B) that those potatoes are appropriate for baking. The phrase structure of the sentence differs for the two alternative meanings. The tree diagrams in Figure 7–2 illustrate the two different phrase structures. If you wish to utter this sentence, how could you provide clues to the listener concerning your intended meaning? You should pause at the locations specified in the appropriate phrase structure. Thus, if you intend meaning A, you should pause after *baking*, whereas if you intend meaning B, you should pause after *are*.

DEEP STRUCTURE

Not all ambiguous sentences have different phrase structures for their alternative meanings. Let us now consider a different type of ambiguous sentence—an example is, "Visiting relatives can be a pain." This sentence also has two distinct meanings, one about obnoxious relatives (A: "Visiting relatives are a pain"), and one about going out to visit (B: "Visiting relatives is a pain"). These two different meanings cannot be distinguished by pausing in different locations, since the phrase structure is the same in the two cases, as shown with the following short-hand notation that makes use of parentheses and brackets to indicate the grouping of words into phrases:

(Visiting relatives)[(can be)(a pain)]

Although the phrase structure of the sentence is the same for its two meanings, the underlying or logical relationships among the words of the sentence are different for the two interpretations. If we paraphrase the sentence so as to preserve the meaning of each interpretation in turn we might form for meaning A "Relatives who visit can be a pain," and for meaning B "Going to visit relatives can be a pain." It should be clear from these paraphrases that the relationship between *relatives* and *visit* is different for the two meanings, and the phrase structure does not seem to capture this difference. For interpretation A, *relatives* is the logical subject of the verb *visit* (the ones doing the visiting), whereas for interpretation B, *relatives* is the logical object of *visit* (the ones being visited). The ambiguity is thus due to

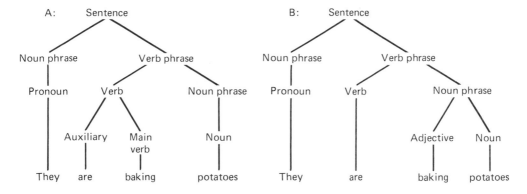

Figure 7-2. Tree diagrams for the two meanings of the sentence, "They are baking potatoes."

the presence of two different sets of underlying or logical relationships among the words corresponding to a single set of superficial relationships.

Examples like this one led Noam Chomsky (1965) and other linguists to draw a distinction between two different phrase structures for each sentence—the surface structure and the deep structure. What we have been referring to as "the phrase structure" to this point is the surface structure, which specifies the superficial relationships among the words and depends on the actual sequence of words produced. In contrast, the deep structure specifies the underlying or logical relationships among the words of the sentence. The two versions of "They are baking potatoes" differ in both surface and deep structures, whereas the two versions of "Visiting relatives can be a pain" have the same surface structure and differ only in deep structure.

This distinction between deep and surface structures can be clarified somewhat by noting that whereas one sentence can have two different meanings, the converse is also true: The same meaning can be expressed by two different sentences. In other words, whereas a single surface structure can stand for two different deep structures (as in "Visiting relatives can be a pain"), a single deep structure can be represented by two different surface structures. An example of this second case is the pair of sentences, "The student read the book" and "The book was read by the student." These sentences share the same meaning although their superficial forms differ. They both have deep structures captured by the tree diagram shown in Figure 7-1. But the two sentences have different surface structures: The surface structure for "The student read the book" is the same as its deep structure, but the surface structure for "The book was read by the student" is different, as shown in the tree diagram of Figure 7-3.

The concept of deep structure seems reasonable when we make a linguistic analysis of a sentence as we just did. However, cognitive psychologists are not merely interested in concepts that describe our language in a reasonable way; they are interested in determining, instead, whether we actually do make use of the concept when

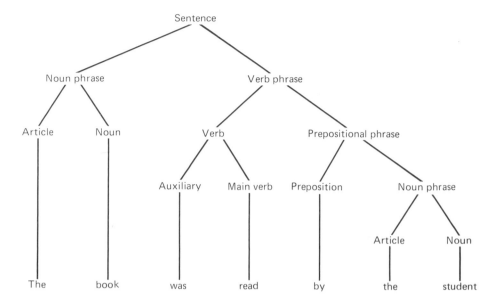

Figure 7-3. Tree diagram specifying the surface phrase structure for the sentence, "The book was read by the student."

we speak and listen. Do we make use of the deep structure of a sentence when we utter it or try to understand it? Is our behavior influenced by the deep structure relationships among the words in a sentence or only their superficial relationships?

An interesting study by Arthur Blumenthal (1967) provided preliminary evidence for the influence on behavior of deep structure by showing that the deep structure of a sentence is important in recalling the sentence. Blumenthal asked subjects to remember a list of sentences and then tested their memory for the sentences by giving them a key word from each sentence as a prompt. Blumenthal found that the effectiveness of a prompt word was dependent on its function in the deep structure of the sentence. He used sentences of two forms that were alike in surface structure but different in deep structure, for example, (A) "Gloves were made by tailors," and (B) "Tables were built by hand." The surface and deep structures of these sentences are illustrated in the tree diagrams of Figure 7-4. Note that *gloves* and *tables* have similar functions in the surface structure of their respective sentences (they are both subjects of the verb, as revealed by the fact that their noun phrase falls immediately under the tree node labeled "sentence"), and these nouns have similar functions in the deep structure of their respective sentences (they are both deep structure direct objects of the verb). On the other hand, the other nouns in the sentences, *tailors* and *hand,* have similar functions in the surface structure (they are both objects of the preposition *by*), but they have very different functions in the deep structure (*tailors* is the deep structure subject but *hand* is object of the preposition *by* in the deep structure as it is in the surface structure).

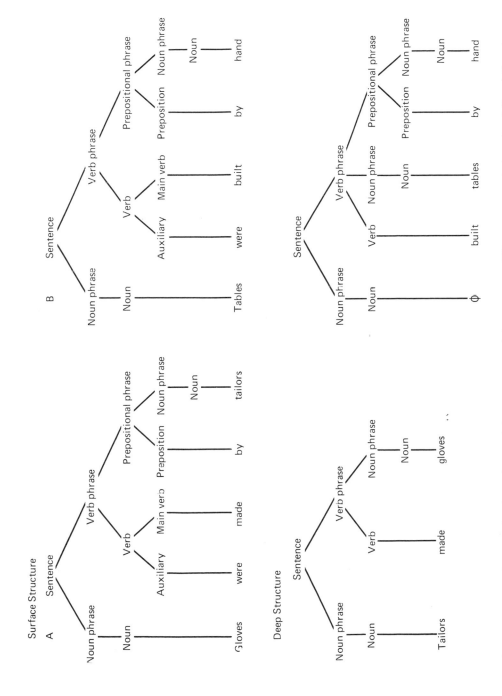

Figure 7-4. Tree diagrams for the surface and deep structures of the sentences, "Gloves were made by tailors" (Panel A) and "Tables were built by hand" (Panel B). Note: φ stands for a word that is missing from the sentence.

203

After studying the sentences, the subjects in Blumenthal's experiment were given one noun from each sentence as a prompt, and were asked to respond with the remaining words. In the control group, subjects were always given the first nouns as prompts (for example, *gloves* and *tables*), whereas in the experimental group, subjects were always given the second nouns as prompts (*tailors* and *hand*). The results of the experiment are summarized in Table 7–1. It is clear that the deep structure function of a word was very influential in determining how effective it would be as a memory prompt. The two sentence types were recalled equally well in the control group for whom the prompt was the initial noun, which had the same surface and deep structure functions in both sentence types. However, sentences of type A were recalled significantly better than those of type B in the experimental group for whom the prompt was the final noun, which had the same surface structure functions in the two sentences but different deep structure functions. Sentences prompted by their deep structure subjects (a very important function) were better recalled than those prompted by nouns that were merely objects of the preposition in the deep structure. Blumenthal argued that the psychological organization of a sentence is determined not only by its surface structure but also according to the relations among its words and phrases as specified in its deep structure.

Table 7–1.   *Mean number of sentences recalled in experiment by Blumenthal (1967).*

	SENTENCE STRUCTURE	
Prompt word	A ("Gloves were made by tailors")	B ("Tables were built by hand")
Final noun (Experimental)	7.2	3.9
Initial noun (Control)	7.1	6.9

(Source: Blumenthal, A.L. [1967]. Prompted recall of sentences. Journal of Verbal Learning and Verbal Behavior, 6, *203–206. Adapted by permission of the author and Academic Press.)*

CASE GRAMMAR

Blumenthal's study, along with similar subsequent experiments, has been taken as convincing support for Chomsky's (1965) concept of deep structure. However, there is one problem with this work which makes it difficult to interpret. This problem is the fact that the prompt words varied both in their grammatical function as specified in the deep structure and in their meaning. More specifically, the final nouns in Blumenthal's study not only differed grammatically, they also differed in terms of their semantic roles. For example, *tailors* differs from *hand* not only because *tailors* is deep structure subject whereas *hand* is deep structure object of the preposition, but also because *tailors* plays the important semantic role of "agent" (roughly, the individual responsible for carrying out the action) whereas *hand* plays the more minor semantic role of "instrument" (roughly, the object used by the agent to perform the action). The importance of such semantic roles is made clear in a linguistic theory that opposes Chomsky's (1965) theory in several regards. This theory, called "case grammar," was first proposed by Charles Fillmore (1968). The central postulate of case grammar is that deep structure representations of sentences should be described in terms of "cases," which are semantic relationships, instead of purely syntactic relationships, such as the grammatical concepts of subject and object, which are derivable from the phrase structure diagrams we have been using. In order to appreciate the difference between case and syntactic relationships, let us examine a triplet of sentences (adapted from Langendoun, 1970):

(1) The congressman received a message by telegram.
(2) A message reached the congressman by telegram.
(3) A telegram conveyed a message to the congressman.

The three nouns *congressman*, *message* and *telegram* maintain the same case relations across the three sentences, but their surface and deep structure grammatical relations change drastically. *Congressman* is in the "goal" case (roughly, the receiver of something that has been transferred or moved) in each sentence; *message* is in the case labeled "patient" (roughly, the person or thing affected by the action), and *telegram* is in the "instrument" case. On the other hand, the syntactic deep structure function of each noun varies from sentence to sentence, as illustrated by the fact that there is a different deep structure (and surface structure) subject in each sentence; *congressman* is the subject of (1), *message* is the subject of (2), and *telegram* is the subject of (3). These three sentences are similar in meaning; the three nouns are playing identical roles in each case. Nevertheless, Chomsky's (1965) grammar in unable to account for these similarities. One powerful argument for Chomsky's theory of deep structure was that it could relate sentences like "The student read the book" and "The book was read by the student," sentences with different surface structures but the same deep structure. The three sentences about the *congressman*, *telegram*, and *message* seem to be related to each other in a similar way, but Chomsky's theory cannot account for this relationship. For that reason, Fillmore argued that the deep structure description of a sentence should not only specify its syntactic relations but should further identify its cases, or semantic roles.

The debate between competing linguistic theories, like those of Chomsky (1965) and Fillmore (1968), cannot be settled by psychological experiments. But psychological experiments can tell us if the concepts put forth by the linguists have any influence on our behavior. Towards that goal, Healy and Levitt (1978) conducted an experimental study to determine the relative extent to which Fillmore's cases and Chomsky's deep structure syntactic relations are accessible to subjects during learning and memory tasks. In one experiment, subjects were divided into four conditions, "surface," "semantic," "deep-structure syntactic," and "arbitrary." The subjects in all four conditions were given five minutes to study a set of 64 different sentences, each printed on a different index card, and with exactly half describing "John" and half describing "Sam." The following instructions were given to the subjects: "You will be presented with a stack of cards. On each card is a sentence which involves either *John* or *Sam*. You are to study these sentences for five minutes. At the end of that time you will be given two sheets of paper which include each of the sentences on the cards with the words *John* and *Sam* replaced by *John/Sam*. Your task will be to recall for each sentence whether *John* or *Sam* was involved in that sentence as it appeared on the card." The subjects in all four conditions saw the same sentences, except that the assignment of *John* or *Sam* to the sentences differed across groups (see Table 7–2 which shows eight sample sentences). For subjects in the surface condition, the assignment of *John* or *Sam* to a sentence depended on the surface structure function of that word in the sentence. *John* was selected whenever the word was the surface structure subject, and *Sam* was selected whenever it was the surface structure object of the preposition. For subjects in the semantic condition, *John* was selected whenever the word was in the "experiencer" case (roughly, the person who undergoes a genuine psychological event or mental state), and *Sam* was selected whenever it was in the "goal" case. For the deep structure syntactic condition, *John* was always the deep structure subject, and *Sam* was always the deep structure object of the preposition. Finally, for the arbitrary condition, neither *John* nor *Sam* was in the same surface, semantic, or deep structure syntactic category through all the sentences.

Table 7-2. *Eight sample sentences shown to subjects in the four conditions of the experiment by Healy and Levitt (1978).*

SURFACE CONDITION	SEMANTIC CONDITION
1. John was sleepy near the fire.	1. John was sleepy near the fire.
2. The accident was imagined by Sam.	2. The accident was imagined by John.
3. The roar was deafening to Sam.	3. The roar was deafening to John.
4. John was the recipient of the grant.	4. Sam was the recipient of the grant.
5. John was given the book.	5. Sam was given the book.
6. The property was leased to Sam.	6. The property was leased to Sam.
7. John was assured misery.	7. John was assured misery.
8. The fruit was obtained by Sam.	8. The fruit was obtained by Sam.

DEEP-STRUCTURE SYNTACTIC CONDITION	ARBITRARY CONDITION
1. John was sleepy near the fire.	1. Sam was sleepy near the fire.
2. The accident was imagined by John.	2. The accident was imagined by John.
3. The roar was deafening to Sam.	3. The roar was deafening to Sam.
4. John was the recipient of the grant.	4. John was the recipient of the grant.
5. Sam was given the book.	5. Sam was given the book.
6. The property was leased to Sam.	6. The property was leased to John.
7. Sam was assured misery.	7. John was assured misery.
8. The fruit was obtained by John.	8. The fruit was obtained by Sam.

(Source: Healy, A.F., & Levitt, A.G. [1978]. The relative accessibility of semantic and deep-structure concepts. Memory & Cognition, 6, 518–526. Adapted by permission of the author and the Psychonomic Society.)

The performance of subjects on the memory test (when they were asked to decide whether *John* or *Sam* was in each sentence) depended strongly on condition; subjects in the surface or semantic conditions made many fewer errors (3 percent errors for the surface condition and 8 percent for the semantic condition) than did those in the deep structure syntactic condition (24 percent errors) or in the arbitrary condition (28 percent errors). These results suggest that subjects can easily access for use in a memory task surface and semantic relations, but they have much more difficulty making use of deep structure syntactic relations, which are not significantly more accessible than arbitrarily defined relations. Another implication of these findings is that the prompted recall studies by Blumenthal (1967) and others were misleading because they confounded deep structure syntactic and semantic relations. When deep structure syntactic relations are varied independently of semantic relations, as in the study by Healy and Levitt (1978), the syntactic relations do not play a major role in memory (see also Elio & Healy, 1982, for a similar finding in a prompted recall paradigm).

TRANSFORMATIONAL GRAMMAR

The deep structure syntactic relations included in Noam Chomsky's (1965) influential theory of language received initial support from psychological experiments and later were seen to have problems. The same was true also for another crucial aspect of his grammar. According to Chomsky (1957), by means of certain linguistic rules the deep structure of a sentence is transformed into the surface structure. The rules linking the deep and surface structures are known as "transformational rules." In some sense, these rules specify the steps according to which thought or meaning is related to the actual words produced. A simple active declarative sentence like "The student read the book" is assumed to have a surface structure which is the same as its deep structure (see Figure 7–1), unlike a passive sentence like "The book was read by the student" which has different deep and surface structures (see Figures 7–1 and 7–3), as do negative sentences and questions. The deep structure of a passive sentence can be changed into its surface structure by means of a passive transformation. Additional transformations are required to change the deep structures of more complex sentences into their surface structures.

The concept of transformation proposed by Chomsky is reasonable on theoretical grounds and provides an efficient way of describing language, but the cognitive psychologists who study language (psycholinguists) are concerned with determining whether we actually use transformations when we construct or understand sentences. In order to determine whether our behavior reflects the use of transformational rules, Jacques Mehler (1963) hypothesized that the transformational complexity of a sentence would determine how easily the sentence could be recalled; a sentence whose surface structure is further away from its deep structure should be harder to remember than one whose surface and deep structures are closer. Mehler's subjects listened to lists of eight sentences. In each list of eight sentences there was one simple active declarative sentence—a "kernel" sentence with the same surface and deep structures. Each of the remaining sentences included one or more transformations. Only three transformations were employed—passive, negative, and interrogative (question)—but these allowed for seven different kinds of transformed sentences because the transformations could be combined. For example, a sentence containing both passive and negative transformations was "The passenger hasn't been carried by the airplane," and one containing both negative and interrogative transformations was "Hasn't the girl worn the jewel?" Memory for the sentences in Mehler's experiment was tested by means of a prompted recall technique like that used by Blumenthal—for each sentence there was a prompting word (for example, *passenger*).

Most of the recall errors made by subjects were syntactic; the incorrect responses differed from the correct sentences in terms of transformations. For example, "The girl hasn't worn the jewel" might replace "Hasn't the girl worn the jewel?" More important is Mehler's finding of a tendency to simplify the syntactic structure. This tendency took several forms. First, subjects made fewer errors on kernel sentences than on any other type; that is, subjects often replaced a transformed sentence with its kernel but rarely made an error in the opposite direction. Second, even for errors that did not involve the kernel there was a "move toward" it; the erroneous sentence recalled by the subject usually contained fewer transformations than did the correct sentence. These results suggest that grammatical transformations constitute additional information which must be stored along with the deep structure information contained in the kernel. Mehler concluded that a sentence is represented in memory as a simple active declarative sentence, plus a mental tag or footnote indicating its transformations. These findings therefore provide support for the hypothesis that our behavior reflects the use of transformational rules.

Despite the early support for transformational grammar provided by this study and others, and despite the important role these studies played in moving psychology away from behaviorism (see Chapter 1), subsequent experiments on this topic were plagued with problems and inconsistencies, and the linguists themselves found problems with some of the theoretical constructs in the grammar. In fact, more recent investigators have argued that in many situations closer to those occurring in everyday life individuals do not remember the transformations of a given sentence or even its grammatical deep structure but rather something more abstract.

Consider, for example, the demonstration illustrated in Table 7–3, which occurred in an article by James Jenkins (1974) entitled, "Remember that Old Theory of Memory? Well, Forget it." Before reading further, follow the directions in Table 7–3.

How many of the sentences did you rate as old? Most subjects so rate at least ten sentences. In fact, you will be surprised to learn that not one of the sentences was old. This demonstration is based on an experiment by Bransford and Franks (1971), which differed from the demonstration in two major respects: Both old and new sentences were included on the test, and subjects were required to give a confidence rating for each old/new judgment they made. As in the demonstration, the

Table 7-3. *Demonstration experiment by Jenkins (1974).*

SENTENCE	QUESTION
Acquisition sentences: Read each sentence, count to five, answer the question, go on to the next sentence.	
The girl broke the window on the porch.	Broke what?
The tree in the front yard shaded the man who was smoking his pipe.	Where?
The hill was steep.	What was?
The cat, running from the barking dog, jumped on the table.	From what?
The tree was tall.	Was what?
The old car climbed the hill.	What did?
The cat running from the dog jumped on the table.	Where?
The girl who lives next door broke the window on the porch.	Lives where?
The car pulled the trailer.	Did what?
The scared cat was running from the barking dog.	What was?
The girl lives next door.	Who does?
The tree shaded the man who was smoking his pipe.	What did?
The scared cat jumped on the table.	What did?
The girl who lives next door broke the large window.	Broke what?
The man was smoking his pipe.	Who was?
The old car climbed the steep hill.	The what?
The large window was on the porch.	Where?
The tall tree was in the front yard.	What was?
The car pulling the trailer climbed the steep hill.	Did what?
The cat jumped on the table.	Where?
The tall tree in the front yard shaded the man.	Did what?
The car pulling the trailer climbed the hill.	Which car?
The dog was barking.	Was what?
The window was large.	What was?

STOP—Cover the preceding sentences. Now read each sentence below and decide if it is a sentence from the list given above.
Test set. . . . How many are new?

1.	The car climbed the hill.	(old__, new__)
2.	The girl who lives next door broke the window.	(old__, new__)
3.	The old man who was smoking his pipe climbed the steep hill.	(old__, new__)
4.	The tree was in the front yard.	(old__, new__)
5.	The scared cat, running from the barking dog, jumped on the table.	(old__, new__)
6.	The window was on the porch.	(old__, new__)
7.	The barking dog jumped on the old car in the front yard.	(old__, new__)
8.	The tree in the front yard shaded the man.	(old__, new__)
9.	The cat was running from the dog.	(old__, new__)
10.	The old car pulled the trailer.	(old__, new__)
11.	The tall tree in the front yard shaded the old car.	(old__, new__)
12.	The tall tree shaded the man who was smoking his pipe.	(old__, new__)
13.	The scared cat was running from the dog.	(old__, new__)
14.	The old car, pulling the trailer, climbed the hill.	(old__, new__)
15.	The girl who lives next door broke the large window on the porch.	(old__, new__)
16.	The tall tree shaded the man.	(old__, new__)

Table 7-3. *(Cont.)*

SENTENCE	QUESTION
17. The cat was running from the barking dog.	(old__, new__)
18. The car was old.	(old__, new__)
19. The girl broke the large window.	(old__, new__)
20. The scared cat ran from the barking dog that jumped on the table.	(old__, new__)
21. The scared cat, running from the dog, jumped on the table.	(old__, new__)
22. The old car pulling the trailer climbed the steep hill.	(old__, new__)
23. The girl broke the large window on the porch.	(old__, new__)
24. The scared cat which broke the window on the porch climbed the tree.	(old__, new__)
25. The tree shaded the man.	(old__, new__)
26. The car climbed the steep hill.	(old__, new__)
27. The girl broke the window.	(old__, new__)
28. The man who lives next door broke the large window on the porch.	(old__, new__)
29. The tall tree in the front yard shaded the man who was smoking his pipe.	(old__, new__)
30. The cat was scared.	(old__, new__)

STOP. Count the number of sentences judged "old."

study sentences, which occurred in random order, could be classified into four interrelated groups. Each of these groups consisted of some "elements" of an overall event or scene, taken one, two, or three at a time. The results of the experiment were exactly the opposite of what one would expect given the earlier studies of transformational grammar like Mehler's. In general the subjects were most confident about (gave the highest ratings to) the most complex sentences, which included the most complete representation of one of the events (in the demonstration, the 5th, 15th, 22nd, and 29th test sentences), even when these sentences had not been studied originally. Whether or not a given sentence actually occurred seemed to have very little influence on the ratings, as long as it correctly described one of the scenes or events. Only the sentences that contained mixtures of elements from different scenes (for example, "The old man who was smoking his pipe climbed the steep hill") or those that introduced some new arbitrary fact (for example, "The pretty girl broke the window") were consistently recognized as new.

How did Bransford and Franks account for their startling findings? They proposed that subjects actively integrated the ideas in the specific sentences they had studied and pulled these ideas together to form abstract structures describing the four separate events. The subjects remembered these integrated event structures, *not* the specific sentences from which they had been constructed. After the fusion or integration into the event structures took place, subjects were not able to conduct an analysis which would allow them to recover the original sentences. Test sentences that corresponded most closely to the entire event structures were given the highest recognition ratings.

Comprehension: Text Structure

How are event structures formed and what are their parts? When we read or listen to a story or text, how do we represent it in memory? These are not simple questions, but in recent years a model of text comprehension has been proposed by Walter Kintsch, Teun van Dijk, and their colleagues (see, for example, Kintsch & van Dijk, 1978; Kintsch & Vipond, 1979; Miller & Kintsch, 1980; van Dijk & Kintsch, 1983), and this model provides a set of answers to these complex questions. There are many other theoretical accounts of text processing that have been proposed, but we will concentrate our attention on this single account because it is the most complete and comprehensive psychological theory, it is well supported by experimental evidence, and it will provide us with a meaningful framework in which to interpret and understand additional observations about text processing. First, we will examine the assumptions included in the text comprehension model and then we will review some experimental support for it.

ASSUMPTIONS OF TEXT COMPREHENSION MODEL

The model, unlike transformational grammar, ignores surface representations entirely and works instead with meaning representations. The method used to represent meaning in this model is based on the notion of "proposition," which we discussed in Chapter 6. In fact, the meaning of a text is described as a structured list of propositions. Propositions are made up of concepts (which are given word names but should not be confused with the words themselves), and each proposition includes a predicate (or relational concept) and then one or more arguments (which coincide roughly with Fillmore's cases). The predicates correspond in the surface structure to verbs, adjectives, adverbs, or sentence connectives, whereas the arguments correspond to nouns, noun phrases, or clauses. Further, one proposition can be embedded as an argument within another proposition. For example, (HIT, MARY, BALL) would be the propositional notation for the sentence "Mary hit the ball;" (PINK, BALL) would be the proposition for the sentence "The ball is pink," and (THOUGHT, JUDY, (HIT, MARY, BALL)) would be the proposition for the sentence "Judy thought that Mary hit the ball." The predicates in these propositions are HIT, PINK, and THOUGHT; the arguments are MARY, BALL, JUDY, and the entire proposition (HIT, MARY, BALL). Propositions like these, ordered in the way they are included in the text, are used to form what Kintsch, van Dijk, and their colleagues call the "text base."

Text Base.   An essential property of a text base is that it be coherent. In order for us to form a meaningful representation of a text or story, we must be able to interrelate its separate parts. If we are given a jumble of sentences to read and cannot determine how one sentence relates to another, we cannot form a text base from that jumble. The sentences comprising a text must stick together or cohere. Kintsch, van Dijk, and their colleagues use a straightforward criterion for coherence, which they call "referential coherence" and which corresponds to argument overlap. If two propositions share the same argument or if one proposition is embedded as an argument in another proposition, then we have satisfied the criterion for referential coherence. For example, (P, A, B) is referentially coherent with (Q, B) because the two propositions share the argument B, or with (R, C, (P, A, B)) because the first proposition is embedded as an argument in the second proposition. More concretely, the propositions we examined earlier, (HIT, MARY, BALL) and (PINK, BALL), are referentially coherent because of the overlapping argument BALL. Likewise (THOUGHT, JUDY, (HIT, MARY, BALL)) is referentially coherent with the proposition (HIT, MARY, BALL) because the shorter proposition is embedded as an argument in the longer proposition.

Kintsch, van Dijk, and their colleages propose that the first step in constructing a text base consists in checking its referential coherence. If there are gaps in the text so that some of its propositions do not have argument overlap with others, then the reader will engage in inference processes to add any necessary links or glue to the text base so that the propositions will cohere. For example, if the text includes the proposition (HIT, MARY, BALL) followed by the proposition (BROKE, WINDOW), the reader must add some inference like (WENT-THROUGH, BALL, WINDOW) to link the two propositions given in the text. The process of bridging gaps by forming inferences is more common than you might think. For a more complete description of this process, see the book by Crothers (1979). It is important to keep in mind that propositions are composed of concepts, not specific words, but specific words are necessarily used to represent the concepts when we write about them. Thus, argument overlap requires that the same concepts be shared by different propositions but not that the same words be shared. For example, one sentence in the text may contain the word *Reagan* and another *the President,* and the propositions representing these sentences would be assumed to have argument overlap because the same concept or person is being referred to in each case.

The network of coherent propositions that forms the text base is represented in the text comprehension model as a "coherence graph," the nodes of which refer to propositions and the connecting lines of which indicate argument overlap. See Figure 7–5 for an example of a sentence of text, the ordered list of propositions used to represent it, and the coherence graph revealing the relationships among the propositions. The number at each node of the graph stands for the ordinal position of the proposition in the text. The first step in forming the graph is to select the top-most proposition. The most important proposition, or the one that leads to the simplest graph structure, is selected for that purpose. Next the second level is constructed by selecting all the propositions that have argument overlap with

Text: "A series of violent, bloody encounters between police and Black Panther Party members punctuated the early summer days of 1969."

Propositions:

    (1) (series, encounter)
    (2) (violent, encounter)
    (3) (bloody, encounter)
    (4) (between, encounter, police, black panther)
    (5) (time: in, encounter, summer)
    (6) (early, summer)
    (7) (time: in, summer, 1969)

Coherence Graph (Nodes are proposition numbers from list above):

Figure 7-5. Sentence of text, corresponding list of propositions, and coherence graph. (Source: Kintsch, W., & van Dijk, T.A. [1978]. Toward a model of text comprehension and production. *Psychological Review, 85,* 363–394. Copyright 1978 by the American Psychological Association. Adapted by permission of the publisher and author.)

the proposition at the top level. The third level is then formed by finding all the propositions having argument overlap with propositions at the second level (but not at the first level), and so on. For convenience, connecting lines are made between levels, not within levels, even if there is argument overlap among the propositions at the same level. Further, if one proposition at a lower level has argument overlap with several propositions at the higher level, only a single connecting line is drawn.

    Memory Processes. We cannot form the coherence graph for a long text all at once. Rather, the model assumes that the text is processed in chunks of several propositions at a time. The number of propositions processed together in each cycle is not constant but has a maximum size, represented in the model as n, a free parameter or variable with a value that is assumed to depend on the specific subjects and text employed. For simplicity, when working with specific texts, Kintsch, van Dijk, and their colleagues have assumed that each cycle contains the propositions from a single sentence, since most sentences (like the one illustrated in Figure 7-5) are long enough to include a number of propositions.

    Because the text is processed in multiple cycles, the model must provide for a way to connect one cycle to the next. The mechanism chosen for this purpose is a short-term memory buffer of size s like that contained in the buffer model of

Atkinson and Shiffrin, which was discussed in Chapter 3. After a chunk of propositions is processed in one cycle, a subset of size s of them is selected to be stored in the buffer. Only the propositions in the buffer are available for connecting the new chunk of propositions with the text processed in previous cycles. The coherence graph can be easily constructed if there is argument overlap between the new chunk of propositions and the propositions in the buffer. But if one or more of the new propositions cannot be linked to those currently available, then a time-consuming "reinstatement search" is made of all previous propositions held in long-term memory. This search of long-term memory is assumed to be time-consuming and costly in terms of resources, so that it adds to processing difficulty whenever it occurs. If the search of long-term memory successfully leads to an old proposition that has argument overlap with the new proposition, then the old proposition is reinstated and the new proposition is linked to it in the coherence graph. On the other hand, if the search of long-term memory fails to reveal any old propositions with the requisite argument overlap, then inference processes are initiated to add connecting propositions to the text base, as in the example above involving the inference (WENT-THROUGH, BALL, WINDOW). These inference processes are also costly and add to processing difficulty.

Which propositions are selected for the short-term memory buffer? In order to avoid costly reinstatement searches which make reading more difficult, it would be best to select those propositions for the buffer that have the greatest argument overlap with the propositions in the next cycle. But it would be impossible for the reader to anticipate the overlap at the time when selection for the buffer must be made. A simpler strategy must be chosen and a number are available (see Fletcher, 1984, for a discussion of alternative strategies). The text comprehension model employs a particular strategy which makes use of two principles: The most important propositions (those highest in the graph) and the most recent propositions (those at the bottom edge of the graph) seem most likely to have argument overlap with the new propositions in the next chunk. This "leading edge" strategy selects the s propositions for the buffer by starting with the top proposition in the graph (for example, proposition 4 in the graph shown in Figure 7–5) and then adding all the propositions along the graph's bottom edge (in our example, proposition 5 would be selected and then proposition 7). When the end of the graph is reached, selection is returned to the highest level available and propositions are chosen from that level in order of their recency (in our example, selection would return to the second level, since no propositions remain at the highest level, and the most recent proposition 3 would be added first, then the next most recent proposition 2, and so on).

Which propositions are stored in long-term memory? Just as only a small number of propositions are held in short-term memory at any given instant, not all propositions in the text are stored in long-term memory. The model includes another parameter, p, which represents the probability that any of the propositions processed during a specific cycle will be stored in, and later retrieved from, long-term memory. The parameter p is called a "reproduction" probability because it combines retrieval information with storage information instead of separating the probabilities for each of these crucial memory operations, since these would be difficult to distinguish. If a specific proposition is processed during more than one cycle (as it will be if it is selected for the short-term memory buffer), then it has a separate reproduction probability p for each of these cycles, so the probability of finding it in long-term memory is increased.

To summarize the properties of the text comprehension model which we have discussed to this point, let us review the three free parameters that we have mentioned: n, the maximum number of new propositions processed in a single cycle; s, the number of propositions held in the short-term memory buffer during a cycle; and p, the probability that a proposition processed during a cycle will subsequently be reproducible from long-term memory.

Macroprocesses.   Along with these processes that involve the specific propositions contained in the text, their interrelationships and storage in memory, the model postulates another set of processes called "macrorules" which are responsible for condensing the details of the text to derive its essential meaning or gist. These macrorules constitute the means by which a "macrostructure" of the text is constructed. The macrostructure is composed of a set of macropropositions that together represent the gist of the text. Macropropositions are sometimes identical to the specific propositions included in the text base, which are also known as "micropropositions." But macropropositions are not restricted to those occurring in the text itself. Macropropositions may also be generalizations of the original micropropositions. For example (IN, COLORADO) is a generalization based on the proposition (IN, BOULDER). Alternatively, macropropositions may be derived by means of inferences, as in the case of the proposition (WENT-THROUGH, BALL, WINDOW) discussed earlier.

Which propositions are eligible for the macrostructure of a text? Just as the important parts of a story are different for different readers and for the same reader on different occasions, the macrostructure formed by the readers depends on their "schema" when they encounter the text. The reader's schema is his or her goal or set and is determined, for example, by instructions provided by the experimenter, expectations based on previous reading, or the like. The schema can be used to classify each potential proposition as relevant or irrelevant to the gist. Irrelevant micropropositions can *never* be macropropositions, but irrelevant generalizations or inferences based on micropropositions may become macropropositions and they do so with probability g, which is another free parameter in the model. In any event, relevant micropropositions, generalizations, and inferences enter the macrostructure with probability m. Like parameter p, parameters g and m are reproduction probabilities that depend on both storage in long-term memory and retrieval from long-term memory, where the macrostructure is held.

The text comprehension model is not limited to a single level of macropropositions. Rather, it includes the assumption that macrostructures are hierarchical, with the criteria concerning relevance becoming increasingly stringent as higher levels in the structure are involved. Relatively many propositions are deemed relevant to the schema at the lowest level of the macrostructure; at the next level more stringent criteria for relevance apply; and the stringency of the criteria is increased further until only one macroproposition is left, which can be viewed as equivalent to a title for the text. For an example, consider a situation when a psychology journal article is read and the reader approaches the article with a research report schema. At one level of the macrostructure, only propositions relevant to the usual components of a research report are considered relevant. Thus, for example, material relevant to the method, results, and discussion would be included in the macrostructure. At a lower level, material relevant to the subparts of these sections, such as the subjects and apparatus subsections of the method, would be included, and at a higher level, only the most essential information, such as that contained in the abstract, would occur. A proposition that is appropriate for several levels of the macrostructure is assumed to have a separate reproduction probability m for each of the levels.

EXPERIMENTAL SUPPORT FOR TEXT COMPREHENSION MODEL

Fit of Text Comprehension Model to Recall Protocols.   The model with these parameters and assumptions was tested by Kintsch and van Dijk (1978) by comparing its predictions to data from an experiment in which subjects read a 1,300-word research report called "Bumper Stickers and the Cops" and later recalled and summarized this text. The report followed the conventions of journal articles reporting research in psychology except for a more informal and less technical style. Subjects read the report at their own speed and later were asked to recall it as well as they could. Following the completion of their recall protocol, the subjects were asked to write a brief (60 to 80 words long) summary of the report. The subjects were divided into three groups that differed in terms of how much time passed between reading the text and recalling it. One group was tested immediately after reading the report; the second group was tested after one month; and the third group after three months.

The recall protocols and summaries were analyzed into propositions and compared to predictions from a version of the model in which the sentence was taken as the chunk size for each cycle (so n, the maximum cycle chunk size, was equal to the largest number of propositions that occurred in a sentence of the report) and s (the size of the short-term memory buffer) was set equal to 4. In addition, with the aid of a computer, many different values of the parameters representing the reproduction probabilities (p, m, and g) were compared and evaluated to determine which set of values yielded predictions that came closest to the observed data. Three levels of macrostructure were assumed, and propositions were deemed relevant or not to each level of the macrostructure according to a report schema that looked for the components of a typical psychological report, as outlined earlier. The data of concern were the frequencies in the recall protocols and summaries of the various specific propositions in the first paragraph of the report and generalizations of these propositions. In other words, for each group of subjects, a count was made of the number of times each proposition or generalization in the first paragraph was included in the recall protocols and summaries, and these numbers were compared to those predicted by the model with different values of p, m, and g. Separate evaluations of the parameters were conducted for the recall protocols and the summaries and for each of the three groups of subjects. The best-fitting parameter values are provided in Table 7-4. For five of the six conditions, a statistical test did not yield a significant difference between the obtained and predicted values; only the data from the immediate recall condition differed reliably from the predictions.

Table 7-4. *Best-fitting parameter values for data reported by Kintsch and van Dijk (1978)*

	PARAMETER ESTIMATE		
PROTOCOL TYPE AND DELAY	P	M	G
Recall			
Immediate	.10	.39	.20
1 Month	.03	.31	.10
3 Months	.02	.32	.04
Summary			
Immediate	.02	.28	.03
1 Month	.02	.20	.04
3 Months	.00	.16	.02

(Source: Kintsch, W., & van Dijk, T.A. [1978]. Toward a model of text comprehension and production. Psychological Review, 85, *363-394. Copyright 1978 by the American Psychological Association. Adapted by permission of the publisher and author.)*

The pattern of parameter estimates shown in Table 7-4 is meaningful and can be interpreted in a straightforward manner. The probability of reproducing a microproposition (p) or a generalization irrelevant to the report schema (g) is about five times as high in the immediate recall test as in the recall test conducted after three months. In contrast, the probability that relevant macropropositions are reproduced in the recall protocols (m) changes little as a function of test delay. In other words, the forgetting rate for irrelevant propositions is almost five times greater than that for relevant propositions included in the macrostructure. Further, the summaries do not show much change with delay, and their best-fitting parameter values closely resemble those for the three-month recall protocols.

Kintsch and van Dijk also compared the results of this experiment to one in which subjects read only the first paragraph of the report and recalled it immediately afterward. In this case, the macroprocesses included in the model are unlikely to apply—the subjects probably did not operate under a report schema because it was not made clear to them that what they were reading was part of a research report. As you would expect under these circumstances, the model did not discriminate between the relevant and irrelevant propositions, and the overall fit of the model was very poor. The best-fitting parameter estimates were nearly the same for p, m, and g ($p = .33$, $m = .30$, and $g = .36$), suggesting that the report schema was not employed in this case.

What do these results imply about text comprehension and memory? As time progresses, we lose increasingly more of the specific details of what we read but retain well the gist. In fact, what we recall after a long time-interval matches closely what we produce if asked soon after reading the text for a brief summary. These conclusions apply when we are reading a lengthy report and have a framework with which to interpret it. If, in contrast, we are reading a segment of a report and have essentially no framework in which to make sense of it, all statements in the report will seem equally important so we can do little in terms of condensing the ideas or organizing them to derive their gist.

Analysis by Propositions. The results we have reviewed from the study by Kintsch and van Dijk (1978) provide general support for the assumptions of the text comprehension model. In addition, other experiments provide tests for specific assumptions of the model. Probably the most fundamental assumption of the model is that the relevant memory units are propositions, rather than, say, words or sentences.

An elegant experiment by Kintsch and Keenan (1973) provides support for the proposition as a memory unit. In one part of this study, subjects read a set of ten sentences all approximately the same length in terms of number of words (16 to 17 words), but varying substantially in terms of number of propositions (4 to 9), as well as in other extraneous variables, such as syntactic structure. Each sentence was placed on a slide, and the subjects were free to project the slides at the reading rate most comfortable for them. A timer kept track of how long each slide was projected. Immediately after a slide was removed, the subjects were required to recall in writing the sentence on that slide. Although all sentences were equally long in terms of number of words, the reading time varied appreciably across sentences, and the number of propositions in each sentence was a reliable predictor of the reading time for that sentence, as shown in Figure 7–6. Beside the observed reading time data points in the figure is a relatively close-fitting straight line which can be described by the following equation:

$$t = 6.37 + .94p$$

where t stands for reading time in seconds and p stands for the number of proposi-

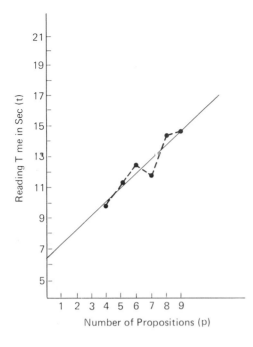

Figure 7-6. Mean reading time as a function of number of propositions per sentence in an experiment by Kintsch and Keenan (1973). (Source: Kintsch, W., & Keenan, J. [1973]. Reading rate and retention as a function of the number of propositions in the base structure of sentences. *Cognitive Psychology, 5,* 257–274. Reprinted by permission of the author and Academic Press, Inc.)

tions. The equation implies that each additional proposition in the sentence increased reading time by about 1 second (.94 second precisely). By this analysis, propositions certainly are important processing units for comprehending sentences.

Assumptions Concerning Coherence and Bridging Inferences.   Central to the model are its assumptions concerning the coherence of a text. As mentioned earlier, it is assumed that it is necessary for the reader to establish referential coherence among the propositions in the text base, and that the reader engages in the time-consuming process of constructing inferences if referential coherence does not exist. An important study by Haviland and Clark (1974) provides support for these assumptions. In their first experiment subjects were presented with pairs of sentences, the sentences in each pair being shown one after another on a display screen. As in the study by Kintsch and Keenan (1973), the subjects controlled the duration of each sentence display by pressing a button which activated a timer. Two types of sentence pairs were employed. In the first type, there was argument overlap between the two sentences in a pair, as in the following example: "Ed was given an alligator for his birthday. The alligator was his favorite present." In contrast, there was no argument overlap in the second type, as in the matched example: "Ed was given lots of things for his birthday. The alligator was his favorite present." In order to make these latter two sentences cohere, the reader must add a bridging inference like "Ed was given an alligator for his birthday." The investigators were primarily concerned with the time it took the subjects to read the second sentence in each pair. Because of the clever matching of sentence pairs, as in the example,

Haviland and Clark could ensure that any differences between the two pair types were due to the preceding sentence contexts and not to the second sentences themselves, which were always the same within a matched set. As expected on the basis of the model, the mean reading time was faster for the pairs with argument overlap (mean = 835 msec) than for the pairs that required a bridging inference to be constructed (1016 msec).

As mentioned earlier, the argument overlap required by the model is an overlap in concepts but not necessarily in words. Because the differences found by Haviland and Clark in their first experiment could be attributed, at least in part, to word repetition, these investigators conducted a second experiment to control for the effects of repetition. In this experiment, there was word overlap, or repetition, in each pair type although the pair types still differed in argument overlap. Thus an example of the pair type without argument overlap in this experiment would be: "Ed wanted an alligator for his birthday. The alligator was his favorite present." Even though the word *alligator* occurs in both sentences, a specific alligator is referred to in the second sentence but not in the first, so that for coherence a bridging inference must be added such as "Ed was given an alligator for his birthday." The alligator referred to in this inferred sentence is the same as that referred to in the second sentence of the pair. Again, as expected on the basis of the model, Haviland and Clark found with these new materials that pairs with argument overlap were read more quickly (1031 msec) than were pairs without argument overlap (1168 msec).

Short-term Memory Processes. An important set of assumptions in the model concerns the role of short-term memory in text comprehension. Specifically, the model postulates a memory buffer which contains s propositions that are selected in accordance with the leading edge strategy. Fletcher (1981) has reported an interesting study which provides strong support for this aspect of the model. In one of his experiments he employed a timed recognition memory test similar to that used previously by Sternberg (1969) in his investigations of short-term memory scanning, which were discussed in Chapter 3. Subjects read short paragraphs (about 80 words long) selected from the *Reader's Digest,* one sentence at a time. As in the studies by Kintsch and Keenan and by Haviland and Clark, the sentences were presented on slides, and the subject pressed a button after reading one sentence as a request for the next. Embedded in the sequence of slides containing sentences were slides containing probe words, which were either words that had already occurred in the text (positive probes) or words that had not yet occurred (negative probes). When a probe appeared, the subject was to decide as rapidly as possible if it had occurred in the text just read and to press one button with the right hand if it had and another button with the left hand if it had not. Four critical types of positive probes were included: words that according to the model were processed during the last cycle but were not included in the short-term memory buffer, words that were processed in the next-to-last cycle but were in the memory buffer, words in the next-to-last cycle not in the memory buffer, and, finally, words from a prior cycle not in the buffer.

The results of this experiment are summarized in Table 7–5, which provides the proportion of correct responses and the mean latency to respond to each type of positive probe. These two measures showed the same pattern: Subjects responded more quickly and accurately to words in the last cycle than to those in a prior cycle, which would be expected since the words in the last cycle should still be retained in short-term memory even if they were not selected for the buffer. And the words in the next-to-last cycle not selected for the buffer were not processed significantly more rapidly or accurately than words from a prior cycle not selected for the buffer, which is in agreement with the assumption that neither of these types of words would be currently available in short-term memory. Most crucially, the words from the next-to-last cycle selected for the buffer were responded to faster and with greater accuracy than words from the next-to-last cycle not selected for the buffer. These data are consistent with the text comprehension model which predicts that propositions selected for the buffer should be in short-term memory when the test probe appears but not those not selected.

Table 7–5. *Proportion of correct responses and latency (in msec) to respond to positive probes of the four types in experiment by Fletcher (1981)*

PROBE TYPE	P (CORRECT)	LATENCY (IN MSEC)
Prior Cycle		
Not in Buffer	.68	1478
Next-to-Last Cycle		
Not in Buffer	.67	1462
Next-to-Last Cycle		
In Buffer	.79	1385
Last Cycle		
Not in Buffer	.91	1234

(Source: Fletcher, C., R., [1981]. Short-term memory processes in text comprehension. Journal of Verbal Learning and Verbal Behavior, 20, 564–574. Reprinted by permission of the author and Academic Press.)

The Notion of Schema. The subject's schema, or set, when reading text plays a crucial role in the model because the schema determines which propositions are eligible to be included in the macrostructure. Probably the most dramatic support for the importance of schema comes from an ingenious series of experiments by Bransford and Johnson (1973). In one experiment in this series subjects were instructed to listen carefully to the following passage and try to comprehend and remember it:

> The procedure is actually quite simple. First you arrange things into different groups. Of course, one pile may be sufficient depending on how much there is to do. If you have to go somewhere else due to lack of facilities, that is the next step, otherwise you are pretty well set. It is important not to overdo things. That is, it is better to do too few things at once than too many. In the short run this may not seem important but complications can easily arise. A mistake can be expensive as well. At first the whole procedure will seem complicated. Soon, however, it will become just another facet of

life. It is difficult to foresee any end to the necessity for this task in the immediate future, but then one never can tell. After the procedure is completed one arranges the materials into different groups again. Then they can be put into their appropriate places. Eventually they will be used once more and the whole cycle will then have to be repeated. However, that is part of life. (p. 400)

This passage is difficult to comprehend without the proper schema but given the appropriate schema (washing clothes), it should be easy to understand and re-member. In order to test this hypothesis, subjects were divided into three test groups. In one group ("No Topic"), no schema was provided for the subjects. In the second group ("Topic After"), subjects were told after hearing the passage that its topic was washing clothes (just as you were given this information after you read the pass-age). In the last and most critical group ("Topic Before"), subjects were provided with the appropriate schema before listening to the passage. All subjects heard the passage one time and were required to rate it on a seven-point scale for compre-hension, with the bottom of the scale (1) indicating "very hard" to comprehend and the top (7) "very easy." Following this rating task was a recall test in which subjects were asked to write down as many ideas as they could remember from the passage. The results are summarized in Table 7–6 in terms of mean comprehen-sion ratings and mean number of ideas recalled from the passage. It is clear from the results that being provided with the appropriate schema greatly aids compre-hension and recall, since subjects in the "Topic Before" group scored higher than those in the other groups. The "Topic After" group, which performed no better than the "No Topic" group, provided an important control for the possibility that during the recall test subjects merely guessed ideas consistent with the topic pro-vided. This study indicates clearly that an appropriate schema can successfully guide the comprehension process. Note that this experiment, unlike the others reviewed so far, did not involve reading; subjects listened to (they did not see) the passage. But text comprehension is important in listening as well as reading, and the model of Kintsch, van Dijk, and their colleagues applies to both situations.

Predictions of Readability.   Probably the most crucial test of a model of text comprehension is whether it can predict how difficult a particular text will be to comprehend. Educators have devised numerous "readability" indices so that they

Table 7-6. *Mean comprehension ratings and number of ideas recalled in experiment by Bransford and Johnson (1973).*

Task	SUBJECT GROUP			
	No Topic	Topic After	Topic Before	Maximum Score
Comprehension	2.29	2.12	4.50	7.00
Recall	2.82	2.65	5.83	18.00

(Source: Bransford J.D., & Johnson, M.K. [1973]. Considerations of some problems of comprehension. In W.G. Chase [Ed.], Visual information processing. New York: Academic Press. Reprinted by permission of the author and Academic Press.)

can decide, for example, which texts will be suitable for students of different reading ability. These indices are not based on a psychological theory of comprehension but rather make reference to obvious surface features of text, such as average word length and average sentence length. Comprehension difficulty is predicted by these indices surprisingly well, but they do have their limitations, and the text comprehension model provides an alternative method for computing readability which overcomes these problems. Kintsch and Vipond (1979) describe an interesting set of analyses illustrating this point.

There is no doubt that the comprehensibility of a speech will affect its persuasiveness. If we cannot understand the arguments made by a speaker, it is doubtful that we will be persuaded by them. Clearly, then, it is important for political candidates to speak in a way that can be easily understood. In fact, it has been argued that Stevenson lost the presidential race in 1952 to Eisenhower in part because Stevenson's speeches were too difficult to understand. In order to test this hypothesis, Kintsch and Vipond (1979) selected one of Eisenhower's speeches and one of Stevenson's speeches and computed one of the standard readability indices for each speech. By this index Eisenhower did slightly worse, since he used somewhat longer words and sentences. However, Kintsch and Vipond argue that this outcome was misleading because by their own intuitions, like those of the political analysts, the Stevenson text was harder to understand. And, in fact, when they analyzed these speeches in accord with the text comprehension model, Kintsch and Vipond found support for their intuitions. For example, no inferences and only two reinstatement searches are required to comprehend the Eisenhower speech, according to the model, whereas the Stevenson speech requires two inferences and three reinstatement searches. Thus, the text comprehension model was able to discriminate between the two speeches in a way that coincides with our intuitive judgments, but the standard readability index failed this test. Further, the model provides a framework in which to understand why Stevenson's speech was difficult to comprehend: The speech was poorly organized, so that the listeners had to tax their memories and draw inferences that were not explicitly stated. This finding, though only preliminary since it is based on such a limited sample, has far-reaching implications that are relevant to many aspects of our everyday life because we spend so much time trying to understand what others have to say.

Language and Thought

It is clear when we consider persuasive speeches that language influences thought. However, some have argued for an even more profound relationship between our language and our non-linguistic cognitive behavior.

Probably the most extreme and most controversial hypothesis about the relationship between language and thought is the linguistic relativity principle, popularized by Benjamin Whorf (1956) and often referred to as the "Whorfian hypothesis." According to this principle, the language we speak influences the way we perceive and think about the world around us. In its strongest form, the Whorfian hypothesis posits a causal developmental relation between our language and our non-linguistic cognitive behavior. In other words, the languages children learn mold the way they view the world. We shall review some of the early evidence provided for this hypothesis and then some of the more recent arguments made against it. Then we shall closely examine three studies in different language domains that should make us hesitant to dismiss the Whorfian hypothesis, even in its strongest form.

EARLY EVIDENCE SUPPORTING
THE WHORFIAN HYPOTHESIS

Despite the important role of non-linguistic cognitive data in Whorf's hypothesis, as Brown (1976) remarks, the data Whorf himself provided to support this principle were entirely linguistic. For instance, Whorf's most well-known example concerns the words for snow in different languages:

> We have the same word for falling snow, snow on the ground, snow packed hard like ice, slushy snow, wind-driven flying snow—whatever the situation may be. To an Eskimo, this all-inclusive word would be almost unthinkable; he would say that falling snow, slushy snow, and so on, are sensuously and operationally different, different things to contend with; he uses different words for them and for other kinds of snow. (1956, p. 216)

From this example, the argument could be made that speakers of Eskimo can make finer perceptual discriminations among snow types than can speakers of English. But this conclusion is not totally warranted. There is no doubt that Eskimo speakers can discriminate among many different kinds of snow, but it is quite possible that English speakers would do just as well in this regard. In fact, a discussion with a group of children building a snow fortress or a group of cross-country skiers about to embark on a vacation would leave little doubt as to their discriminating abilities with respect to snow classification.

What is needed for an adequate test of the Whorfian hypothesis is a measure of non-linguistic discrimination ability that can be related to linguistic categorization. In their important work on this topic, Brown and Lenneberg (1954) provide just this necessary measure. The domain in which Brown and Lenneberg chose to work was that of color vision, which has two important virtues: There is a complete and precise physical description available for color, and there are known clear-cut differences in color classification across languages. This last property is illustrated schematically in Figure 7–7, which provides the basic color terms from three languages, English, Shona, and Bassa (both African languages). As Figure 7–7 shows, languages differ markedly both in terms of the number of color categories they use (just as they differ in the number of words for snow) and in terms of where on the physical wavelength continuum they place the boundaries separating different color categories. In view of these well established differences among languages, Brown and Lenneberg decided for simplicity to work within a single language, English.

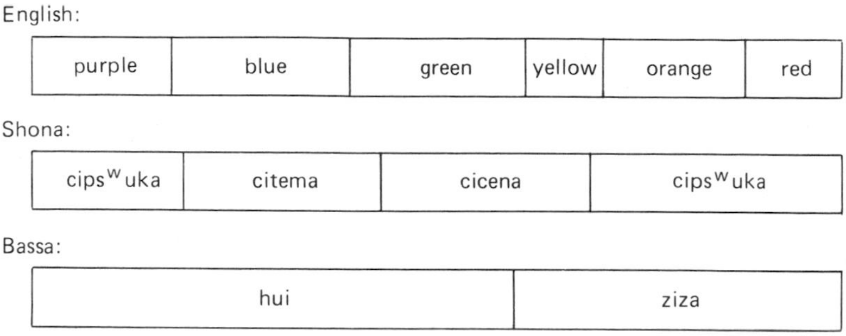

English:

purple	blue	green	yellow	orange	red

Shona:

cips^{w}uka	citema	cicena	cips^{w}uka

Bassa:

hui	ziza

Figure 7-7. Different ways to categorize colors. (Redrawn from Gleason, H.A. *An Introduction to descriptive linguistics, revised edition.* Copyright 1955, 1961 by Holt, Rinehart and Winston, Inc. Reprinted by permission of Holt, Rinehart and Winston, CBS College Publishing.)

The measures of non-linguistic discrimination ability chosen by Brown and Lenneberg were derived from recognition memory tests, and they compared these measures with several different indices of linguistic "codability," which is the ease of finding an appropriate term or expression to describe a given color.

Subjects in the study by Brown and Lenneberg were presented with an array including twenty-four chips of different colors. The subjects were then shown each chip separately and asked to give it a name or label. With these naming data, Brown and Lenneberg derived five different indices of color codability, including, for example, the number of syllables comprising the color name and the latency to make a naming response. The index of codability they found most useful involved interpersonal agreement on a color name. To compute this index, the investigators counted the number of different names given to a specific color chip and also the number of subjects who agreed on the modal response. Then the first number was subtracted from the second. To derive their measure of non-linguistic color discrimination, they used a recognition test and varied both the number of different color chips shown on a given trial (one or four) and the length of the retention interval separating the initial presentation of the stimulus and its test (7 sec, 30 sec, or 3 min). In support of the Whorfian view, they found a high correlation between the non-linguistic measure of recognition and the linguistic measure of codability. Further, they found that this correlation improved as the number of to-be-remembered color chips and the length of the retention interval increased, which implies that memory processes, rather than purely perceptual processes, are at the heart of this relationship between language and cognition.

MORE RECENT ARGUMENTS AGAINST THE WHORFIAN HYPOTHESIS

Despite this strong initial support for the Whorfian hypothesis, in a more recent article Brown (1976) described a number of subsequent studies which led him to just the opposite conclusion—namely, that there is a universality in our perception of colors. The research that was most influential in persuading Brown of this conclusion was performed by one of his former students, Eleanor Rosch Heider. (We discussed some of this work in Chapter 5 when we considered natural categories.) Probably the most decisive study was one in which Heider (1972) computed codability scores of colors by twenty-three native speakers of languages other than English, each speaking a different language. Her array of stimuli included eight focal colors (American and foreign students' selections of the best instances or prototypes of color categories; see Chapter 5) along with twenty-one nonfocal colors, and she used two different indices of codability—name length and response latency (since she used only one speaker of each language she could not make use of Brown and Lenneberg's index of interpersonal agreement). She found that the focal colors had significantly better codability scores by both of her indices than did the nonfocal colors, and this advantage for the focal colors held for all language families tested. This finding made Brown wonder whether the demonstration by Lenneberg and himself of a correlation between codability and recognition really had any implications concerning language per se. Brown and Lenneberg had assumed that the codability scores they derived were dependent on the language they employed, but Heider's results seem to imply that the scores were not dependent on language but on some other psychological factors. Rather, it seems that focal colors are human universals and that these colors are perceived more easily than other colors, not because of the names we give them, but rather because of some physiological characteristics of the human eye and brain. Work by anthropologists (Berlin & Kay, 1969) supports the hypothesis that there is a universal set of focal colors. Although languages differ in the number of color categories they employ and where they place the boundaries between categories, they do not differ as to which colors are the best instances or prototypes of the color categories.

Thus, the original support for the linguistic relativity principle provided by Whorf (1956) himself was insufficient because non-linguistic data were not considered. Likewise, the work by Heider (1972) suggests that the early work by Brown and Lenneberg (1954) was insufficient because only a single language community was tested. A proper and sufficient test of the Whorfian hypothesis requires that at least two different language communities be tested and that non-linguistic cognitive tests be performed with these communities. Although there are not many experiments that meet these requirements, there are at least three studies that are sufficient by these criteria. They suggest that it may be premature to reject the Whorfian hypothesis until additional experiments are conducted.

PROPER TESTS OF THE WHORFIAN HYPOTHESIS

As we remarked at the start of this chapter, language is hierarchical, with many different levels of analysis. The tests of the Whorfian hypothesis that we have considered so far are all relevant to the same linguistic level—the lexical level, or level of word meanings. The studies that we shall discuss next are located at three different levels of the linguistic hierarchy: the lexical level, the syntactic or grammatical level, and the phonetic level or level of the phoneme.

Lexical Level.   Since anthropological studies indicated that languages agree in their placement of focal colors but differ in terms of boundary colors, the best way to test the Whorfian hypothesis with color terms would seem to involve the color boundaries. Just such a test was provided by Kopp and Lane (1968) who worked with two groups of subjects—a pair of English-speaking college students and a pair of adult speakers of Tzotzil, a Mayan language with color categories different from those in English. The procedures used to test the Whorfian hypothesis in this experiment were similar to those traditionally used to test for categorical perception of speech sounds, as described in Chapter 2. Two separate tasks were employed. The first was an identification test, in which color stimuli varying in wavelength were shown to the subjects one at a time, and the subjects were to select one of several category names for each stimulus. The English speakers were restricted to five category names—*red, yellow, green, blue,* and *violet;* the speakers of Tzotzil were limited to four category names—*coh, k'on, yox,* and *ik'loan.* The identification functions for the four subjects are shown in Figure 7–8. The second task was an ABX discrimination test, in which subjects saw a triplet of stimuli, the first two of which were adjacent stimuli in the identification test (A and B) and the third of which (X) was identical to one of the first two. The subjects were instructed to press one of two response buttons for each stimulus triplet to indicate whether the third stimulus was the same as the first or the second. The ABX discrimination functions are shown below the identification functions in Figure 7–8.

The results of the identification tests confirm that the two languages differ markedly in their placement of color category boundaries. More interestingly, the discrimination functions for the two languages differed considerably but systematically: For both languages, as in the case of categorically perceived speech stimuli, there was poorer discrimination within categories than across category boundaries. Thus, a non-linguistic perceptual discrimination was found to be related to linguistic categorization. Although the results of this study can only be seen as preliminary, because of the small number of subjects employed, they provide dramatic support for the linguistic relativity principle at the lexical level.

Syntactic Level.   Much of the psychological experimentation aimed at testing the Whorfian hypothesis has been at the lexical level. However, Roger Brown (1977) himself admits that

> in other cognitive domains, Whorfian hypotheses may prove to be more nearly correct. And, above all, I never forget that Whorf had relatively little to say, in his work as a whole, about lexical differences. For the most part, he was concerned with semantic differences expressed in the grammars of languages, rather than in their lexicons. (p. 187)

Let us then consider the work that has been accomplished in testing the Whorfian hypothesis at the syntactic level. Very little work has been done in this domain, not, according to Brown, because the ideas are untestable but rather because "no psychologist has yet been sufficiently ingenious" (p. 187).

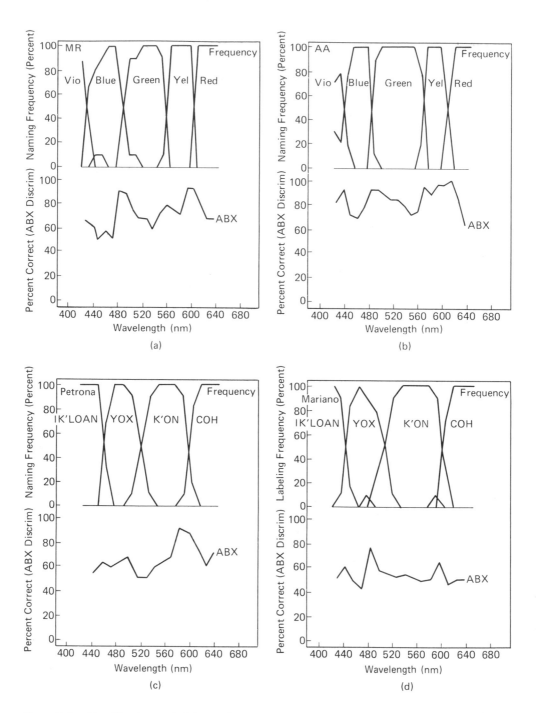

Figure 7-8. Identification probability and ABX discrimination accuracy as a function of wavelength for two English (MR and AA) and two Tzotzil (Petrona and Mariano) speakers, from Kopp and Lane (1968). (Source: Kopp, J., & Lane, H. [1968]. Hue discrimination related to linguistic habits. *Psychonomic Science,* 11, 61–62. Reprinted by permission of the author and the Psychonomic Society.)

Probably the most important, and certainly the most widely cited experiment involving the syntactic level was performed by Carroll and Casagrande (1958). The language they investigated was Navaho. In the Navaho language, when using a verb of handling (*touch* would be one such verb in English), the speaker must select a particular one of a set of endings according to the form or material of the object being handled, just as in English we often must select a verb ending consistent with the number of individuals performing the action described by the verb. Carroll and Casagrande hypothesized that, in light of the obligatory classification of objects in Navaho, Navaho-speaking children would learn to discriminate the form and material of objects at a younger age than would their English-speaking counterparts.

In order to test this hypothesis, Carroll and Casagrande used a modified ABX discrimination task. They selected seven pairs of objects, with the objects in each pair differing from each other in two dimensions, for example in color and material or in size and shape. The subjects were presented the object pairs one at a time. After each object pair was shown, the subjects were given a third object which matched each object from the pair in only one of the two relevant dimensions. The subjects' task was to indicate which object in the pair "went best" with the third object. For example, one pair comprised a yellow stick and a blue rope. The third object was a yellow rope, so the subject could select either on the basis of color (in which case the yellow stick would be chosen) or on the basis of material (in which case the blue rope would be chosen). In Navaho, different verbal endings are used for ropes and sticks, but the verb endings do not vary as a function of object color. The subjects were 135 Navaho children on a reservation in Arizona, ranging in age from three to ten years. The subjects were divided into different groups, two of which are of central concern to us—children who spoke Navaho predominantly (59 subjects) and children who spoke English predominantly (43 subjects). There was also a control group of subjects comprised of 47 middle-class children of the same age range from Boston.

The results comparing the two groups of Navaho children were all in the expected direction (the Navaho speakers more often than the English speakers selected on the basis of the form or material dimension), and the differences between the two groups of Navaho children were statistically significant for five of the seven pairs. In addition, an interesting developmental trend was noted indicating greater reliance on the form or material dimension with increasing age. The one peculiar result concerns the control group of children from Boston. The investigators found that the responses of these children more closely resembled those of the Navaho-speaking children than those of the English-speaking children from the reservation. This finding can be more easily understood if one assumes that the children from Boston had more experience playing with toys varying in shape and material than did the Navaho children of the same age; this might make them more sensitive to the form and material attributes. The authors reached the following conclusions:

> The tendency of a child to match objects on the basis of form or material rather than size or color increases with age and may be enhanced by either of two kinds of experi-

ences; (a) learning to speak a language, like Navaho, . . . because of the central role played by form and material in its grammatical structure . . . , or (b) practice with toys and other objects involving the fitting of forms and shapes. (p. 31)

Although its results were quite promising, this study did not lead to any more conclusive follow-up studies testing the Whorfian hypothesis at the syntactic level.

Phonetic Level.   Although the Whorfian hypothesis has usually been formulated with reference to the lexical and syntactic aspects of language, Healy (1978) has pointed out that the same principle is applicable to an aspect of language lower in the linguistic hierarchy—its phonetic structure. In fact, there are studies in the field of speech perception that are clearly consistent with the Whorfian view. Several groups of investigators have revealed differences in discrimination ability between speakers of different languages. For example, Miyawaki, Strange, Verbrugge, Liberman, Jenkins and Fujimura (1975) investigated the perception of the consonant sounds [r] and [l] by native speakers of English and Japanese. This distinction was selected for investigation because it is a phonemic distinction in English (we have words like *row* and *low* that differ only in these consonants) but not in Japanese. The English speakers were college students at the University of Minnesota, and the Japanese speakers were students and staff at the University of Tokyo, all of whom had received at least ten years' formal training in the English language.

As in tests of categorical perception and in the color perception experiment by Kopp and Lane (1968), two different tasks were employed—an identification test and a discrimination test. These tests were performed on stimuli from two different continua. By means of a speech synthesizer, each continuum was constructed by varying the direction and initial starting frequency of the third formant transition (see Chapter 2 for a discussion of the construction of speech continua of this type). For one continuum, this third formant was combined with first and second formants to yield synthetic speech syllables ranging from [ra] to [la]; for the second continuum, the third formants existed in isolation. All subjects performed the discrimination tests on both stimulus continua, but only the English-speaking subjects performed the identification test, and this test was conducted only with the speech ([ra]—[la]) continuum.

The results of the experiment are summarized in Figure 7–9, which shows the single identification function of the speech sounds by the American subjects along with the four separate discrimination functions (for the two subject groups with the two continua). For the speech continuum, there were large differences in discrimination between the two groups of subjects. English speakers revealed the critical signs of categorical perception: better discrimination across than within the category boundaries determined by the identification test. In contrast, Japanese speakers demonstrated poor discrimination throughout the continuum. The poor discrimination performance of the Japanese speakers cannot be attributed to hearing defects or an inability to discriminate the acoustic patterns, since performance by the Japanese speakers was as high as that of the English speakers on the nonspeech continuum involving the isolated third formants. These findings indicate

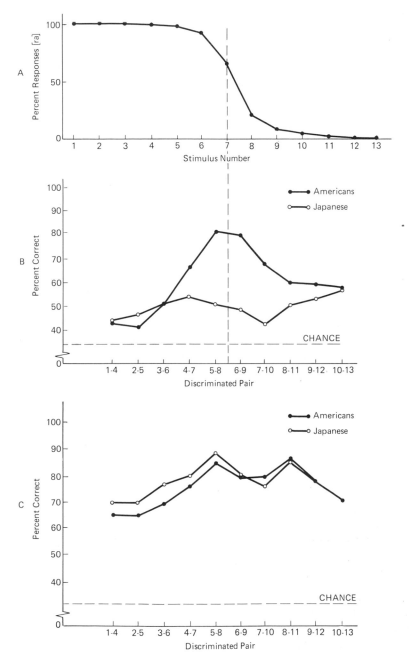

Figure 7-9. Panel A: Identification of speech stimuli by Americans. Panel B: Discrimination of speech stimuli by Americans (closed circles) and Japanese (open circles). Panel C: Discrimination of non-speech stimuli by Americans (closed circles) and Japanese (open circles). (Source: Miyawaki, K., Strange, W., Verbrugge, R., Liberman, A.M., Jenkins, J.J., & Fujimura, O. [1975]. An effect of linguistic experience: The discrimination of [r] and [l] by native speakers of Japanese and English. *Perception & Psychophysics, 18,* 331–340. Reprinted by permission of the author and the Psychonomic Society.)

a clear effect of linguistic experience on speech perception. This experience seems to involve a loss of, rather than an improvement in, discriminability with increased age; Eimas (1975) has shown that American infants perceive the consonant sounds [r] and [l] categorically, and it would only seem reasonable to assume that Japanese infants would behave in the same way.

This study gives clear support to the Whorfian hypothesis at the phonetic level, as do all the studies demonstrating categorical perception of speech, to the extent that they indicate that the category boundaries are not caused by acoustic properties of the stimuli and differ from language to language. We would also not be surprised to discover an effect of language on the perception of printed characters. Imagine, for example, a tachistoscopic experiment in which subjects must discriminate pairs of printed symbols. Presumably, English readers would perform more accurately than Chinese readers when the symbols involved were letters of our alphabet, whereas Chinese readers should perform better with Chinese characters (see Healy, 1978). Note that the symbols involved in this imaginary experiment, like the sounds involved in the study by Miyawaki et al., are linguistic, but they are not meaningful symbols or sounds when presented on their own. Hence, it seems appropriate to classify discrimination tasks involving such symbols or sounds as nonlinguistic cognitive tasks, and this classification is required if those tasks are to be taken as relevant to the linguistic relativity principle.

The studies we have reviewed and the others reported in the literature by no means *prove* Whorf's linguistic relativity principle. But they provide sufficient evidence to warrant further investigation of the hypothesis.

Summary

Language has multiple levels of analysis. The phrase structure level can be described by means of a tree diagram which specifies the location of pauses when a sentence is uttered and illuminates the meaning of a sentence that has more than one surface structure. In order to disambiguate other sentences, a deep structure must be postulated that reveals the underlying or logical relationships among the words of a sentence. Some experimental support has been provided for the linguistic notion of syntactic deep structure, but this support can be attributed to the normal confounding of grammatical function with semantic role. When the two variables are unconfounded, semantic role, as captured by Fillmore's case grammar, seems to be more important. Similarly, the linguistic notion of transformation, the mainstay of Chomsky's transformational grammar, received initial support from laboratory experiments. But later studies indicated that, when given a series of sentences, we remember something more abstract than their transformations or deep structure. Our memory in such a situation may best be described in terms of an integrated event structure.

Kintsch, van Dijk, and their colleagues have proposed a model of text comprehension that provides for the construction of an integrated event structure, or a coherent text base. Argument overlap is necessary for coherence, and inferential processes are instituted whenever needed to assure such overlap. A long text is processed in cycles, each of which consists of a chunk of new propositions (usually those contained in a single sentence) along with a small number of old propositions that are held in a short-term memory buffer. Propositions are selected for the memory buffer in accord with a leading edge strategy that gives precedence to the most recent and most important propositions, as specified in the coherence graph that defines the text base. The propositions held in long-term memory are determined probabilistically as a function of the number of cycles that a given proposition participates in. Along with these microprocesses, the model postulates a set of macroprocesses that are responsible for constructing a hierarchical representation of the gist of the text, in accord with the reader's schema.

General support for this text comprehension model has been provided by a study which compared the predictions of the model to the observed frequencies with which subjects recalled the propositions in the first paragraph of a research report. Experimental support was also provided for the more specific assumptions of the model. In particular, there was evidence that propositions are processing units for comprehending sentences, that argument overlap facilitates comprehension of sentences, that the leading edge strategy determines which propositions will be held in the short-term memory buffer, and that an appropriate schema can effectively guide comprehension. The model has also been used successfully to predict readability, or the ease with which a text or speech can be comprehended.

Undoubtedly, linguistic messages influence our thoughts, but it is not clear whether the language we speak influences our view of the world. According to the Whorfian hypothesis there is a causal developmental relationship between language and non-linguistic cognitive behavior. Initial support was provided for the Whorfian hypothesis, but the initial studies were inadequate either because they did not provide tests of non-linguistic cognitive behavior or because they tested only a single language community. Three studies that are adequate by these criteria provide evidence for the Whorfian view at the lexical, syntactic, and phonetic levels of language. Additional experimentation is needed to settle this important issue.

EIGHT

Problem Solving

The essence of a problem is that a person must discover what must be done in order to achieve some goal. People face a variety of problems in the ordinary course of living—trying to figure out why the car won't start, working on a mathematics exam in school, looking for the screwdriver that isn't in its usual place, planning a holiday party, or searching for a friend's house in an unfamiliar neighborhood. In addition to the problems presented by everyday living or by the demands of occupations, people often seek out problems to solve—crossword and jigsaw puzzles, or games such as checkers, chess, and bridge.

Obviously, problems come in many shapes and sizes and vary in difficulty and importance. Because of the variety of tasks that may appropriately be called problems, it should be clear that there is no neat, clearly-defined process called problem-solving. Rather, solving problems involves a complex of processes, and the importance of any component process will vary from one problem to the next. There are three important consequences of this way of thinking about problems.

1.   First, the details of what an individual does in trying to solve a particular problem are likely to be determined largely by the nature of the problem being attempted. For example, the details of what a person does when trying to choose a move in a game of chess are really quite different from the details of what will be done when trying to fix a car. The activities involved in solving any single problem can, in principle, be divided into two classes: Those aspects that are specific to that particular problem, and those aspects that are similar to processes seen in solving some other problems. This chapter will focus on the more general characteristics of problem-solving. We will discuss processes that are relevant to solving a number of different problems; no attempt will be made to describe in detail the solution to any particular problem. In effect, we will provide you with a set of ideas for understanding problem-solving. If there is some problem of special interest to you, you can then use these ideas to help you better understand performance on that task.

2.   Second, researchers who study problem-solving may select tasks to use in their research either because the tasks are similar to common problems or because the tasks appear useful for investigating some process of theoretical interest. Real-life problems are often very complicated, with the result that it is hard to develop a reasonably clear account of what people do when attempting such problems, what makes such problems hard or easy. Therefore, researchers frequently employ simple problems, either stripped-down versions of common problems or specially constructed tasks. This is done in order to get a clearer picture of some particular problem-solving process. In this chapter, we will sometimes describe research using rather artificial problems because the special context provides a very good illustration of the process under discussion. In other instances, however, the findings will be based on problems that are more familiar to you.

3.   Third, emphasizing the differences among problems and their unique features raises important questions about learning to solve problems. Perhaps all of us would like to be good problem-solvers, and we may wonder how one improves. Consider two extreme positions: First, the broadest, most optimistic—there is something called problem-solving ability which, once acquired, allows one to solve any problem efficiently; second, the narrowest, most pessimistic—every problem is unique, thus a person learns to solve problems one by one. Stressing the uniqueness of problems suggests that the correct answer lies closer to the second, pessimistic alternative; we will consider this topic at the end of this chapter.

Problem Characteristics

It is useful to examine some of the ways in which problems can differ, keeping in mind that problems do not fit nicely into any simple classification scheme. There are several ways of considering variation among problems, each of which suggests differences in the processes that are likely to be involved.

DEGREE OF CONSTRAINT

Problems may be arranged along a complex dimension from well-defined to ill-defined (see, for example, Reitman, 1965). For a very well-defined problem, everything is clearly specified such that the accuracy of a proposed solution can be judged easily. A jigsaw puzzle is an example of a well-defined problem—the issue is to make the pieces fit and there is no difficulty in deciding when the puzzle is complete. Mathematical proofs are also well-defined problems; in such a problem, the initial state and the desired final state are identified, and a rigorous set of rules governs allowable operations.

At the other extreme are tasks which are in some sense vague—for example, "Given a description of the set of jobs done by a work crew of three men, find a way of organizing the crew's work so that productivity is high, the men's preferences and skills for various tasks are taken into account, and morale among crew members is good." (Maier & Janzen, 1969, present a more detailed version of such a problem). There are a number of uncertainties here, related to evaluating any proposed solution (for example, how should morale be balanced against productivity?) as well as to constraints which might apply (for example, does the company require that each man spend at least some time on each job, must the tasks be done in a particular order?) As problems become less well-defined, greater importance is attached to activities such as interpreting the problem, generating solution possibilities that are minimally suggested by the information given, and evaluating solution attempts. For well-defined problems, there might exist a solution procedure, often called an *algorithm*, which can unerringly lead to a solution (although a person may or may not know the algorithm). Such procedures will not exist for ill-defined problems.

SOLUTION LENGTH

A different way of looking at problems is in terms of their length or complexity—the number of steps required for solution. A problem might have just a single, critical step or might require a lengthy, fairly complicated series or operations. Examine the description of the "hatrack problem" in Figure 8–1. This problem is actually rather difficult—about 50 percent of college students fail to solve it within 45 minutes (Burke & Maier, 1965). Success seems to depend strongly on coming up with a single idea: using the ceiling in building the hatrack (see Dominowski & Jenrick, 1972).

The pyramid puzzle described in Fig. 8–2 presents a different picture. For this problem, a perfect, error-free solution requires 31 moves—but people usually make mistakes and thus require more. The length of a required solution does not determine problem difficulty in any simple fashion; for example, the hatrack problem has a short but difficult solution. What does happen is that, as required solutions become longer, processes such as organizing sequences of moves, setting

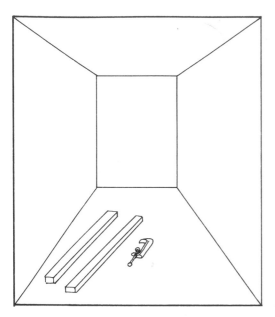

Figure 8-1. The hatrack problem. In a room measuring 8′ × 8′ × 8′ are two strong sticks, each 5′ long, and a C-clamp. The task is to construct a hatrack stable enough to hold a winter coat.

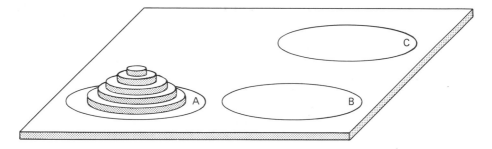

Figure 8-2. The pyramid puzzle. On a table are three circles A, B, and C. On circle A five discs are stacked in order of size, the largest on the bottom. The task: Move one disc at a time, moving only the top disc in any stack, and moving a disc only from one circle to another, get the discs stacked exactly the same way on circle C. Important restriction: No disc may be placed on top of another disc that is smaller. The solution is at the end of the chapter.

subgoals, monitoring progress toward a solution, and remembering outcomes of previous operations become more relevant.

WHAT MUST BE DONE

Three types of problems discussed by Greeno (1978) are illustrated in Figure 8–3. Greeno focussed on what the problem-solver is given and asked to do to achieve a solution; as these requirements change, so do the processes highlighted in problem-solving. Problems of inducing structure require the person to identify the rela-

A. PROBLEMS OF INDUCING STRUCTURE

1. What number comes next in this series?

   142434445464__

2. Complete the analogy:
   baseball is to bat as tennis is to

   a. kick
   b. court
   c. racket

B. TRANSFORMATION PROBLEMS

1. HOBBITS AND ORCS:

Three hobbits and three orcs stand on one side of a river. On their side of the river is a boat which will hold up to two creatures. The problem is to transport all six creatures to the other side of the river. However, if orcs ever outnumber hobbits, orcs will eat the hobbits. How should they get across?

2. WATER JARS

A person has 3 jars having the capacities listed. How can the person measure exactly 11 ounces of water?

Jar A—28 ounces
Jar B— 7 ounces
Jar C— 5 ounces

C. ARRANGEMENT PROBLEMS

ANAGRAMS: Rearrange the letters in each set to make an English word:

EFCTA
IAENV
BODUT
LIVAN
IKCTH

Figure 8-3. Examples of three types of problems. The solutions are given at the end of the chapter.

tions existing among the elements presented and to construct a coherent representation of the pattern of elements. To solve a series-completion problem, one must determine both the kinds of relations among items and the period length (the number of items involved in some regularity) of the series. In the example in Figure 8–3, the period length is two (the series can be segmented as 14/24/34/44/54/64) and the relations between any pair and the preceding pair are "next, same"—that is, the first item in each successive pair is the next number in a simple counting scheme whereas the second number in each pair is the same. Therefore, the series would be continued with "74." Both relation-type and period length are important determinants of the difficulty of series-completion problems (see Kotovsky & Simon, 1973).

Solving an <u>analogy problem</u> involves such processes as encoding the meanings of the terms, inferring the relation between the A and B terms, mapping the relation between the A and C terms, and applying the relation inferred between A and B to C in order to select the appropriate alternative (Sternberg, 1977). In the example, the A term, baseball, includes in its meanings "name of a game," "round object," "ball that is hit, thrown"; the meanings of the B term (bat) include "long object used to hit balls," "to hit something sharply," "small animal that flies." Possible relations between the A and B terms that might be inferred include "baseball is played with a bat," "baseball is hit with a bat," "(in) baseball an activity is to bat." As encoding and relation-finding continue, one arrives at the solution, noting that "the game of baseball is played with a bat, as the game of tennis is played with a racket." Analogies are not always solved with a rigid sequence—first determine the A—B relation, then A—C, and so on. Especially for more difficult analogies, people may make more use of the A—C relation than the A—B relation, and may even generate relations between C and the alternatives in searching for a solution (Grudin, 1980; Whitely & Barnes, 1979). Analogies and series-completion problems can be presented with a variety of content, including numbers, letters, geometric forms, and words. Consequently, performance on such problems depends, not only on processes related to finding relations and constructing pattern descriptions, but also on a person's semantic knowledge, to differing degrees and in different aspects. Problems like these are often included in tests of "reasoning abilities"; we will discuss a number of reasoning processes in Chapter 9.

In a <u>transformation problem</u>, the person is given both an initial situation and a goal state and must find a sequence of operations that will, within some set of rules, change the initial state into the goal state. Thus, in the hobbits-and-orcs problem, one must find a series of moves of creatures and boat, back and forth across the river until all are on the other side. For a water-jars problem, one must discover a series of pourings that will result in the desired distribution of water. Mathematical proofs and the pyramid puzzle mentioned earlier also have specific start and goal states. For transformation problems, a key question concerns how moves or operations are chosen, and we will discuss strategies that are used to solve such problems later in this chapter.

<u>Arrangement problems</u>, as the name implies, require that the elements presented be recombined or rearranged to satisfy a stated criterion. In addition to anagrams like those in Figure 8–3, arrangement problems include jigsaw puzzles and construction problems like the hatrack problem. Notice that, although the criteria for a solution are provided, the precise nature of the goal state must be produced by the problem-solver (in contrast to transformation problems where the goal state is specified). Therefore, these problems emphasize generating possible solutions or part-solutions and evaluating these to determine if they satisfy the criterion or might be elaborated to produce a solution. We will discuss these processes in detail very shortly.

This brief survey of ways in which problems differ illustrates the variety of processes that can be involved in solving problems. In a real sense, solving a problem can require successful execution of many cognitive processes. We will now consider some of the more important components of problem-solving in greater detail.

Problem-Solving Processes

In earlier chapters we discussed some basic features of the human information-processing system. Problem-solving, like any human activity, is constrained by the nature of the system. For example, attention to environmental information is limited and selective (see Chapter 3); if a problem situation is information-rich, a person might fail to attend to important information or select poor information on which to base problem-solving efforts. This is a limit to the amount of information that can be held in short-term (working) memory; processing resources are required to maintain content in short-term memory, and maintaining content competes with operating on that content for the resources available (Chapter 3). Problem-solving is a real-time activity that utilizes active memories and quite clearly requires, not just remembering, but operating on those active memories. We might therefore expect that problems can easily overload a person's capacity for processing current information. Long-term memory has unlimited capacity, but constructing a long-term memory representation requires processing resources, and, while some information in long-term memory is retrieved automatically, retrieval may fail. Retrieval depends both on the quality of the cues available and the nature of the organization of long-term memory (see Chapter 4). A problem may call for considerable retrieval of information from a person's store of general knowledge; alternatively, to minimize the load on short-term memory, it may be advantageous to store intermediate results of a solution attempt in long-term memory, provided that the information can be retrieved successfully. In both of these ways, long-term memory processes can have important effects on problem-solving.

Two general points are worth keeping in mind as we discuss problem-solving. First, the major processing steps in problem-solving occur in an essentially serial, rather than parallel, fashion. Although some mental operations seem to function in parallel and thus without mutual interference (see Chapter 3), many problem-solving processes work in a serial manner and thus involve competition for processing resources (Newell & Simon, 1972). If we consider what appears to us as conscious work, our own intuition suggests that we tend to work on one thing at a time (serial processing), with clear limits on how much we can do.[2] Second, our limited capacity for processing current information can have a somewhat indirect effect on problem-solving. Bruner, Goodnow, and Austin (1956) proposed that a person faced with a mental task can have a conflict of goals. One goal is to complete the task as efficiently as possible, but this can conflict with the goal of minimizing cognitive strain (mental effort or stress on processing capacity). An ideal solution strategy is one which both leads to an efficient solution and minimizes cognitive strain. However, a person might elect to use a less efficient approach in order to keep cognitive strain within acceptable bounds.

REPRESENTING A PROBLEM

Logically, the first step in solving a problem is to determine what the problem is, which involves identifying what is given, what are the characteristics of the desired solution, and what constraints apply to solution attempts. There are two distinctions worth making among several ways of describing a problem. First, one can distinguish between the problem *as presented* and the problem described at a slightly more abstract or formal level. For example, suppose we choose the word *budget* to be the solution to an anagram; the problem would thus involve presenting the six letters in some scrambled order and asking the person to rearrange them to make a word. Quite clearly, we can present this problem in many different ways, depending on the specific arrangement of the letters that a person is given; *udgetb* and *degtub* are two different ways to present the "same" problem. Another, probably familiar, example is that mathematical problems can be presented in either equation format or as word problems. Second, we can distinguish between the problem as presented (what we might call the *surface description*) and the *representation* of the problem adopted by the problem-solver. Suppose two people are given the same objective problem in mathematics— that is, they are presented with precisely the same information. One person starts trying to formulate equations, whereas the other starts drawing diagrams; although they were presented with the same problem, they are representing it in different ways. Thus, a problem, described in an abstract or formal manner, can be presented in different ways (given different surface descriptions), and, given any particular surface description, people can represent the problems to themselves in different ways.

The central point is that actual problem-solving makes use of the representation of the problem that is constructed by the problem-solver. The questions which arise are: Does the adoption of one or another representation of a problem affect problem-solving? Does the presentation of one or another surface description of a problem affect problem-solving? The answer in each case is "yes." We will first consider the effects of presenting different versions (surface descriptions) of a problem.

Effects of Surface Features.   There is ample evidence that presenting different surface descriptions of a problem results in differences in problem difficulty. Some of these effects depend on a form of pattern recognition (see Chapter 2). Recall that familiar patterns are recognized or encoded quickly and relatively automatically. For example, it is very difficult to look at the following visual information—A—without recognizing the letter "A." Our perception of the environment is highly organized; in a related fashion, the presentation of a particular surface description of a problem elicits a particular organization or interpretation of the information by the problem-solver. Different surface descriptions can lead to different representations and thus affect the course of problem-solving. Let us consider some examples.

For the "candle problem," the person sits at a table on which there are tacks, a box, matches, and candles, and is asked to attach a candle to a "wall" (a piece of cork or cardboard placed vertically at the side of the table) in such a way that the candle will not drip wax on the table or floor when it is lighted (Figure 8–4).

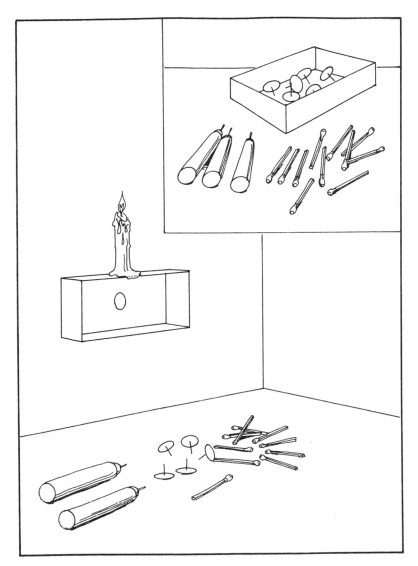

Figure 8-4. The candle problem. The upper panel shows equipment available for mounting a candle on a wall. The lower panel shows the solution. (From Bourne, Ekstrand, & Dominowski, 1971.)

What is important is how the tacks and box are arranged when the materials are presented. The inset in the upper right portion of Figure 8–4 shows how the materials are arranged for the "box-filled" presentation—the box holds the tacks. Alternatively, the box can be empty with the tacks lying on the table when the problem is presented. This problem is quite easy when the box is presented empty, but it is much more difficult when the tacks are in the box. Glucksberg and Weisberg

(1966) found that, when the box holds the tacks, people do not really notice the box as a separate object and thus they do not think of using the box as a platform for some time.

Two related findings have been obtained using anagram problems. The letters in an anagram can be ordered in many different ways, and some orders are easier to work from than others. People are likely to find the solution *bacon* faster if given the anagram *aconb* than if presented with *nobca*; the anagram *bocan* is also likely to yield faster solutions than *nobca*. Notice that *aconb* contains a very useful clue, the letter sequence *acon* which is also part of the solution; *bocan* has three of the five letters in the same positions that they occupy in the solution word *bacon*. In contrast, *nobca* has no useful clues and might contain misleading information (if, say, people try to think of words having *ca* in them), which makes finding the solution more difficult (LeMay, 1972). These examples illustrate that the kinds of clues included in a problem presentation can affect success on the problem.

The second finding stemming from work with anagrams concerns, not specific clues, but the level or quality of organization of the problem's surface description. The proposal, originally made by the Gestalt psychologists, is that the better organized the initial presentation is, the harder it will be to reorganize, and thus the harder the problem will be to solve. For example, anagrams that are easier to pronounce are harder to solve. Try pronouncing *rlfuo, lrufo, lurof*; *rlfuo* and *lrufo* do not conform well to the structural rules for English words and are hard to pronounce, but *lurof*, while not a word, has good structure and is fairly easy to pronounce. All three could be used as anagrams for *flour*, and research shows that *lurof* would be the hardest to solve.

In a study by Dominowski (1969), subjects were given a list of anagram letter strings and were asked to pronounce them as best they could, as if they were English words; the time needed to pronounce the strings was measured. The participants were not told that the letter strings were anagrams (that is, that each string could be arranged to make an English word) or that they would later be asked to solve anagram problems. They practiced pronouncing the letter strings, several times. When this practice was over, they were told that they would now be given a second task, and were given each of the letter strings with instructions to find the word that could be made by rearranging the letters. The results were clear-cut; with practice, people were better able to pronounce the anagrams, and pronunciation practice made the anagrams harder to solve (compared to performance without pronounciation practice).

A related finding is that word anagrams tend to be harder to solve than non-word anagrams (Ekstrand & Dominowski, 1968). A word anagram is a problem where the letter string that is presented is itself a word, with the person required to make a different word by rearranging the letters—for example, given *night*, find *thing*. In an ordinary, non-word anagram like those we have previously discussed, the presented letter string does not constitute a word. Word anagrams not only tend to be easier to pronounce than non-word anagrams, but they also have meaning, which non-word anagrams clearly lack. However, the difference in difficulty between the two kinds of anagrams appears to stem primarily from the fact that word anagrams are easier to pronounce (Fink & Dominowski, 1974). These findings indicate that, for arrangement problems like anagrams, given that few or no useful clues are present in the initial surface description, increased organization of the initial presentation inhibits reorganization and thus increases problem difficulty.

There is an especially interesting aspect of these findings. When people are given anagrams to solve, the problems are usually presented visually, with no requirement to pronounce the anagrams; people are simply told that the letters must be rearranged to make an English word. People given the candle problem (with the box containing the tacks) do not have their attention deliberately drawn to "the box of tacks"; rather, they are simply told to solve the problem. A similar finding, not concerned with problem-solving, is that acoustic similarity produces errors in short-term memory recall when items are presented visually (see Chapter 3). What these results indicate is that certain aspects of information encoding occur quite automatically, even when doing so is detrimental to task performance.

The findings we have reviewed suggest that the surface description of a problem can suggest useful or inappropriate internal representations, and that, given few or no useful clues, greater organization retards adoption of an appropriate representation, and therefore solution of the problem. Research on solving simple algebra problems indicates that variation in problem presentation can have additional effects. Consider the "word" and "equation" versions (Mayer, 1982, p. 448) of the same problem:

"Find a number such that if 3 more than 4 times the number is divided by 3, the result is the same as 5 less than 2 times the number."
"Find X given $(3 + 4X)/3 = 2X - 5$"

There are two common assumptions about the difference between the two problem formats. First, we expect that word problems will be somewhat harder to solve, which Mayer (1982), among others, found to be correct. Second, we expect that word problems will be solved by first translating the words into an equation and then solving the equation. In other words, word problems will tend to be harder because they involve the extra step of translating from words to equation format. This assumption, however, is not correct, at least when people are not allowed to use pencil and paper in solving the problems.

Mayer (1982) presented both kinds of problems on a computer screen, with people typing their answers on the keyboard. He found that people tend to use different kinds of approaches for the two types of problems. To understand the various strategies, examine the problem state shown below:

$5X = 27 + 2X - 12$

There are two, fundamentally different operations that can be applied to this expression. One could "move" 2X to the other side of the equals sign (or, subtract 2X from both sides of the equality), producing

$$5X - 2X = 27 - 12$$

This operation is a fundamental component of what Mayer called the "isolate" strategy. Alternatively, one could perform a computation on one side of the equality, subtracting 12 from 27 and producing

$$5X = 15 + 2X$$

Computations on one side of the equality are basic operations of the "reduce" strategy described by Mayer. The central finding was that people preferred an "isolate" strategy for equation problems but a "reduce" strategy for word problems. This illustrates the point that different surface descriptions of "the same" problem can lead to the adoption of different solution strategies.

Organizing Information.   We have been stressing the effects of varying the presentation format of a problem, and with good reason, because there is ample evidence that problem-solvers tend to adopt the representation most directly suggested by presented, surface description (Simon & Hayes, 1976). It is, however, possible for people, all given the same initial presentation, to form different representations. This is illustrated by research using matching problems (see Figure 8–5 for an example). This kind of problem involves figuring out the relations among a number of items of information. It will be worthwhile for you to study the problem and try to solve it before reading further.

Sitting at a bar, from left to right, are George, Bill, Tom, and Jack. Based on the information below, figure out who owns the Cadillac.

1. George has a blue shirt.
2. The man with a red shirt owns a VW.
3. Jack owns a Buick.
4. Tom is next to the man with a green shirt.
5. Bill is next to the man who owns a Cadillac.
6. The man with a white shirt is next to the Buick owner.
7. The Ford owner is furthest away from the Buick owner.

Figure 8-5. A matching problem. The solution is given at the end of the chapter.

The information for a matching problem is presented in sentences. The question is what people do with this sentential information when trying to determine the relations needed to solve the problem. Schwartz (1971) gave people problems of this sort, allowing them to use pencil and paper so that he could examine how they represented the information. He found that three kinds of representations were used with some frequency. (Typical representations for the first three sentences of the sample problem are given in Figure 8–6).

Schwartz observed that people used either list, network, or matrix formats to represent the information given in the sentences, as well as the relations they determined by working on the problem. The list format is essentially a shorthand version of the sentences themselves. The network format includes one line for each dimension of variation in the problem content. The names are on one line, ordered according to the information stated in the problem; on separate lines, the shirt colors and car names are listed, in arbitrary order, and lines connecting matched items are drawn. For example, the line between *Jack* and *Buick* represents the information in sentence 3. A matrix format, one version of which is shown in the figure, represents existing relations (marked with "yes" in the appropriate box) as well as nonexistent or impossible relations (indicated by filling in a box).

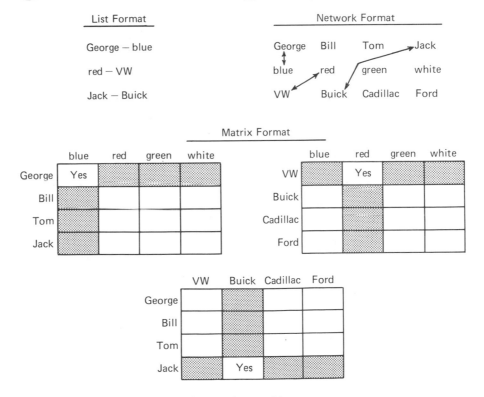

Figure 8-6.   Representations used for matching problems.

The list format is unorganized and need not even include all of the items involved in the problem. In contrast, both the network and matrix formats represent all items in a reasonably organized fashion, which provides some idea of which matches need to be found and facilitates checking which relations have already been determined. The matrix format is, however, the only representation that conveniently allows nonexistent relations to be included. For example, consider sentence 4, "Tom is next to the man with a green shirt." None of the formats allows a convenient representation of the "next to" relation, but a partial meaning of the sentence, "Tom does *not* have a green shirt," is easily included in the matrix format, by filling in the "Tom-green" box. It is difficult to include such information in the network; one might invent "negative" (isn't matched with) lines, but doing so makes the network cluttered and confusing. The ease with which nonexistent relations can be included in the matrix format allows the problem-solver to restrict the number of possible relations to be explored. Schwartz (1971) found that people who use the matrix representation are much more successful at solving matching problems. The matrix format represents problem information, presented and derived, more completely and thus reduces the load on short-term memory.

Changing a Representation.   The initial representation adopted by a problem-solver has strong impact on solution attempts and thus affects the chances of reaching any, or an efficient, solution. Obviously, people can and do change their approaches to problem-solving. Anagrams containing misleading clues can be solved, and people can solve the box-filled version of the candle problem, even though solution is slower in these cases. The fact that such problems are eventually solved, despite initial, inappropriate representations, indicates that changes take place. How do problem-solvers change representation? This is an interesting and important question, but at present, this aspect of problem-solving is not well understood. There have been suggestions regarding what might influence such changes; for example, Simon and Hayes (1976) obtained evidence supporting the idea that problem-solvers will consider changing representations that place too heavy a load on short-term memory when working toward a solution. But attempts to deal formally with changes in representation have not fared well.

Consider a suggestion made by Weisberg and Alba (1981). They proposed that the initial representation determines a particular, finite-but-possibly-large domain of possible solution attempts. They further proposed that a problem-solver will remain in that domain until all of the alternatives have been tried, and will change when the domain has been exhausted. Unfortunately, people's behavior does not conform to this proposal. They frequently change approaches long before a domain has been exhausted; for example, given the anagram *nobca*, you might "try something different" well before considering all possible letter strings containing *no*, as suggested by the anagram. Conversely, people sometimes persist in repeating attempts previously tried and found wanting. For a familiar, homey example, have you ever, when seeking a misplaced object, searched repeatedly in a particular place even though you know you looked there before without success? For most people, the answer is "yes," perhaps with a sigh. Both kinds of behavior—changing before a domain is exhausted and repeating prior, unsuccessful attempts—indicate that the proposed, simple mechanism cannot adequately account for when changes will or will not occur. We will have a bit more to say about this question later, when processes of evaluation are discussed.

Changes in representation, or perception of a problem, were stressed by the Gestalt psychologists. They emphasized the need to alter perceptions of problems in many circumstances, as well as the organized, principled nature of both initial perceptions and reorganizations. Consider a classic example of Wertheimer's (1982), dealing with the problem of determining the area of a parallelogram. Suppose a student, who already knows how to determine the area of a rectangle, is asked to find the area of the figure shown in Figure 8-7.

When given this problem (with a ruler available to measure any desired line lengths), one common response is of the form, "I can't do this—I haven't learned this yet." More productive thinking is exhibited by those students who, either immediately or after a delay, react roughly as follows: They remark that there's something wrong with the figure, referring to the sides. They note that there is "an extra part" on the left, perhaps also that there is "a part missing" on the right. Finally, they state, in effect, that the extra part on the left is just what is needed to fit into the gap on the right to make the figure a rectangle. At this point, finding the area is an easy step.

Wertheimer points out that the parallelogram induces the perception of the two horizontal lines having an oblique reference to each other. Of course, in a rectangle, the horizontal lines are related vertically. It is when one changes perception of the relation of the horizontal lines of the parallelogram, viewing them as having a vertical reference, that the "extra part," the triangle on the left, becomes apparent. Wertheimer (1982) describes other examples of changes in representation, much more fully than we can do here. Useful changes, which lead toward solutions, do not occur haphazardly but reflect structural relations present in the problem situation. In our example, comparing the structural relations of the parallelogram that is presented with the structural relations of the rectangle that might be created is a critical step in finding the solution.

It is clear that changes in representation occur, and that they are often necessary for successful problem-solving. We can agree with Wertheimer that this behavior is organized, and that productive representations reflect important situational relations. But, referring to our example, consider the following question: What happens that leads the students to view the parallelogram as a possible rectangle? It is questions of this form for which we currently lack complete answers.

Hints. One way to try to "force" a change in representation is by giving a hint to a problem-solver. Giving a hint may be viewed as changing the problem

Figure 8-7. Using a ruler to measure distances, find the area of the parallelogram.

situation by introducing a new element. Usually, hints are given with the intention of helping the problem-solver, although a hint might have no effect or even be misleading. There is a potentially critical difference between the hint-giver's representation of a problem and that of the person trying to solve the problem. Very simply, the hint-giver knows the solution but the problem-solver does not. Consequently, the connection between a hint and the solution might be clear to the hint-giver, but the clarity of this relation might be lost to the problem-solver. Hints can be ignored, lead to a different and incorrect representation, be interpreted as consistent with the problem-solver's current approach, or yield a solution (Burke, Maier, & Hoffman, 1966). It is neither surprising nor informative if people given a hint do not solve a problem more efficiently than those left alone.

We will use the hatrack problem to illustrate what can happen when a hint is given. This problem was described in Figure 8–1 and is reproduced in Figure 8–8, together with the solution—and some popular, incorrect attempts.

Recall that the task is to use the two sticks and the clamp to erect a hatrack

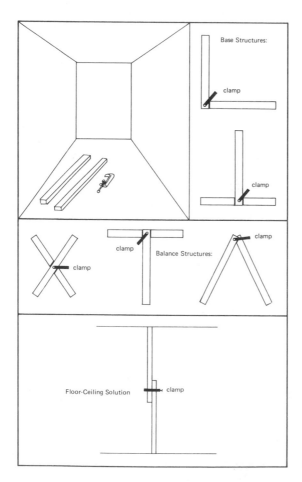

Figure 8–8.   The hatrack problem.

stable enough to hold a winter coat. The way to solve the problem is to wedge the sticks between the floor and the ceiling, joining them in the middle with the C-clamp which also serves as the coat hook. People given this problem often try other solutions, such as "balance" structures or "base" structures, but these are unstable and thus incorrect.

One hint that has been used with this problem is the "clamp hint," which involves telling the problem-solver that, in the solution, the clamp serves as the coat-hook. This hint is incompatible with base structures (where the clamp is near the floor), but it is consistent with both the correct, floor-ceiling structure and incorrect, balance structures. Giving this hint to someone already trying a balance structure is unlikely to have any effect, since the hint is consistent with what the person is already doing. If the clamp hint is given to people trying base structures, they are likely to change, but research shows that they are most likely to change to balance structures, which are also incorrect (Burke et al., 1966; Dominowski & Jenrick, 1972).

Various hints have been tried with several different problems, usually with only modest improvements in problem-solving success (see, for example, Weisberg & Alba, 1981). Not surprisingly, some hints are "better" than others, and it has been suggested that the effectiveness of a hint for aiding solution is directly related to the number of incorrect approaches it eliminates (Burke, 1969). That is, the ideal hint would be consistent only with the solution to the problem, whereas a poor hint would be consistent with the solution but also with a number of incorrect representations. For example, for the hatrack problem, we have seen that the clamp hint, which does not help solving very much, is inconsistent with base structures but compatible with both the solution and incorrect, balance structures. In contrast, the ceiling hint, which is the statement that the ceiling must be used to solve the problem, is incompatible with both base and balance structures. The ceiling hint is very effective, typically producing very rapid solutions to the problem (Burke, 1969; Dominowski & Jenrick, 1972).

Do hints alter problem representations? Provided that the hint is incompatible with the person's existing representation and is not ignored, the answer is "yes." Do hints help people solve problems? Not necessarily, for reasons that are perfectly understandable.

Incubation.   We will very briefly discuss an idea with considerable intuitive appeal, namely the notion of an incubation effect—that it is better to leave an unsolved problem than to continue working on it. The memoirs of a number of important, creative individuals refer to having the solution to a problem come to them "out of the blue" or easily finding the solution after a period of inactivity (Rothenberg, 1982 presents a detailed and interesting discussion of these reports). Several different theories have been proposed as to why there should be incubation effects; one of them concerns the issue of representation. A person who has worked on a problem without success is likely to have an inappropriate representation of the problem. By "leaving the situation," the person, upon returning to the problem, has an opportunity to interpret the problem in a new, and perhaps more productive way.

Unfortunately, research on incubation effects has typically failed to identify any such effect (for example, Dominowski & Jenrick, 1972; Fulgosi & Guilford, 1968). That is, people given time off from an unsolved problem are not more successful than those who continue work on the problem. A possible reason for such discouraging findings is suggested by results from the Dominowski and Jenrick (1972) study. Here, people worked on the hatrack problem for a short while, without finding the solution; they were told to stop work and were taken to a different room where another task was presented—they were not told that they would return to the hatrack problem. When they renewed work on the hatrack problem, 73 percent continued the incorrect approach they had been trying before the "time off"; the vast majority of the remainder changed to a different, incorrect approach. Of course, under different circumstances, more positive results might be obtained. In autobiographical accounts of incubation (see Chapter 1), working time and time off were much longer than those used in the research studies, so the negative research results do not necessarily invalidate these accounts. At the present time, we cannot be sure if or when incubation effects might occur.

SEARCH PROCESSES

For a meaningful problem to exist, there must be more than one way to proceed, with the problem-solver not knowing the correct alternative. It is perhaps not surprising that problem difficulty increases as more apparent alternatives are available (provided that only one will yield a solution). Researchers have tried to determine the precise form of the relation between difficulty and the number of alternatives; while all studies show that difficulty increases with more alternatives, the precise form of the relation depends on the type of task.

Suppose you have the problem of finding the piece of a jigsaw puzzle that fits a particular, target piece, or finding the word that meets stated criteria from a list that is provided. In such cases, difficulty is linearly related to the number of available alternatives (e.g., Dominowski, 1972). Each alternative must be separately considered to determine if it is the solution, so each additional alternative adds a constant amount to problem difficulty. If, however, a problem-solver can eliminate multiple alternatives simultaneously, difficulty then shows a negatively accelerated relation to the number of alternatives (e.g., Neimark & Wagner, 1964), that is, each additional alternative increases difficulty by a smaller amount.

We can illustrate the difference between these two relations by referring to a modified game of "battleships." Suppose your opponent has placed a ship on one of the squares of a board, and you must guess where it is. If you are required to guess one square at a time, it is clear that the difficulty of your task will be a direct, linear function of the number of squares on the board. Suppose, however, that you were allowed to ask a different kind of question—for example, "Is your ship is on the left half of the board?"—with your opponent responding "yes" or "no." With this kind of question, whether you are told "yes" or "no," you can eliminate half of the squares on the board with just one question. If you continue asking questions like this, guessing that the ship is on the left half of the remaining squares (or the right half, or the top half), you would be able to find where the ship is with a relatively small number of guesses. If you used this "half-split" strategy, finding the correct square on boards having 8, 16, and 32 squares would require only 3, 4, and 5 guesses, respectively. When the half-split strategy is used, doubling the number of alternatives increases problem difficulty by only one step because they need not be tested individually.

The alternatives to be considered do not have to be presented in an obvious way; the number of alternatives might exist only "in the head" of the problem-solver. For example, a better hint eliminates more incorrect representations, which is equivalent to reducing the number of alternatives to be considered (see, for example, Burke, 1970). Anagrams are easier to solve when the anagram letters enter into fewer combinations in the language (Ronning, 1965). For example, *hckit* is a fairly easy anagram because many letter combinations (here, *hc, tc, tk, kt, ctk, kh,* etc.) simply do not occur in English words, reducing the number of alternatives. Telling a person that the solutions to an anagram belongs to a a particular category (for example, animal names) reduces the number of possible solutions and thus makes the problem easier (Safren, 1962). To illustrate, consider the difficulty of the anagram *sulraw*, depending on whether one knows or does not know that the solution is an animal name *(walrus)*; you might try this on a number of your friends. If you give them the anagram without the extra information and they seem to be having trouble finding a solution, you could then give them a hint. A number of findings indicate that, whether the alternatives are physically present or "in the head," the number of alternatives plays an important role in determining the difficulty of a problem.

Working through a mathematic proof or solving a problem like the pyramid puzzle (see Figure 8–2) involves more than simply selecting the correct alternative or retrieving the right idea from long-term memory. Solving such problems requires an extended sequence of moves or steps. Consequently, for such multi-step problems, the issue of problem size is more complex. One can "count the number of alternatives," such as the number of chess pieces or the number of coins in a pyramid puzzle, but here the additional items typically *must* be used to solve the problem, rather than just serving as distractors. A larger problem might present more blind alleys or longer blind alleys, so choosing an incorrect alternative may be more costly; recovering from the error could require many extra steps.

The difficulty of multi-step problems tends to have a positively accelerated relation to the number of required solution steps. Successive increases in the number of required steps produce larger and larger increases in difficulty. With a pyramid puzzle, the number of necessary moves for a solution increases sharply with the number of coins; problems having 3, 4, and 5 coins require 7, 15, and 31 moves respectively. People usually need more than the minimum number of moves, and the number of unnecessary (extra) moves increases with the number of coins (Gagné & Smith, 1962). The size of a matching problem (see Figure 8–5) can be varied over a wide range by changing the number of attributes (for example, cars, pets, jobs, hobbies) or the number of values per attribute (information might be given about two, three, four or more pets, cars, or what have you). As the number of required matches increases, difficulty increases ever more markedly. (Polich & Schwartz, 1974). Increasing from 9 to 21 the number of matches which must be worked out produces a slight increase in difficulty, but a further increase to 35 results in a dramatic increase in difficulty (Figure 8–9).

In all the examples we have considered, increasing the size of a problem space leads to greater solution difficulty, although the precise relation depends on the kind of problem. If a problem is quite large, however, further increases in its size will probably have no effect. The general reason is that limited-capacity, serial-processing systems (like human problem-solvers) are unlikely to search a large problem space exhaustively (Newell & Simon, 1972). There are several, more specific reasons why this is so. Serial searches are relatively slow, and time or lack of interest may prohibit complete search of a large space. In addition, lengthy searches pose serious difficulties for limited capacity systems with respect to monitoring and management; in ordinary terms, it is easy to lose track of what has been done and what is left to do. On a more positive note, people make use of information available in the problem situation to limit search to likely alternatives—they use selective search strategies, often called *heuristics*. These are rules of thumb, or hypotheses, that guide search and may lead to an efficient solution or no solution at all. We are all familiar with search behavior having such characteristics. For example, if you believe you lost something while walking through a field, you would search where you had walked rather than starting at a corner of the field and relentlessly checking every inch. If looking for a missing person, a reasonable detective would

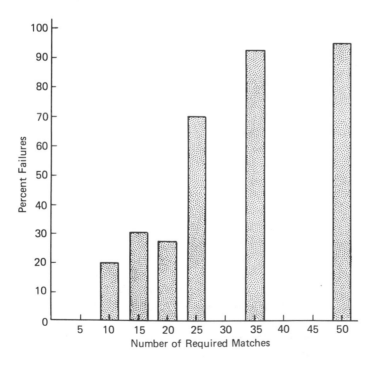

Figure 8-9. Likelihood of failing a matching problem as a function of the number of matches required. (Adapted from Polich, J.M., & Schwartz, S.H., [1974]. The effect of problem size on representation in deductive problem solving. *Memory and Cognition, 2,* 683–686. Reprinted by permission of the author and the Psychonomic Society.)

follow a set of footprints or other clues to the person's likely location. For large problems, the appropriateness of one's heuristics plays a critical role, whereas the precise size of the possible space is not crucial.

Earlier we introduced the notion of algorithms—specific solution procedures that guarantee success for particular problems—pointing out that such procedures will exist only for well-defined problems. If an algorithm is relatively simple and easy to follow, people will learn to use it (as we will discuss later in the chapter). In many circumstances, however, even though an algorithm might exist, people are not likely to use it. With respect to search behavior, an algorithm is a systematic and exhaustive search pattern; in contrast, heuristic search is highly selective and probably incomplete. As noted above, human problem solvers usually do not use exhaustive search patterns for large problems and may not do so even for smaller problem spaces. In general, people use heuristic methods, for better or worse, in trying to find solutions.

Means-End Analysis. A transformation problem involves presenting both an initial state and a desired goal state; the problem consists of finding a sequence of operations that will transform the initial state into the goal state (refer back to Figure 8–3 for examples). For such problems, a generally useful strategy is means-end analysis, which consists of identifying differences between the initial and goal states and then choosing operations that will reduce the differences. Solving transformation problems requires a sequence of operations or moves, and means-end analysis can be applied repeatedly. At each step, one tries to find a next step that will reduce the difference between the current state and the goal state. For example, for a hobbits-and-orcs problem, means-end analysis would lead to the following selections of moves: When the boat is on the initial (left) bank and will be moved toward the goal (right bank), select moves that transport the maximum number of creatures across. When the boat is on the right bank and must be returned to the left bank, select moves that transport the minimum number of creatures (namely, one) in this "backward" direction.

For a different example, consider the following water-jars problem: Suppose you have three jars with the following capacities (in pints): A, 8; B, 5; C, 3. In the initial state, A is filled with water; the desired goal is to have four pints of water in Jar A and in jar B. Since the only kind of operation possible is to pour water from one jar into another, from the initial state there are two possible moves: Fill B from A, or fill C from A. Which would you choose? According to means-end analysis, you should select the move of filling jar B. The desired goal state is 4 pints in A and 4 in B; if you fill B from A, the result would be 3 pints (left) in A and 5 in B; if you fill C from A, the result would be 5 pints in A, 0 in B, and 3 in C. Because, after filling B, the amounts in jars A and B are closer to what is desired, filling B is the move preferred by means-end analysis.

In effect, means-end analysis is a strategy of trying to move closer to the goal with each step that is taken. For problems with clearly-specified initial and goal states, it can be a very effective strategy. There are research findings suggesting that problem-solvers tend to use such an approach when working on water-jar problems (for example, Atwood, Masson, & Polson, 1980) and, in some circumstances, on hobbits-and-orcs (for example, Jeffries, Polson, Razran, & Atwood, 1977; Simon & Reed, 1976).

Although means-end analysis can be helpful, this approach cannot by itself lead to solutions in many instances. For example, at various points in some problems, it may be necessary to take an intermediate step that leads temporarily away from the final goal, much like taking a detour or roundabout route to a destination. The existence of such states in a problem tends to produce difficulty (Jeffries, et al., 1977), and it is clear that to get through such difficult states one must use something other than a pure means-end approach. In addition, using a means-end strategy can prevent a person from gaining useful knowledge about the structure of a problem. Sweller and Levine (1982) gave people maze problems which required noticeably roundabout paths to be followed to get from the start to the goal. Some subjects were shown where the goal state was, whereas others were not (of course, nobody was shown the overall structure of the maze with its roundabout solution path). People who were shown the location of the goal state, when they faced choice points in the maze, tended to try moving directly toward the goal (the means-end choice), but these moves were nearly always wrong because of the structure of the maze. There were two major findings: People shown the goal, and thus trying to use a means-end approach, performed more poorly on the maze problems than those not knowing the goal's location. In addition, people using the means-end approach learned less about the structure of the maze, as evidenced by their performance when given the maze a second time. Even though all subjects had solved the maze once, those who had done so without knowing the goals location were better at solving the maze a second time. This result reflects the relatively low level of processing required by a means-end approach. In somewhat oversimplified terms, a means-end strategy is this: Wherever you are in a problem, try to move closer to the goal (reduce differences between the current and goal states). With this approach, there is no obvious need to attend to any information about the structure of the overall problem—at each point, one just tries to make a forward step. Consequently, a person using this approach is less likely than others to learn possibly useful information about the problem structure.

Means-end analysis is essentially a forward-moving strategy—you try to alter what you have in order to make it more similar to the desired goal. Transformation problems allow the converse strategy—working *backward* from the goal to what has been given as the starting state. Malin (1979) had people memorize sets of equations relating a number of variables to one another; she then gave them problems to solve in which the values of some variables were given and the value of an unknown variable was to be determined. She found that, for a considerable number of problems, the most efficient strategy was a combination of working forward and working backward. Among the advantages of the mixed strategy were such features as constraining search in more productive ways and minimizing the load on short-term memory.

GENERATING POSSIBLE SOLUTIONS

Many problems require people to generate ideas or alternatives on the basis of the information given. For example, if your car won't start, you must think of possible reasons for this sad state of affairs (unless you refuse to accept the problem and turn it over to your local mechanic). If you turn on your television, radio, or iron and nothing happens, you must generate and test hypotheses about possible reasons for that event. (It is perhaps a reflection of manufacturers' beliefs about their customers' problem-solving skills that many electrical appliances now come with instruction booklets suggesting that if the appliance doesn't work, you should check to see if it is plugged in!)

We saw earlier in this chapter that problem-solvers are strongly influenced by cues present in the problem-as-presented. The examples we discussed illustrated the point that "the same problem" can be presented in different ways that are harder or easier to solve, depending on the usefulness of the cues contained in the initial surface description. We will now discuss some additional factors that influence the generation of ideas in problem-solving.

Familiarity.   As a general rule, problems are easier when their solutions require the production of more familiar ideas. Familiarity effects have often been studied with simple verbal problems such as anagrams or word-guessing tasks such as "think of a word starting with W that is the name of a tree." The effects of familiarity can be illustrated with the two sets of anagrams shown in Table 8–1. Most people will solve the problems in Set A more quickly than those in Set B (you can test this by giving the problems to some friends). The solution words for Set A problems occur far more frequently in general language use than the solutions for Set B problems. Set A solutions are more familiar and are produced more readi-

Table 8-1. *Anagrams: Each letter set can be rearranged to make an English word.*

GROUP A	GROUP B
monye	goudr
tnkih	humko
udjge	acoem
nfacy	hemty
ohswn	cafet
iusmc	aoclf

Solutions, Group A: money, think, judge, fancy, shown, music. Group B: gourd, hokum, cameo, thyme, facet, focal.

ly. Using word-guessing problems, Duncan (1973) showed that more familiar items have a kind of double advantage: People are more likely to retrieve from long-term memory a more familiar item, and if they produce items of varying familiarity, they tend to generate the more familiar items earlier. For example, if trying to "think of a tree-name starting with W," people are more likely to come up with *willow* than with *walnut*, and if they produce both names, they are likely to generate *willow* before *walnut*.

Familiarity effects have also been demonstrated in other ways. In a study by Maier and Janzen (1968), people were given the two-string problem. For this problem, a person is brought into a large, bare room with two strings hanging from the ceiling, just far enough apart so that it is impossible to grasp one and stretch out to reach the other. The problem is to tie the strings together; one or more objects are made available that may be used to help achieve this goal. The solution to the problem depends on what objects are available, but here are two alternatives. One solution involves extending one of the strings, with some additional string, or with a ruler tied to the end, so that this extended string becomes just long enough to allow the person to hold onto it and reach the other. Another solution is to tie an object near the end of one string and make this string swing back and forth like a pendulum; this allows the person to grasp the other string and simply wait for the swinging string to come within reach. Any object with sufficient mass can be used as the "pendulum weight."

Maier and Janzen found that, if both a ruler and a bar of soap were made available, people were more likely to try using the ruler than the soap, presumably because they viewed the ruler as a potentially useful object whereas soap is "just for washing up." This is a general effect of past experience or familiarity. As a more specific example, people were more likely to use a small ball of twine to extend one of the strings (unwinding twine and using its length properties is quite familiar) rather than using the ball of twine as a pendulum weight, a function it could serve quite well.

These familiarity effects arise from general, long-term experience. It is also possible to make items "locally familiar." For example, Dominowski and Ekstrand (1967) gave some subjects the opportunity to learn a list of words prior to trying some anagrams; the words were the solutions to the anagrams. Subjects who had had prior word-list presentation took an average of two seconds to solve each anagram, compared to one-half minute for those who had not. Prior exposure made the words more familiar in that situation and thus facilitated their retrieval in the same situation.

These findings show that people are more likely to think of familiar ideas—and to think of them earlier—in a problem situation. It is worth noting, however, that familiarity is not necessary for problem-solving. For example, even though people considered the bar of soap a rather useless object when other objects were also available, they quite readily used it as a pendulum weight to solve the two-string problem when it was the *only* object available (Maier & Janzen, 1968). By using the context provided by the problem setting, people arrived at an unfamiliar idea.

It is also important to realize that familiarity does not guarantee solution. For example, when asked to list possible uses for an object people may produce "using it as a weight" but fail to think of using the object as a pendulum weight when later given the two-string problem (Duncan, 1961). To understand these results, we need only remember that every situation, including a problem setting, provides a context which influences the production of ideas. A person may use that context to arrive at a productive, unusual idea, or the context may inhibit the retrieval of what is *in other circumstances* a very familiar idea.

Original and Creative Production. Original ideas are statistically infrequent—the less often an idea is produced, the more original it is, with maximum originality identified with the unique idea offered by only one person. It is worthwhile to distinguish original ideas from creative ideas, the latter being defined as both original and useful (relevant to some goal, appropriate to the situation). Both originality and usefulness exist in degrees—ideas are more or less original and more or less useful. To simplify discussion, it is common to select minimum levels of originality and usefulness as criteria such that an original idea meets the criterion for unusualness and a creative idea meets the criteria for *both* unusualness and usefulness.

As we have already seen, when people produce ideas they tend to think of familiar ideas first, with less common ideas occurring later. The familiar ideas are produced fairly rapidly whereas the more original ideas occur at a slower rate. Relative to any situation, only a few familiar or common ideas but a great many unusual ideas are possible; as a rule, people give a greater number of original responses as they continue to work at the task. Therefore, there is a tendency for the number of original ideas to be strongly related to the total number of ideas produced (Christensen, Guilford, & Wilson, 1957). Since creative ideas must be original (as one of the criteria), you might expect that more creative ideas will be produced with continued responding, but this is only partly correct. Continued effort results in the production of ideas of all levels of quality (usefulness, relevance). As more ideas are generated, there will be an increase in the sheer number of creative ideas, but a larger increase in the number of poor ideas. The *average* quality of ideas decreases as more ideas are produced (Johnson, Parrott, & Stratton, 1968).

The difference between generating original ideas and producing creative (original and useful) ideas was nicely demonstrated in a study by Manske and Davis (1968). People were asked to give uses for an object under different instructional conditions: Neutral ("give uses"), "Be practical," "Be original," "Be original and practical," and "Use your wildest imagination." Some of the results are shown in Figure 8–10. Changing the instructions resulted in large differences in the number of uses given, and thus the number of original uses. But the number of creative ideas was quite small and constant across conditions. These results and others imply that, although generating original ideas is fairly easy, producing creative ideas is a process that is both quite difficult and hard to influence. Simply put, most original ideas are not useful and thus fail to meet the dual criteria for creativity.

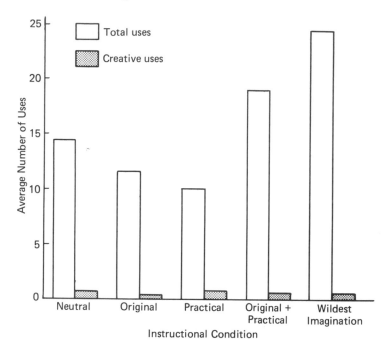

Figure 8-10. Effects of different instructions on production uses for an object. (From data by Manske & Davis, [1968]. Effects of simple instructional biases upon performance in the Usual Uses Test. *Journal of General Psychology, 79,* 25–33.)

Campbell (1960) pointed out that, if a problem requires a creative solution, then, virtually by definition, it must be one which can elicit a very large number of ideas, most (all but one?) of which won't work. He therefore argued that producing a creative solution requires sufficient knowledge (to be able to generate possibly relevant ideas), generating very many ideas (even though most will be inadequate), and selective retention (of the better ideas). The last factor, selecting better ideas, suggests a role for evaluation in creative problem-solving, a topic we will discuss shortly. Keeping in mind that generation of many ideas is necessary, what can be done to increase the potential productivity of those ideas? One popular technique is the *checklist*, which is typically a series of questions added to the basic problem. For example, given the task of redesigning a product, the checklist might include questions like: New material? Make smaller? Make larger? Add a part? Rearrange parts? Change the shape? The basic notion is to suggest a variety of directions along which to think of new ideas; the technique both encourages production of a variety of ideas and provides some guidelines for relevance (see Adams, 1979, for an extended discussion).

There are many suggestions that finding new relations is an important part of creative problem-solving. Rothenberg (1982) has proposed that finding creative solutions frequently involves simultaneous consideration of opposite or contrary ideas, with the goal of resolving or synthesizing the conflict and thereby producing a new, useful idea. In more general terms, writers have suggested "forcing" attempts to find new relations among ideas. For example, Mednick (1962) reports an anecdote about a physicist who wrote the names of theoretical concepts on slips of paper and put them in a fishbowl. Periodically, he would draw some slips from the fishbowl and try to find ways of relating the random combination of concepts that resulted. In a similar fashion, people who have used a checklist to generate a variety of ideas are often asked to then select ideas produced in response to different questions and try to generate a way to interrelate them (see, for example, Adams, 1979). Such techniques by no means guarantee a successful outcome, but, by encouraging the production of contextually-relevant ideas, they have the potential for facilitating the generation of creative ideas.

EVALUATING IDEAS

Whenever a possible solution has been generated, its adequacy must be judged. Evaluation can occur many times in the course of work on a problem, applying not only to potential "final solutions" but also to intermediate steps. When a person has worked on a problem for a time without success and decides to try a different approach, this act implies that an evaluation has been made of the likely usefulness of the current approach (Dominowski, 1981). Burke (1970) suggested that people judge the "nearness-to-success" of their attempts in deciding whether or not to change the direction of their approach to a problem—people persist longer in an incorrect approach if it seems to come closer to solving the problem. It is also possible for a person to be pursuing a proper approach to a problem but to abandon it, which is an error in judgment. For example, to solve the nine-dot problem (Figure 8–11), it is necessary to extend some lines beyond the "square" made by the dots. Some people extend a line, even a correct line (one that is part of the final solution), but then switch to an approach of drawing lines completely confined to the area of the dots, which cannot work (Lung & Dominowski, 1985). Such evaluation errors—persisting in an incorrect approach or abandoning a correct approach—may occur simply because the problem-solver is dealing with part-solutions or initial steps for which clear criteria are not readily available. The use of inappropriate criteria will clearly lead to less-than-optimal choices (see Simon & Reed, 1976). There are also suggestions that judgmental errors are more likely when the problem-solver lacks a coherent understanding of the problem's structure (see Greeno, 1977; Wertheimer, 1982).

Evaluating complete or final solutions varies in complexity, depending on the problem. For well-defined problems with clear-cut solution criteria, deciding whether a problem has been solved can be rather easy, almost automatic. For example, a person working on the anagram *trawe* who produces the arrangement *water* will have little difficulty in deciding that it is an English word having the appropriate

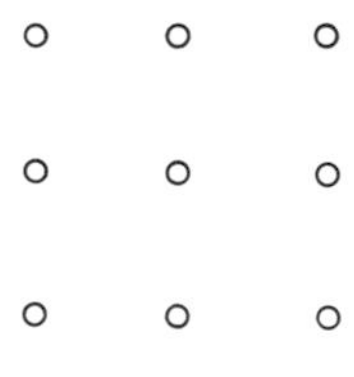

Figure 8-11. The nine-dot problem: Connect all the dots by drawing four straight lines without lifting your pencil from the paper. The solution is given at the end of the chapter.

five letters. In contrast, when solution criteria are somewhat vague, evaluation plays a more critical role in determining the quality of solutions that are given. Johnson, Parrott, and Stratton (1968) gave people relatively ill-defined tasks such as writing story titles, asking them to generate many different alternatives and then to select the one that was the best. Results showed that people were not very successful in judging their own ideas. Differences in quality between preferred and non-preferred ideas were either nonexistent or only slightly favored the ideas preferred by the people who produced them. To state this differently, the typical person would have produced a solution better than the one he or she had picked as "best."

Subsequent research by these investigators focused on improving people's evaluation through training. The training consisted of presenting people with examples of ideas of different levels of quality, explanations of the quality differences, and practice in judging ideas, with corrective feedback. Introducing such training between the production of solutions to a problem and choosing one's best solution resulted in a larger difference in quality between subjects' preferred and non-preferred ideas (Johnson, Parrott, & Stratton, 1968). In addition, those who received evaluation training, when given a new task, produced fewer ideas but ideas of better average quality, compared to untrained people (Johnson, Parrott, & Stratton, 1968; Stratton, Parrott, & Johnson, 1970). Evaluation training improved later production of ideas presumably because trained people were better able to reject inferior solution possibilities and to focus their efforts on ideas more likely to meet quality criteria.

Knowledge, Experience, and Expertise

✓ Problem-solving concerns behavior in relatively novel situations. In some sense, a problem-solver must do something "new"; discovery of solutions is the essence of problem-solving. It is nonetheless obvious that problem-solving is strongly influenced by what a person already knows, by the experiences he or she has had previously.✓ For example, consider some topics already discussed—the positive and negative effects of cues present in the surface description of a problem, the role of familiarity, or the influence of evaluation training on later production. Although presented to illustrate different aspects of problem-solving processes, each reflects in part an influence of past experience. In this section we will focus on the effects of experience, considering questions such as the following: What do people learn from solving a problem? How does the form of a person's knowledge affect problem sovling? What distinguishes experts from novices?

PRACTICE EFFECTS

Problem-solving research usually concentrates on a person's behavior when given a problem for the very first time. The simplest extension of research, in order to study practice effects, would be to present the same problem a second time. Surprisingly, relatively little is known about solving a problem "the second time," so our discussion must be a bit speculative. What might a person learn from solving a problem that would help when it is repeated? The possibilities include remembering the solution and thus being able to simply retrieve it from long-term memory; acquiring some strategy that will allow a more efficient solution; and, in a more general sense, learning something about the structure of the problem that will help in finding the solution. The relevance of these ideas must depend on the kind of problem under consideration. If a problem has a simple solution, perhaps resting on a single, critical idea, it is plausible that people might remember the solution (for example, do you remember the solution to the hatrack problem?). But for problems with more complex solutions, there is little evidence that people simply recall the solution when given the problem a second time (Thomas, 1974; Weisberg & Alba, 1981). The fact that people given a problem such as hobbits-and-orcs tend to do better on the second attempt has been interpreted as resulting from acquisition of a better strategy—for example means-end analysis (Simon & Reed, 1976)—and as a consequence of learning the general features of the structure of the problem (Thomas, 1974). It is important to note that people can solve a problem but learn very little about its structure, with the result that they show only modest improvement when the problem is repeated (Sweller & Levine, 1982).

Most research on practice effects has concerned transfer between different problems. A critical factor is the type and degree of similarity or difference between problems. The similarity of problems' surface descriptions is important because transfer between problems depends on the perception of similarities by the problem-solver (Maier, 1940). In addition, the type of relation between solutions to different problems affects the kind of transfer to be expected. These points will be explained as we consider various problem-solving transfer situations.

Problem-Solving Set.   Suppose a set of problems has very similar surface descriptions and relatively simple, nearly identical solutions. In effect, the problems will be perceived as strongly related to one another, and a set procedure or algorithm can be used to solve each and every problem. Under these circumstances, people will learn the solution procedure and apply it, more and more readily, as they proceed through the problems. This behavior is referred to as the development of a *problem-solving set*. This phenomenon can be illustrated with the problems shown in Table 8–2.

All of these problems have the same general description—there are three jars with different capacities, and the task is to figure out how to pour water among them to arrive at the desired amount. Each problem can be solved by filling the largest jar (A), then pouring water from it into the medium-sized jar (B) once and the smallest jar (C) twice, leaving the desired amount in the largest jar. In other words, an algorithm for solving these problems is A - B - 2C. Research has shown that people learn the algorithm as they work through the problem series; solutions for the fifth problem will be faster than those for the first problem. Problem six has special interest; if presented after a number of (A - B - 2C) problems, people will use this algorithm to solve it even though a simpler solution (B - C) will work. In fact, if the set-inducing problem series is followed by a water-jar problem that

Table 8-2. *Water jar problem.*

General Format: A person goes to the river with three jars having the capacities listed. How should the person go about measuring the desired amount of water? Examples:

| | Jar Capacities | | | |
	A	B	C	Desired Amount
(1)	17	7	4	2
(2)	22	9	3	7
(3)	30	19	3	5
(4)	20	7	5	3
(5)	28	7	5	11
(6)	17	7	3	4

cannot be solved with the algorithm, people will try to use the algorithm and thus have greater difficulty in reaching a solution (Gardner & Runquist, 1958). The general statement is that, given experience with a number of very similar problems, people will adopt a fixed approach; doing so will be advantageous for the restricted set of problems for which the algorithm is appropriate but will be detrimental for problems having some surface similarity but requiring different solutions.

Learning to Solve.   The problems used in studying set are quite special in that they are highly similar to one another. A lower level of similarity is involved in discussing problems belonging to the same class or category. For example, consider the class of water-jar problems, or the class of anagram problems, or that of multiplication problems. In each class, there is some similarity among surface descriptions (as well as formal characterizations), but the details of the solutions vary to a degree from problem to problem. An important question that has arisen is whether, with practice, people get better at solving problems belonging to the same class.

A brief aside. This kind of analysis might be extended to higher-order classes, such as verbal problems, or numerical problems, or spatial problems. Such higher-order classes will not be considered here, for two reasons: First, little is known about practice effects for these more abstract classes, and, second, there are reasons to expect that little transfer would occur.

Ordinary experience seems to suggest that people do get better at solving problems of the same class (as defined above). It can therefore be surprising to encounter research reports indicating that people do *not* improve with practice in solving problems such as anagrams (for example, Mayzner & Tresselt, 1962) or word-guessing tasks (Duncan, 1966). Such negative results have led cognitive psychologists to be quite cautious about expecting people to learn to solve a class of problems. However, the negative reports themselves must be treated with caution since they come from studies in which minimal practice was given.

Consider tasks like the hatrack problem, the two-string problem, and the candle problem. Each problem involves using an object in a fairly unusual fashion, although the specific object, the particular use, the other objects and the situation vary among the tasks. These problems, together with some others, can be said to define a class of "object-use problems." Do people get better at solving such problems with practice? An earlier report suggested that there was no transfer from one problem to another (Duncan, 1961) but, in that study, each person was given only two problems. In a later study (Jacobs & Dominowski, 1981), each person attempted seven object-use problems, with the result that, eventually, there was modest improvement in performance. There was no clear improvement from the first to the second problem (consistent with Duncan's 1961 finding); however, solution times for problems at the end of the series were moderately faster than solutions for problems at the beginning of the series. A related finding is that performance on the nine-dot problem (see Figure 8–11) is improved by prior practice on a series of dot-connecting problems varying in the number and arrangement of dots as well as in the pattern of lines forming the solution (Lung & Dominowski, 1985).

These preliminary results suggest that, with enough and varied practice, people can learn to solve a class of problems more effectively. There is, however, little reason for unbridled optimism, and there are good reasons for expecting any general transfer to be slow and difficult. Recall that people tend to represent a problem in terms of its surface description; over the problems in a class, such as object-use problems, the surface descriptions are a little similar but a lot different, which does not make it likely that people will readily perceive them as related. Furthermore, since the details of the solutions are largely different, what one could learn that might help solve the class of problems is likely to be rather vague and only a part of the solution to any individual problem. For these reasons, substantial improvement is likely to require extensive experience with the class of problems. In addition, it seems critical that people *solve* the practice problems; attempting a series of practice problems without much success has no clear benefit, even if answers to unsolved problems are provided (Anthony, 1973; Lung & Dominowski, 1985).

Solving by Analogy. A form of problem-solving that usually impresses people involves using an analogy between semantically-distant domains; for a hypothetical example, solving a problem in interpersonal relations by using a model drawn from physics. The possibility of an analogical solution exists when the formal representation of one problem can be mapped onto that of another problem. The key idea is that mapping applies to relatively abstract representations of the problems and *not* to their surface descriptions. For a simplified schematic illustration, examine the diagram in Figure 8–12.

This diagram represents the solution to Duncker's (1945) "radiation problem"—destroying a tumor in a patient's body (the center of the diagram) by simultaneously sending a number of low-intensity x-rays from different directions (so healthy tissue around the tumor is not damaged) so that they intersect at the tumor, yielding a combined high-intensity radiation which will eliminate the tumor. It also represents the solution to the "attack-dispersion" problem devised by Gick

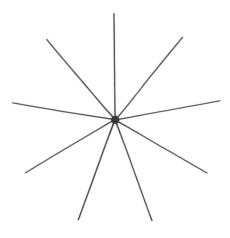

Figure 8-12. The solution to Duncker's (1945) "radiation problem."

and Holyoak (1980)—dividing an army into small groups which then simultaneously charge a fort (center of the diagram) along different roads so that they all reach the fort at the same time, resulting in a concentrated and effective attack. Gick and Holyoak (1980) used these problems to study analogical problem-solving, with clear-cut results. Subjects first solved the "attack-dispersion" problem (or read the problem, with the solution provided). When they were given a hint to use that story when working on the radiation problem, the vast majority transferred the solution and proposed the dispersion solution to the radiation problem. However, when no hint was given, the odds were against subjects' using the analogy to solve the radiation problem. In the "worst case," fewer than 10 percent of subjects spontaneously noticed the analogy and used it to solve the radiation problem. Similar results suggesting that people are not very likely to use analogies to solve problems were obtained by Reed, Ernst, and Banerji (1974), using different "cover stories" for river-crossing problems like hobbits-and-orcs. The most likely reason for the difficulty of solving by analogy is that people tend to respond to the surface description of a problem, whereas noticing the analogy requires going beyond the obvious, surface description.

KNOWLEDGE STRUCTURES

We have already discussed many examples of the ways in which the knowledge a person variously acquires may or may not help with solving problems. People can learn algorithms useful for solving a quite limited set of problems, may acquire broader knowledge applicable to a class of problems, or may know the solution to one problem but fail to realize that it would be useful in solving another. The pattern of findings suggests that the structure of knowledge that a person accumulates may have important implications for subsequent problem-solving. At this point we want to emphasize a potentially important distinction; that between procedural knowledge and declarative knowledge (see Greeno, 1973). Procedural knowledge, as the name implies, refers to knowing *how to do* things, whereas declarative knowledge refers to knowing *about* things, facts, concepts, and their interrelations (as discussed in Chapter 6).

A number of studies have been concerned with the effects of instruction on subsequent problem-solving, where the instruction emphasizes either procedural knowledge or declarative knowledge. Students received instruction concerning a mathematical formula that could be used to calculate answers to a variety of problems. *Procedural* instruction began with presentation of the formula and continued with step-by-step lessons in calculation. *Declarative* instruction stressed relating the terms of the formula to concepts from everyday life; the formula itself was not presented until the very end, as a summary of the concepts which had been discussed. After instruction, various kinds of test problems were given. Problems were given solely using the symbols of the formula, as well as word problems to which the formula could be applied.

For problems requiring fairly straightforward use of the formula, students receiving procedural instruction performed better. Those receiving declarative instruction were better at recognizing unanswerable problems or answering questions about the formula (Mayer & Greeno, 1972). Students receiving procedural instruction found word problems much harder than those stated in terms of the formula, whereas those receiving declarative instruction did about equally well on the two types of problems (Mayer, Stiehl, & Greeno, 1975). As Mayer (1975) has pointed out, if the goal of instruction is understanding which will transfer to novel situations, the learner must have an adequate base of relevant, prerequisite knowledge (or have it provided). Moreover, the instructional method should encourage a broad assimilative set (so that the knowledge base will be activated) and provide information that supports the formation of new relations as well as the development of procedural skills.

EXPERTISE

An expert is a person who is extremely skilled or knowledgeable in some field. Two general remarks about expertise are worth noting. First, the notion of the "all-purpose expert" has little merit; expertise is relative to some domain which is reasonably broad but has clear limits. Second, experts acquire their exemplary knowledge and skills through substantial amounts of study and practice over long periods of time. Although expertise is acquired, and it is reasonable to suppose that features of expertise would gradually emerge as a person's relevant knowledge and experience grow, full-blown expertise is the product of an enormous amount of learning. The studies we have previously discussed, dealing with the effects of practice and training, are relevant to modest improvement in the performance of ordinary problem solvers but barely scratch the surface of what is involved in developing expertise.

By definition, experts are very good at solving a particular domain of problems. For cognitive psychology, a meaningful question concerns how experts accomplish their feats—what do experts do differently from ordinary, less-skilled problem-solvers? Possession of a vast amount of procedural and factual knowledge can give a person multiple advantages in solving problems. Quite clearly, an expert may know solution procedures that are simply not available to the ordinary problem-solver. Factual knowledge can greatly reduce problem difficulty by changing the processes involved in reaching a solution. Consider the problem of multiplying 27×39. For most people, this problem might be nearly impossible to do "in the head" and perhaps modestly difficult if paper and pencil are used. The difficulty in doing this problem in the head stems from overloading short-term memory. Doing the necessary arithmetic processing and remembering intermediate products compete for the limited resources available to the extent that a person may not be able to complete the solution. In contrast, suppose a person knew (had previously learned the fact) that $27 \times 39 = 1053$. For this person, the problem is trivial; the answer can readily be retrieved from long-term memory with very little interference with other information-processing activities. Such observations were made in the study of Professor Aitken, an expert at mental arithmetic whose astonishing feats were described in Chapter 1. One of the reasons why Professor Aitken could accomplish mental calculations that seem impossible is that he had a tremendous store of number facts. Without calculating, he could recognize that $1961 = 37 \times 53 = 44^2 + 5^2 = 40^2 + 19^2$ (Hunter, 1968). The ready availability of number facts eliminated the need for some calculations, provided a basis for identifying problem structure, and allowed Professor Aitken to focus processing on other aspects of the calculations.

Processes of perception and memory have been emphasized in recent accounts of expertise. Schoenfeld and Herrmann (1982) asked mathematics professors and college-level mathematics students to sort a set of math problems in terms of their similarity to one another. The students clustered problems on the basis of their surface, whereas the mathematicians clustered problems on a more abstract basis related to principles or methods relevant to solving the problems. After an intensive course in mathematical problem-solving, the students' sortings were more similar to those of the experts, although still far from demonstrating expertise. Similar findings have been obtained in a study of novice and expert computer programmers; novices organize program statements on the basis of syntax (surface structure) whereas experts employ an organization reflecting principles of program function (Adelson, 1981). We have previously described research showing that ordinary problem-solvers are heavily influenced by the surface description of a problem, a finding repeated in the above-mentioned results for novices. In contrast, experts go beyond the surface description; their representations are more likely to capture problem structure and to facilitate the identification of relations, both within the problem and between the current problem and others, that will aid finding a solution.

Quite striking results have been reported from research on chess masters' perception and memory. Beginning with the research by DeGroot (1965), it has repeatedly been found that chess masters have a remarkable ability to reproduce the positions of the pieces on the board after only a few seconds' glance. The research procedure is to present a board showing a middle-game arrangement for a few seconds, then to cover the board and ask the person to reproduce the positions of the pieces. Some illustrative findings from a study by Chase and Simon (1973) are shown in the upper half of Figure 8–13.

The figure shows, that, after just one five-second glance at the board, the master could correctly place sixteen of the twenty-four pieces, compared to eight for a class-A player and only four for a beginner. One possible explanation is that better chess players just have generally better short-term memories, but this explanation is ruled out by examining reproductions of randomly-arranged pieces. As shown

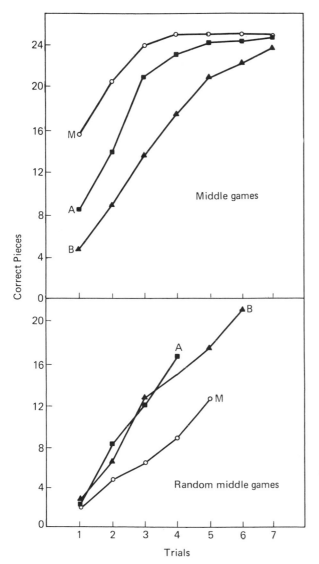

Figure 8-13. Learning curves of the master (M), class A (A), and beginner (B) for the middle-game and random middle-game positions. The brackets are standard errors on five positions. (Source: Chase, W.G., & Simon, H.A., [1973]. Perception in chess. *Cognitive Psychology, 4,* 55–81. Reprinted by permission of the author and Academic Press, Inc.)

in the bottom half of Figure 8–13, expertise was of no advantage when reproducing random arrangements. The master player remembers better only when the arrangement reflects the structure of chess; under these conditions, the master perceives configurations among the pieces and uses these organized chunks for recall. These findings led to the theory that pattern recognition is the foundation of chess skill (Chase & Simon, 1973; deGroot, 1965; Frey & Adesman, 1976). The expert player, through years of study and practice, acquires a very large number (tens of thousands) of recognizable patterns, with plausible moves associated with each pattern. The essential step in playing a game is thus recognition of a pattern and retrieval of the associated moves. It should be noted that deGroot (1965) did *not* find differences between players of varying skill in such aspects of chess as number of moves considered or depth of search regarding a possible move. These no-difference findings, coupled with the striking skill-level differences observed on chess memory tasks, led to the emphasis on memory as the basis of expertise.

Recently, however, the recognition-association view of expertise has been challenged. Holding and Reynolds (1982) found that expert players chose better moves than less skilled players under conditions where there were no skill-level differences in memory for arrangements. They also found that only about 20 percent of the pieces moved (when a player was choosing) were accurately remembered (when reproducing the arrangement). A related finding was reported by Charness (1981), who gave both move-selection and arrangement-reproduction tasks to chess players of varying skill levels and varying ages (sixteen to sixty-four years old). He found that, on the memory task, performance was positively related to skill level but negatively related to age; in contrast, on the move-selection task, only skill level mattered. To state this differently, for any given skill level, the older players showed a deficit on the memory task but not with respect to choosing moves. These findings suggest that chess expertise (choosing good moves) does *not* depend on a recognition-association process. Rather, the results suggest that accurate evaluations of positions and moves play a critical role in expertise. Better evaluations could be based on recognition of previously-seen favorable and unfavorable positions, but these findings suggest that this cannot be the complete answer. The implication is that experts possess better rules or criteria for making evaluations, and that expertise involves more than just the accumulation of meaningful patterns.

Summary

Problem-solving emphasizes the discovery of correct responses in various situations. Problems vary from being very well-defined to vague and ill-defined, differ in the number of steps required for their solution, and pose various kinds of difficulties—for example, inducing structure, transforming a given situation into a desired state, or rearranging problem elements. As task characteristics change, so do the processes that are most relevant to finding a solution.

Solving problems involves both short-term and long-term memory processes

Table 8-3. Solutions to chapter problems.

A. **Pyramid Puzzle** (Figure 8–2). (Using five discs numbered 1 through 5, with 1 the smallest; 1-C means move disc 1 to circle C, etc.): 1-C, 2-B, 1-B, 3-C, 1-A, 2-C, 1-C, 4-B, 1-B, 2-A, 3-B, 1-C, 2-B, 1-B, 5-C, 1-A, 2-C, 1-C, 3-A, 1-B, 2-A, 1-A, 4-C, 1-C, 2-B, 1-B, 3-C, 1-A, 2-C, 1-C.

B. **Hobbits and Orcs** (Figure 8–3). (Using h = hobbit, o = Orc, F = forward boat move, B = backward boat move; F/2o means move the boat forward with two orcs): F/2o (or F/1h, 1o), B/1o (or B/1h), F/2o, B/1o, F/2h, B/1h,1o, F/2h, B/1o, F/2o, B/1h (or B/1o), F/1h,1o (or F/2o).

C. **Water Jars** (Figure 8–3). Fill 28; from this, fill 7 once, 5 twice, leaving 11 in largest (28) jar.

D. **Anagrams** (Figure 8–3). Facet, naive, doubt, anvil, thick.

E. **Matching problem** (Figure 8–5). Tom owns the Cadillac.

| | SHIRT | |
PERSON	COLOR	CAR
George	Blue	Ford
Bill	Red	VW
Tom	White	Cadillac
Jack	Green	Buick

F. **Nine-dot problem** (Figure 8–11).

and often stresses capacities for processing current information. People develop representations of problems that are strongly influenced but not completely determined by the problem-as-presented. People tend to focus on the surface description of a problem; consequently, different ways of presenting a problem can produce differences in difficulty. The surface description can suggest useful or inappropriate representations; a good representation captures the essential features of a problem while placing minimal demands on working memory. Changing inadequate representations is a critical part of problem-solving, but we do not yet understand precisely how such changes occur. Hints tend to produce changes although they do not necessarily aid in solving a problem; the effectiveness of a hint depends on how many incorrect ideas it eliminates.

The size of a problem is defined in terms of the number of alternatives that must be examined (and rejected) to find the solution or by the number of steps required to produce a solution. For small to medium-size problems, difficulty increases with problem size. The precise relation depends on the kind of search strategy employed, and once problems are relatively large, success depends critically on the effectiveness of strategies or heuristics. Means-end analysis is a generally useful strategy which involves identifying differences between current and desired states and then finding ways to reduce or eliminate those differences.

Problems are easier to solve when required solutions are more familiar. People are more likely to think of familiar ideas and to produce them earlier; unusual ideas tend to occur later and relatively slowly. Creative solutions are those which are both unusual and practical, and, since most unusual ideas are not practical, finding creative solutions is quite difficult. One key is to keep idea production within potentially useful directions. Judging the adequacy of ideas varies greatly in complexity across tasks; evaluation training improves both the production and evaluation of possible solutions for ill-defined tasks.

Solving a series of highly similar problems typically leads to the acquisition of a fixed solution procedure, a problem-solving set. For less similar problems, however, practice effects are less likely to be observed. With enough, varied practice, people can learn to solve a class of problems more effectively. Real expertise requires extensive experience in some domain, for example, chess, mathematics, or verbal problems. Experts have broad and highly-organized knowledge about their fields of expertise, enabling them to solve some problems "from memory" whereas novices must expend considerable effort in trying to find a solution. Experts also develop repertoires of efficient strategies for accomplishing tasks within their fields of expertise. In addition, research suggests that an important difference between experts and novices may be experts' ability to quickly and accurately evaluate alternative ideas.

NINE

Reasoning and Judgment

Evaluating arguments, drawing conclusions from facts, and making a variety of judgments, choices, and decisions are important aspects of human behavior. These activities occur in many forms, ranging from relatively automatic processes to much slower processing with substantial conscious components. For example, a person given the task of noticing a weak signal (for example, a spot of light) that occurs only infrequently could be described as making a judgment (regarding the amount of stimulation perceived) and a decision (regarding the criterion for responding *yes* or *no*). With simple signal-detection tasks, the processes corresponding to judgment and decision-making are rapid and fairly automatic. Similar, rapid processes are included in some models of semantic memory processing, sometimes coupled with slower, more deliberate, "second-stage" comparison and choice procedures (Chapter 6). Concept-learning strategies (Chapter 5) involve drawing conclusions about hypotheses or the relevance of features on the basis of information contained in the features of an instance and the feedback concerning the instance's category membership. As these examples illustrate, reasoning and judgment play a part in many other cognitive activities; models of attention, perception, and memory commonly postulate mechanisms or procedures for comparing, selecting and the like. Typically, these processes have an automatic character, and a rough generalization is that they are assumed to work rather well, except perhaps for random distortions in the system.

In this chapter we will be concerned with more deliberate cases of reasoning and judgment. That is, we will focus on people's behavior when their primary task orientation is to reach a conclusion or make a choice, often using a complex set of verbal or numerical information. In these contexts, in everyday life and in research, we frequently refer to making a reasoning *error*, a *poor* judgment, or a *bad* decision. Such descriptions imply the existence of normative standards for proper or correct behavior. Indeed, such standards have existed for a very long time, and they arise from logic and mathematics.

Formal logic is a discipline concerned with systematic methods for reaching correct conclusions. Traditionally, it deals with the truth or falsity of statements and provides rules for relating statements to one another. In a similar fashion, mathematics involves rigorous rules for dealing with numbers and concepts describable with numbers. It is an oversimplification, but the essential idea is captured by the notion that "math tells us how to calculate correct answers." Quite obviously, some people are logicians and others are sophisticated mathematicians, so logic and mathematics describe at least some human behavior. It is also the case, however, that people are sometimes illogical and have intuitions about quantities that are quite discrepant from the answers dictated by mathematical theory.

The psychological issue of primary interest is how "ordinary people" deal with reasoning and judgmental tasks. This chapter will cover two broad areas. We will consider first the reasoning processes involved in evaluating the internal consistency of arguments (sets of statements) and in relating evidence to the truth status of a statement. The second topic concerns dealing with uncertain information—estimating likelihoods of events and relations among events, choosing between complex alternatives. We will describe the agreements and disagreements between people's answers and the dictates of logic and mathematics, and we will discuss the processes people use to arrive at their answers.

Syllogistic Reasoning

A classical task for studying reasoning is the syllogism, which is an argument consisting of two (or more) premises and a conclusion. The premises are assumed to be true, and the task is to determine whether or not, given the truth of the premises, the conclusion follows necessarily. Here is an example:

Premise 1:   All cats are animals.
Premise 2:   Some animals have tails.
Conclusion: Some cats have tails.

To understand what syllogistic reasoning requires, consider what a person given a syllogism is *not* asked to do. The person is not to decide if Premise 1 or Premise 2 is in fact true; rather, the person is required to assume that they are true. Similarly, the person is not asked to decide if the conclusion is factually accurate but only if it follows necessarily from the premises. To emphasize the internal orientation of syllogistic reasoning, consider the following example:

Premise 1:   All dogs are airplanes.
Premise 2:   Some airplanes have leaves.
Conclusion: Some dogs have leaves.

Based on our general knowledge of the world, the statements in the first example seem reasonable (cats are animals, and so on) but those in the second example seem wrong, strange, even bizarre. From the viewpoint of logic, the two examples are identical, fitting the abstract, general form shown below:

Premise 1:   All A's are B's.
Premise 2:   Some B's have C's.
Conclusion: Some A's have C's.

If you found yourself evaluating the conclusions to the two sample syllogisms differently (accepting one but not the other), you were not treating the syllogisms as formal logic requires. Logically, the two examples are identical because, in logic, content does not matter, and the premises are to be assumed correct. Of course, the content of the statements in a syllogism can be psychologically important, as we shall see later. The examples conform to syllogism No. 2 in Table 9–1 (the statement "some airplanes have leaves" can be rewritten "some airplanes are things that have leaves," thus it conforms to "some B are C."). Table 9–1 presents a sample of the syllogisms which can be constructed by varying the types of relations given in the premises (one premise relates A to B, the other relates B to C, and conclusions relate A to C). The logical conclusion for each syllogism is also indicated; as you can see, no logical conclusion follows from the premises of our earlier examples.

As illustrated in the examples, four kinds of statements can be used (all, some, some not, no). With one exception, the statements are ambiguous in that they can refer to more than one relation. Figure 9–1 shows that the statement "All A are B" can refer to either of two relations between sets A and B. The set A might be included within the larger set B, or sets A and B might be one and the same. The first relation (A inside of B) is called class inclusion, as in "All dogs are animals"; the second relation represents equivalence, best illustrated by definitions such as

Table 9-1.

	PREMISES	LOGICAL CONCLUSION		PREMISES	LOGICAL CONCLUSION
(1)	All A are B. All B are C.	All A are C.	(11)	Some A are not B. All B are C.	Can't say.
(2)	All A are B. Some B are C.	Can't say.*	(12)	Some B are A. No B are C.	Some A are not C.
(3)	No A are B. All C are B.	No A are C.	(13)	All B are A. All B are C.	Some A are C.
(4)	Some B are not A. All B are C.	Can't say.	(14)	Some A are not B. Some B are not C.	Can't say.
(5)	All A are B. No C are B.	No A are C.	(15)	Some B are A. Some C are not B.	Can't say.
(6)	No B are A. Some B are not C.	Can't say.	(16)	All A are B. All C are B.	Can't say.
(7)	Some A are B. All B are C.	Some A are C.	(17)	No B are A. Some B are C.	Can't say.
(8)	All B are A. All C are B.	Some A are C.	(18)	Some B are not A. Some C are B.	Can't say.
(9)	No A are B. No B are C.	Can't say.	(19)	All B are A. No B are C.	Some A are not C.
(10)	Some A are B. Some B are C.	Can't say.	(20)	All A are B. No B are C.	No A are C.

*The conclusion "Can't say" means that no specific statement relating A to C necessarily follows from the premises.

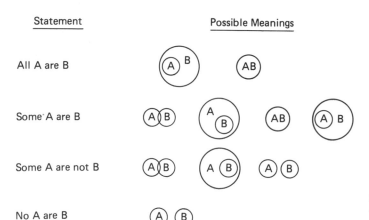

Statement	Possible Meanings

All A are B

Some A are B

Some A are not B

No A are B

Figure 9-1. Diagrams representing the meaning of quantified statements in formal logic.

"All mothers are female parents." The only unambiguous statement form is "No A are B." which can only mean that there is no overlap between sets A and B. Statements involving "some" or "some/not" are highly ambiguous since each type can have several different meanings. Figure 9-1 also shows the meaning of "some" in formal logic; notice that the last two meanings shown for "Some A are B" are the two possible meanings for "All A are B," and that the last meaning shown for "Some A are not B" is the meaning of "No A are B." In logic, "some" means "at least some and perhaps all," quite different from ordinary language where we would not use "some" when we could say "all." Typically, if we say "some are" it implies that "some are not," and vice versa. People may thus fail to arrive at logical conclusions when dealing with statements involving "some," but for an uninteresting reason. Researchers usually explain the special, logical meaning of "some" to subjects when presenting syllogisms, although it is not clear that doing so makes any difference in the kinds of conclusions people reach. Notice that, even if we restrict the meanings of "some" and "some not" to the first, two, "natural" meanings, both statements are still ambiguous.

In logic a conclusion follows only if it applies to all possible combinations of all possible meanings of the premises. This suggests that "being logical" will require considerable information-processing. The person must consider all possible meanings of each premise, construct all possible combinations of those meanings, and determine whether a conclusion is consistent with all the combinations generated. Figure 9-2 shows a logical analysis of syllogism 8 from Table 9-1.

We can state the logical requirements in the opposite way as well: A conclusion does not follow if it is possible to construct at least one combination of the premise meanings to which the conclusion does not apply. For the example in Figure 9-2, the conclusion "All A are C" fits the fourth combination of the premise meanings but does not fit the first three—it is therefore *not* a proper, logical conclusion. The many syllogisms in Table 9-1 for which "can't say" is the logical response do not allow any specific conclusion because no statement covers all the possible premise combinations; such syllogisms are called *invalid* because no conclusion

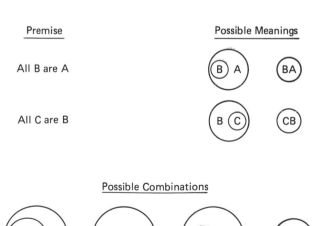

Conclusion:
    Some A are C (true no matter which combination is considered)

Figure 9-2. Logical analysis of a syllogism.

follows logically from the premises. Researchers have consistently found that people have particular difficulty with invalid syllogisms; for example, Ceraso and Provitera (1971) obtained 77 percent correct conclusions for valid syllogisms (where some conclusion does follow logically from the premises) but only 36 percent correct conclusions (namely, "can't say") for invalid syllogisms. As these results suggest, a common error in syllogistic reasoning is to accept a conclusion that does *not* follow logically from the premises.

There are three major steps to syllogistic reasoning: Interpreting the premises, generating combinations of premise meanings, and comparing conclusions to the combinations generated. As we have seen, logic requires that all steps be done completely. Given what we know about the limits of human processing capacity, we should not be surprised if people fail to reach logical answers, not because logic is irrelevant to their behavior but because they fail to complete all the processing required by logic. Indeed, research suggests that, among college students untrained in logic, only about 10 percent perform in a thoroughly-logical fashion on syllogisms (Dominowski, 1977). We will discuss what "most people" do with respect to the three phases of syllogistic reasoning, dealing primarily with research using abstract statements (for example, All A are B, or Some X are Y). Later we will consider the effects of using meaningful statements that relate to people's world knowledge and beliefs. Before beginning this discussion, however, we will first present a quite different view of human reasoning, one that implies that people do very little processing on syllogisms.

Atmosphere Hypothesis.   An idea initially proposed many years ago is that people arrive at conclusions on the basis of the atmosphere or global impression created by the premises. For example, premises containing "some" are assumed to create an atmosphere for accepting conclusions containing "some." Begg and Denny (1969) stated the atmosphere hypothesis in terms of two principles: (1) When one or more of the premises is negative, a negative conclusion will be (most frequently) accepted; (2) when one or more of the premises is particular (includes "some"), a particular conclusion will be (most frequently) accepted. When the premises do not include negative or particular statements, a universal affirmative (all) conclusion will be chosen. The atmosphere hypothesis thus makes a prediction concerning the conclusion people will accept for any pair of premises; for example, a "some" premise and a "no" premise should lead to accepting a "some not" conclusion. Notice that the atmosphere hypothesis implies that people do not even attempt analyses of syllogisms that faintly resemble logical processing; in effect, all that presumably matters is the nature of the modifiers (some, no, and so on) found in the premises.

People's errors in accepting conclusions for invalid syllogisms often have been found to agree rather well with atmosphere predictions. Illustrative data are presented in Table 9–2. Several comments are in order concerning these findings. First, the data stem from only invalid syllogisms, a point we will return to shortly. Sec-

Table 9-2. *Errors made for invalid syllogisms.*

Premise Pair	OBSERVED FREQUENCY OF CHOICES			
	All	*Some*	*No*	*Some Not*
All, All	22*	3	1	1
All, Some	6	91*	2	19
All, Some Not	3	34	6	147*
Some, Some	2	89*	4	40
Some, No	3	15	34	72*
All, No	1	3	51*	4
Some Not, No	8	76	44	98*
No, No	15	15	47*	15

Note: Frequencies vary from row to row partly because different numbers of syllogisms of each type were used in the study. The choice marked with an asterisk is the atmosphere prediction. (Source: Begg, I. & Denny, J.P. [1969]. Empirical reconciliation of atmosphere and conversion interpretations of syllogistic reasoning errors. *Journal of Experimental Psychology, 81,* 351–354. Copyright 1969 by the American Psychological Association. Reprinted by permission of the author and American Psychological Association.)

ond, the syllogisms included only abstract terms, for example, "All X are Y." Third, there is not complete agreement between atmosphere predictions and data, and the level of agreement varies across syllogisms—responses to syllogisms including premises of the form "No A are B" tend to show less agreement with atmosphere predictions than other forms.

Despite the fact that data like those in Table 9–2 fit atmosphere predictions to some degree, the atmosphere hypothesis is not now considered to be a very good account of human reasoning (although atmosphere may affect the choice of conclusion under limited circumstances—see Guyote & Sternberg, 1981). There are several reasons. Atmosphere cannot explain why people do better on valid syllogisms than on invalid syllogisms (for the atmosphere hypothesis, there is no distinction between valid and invalid syllogisms). Nor can atmosphere explain the effects of introducing certain kinds of meaningful content into the premises (we will explain the details shortly; for now, the point is that content is not supposed to matter, according to the atmosphere hypothesis). In general, data consistent with atmosphere predictions can also be explained in terms of other theoretical ideas which do a better job of providing an overall account of syllogistic reasoning. It is these ideas to which we will now turn our attention. A final comment about atmosphere—although it does not seem to be a good account of performance when people are given syllogisms with relatively ample time to work on the problems, it might be relevant to what people do when they have little time to consider an argument. For example, when listening to a political speech, a person has little opportunity to process very thoroughly the arguments contained in the speech. Perhaps atmosphere is quite relevant under such circumstances; at present, this is just speculation.

PREMISE MISINTERPRETATION

There is ample evidence that people frequently misinterpret the premises of a syllogism. Rather than considering all possible meanings of a premise, as logic requires, people tend to encode just one meaning. The most common error is to infer that the presented statement and its converse are true; for example, presented with "All A are B," people tend to interpret this as meaning that it is also true that "All B are A" (Ceraso & Provitera, 1971; Chapman & Chapman, 1959; Revlis, 1975). Proposed conversion errors are shown in Figure 9–3.

The theoretical proposal is that people misinterpret (convert) the premises but then combine their (mis)interpretations logically to arrive at conclusions. Premise conversions may or may not lead to a logical error regarding the conclusion, as illustrated in Figure 9–4. For some syllogisms, use of a limited interpretation of the premises will lead to the same, valid conclusion as a complete logical analysis. For other syllogisms, premise conversions will lead to accepting logically invalid conclusions. Models assuming premise conversion have been used successfully to predict not only when people will or will not reach logically-acceptable conclusions but also which conclusions people will reach (Ceraso & Provitera, 1971; Fisher, 1981; Revlis, 1975).

The importance of premise conversion as a source of errors on syllogisms has been shown in several ways. Generally, experimenters try to block conversion in their subjects. Ceraso and Provitera (1971) did this by presenting longer, unambiguous premises such as "All A's are B's, but there are some B's that are not A's." With such unambiguous premises, people reached logically-correct conclusions far more often. Revlis (1975) presented meaningful premises, chosen so that people's world knowledge would block conversion. For example, given the premise "All dogs are animals," people will *not* assume the converse "all animals are dogs" and therefore do not make conversion-driven errors.

PARTIAL COMBINATION

Premise misinterpretation is not the only error people make in processing syllogisms. The most difficult syllogisms are those for which "can't say" is the proper response even if premise conversion is assumed. For example, no logical conclu-

Premise	Postulated Misinterpretation	
All A's are B's	All A's are B's and All B's are A's	(AB)
Some A's are B's	Some A's are B's and Some A's are not B's	(A)(B)
Some A's are not B's	Some A's are not B's and Some A's are B's	(A)(B)

Figure 9–3. Proposed misinterpretations of premises.

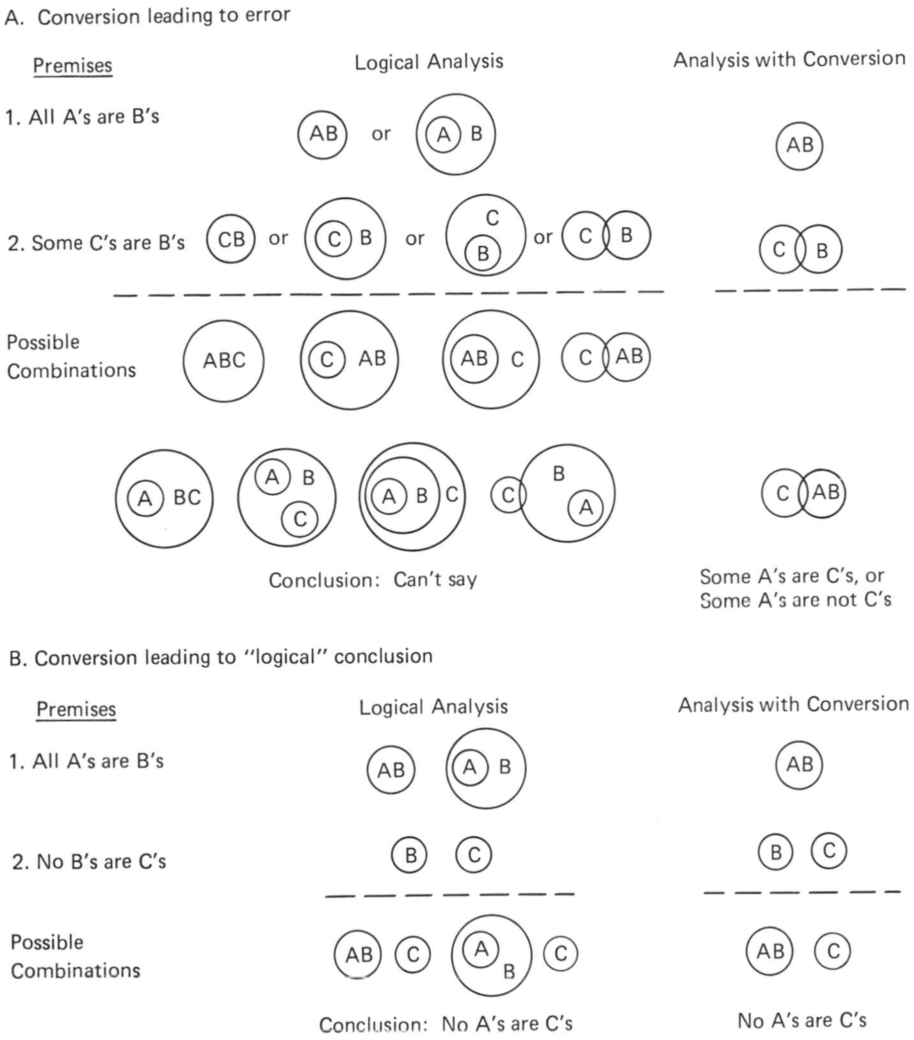

A. Conversion leading to error

Conclusion: Can't say

Some A's are C's, or
Some A's are not C's

B. Conversion leading to "logical" conclusion

Conclusion: No A's are C's

No A's are C's

Figure 9-4.   How premise conversion can effect reasoning.

sion can be drawn from the premises "Some A are B" and "Some B are C" whether one considers all possible meanings of each premise or just the limited meaning (partial overlap) postulated by premise conversion. If A and B partly overlap and B and C partly overlap, A and C might completely overlap, partly overlap, or not overlap at all; thus, even with limited premise meanings, no conclusion necessarily follows. Furthermore, premises of the form "No A are B" are unambiguous and not subject to misinterpretation; nonetheless, people make mistakes in dealing with such premises. Premise misinterpretation cannot explain such results; another process must be involved.

Many researchers have obtained evidence that people may generate only some (rather than all) combinations of premise meanings (Ceraso & Provitera, 1971; Erickson, 1978). Guyotte and Sternberg (1981) proposed that limitations of working memory lead to selecting just a few premise pairings. Incomplete combining strategies can lead to a variety of errors, which can be illustrated with the pair of premises shown in Figure 9–5. Ceraso and Provitera (1971) gave this premise pair to people with the instruction to select an answer from "All A's are C's," "Some A's are C's," "No A's are C's," and "Can't say" (the logically correct answer). The percentages of subjects making each choice were: "All," 5 percent; "Some," 10 percent; "No," 35 percent; and "Can't say," 50 percent. Figure 9–5 illustrates that each conclusion could be reached in any of several ways; for example, a person who considered just combination 1 would accept the conclusion "All A's are C's." Incomplete strategies can lead not only to viewing as "necessarily true" conclusions that are only "possibly true" but also to rejecting as "impossible" other conclusions that are also "possibly true." For example, a person who considers just combinations 2 and 3

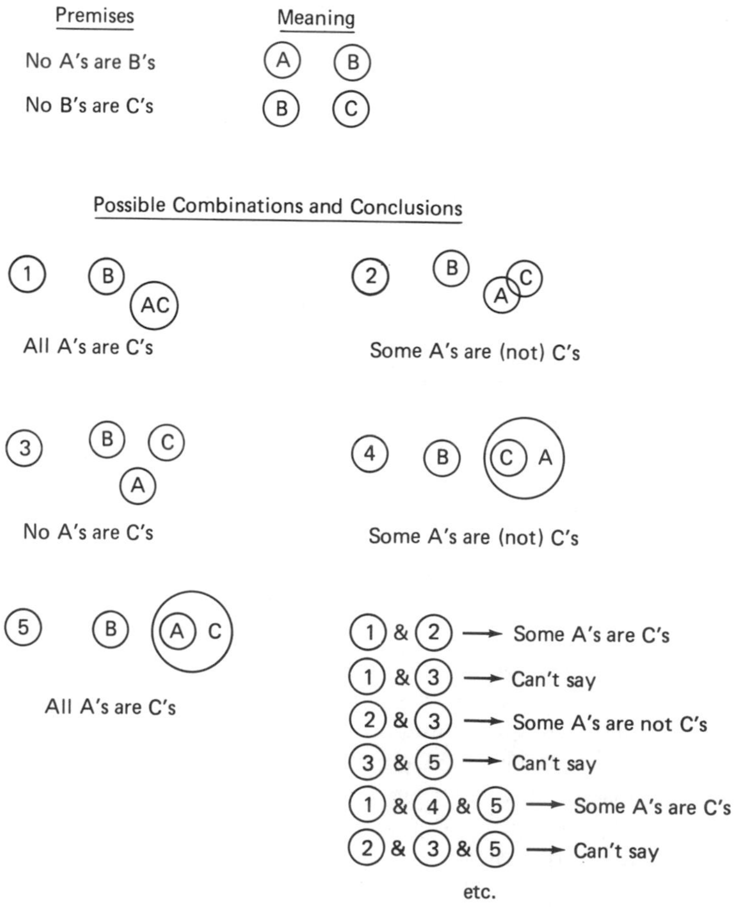

Figure 9-5. Partial combinations of premise meanings.

might say that it is impossible that "All A's are C's" might be true. Partial combination of premise meanings accounts for a substantial proportion of the errors people make in dealing with premise pairings (Fisher, 1981; Johnson-Laird & Steedman, 1978). As a consequence, the more premise combinations that are required to arrive at a logically-correct conclusion, the less likely it is that people will do so.

Failure to generate all possible premise pairings is quite consistent with what we know about the limited processing capacity of human information processing. There are, however, other facets to what people do with respect to premise pairings. In some instances, people simply form erroneous, alogical combinations—that is, they consider a combination that cannot logically be made from the premises as being "possibly true" or even "necessarily true" (Erickson, 1978; Fisher, 1981). For example, given that A and B partly overlap and that B is a subset of (is totally contained within) C, it is *not* possible for there to be no overlap between A and C. Yet a minority of subjects consider such a relation as "possibly true."

When people generate only some of the possible premise combinations, they do not form pairings on a random basis. Rather, certain kinds of premise pairs seem to be favored over others (Guyotte & Sternberg, 1981; Johnson-Laird & Steedman, 1978). The general tendency is that "simpler" combinations will be more likely to be considered, or will be generated earlier. For example, forming combinations where class-inclusion relations are generated (one set contained within another) is not favored; this relation is arguably more complex than others because of the asymmetical relations involved—for example, if A lies within C, then "All A are C" but "Not all C are A." Alternatively, when the nicely symmetrical, partial overlap relation can logically be generated, it is in fact considered more than other possible combinations (Fisher, 1981). Such "biases" for some combinations over others allow predictions of which erroneous conclusions people are more likely to reach; in addition, bias may contribute to the general finding that people tend to consider less than all possible premise pairings. That is, the use of only partial combinations may result both from limitations on processing capacity and from a tendency to consider "preferred" pairings.

EVALUATING CONCLUSIONS

Whether or not premises have been misinterpreted, and whether or not premise meanings have been combined completely, incompletely, or alogically, a person must choose a conclusion or check a given conclusion against the premise pairings that have been considered. According to formal logic, a conclusion follows only if it is consistent with all (possible) premise combinations. At least two error-producing processes related to evaluating conclusions have been identified. First, people might accept a conclusion as "necessarily true" if it fits some but not all of the premise combinations they have considered (Chapman & Chapman, 1959; Dickstein, 1978). In effect, people sometimes fail to completely comprehend the meaning of "logically necessary." Second, people sometimes make an error quite similar to premise conversion; Dickstein (1978) has called this tendency "conclusion conversion." The premises may logically allow a conclusion only in one direction, for example, "Some A are C," but people may erroneously conclude that the converse, "Some C are A," is also acceptable.

We have, implicitly, been presenting a view of syllogistic reasoning in which a person first interprets each premise, then forms a partial or complete set of premise pairings, and finally evaluates conclusions against the combinations generated. This notion is a bit too neat. Johnson-Laird and Steedman (1978) have proposed that people might produce a plausible, tentative conclusion based on a preferred or most-plausible premise pairing; to reach a correct conclusion, a tentative conclusion must then be tested to see if it can be invalidated by any combination of the premises. This test might be incorrectly or inadequately carried out; indeed, Helsabeck (1975) found that people have considerable difficulty with generating counter-examples to a stated conclusion.

Belief-Bias Effect.

The question we will now consider concerns the effect on reasoning of using abstract versus meaningful materials (a question we will encounter again, later in this chapter). With respect to syllogistic reasoning, two broad effects have been obtained when syllogisms contain meaningful statements which tap a person's knowledge of the world. As mentioned previously, meaningful statements can block conversion of premises, for example, people do *not* interpret "All cats are animals" to also mean that "All animals are cats." Consequently, logical errors stemming from premise conversion may be avoided. The second influence is the belief-bias effect.

Many researchers have reported that people may evaluate meaningful conclusions to syllogisms on the basis of their beliefs rather than through logical analysis (for example, Henle, 1962). In simple terms, it is proposed that people will accept conclusions that conform to their beliefs and reject conclusions inconsistent with their beliefs, regardless of the logical status of the conclusion. This view is quite widely held, although some researchers disagree (Revlin, Leirer, Yopp, & Yopp, 1980).

A study by Evans, Barston, and Pollard (1983) provides clarifying information. These researchers gave people complete syllogisms (two premises and a conclusion), asking them to decide whether or not the conclusion followed from the premises. The conclusions were either quite believable (for example, "Some good ice skaters are not professional hockey players") or rather unbelievable ("Some professional hockey players are not good ice skaters"), and were either valid or invalid conclusions, given the premises. Results indicated that belief-bias had a greater effect with invalid syllogisms. That is, people were more likely to accept a believable-but-invalid conclusion than they were to reject an unbelievable-but-valid conclusion. Evans and co-workers (1983) suggested that the results reflect the fact that people face a conflict between logic and belief when working on the syllogisms. For valid-but-unbelievable conclusions, the premises dictate that the conclusion should be accepted, but the conclusion itself is hard to believe. For believable-but-invalid conclusions, logic poses less of a conflict; that is, the conclusion, although not a necessary derivation from the premises, is *not* contradicted by the premises either. The conclusion is "possibly true" (not necessarily true) and, since it is a very believable statement, people tend to accept it. Based on data obtained by having people think aloud while working on the syllogisms, Evans and co-workers found that this account applies best when people try to reason from the premises to the conclusion. This approach is fundamentally logical and thus leads people to the belief-versus-logic conflict, especially with valid-but-unbelievable conclusions. When people focus primarily on the conclusion itself, their responses are largely based on beliefs—believable conclusions are accepted and unbelievable conclusions rejected. On the whole, the findings show that a belief-bias effect exists, although in several different forms. People may face conflict between logic and what they believe about the world, which will make reasoning with meaningful material different from that seen with abstract material.

Testing Statements for Truth

Syllogistic reasoning tasks emphasize the internal consistency of an argument. The person is asked to assume that the premises are true when determining whether or not a conclusion follows logically from the premises. A different but interesting question concerns how people (should) use evidence to determine whether a particular statement is in fact true or false. Most research on this question has employed conditional (if . . . , then . . .) sentences, as well as a selection task in which the person is asked to specify which of a number of items must be tested to find out if the proposition is true or false. Figure 9–6 presents a sample selection task; it will be worthwhile to try this task before reading further.

Figure 9–6. A selection task for testing propositions.

A Selection Task for Testing Propositions

"Assume that each of the boxes below represents a card lying on a table. Each card has a letter on one side and a number on the other side. Consequently, the card with "5" showing has some letter on the other side (which you cannot see) as does the card with "4" showing, while the card with "A" showing and that with "K" showing each has some number on the other side. Here is a rule which might apply to the cards: IF A CARD HAS A VOWEL ON ITS LETTER SIDE, THEN IT HAS AN EVEN NUMBER ON ITS NUMBER SIDE. Your task is to indicate which of the cards you need to turn over in order to find out whether the rule is true or false. Which card or cards would you select?"

Table 9-3 Truth table for a conditional statement.
General form: "If _p_, then _q_." Example: "If vowel, then even number."

POSSIBILITIES		TRUTH VALUE
General	_Example_	
pq	vowel, even number	TRUE
$p\bar{q}$	vowel, not even number (vowel, odd number)	FALSE
$\bar{p}q$	not vowel, even number (consonant, even number)	TRUE
$\bar{p}\bar{q}$	not vowel, not even number (consonant, odd number)	TRUE

To understand the answer to this problem, we must consider the meaning of the rule to be tested and the truth values it assigns to different possibilities. In short form, the sample rule is "If vowel, then even number," which is a particular example of the general form of conditional sentences "If P, then Q." Table 9–3 shows the truth table for conditional statements, according to formal logic. As shown in Table 9–3, a conditional statement implies that only one kind of instance is false (does not exist), P$\bar{\text{Q}}$, or a card with a vowel and an odd number in our example. Any other combination of P or $\bar{\text{P}}$ (vowel or consonant) with Q or $\bar{\text{Q}}$ (even or odd number) is consistent with the rule.

Let us now consider the four cards in Figure 9–6 with respect to the rule, from a logical viewpoint. The card with "A" showing must be examined; if it has a vowel on the other side, this would confirm the rule, but if it has an odd number, that would disprove the rule (In symbolic terms, the issue is whether this P card is a PQ or P$\bar{\text{Q}}$ instance). The card with "K" showing can provide no useful information—it makes no difference whether there is an odd or even number on the other side (K corresponds to $\bar{\text{P}}$; as shown in Table 9–3, both $\bar{\text{P}}$Q and $\bar{\text{P}}\bar{\text{Q}}$ are true in logic). Similarly, the card with "4" showing is not crucial; "4" corresponds to Q, and both PQ and $\bar{\text{P}}$Q instances are consistent with the rule. In contrast, the card with "5" showing is critical because it would falsify the rule if it has a vowel on the other side (the issue is whether this $\bar{\text{Q}}$ card is a P$\bar{\text{Q}}$ or $\bar{\text{P}}\bar{\text{Q}}$ instance). Thus, the logically correct answer is that the "A" and "5" cards (in general, the P and $\bar{\text{Q}}$ cases) must be examined.

When people are given the selection task with abstract, arbitrary materials like those in our example, only about 10 percent or fewer make the correct selections. About 50 percent of subjects say they would turn over the "A" and "4" cards (P and Q), about 35 percent select just the "A" card (P only), with the rest making a variety of other choices. What is most striking is that very few people propose examining the "5" card ($\bar{\text{Q}}$), which must be examined (Johnson-Laird & Wason, 1970).

There are many problems associated with the use of conditional sentences. People may convert the conditional sentence, interpreting "If P, then Q" to also mean that "If Q, then P" (Taplin & Staudenmayer, 1973). This behavior is identical to premise conversion in syllogistic reasoning (interpreting "All A are B" to also mean "All B are A"); however, conversion occurs less often with "If, then" statements than with "All" or "Some" statements. People may fail to comprehend the conditional rule and the nature of the task, merely naming as their "selections" the terms mentioned in the rule; such alogical behavior may be most likely when abstract materials are used (Evans, 1972; Reich & Ruth, 1982). When conditional sentences have meaningful content, the nature of that content affects how people interpret them; also, conditional statements are not interpreted in the same way as other, logically equivalent, statements (Evans, 1977; Roberge, 1982). All of these factors can affect how people interpret conditional sentences and thus may influence performance when people are asked to indicate how they would test a statement. Notice that none of the above factors tells us anything about how people use evidence to decide whether a statement is factually true or false. Despite the problems which stem from the factors mentioned above, research on testing conditional statements has generated two broad issues, to which we will turn our attention.

Assume that we are dealing with an "If P, then Q" statement. To make discussion simpler, we will ignore "not-P" instances ($\overline{P}Q$ and $\overline{PQ}$); logically, there is no need to test "not-P" instances, and many people consider $\overline{P}Q$ and $\overline{PQ}$ to be irrelevant (Wason & Johnson-Laird, 1972). The critical instances are thus PQ and $P\overline{Q}$; PQ instances confirm the rule, whereas any $P\overline{Q}$ instance disproves the rule. Logic states that it is impossible to prove that an "If P, then Q" rule is true by observing a finite number of PQ instances. However, just a single $P\overline{Q}$ instance proves the rule is false. For example, suppose you are testing the statement "If a female bird has spots on her feathers, then her eggs have spotted shells." The logical point is that, no matter how many spotted-birds-who-lay-spotted-eggs you have observed, that does not prove that the rule is necessarily true—there still might be, somewhere, not yet observed by you, a spotted bird who lays non-spotted eggs. However, if you see just one spotted bird that lays non-spotted eggs, that does prove that the rule is false. Logic thus stresses the importance of evidence that falsifies a statement. Let us now relate this to performance on the selection task.

Given the rule "If vowel, then even number," cards with a vowel/even number combination (PQ) are confirming instances, whereas cards with a vowel/odd number combination ($P\overline{Q}$) disprove the rule. Emphasis on falsification suggests that the appropriate behavior is to seek potentially-falsifying instances; in other words, check the vowel (P) card because it could be ($P\overline{Q}$) and check the consonant ($\overline{Q}$) card for the same reason—it could be a ($P\overline{Q}$) instance. As noted earlier, the initial research with the selection task indicated that very few people check the $\overline{Q}$ card, whereas people frequently check the P card and the Q card. The explanation of such behavior was roughly that people tend to seek confirming evidence and fail to appreciate the value of falsifying evidence. Notice that one could obtain a confirming (PQ) instance from the P card and from the Q card; the $\overline{Q}$ card could provide only a falsifying ($P\overline{Q}$) instance. It is primarily the finding of a general tendency to avoid checking the Q card that has led to the notion that people have a "confirmation bias" (Wason & Johnson-Laird, 1972). We will consider this idea in greater detail shortly.

The second finding stemming from research may be termed the "realism effect." Wason and Shapiro (1971) gave British subjects a version of the four-card task using what they called "thematic materials." Each card referred to a journey, having a city on one side and a mode of transportation on the other, and the rule to be tested concerned how journeys were made—for example "Every time I go to Manchester I travel by train." Presented with cards showing "Manchester," "Leeds," "train," and "card," 62 percent of the subjects made the correct choice of the P card and the $\overline{Q}$ card ("Manchester," "car"). This was substantially better performance than that observed with the abstract version of the task (about 10 percent correct), leading to the idea that people reason better when testing realistic statements. We will now discuss this idea.

REALISM EFFECT

If people reason better with realistic rather than abstract materials, why might this be so? One proposal is that people are capable of reasoning properly but are prevented from doing so when abstract materials are used, for various reasons (Wason & Johnson-Laird, 1972). If this proposal is accurate, then the relatively good performance with realistic materials, and not the very poor performance with abstract materials, indicates the "true level" of people's reasoning abilities. Later research, however, has shown that there are serious problems with this proposal.

Although there have been reports of very good performance on realistic versions of the four-card task (Van Duyne, 1974), several researchers have found little or no difference in performance between abstract and more realistic versions of the task (Gilhooly & Falconer, 1974; Manktelow & Evans, 1979). A possible resolution to this confusing pattern of results has been offered by Griggs and Cox (Cox & Griggs, 1982). They propose a "memory-cuing hypothesis" which states that people will be likely to make correct selections when (1) the rule to be tested is familiar to them and (2) they have had experience with violations (counter-examples) of the rule. For example, American college students did poorly with the "journeys" version of the task (with which they presumably had little or no experience) but made a high percentage of correct selections with a "drinking-age-rule" version (which was the law in their state and for which virtually all subjects could remember experiencing violations). The implication of this hypothesis is that, when and if people perform better with a realistic version of the selection task, it is *not* because they more thoroughly analyze the conditional statement and the possible implications of each card, but rather because they already know what to check. It seems likely that there will be continued debate about what is involved in the elusive "realism effect." Quite clearly, it is *not* correct to state simply that "people will reason better with realistic materials."

CONFIRMATION BIAS

With the selection task, a common finding is that people fail to test the $\overline{Q}$ card but do test the P card and the (unnecessary) Q card. These tendencies, especially the failure to test the $\overline{Q}$ card, have been attributed to a "confirmation bias"—a desire for confirming evidence and a failure to appreciate contradictory evidence. Behavior consistent with a confirmation bias has been observed with a number of "realistic" versions of the task (Krauth, 1982; Reich & Ruth, 1982). Indeed, the idea of confirmation bias has been proposed in regard to behavior in a variety of tasks. For example, confirmation bias has been suggested as one possible reason why people fail to consider all premise combinations in syllogistic reasoning. Having generated one conclusion that is consistent with the premises, people may cease processing and accept the possible, but not logically necessary conclusion (Dominowski, 1977). As mentioned in the previous section, people find it difficult to generate counterexamples to a given conclusion (Helsabeck, 1975). When testing their own hypotheses in concept-learning tasks, people tend to behave as if their current hypothesis is likely to be correct, to prefer direct tests of their hypotheses, and to accept their hypotheses as correct after a relatively small number of confirmations, even though other hypotheses are still tenable (Taplin, 1975; Wetherick & Dominowski, 1976).

In several studies (Wason, 1968), people were given the task of discovering a rule which applied to three-digit series. To start, they were told that the series 2 4 6 conforms to the rule to be discovered; people were to propose additional series with the experimenter indicating whether each did or did not conform to the rule. An important point is that the unknown rule was very general—"numbers in increasing order of magnitude." There are many, more specific rules yielding positive instances that will also be positive instances of the general rule; for example, any series that fits "numbers increasing by 2," or any that fits "the second number is twice the first, and the third 1½ times the second" will also conform to the general rule.

When given this task, people typically formulated a more specific rule as a hypothesis, say, "numbers increasing by 2." The interesting finding was that people proposed series that were consistent with their hypothesized rules. For example, given the hypothesis "numbers increasing by 2," a person might propose 4 6 8, 10 12 14, 24 26 28, 7 9 11, and so on. Each series conformed to the hypothesis "numbers increasing by 2" and also conformed to the experimenter's rule "numbers in increasing order of magnitude"; therefore, the experimenter would indicate that each series conformed to the rule to be discovered. The typical result was that people became increasingly convinced that their limited hypotheses were correct, even to the point that some became quite upset when they offered their hypotheses as the solution and were told that they were wrong.

Wason argued that people went about this task by seeking direct confirmations of their hypotheses (as illustrated above) and that this is the wrong way to do the task. A person needs to propose a series inconsistent with the limited hypothesis in order to find out that the limited hypothesis is wrong. For example, proposing 5 6 7, which is inconsistent with "increasing by 2", and finding out that it *does* conform to the rule to be discovered is what allows a person to learn that "increasing by 2" is not the answer. As Wason pointed out, a person could discover the (general) rule by seeking falsification of a current hypothesis (proposing counter-examples) but not by seeking confirmations (proposing consistent examples).

Related observations were obtained by Mynatt, Doherty, and Tweney (1977, 1978) using a much more complicated task involving an artificial universe. Subjects viewed a video screen containing varying numbers of shapes (squares, triangles, and so on) of different brightnesses and could "fire particles" on the screen to see what would happen to them. The task was to discover the "law of the universe" governing the motion of the particles. Each screen-view represented a sample of the total universe; thus, different screen-views had different combinations of shapes in them. In one version of the task, the "law" was that very bright shapes had (invisible) circular boundaries some distance from their centers, and a particle would stop when it "hit" a boundary. However, the first few trials (views) were arranged to encourage people to adopt the hypothesis "triangles have boundaries" because the researchers were interested in what people would do once they had adopted this incorrect hypothesis.

Subjects who initially adopted the "triangle hypothesis" tended to prefer direct tests of the hypothesis. Given the choice of conducting a test (firing a particle) in a sample containing a triangle or one without a triangle, they chose the sample with a triangle most of the time. In general, people showed little interest in testing alternatives to the hypothesis they had under consideration. If, however, they did encounter falsifying evidence (for the triangle hypothesis), people typically made use of this information and modified their hypotheses. A summary of the results of the first study (Mynatt et al., 1977) is that people tended to consider only one hypothesis at a time and to seek evidence in such a way that they were more likely to obtain confirmatory evidence rather than falsifying evidence, although they did reject their hypotheses when (if) falsifying evidence was encountered. In the second study, where a much more complex "universe" was used, the major difference in the finding was that, with greater complexity, there was a greater chance that people would keep and retest a hypothesis after falsifying evidence had occurred (Mynatt et al., 1978). The researchers suggested that this tendency was due to the extreme complexity of the task—specifically, to the difficulty of generating new, plausible hypotheses. It is also possible that people misinterpreted evidence, again because of the complexity of the system.

These findings suggest that it is worthwhile to separate how people seek evidence from how they use falsifying evidence. People do not directly seek contradictory evidence—they tend not to test "universe samples" that could only provide contradictory evidence or to check the $\overline{Q}$ card. Rather, they prefer direct tests of hypotheses, seek some confirmation, and generally test propositions such that confirmations are more likely to occur than falsifications. There is thus a confirmation bias with respect to information-seeking. But there are results showing that people do make proper use of falsifying evidence, abandoning a hypothesis when contrary evidence occurs (less so in difficult situations). This pattern of behavior is not completely inappropriate—it may be fairly reasonable. Wetherick (1970) has argued that we need to know "what might be correct," not just what is wrong; from this viewpoint, we should not seek only falsifying evidence since observing some confirmations of a proposed rule make it worth considering. In addition, direct tests of hypotheses can yield falsifying evidence. If testing a statement of the form "If P, then Q", a check of P's to see if they are Q or $\overline{Q}$ can lead to observing $P\overline{Q}$ if such falsifying instances exist. For a more concrete example, testing the "triangle hypotheses" by consistently firing particles at triangles can result in observing that a triangle does not stop a particle. It is clearly a mistake to ignore or misinterpret falsifying evidence. However, it appears that the main danger with a confirmation bias for seeking evidence is that an encounter with contradictory evidence might be delayed. The danger would be most serious if, on the basis of a number of confirmations, a person concluded that a wrong hypothesis was correct and stopped seeking evidence. This is precisely what happened in Wason's (1968) research on rules for number series (where a subject had to directly seek falsifying evidence in order to observe it); in Mynatt and co-workers' (1977) study, people could encounter falsifying evidence despite a confirmation-seeking bias, and they generally made proper use of contradictions. This suggests that the danger with a confirmation-seeking bias depends on the nature of the rule and the environment in which evidence is obtained, in a fashion that remains to be precisely determined.

Inferences About Uncertainty

Syllogistic reasoning and statement testing concern absolute standards. A conclusion either does or does not follow logically from the premises, and a statement must be judged as either true or false. In contrast, much of the information we deal with is uncertain, more or less correct. The normative standards for processing uncertain information come from mathematics, namely probability theory and statistics. In essence, the correct answers to problems involving uncertainty are determined via mathematical formulas. Two broad research questions arise: To what extent do human judgments agree with answers derived from mathematical theory and formulas? How do people go about making judgments about uncertainty? Although earlier research suggested that people are fairly good "intuitive statisticians" (Peterson & Beach, 1967), later studies have shown that human judgments frequently deviate markedly from formally-derived answers. These studies have led to the identification of heuristics (rules of thumb) that people use to make judgments about uncertainty. We will discuss some of this research with respect to the tasks of making probability judgments and estimating statistical relatedness.

PROBABILITY JUDGMENTS

Probabilities are numbers ranging from zero to one; a probability of zero ($p = .00$) means that the event is impossible whereas a probability of one ($p = 1.00$) means that the event is certain to occur. Probabilities between the two extremes apply to things that are more or less likely to happen. Normative, objective probabilities are based on the analysis of a well-specified source of events. For example, if a deck of 52 cards contains 13 spades, then the probability of randomly selecting a spade from the deck is 13/52 or .25. A note on the word "randomly"—probability theory assumes that events are produced by a process yielding uncertainty about the outcome. For example, the answer to the card-deck problem above is based on the assumption that a card is selected from the deck by a process such that every card in the deck is equally likely to be chosen. Clearly, if one looked at the cards' suits before selecting, the "probability" of getting a spade would be quite different. The central point is that objective probabilities are based on formal models assuming a well-specified source and an appropriate (random) process for generating events from that source. Research seeks to relate people's probability judgments, or subjective probabilities, to the objective probabilities.

There are many reasons why human judgments may not correspond to answers derived from probability theory. To start, probability theory is a highly abstract and difficult body of knowledge, and there are still unresolved issues regarding some of its essential concepts (see Lopes, 1982). Even for sophisticated individuals, determining how to calculate the answer to some probability problems can be troublesome (Bar-Hillel & Falk, 1982). There may be aspects of the methods used to collect research data—the way in which problems are phrased, the kinds of responses required, for example—that could produce somewhat distorted information about people's statistical intuitions (Kahneman & Tversky, 1982a). In addition, there are many different meanings of "uncertainty" in everyday life and natural language, with the variations relating differently to formal probability-theory concepts. For example, we distinguish between internal and external uncertainty (Kahneman & Tversky, 1982b); compare "I'm not sure if my old car will start on cold winter mornings" (external), with "I'm not sure if London is the capital of England" (internal). We will return to some of these issues in the discussion to follow.

Probability or Frequency?   In formal terms, a probability is a proportionate frequency; the probability of (randomly selecting) a spade equals the number of spades in the deck (13) divided by the total number of cards in the deck (52), = .25. If there are 12 girls and 9 boys in a classroom, then

$$p \text{ (girl)} = \frac{12}{12 + 9} = \frac{12}{21} = 0.57$$

for random selection. There is, however, evidence that in some circumstances people base supposedly probabilistic judgments not on probabilities but on frequencies. In a series of experiments by Estes (1976), people received information regarding the outcomes of a series of (imaginary) opinion polls. Each poll involved a comparison of two alternatives (two products, two political candidates, and so on), with one of the two winning the poll. The subjects were shown poll results involving different comparisons, one at a time, after which they were asked to make predictions concerning future poll results. The critical predictions concerned alternatives which had not been previously compared and which had different win/loss histories. For example, people were asked to predict which product, A or C, would "win" if they were placed in contrast for a poll. Product A had appeared in 6 polls, winning 5, whereas product C had appeared in 18 polls, winning 9, but subjects had never seen a poll comparing A and C.

If people based their predictions on a comparison of the products' probabilities of winning (using past performance), they would predict that product A would win because product A's proportion of wins is 0.83 (5/6 = .83) whereas product C's proportion is only 0.50 (9/18 = .50). However, subjects' dominant prediction was that product C would win! In general, Estes found that people based their predictions on an alternative's frequency of wins rather than on an alternative's probability of winning. Although it has proved possible to direct subjects' attention to the number of losses (Estes, 1976), and to encourage people to consider the quality of opposition (a win against a "strong opponent" counts more; Neely, 1982), it remains the case that judgments reflect relative frequencies rather than relative probabilities. The implication is that people's intuitions about probabilities for various events will be accurate only if the events have had roughly equal opportunities to occur; in this case, frequency differences and probability differences are highly related. As Estes (1976) remarked, a driver might have an accurate impression of the relative frequencies of accidents on a through-street and a side-street, but have a distorted view of the relative probabilities of an accident occurring because of failure to consider that there are more opportunities for accidents to occur on the through-street.

Representativeness.   Probability theory provides rules for combining probabilities. For example, the *conjunctive rule* states that, given two events A and B, with probabilities p (A) and p (B), the probability of A and B occurring together, p (A&B) cannot be larger than the smaller of the two individual probabilities. If, in a given population, the probability of being Chinese is 0.30 and the probability of being married is .60, the probability of being Chinese *and* married cannot be larger than 0.30. However, under some circumstances, people overwhelmingly make a "conjunctive error," stating that the conjunction is more probable than one of the parts. Kahneman and Tversky (1982a) provide an example: People were given personality sketches like the following:

> Linda is 31 years old, single, outspoken, and very bright. She majored in philosophy. As a student, she was deeply concerned with issues of discrimination and social justice, and also participated in anti-nuclear demonstrations. (Kahneman & Tversky, 1982a, p. 126)

They were then asked which statement about Linda was more probable—that she is a bank teller, or that she is a bank teller who is an active feminist. Over 80 percent of college students chose the second (conjunctive) statement as more likely; objectively, it is not possible for this to be correct. Why did they make this erroneous choice? Apparently because the personality sketch resembled their idea of a feminist bank teller more than their idea of (just) a bank teller. This illustrates use of a representativeness heuristic—judging "probabilities" by the degree to which evidence and outcomes have similar features (Kahneman & Tversky, 1973).

One of the consequences of using a representativeness heuristic is failure to consider "base rates." A formula known as Bayes' theorem provides the probability-theory answer for problems involving hypotheses and observations. The general sense of Bayes' theorem is that the probability that some hypothesis is correct *after* an observation occurs depends on (a) the probability that the hypothesis was correct *before* the observation was made; (b) the probability that the observation would be expected to occur if the hypothesis were correct, and (c) the probability that the observation would be expected to occur if any other hypothesis were correct. The first of these—the *a priori* (before-the-fact) probability that the hypothesis is correct—is the critical base rate. We need not go into the details of Bayes' theorem; rather, here is a sample problem to which it applies:

> It is known that 5 percent of the population is afflicted with the disease rubadubitis. A new diagnostic test has been developed which is rather good. If a person has rubadubitis, the test gives a positive result 85 percent of the time. If a person does *not* have the disease, there is only a 10 percent chance of getting a positive test result from the test. All in all, a pretty good test. Here's the situation: The test has just been given to John Doe and the test result is positive. What is the probability that John has rubadubitis?

Most people say that, given the test result, there is about an 85 percent chance that John has the disease, thinking the odds to be about 6 to 1 in favor of the disease. However, application of Bayes' theorem indicates that after the test result, the probability that John has the disease is only .31—the odds are about 2 to 1 that John does *not* have rubadubitis! The large errors people usually make result from ignoring the base rate—the fact that the disease occurs very infrequently in the population (see for example, Hammerton, 1973; Kahneman & Tversky, 1972).

To make this point clear, let us consider some numbers (in doing so, we will arrive at the Bayesian answer, although without showing the formula). Suppose the population consists of 10,000 people. Since 5 percent have the disease, this means that 500 people have rubadubitis and 9500 do not. Of the 500 afflicted individuals, 85 percent or 425 will yield positive test results, while 10 percent or 950 of the 9500 *non-diseased* people will also have positive test results. For the whole population, there would be 1375 positive test results (425 + 950 = 1375), and only 425 or 31 percent would come from people who actually have the disease.

Of course, one could learn to use Bayes' theorem to calculate answers to problems like that presented above (a good idea!). The point, however, is that when people do not calculate but rather make judgments, they often reach substantially inaccurate answers. The positive test result is psychologically very compelling; a person with a positive test result appears quite representative of the diseased part of the population, leading people to be quite sure that the disease is present. What they are ignoring is that the disease occurs very infrequently, that there will be many "false positives" (positive test results from non-diseased individuals). Research suggests that, when people are given descriptive information about an individual (for example, a test result or personality sketch) they will ignore base rates and judge probabilities on the basis of the representativeness of the individual information for various outcomes (Kahneman & Tversky, 1973). Although there has been some success in identifying conditions that lead people to make greater use of base rates—and thus less use of representativeness (for example, Christensen-Szalanski & Beach, 1982; Tversky & Kahneman, 1980)—the increase in judgmental accuracy has been relatively modest.

Judgment via representativeness occurs in other situations as well. Probability theory indicates that the larger a sample is, the more likely it will resemble the characteristics of the population from which it was drawn. In contrast, people tend to expect even very small samples to be very good representatives of the population, leading them to erroneously overinterpret small samples of information (Tversky & Kahneman, 1971). If told that a sample has been randomly selected, people expect the sample to "look random," having no obvious pattern, having an "appropriate" amount of irregularity or variability (Bar-Hillel, 1980; Kahneman & Tversky, 1972). Such erroneous beliefs about the representativeness of small samples may often be harmless in everyday life, but they can cause difficulties. They underlie the "gambler's fallacy," the belief that "things will self-correct" in the very short run. For a very simple example, if a coin has been tossed twice and produced "tails" both times, the gambler's fallacy would be the belief that there is a better than 50 percent chance that the coin will fall "heads" the third time it is tossed (there is not). Thinking that the next toss "just has to be heads" so that the mini-series of three tosses gets closer to half-heads, half-tails is an excellent way to lose money.

For a different example of a problem that could stem from belief in the representativeness of small samples, consider the following: Suppose that three students must be chosen from a class of eighteen males and twelve females for something pleasant—they will get out of school early or gain some other desirable outcome. The teacher tells the class that the three students have been randomly selected and announces who they are: two females and one male. The whole class is 60 percent males, but the chosen sample has more females. Belief in small-sample representativeness could lead to thinking that the students were not chosen randomly, that the teacher used some biased method, and that the teacher also lied to the students. In fact, randomly drawing samples of three from an eighteen male, twelve female "population" would yield samples with two females and one male about one-third of the time. The outcome is hardly unusual, but it could be difficult to explain this fact to one who erroneously believes that small samples should resemble the population.

Availability.   Judgments of probabilities may be made on the basis of how easily relevant information comes to mind. For example, Tversky and Kahneman (1973) asked people whether the letter K is more likely to occur in the first or third position in English words. By a two-to-one ratio, people said that the first position was more likely, although the opposite is in fact correct. Because of the nature of our word knowledge, it is easier to think of words based on a first letter than on a third letter. Therefore, the explanation of this result in terms of the availability heuristic is that, when asked the question, people tried to think of words starting with K and words having K as the third letter. They could more easily think of words starting with K (or could think of more of them), so they judged that K occurs more often in the first position. This example illustrates that one influence on availability, and thus an influence on probability judgments, is the nature of organization of a person's memory. In principle, one might expect that many other factors which can affect the memorability of information would also affect availability and there-fore probability judgments. There is evidence indicating that this is so.

Tversky and Kahneman (1973) presented subjects with recorded lists of names of public personalities—movie stars, politicians, and so on. Each list had equal numbers of male and female names, but the lists were constructed so that, in one list, the female names were more famous, and in the other the male names. Famous names are easier to remember, so, if people judged the relative frequencies of male and female names in a list on the basis of which names they could recall (avail-ability), they would judge whichever class had more famous names to have been larger. This is precisely what happened, to an overwhelming degree.

In another study, people were asked to judge death rates in the United States from various causes (Lichtenstein, Slovic, Fischhoff, Layman, & Combs, 1978). The researchers obtained evidence showing that the judgments were biased by factors such as disproportionate media coverage, memorability of specific instances, and how easily one could imagine a person dying from a particular cause. For example, college students judged death by tornado to be more frequent than death from asthma (in fact, the latter is twenty times more likely), which can be attributed to the intense media coverage of tornadoes and to the ease with which one can im-agine a person dying in a tornado, among other factors.

As Shanteau (1978) has pointed out, people do not have direct knowledge of official death rate statistics, or of many other facts about which they might be asked to make judgments. Under such circumstances, people may have no real alterna-tive to basing their judgments on availability—the kinds of information they can generate from what they do know. This idea is consistent with the finding that tell-ing people about the possible influence of media coverage, imaginability, and so on, had no effect on their estimates of death rates (Lichtenstein et al., 1978).

When people have information available that seems relevant to making a proba-bility judgment, they find it very difficult to ignore it, as illustrated by the "knew-it-all-along effect." This refers to the finding that, once people know that a particular outcome has occurred, they are inclined to believe that they would have predicted it to happen. In one study (Fischhoff, 1975), people were given background informa-tion about an historical event—a battle between two armies—and were asked to estimate the likelihoods of various outcomes such as a victory for one or the other side, or a military stalemate with or without a political solution. These are before-the-fact judgments. If, however, people were also told a particular outcome, their estimates of the predictability of that outcome were quite different, namely, higher. For example, people getting just the background information might estimate that there was one chance in three that side A would win. Those also told that side A won would estimate that the background information allowed a prediction of better than one chance in two that side A would win.

The knew-it-all-along effect has been obtained with different kinds of materials (historical events, personal stories, answers to obscure questions) and with different methodologies. Knowledge of an outcome biases people's judgments of what their own or others' estimates would be without outcome knowledge (Fischhoff, 1975; Slovic & Fischhoff, 1977; Wood, 1978). Outcome knowledge becomes integrated with a person's other knowledge of the situation and is subsequently difficult to separate out. Consequently, telling people to ignore outcome knowledge has little impact on the knew-it-all-along effect (Fischhoff, 1977).

Confidence.   When people make statements or answer questions, their confidence in the accuracy of what they say can range from "just a guess" to certainty. A question which arises is how well differences in accuracy are related to differences in confidence. The concept of *calibration* refers to the degree of agreement between "percent accuracy" and "percent confidence." A person would be perfectly calibrated if, throughout the range, these two percentages matched; that is, the person is correct 60 percent of the time for answers about which he or she is "60 percent sure," correct 80 percent of the time for "80 percent sure" statements, and so on. Research on confidence and accuracy has shown two things: First, in a general sense, confidence and accuracy are reasonably related, that is, people are generally more accurate about answers in which they have more confidence. Second, people are far from perfectly calibrated. Most noticeably, people exhibit overconfidence at the high end of the scale, being more confident than the accuracy of their answers warrants (Lichtenstein & Fischhoff, 1977). For answers about which people are certain (100 percent confidence), they are correct about 80 percent of the time (Fischhoff, Slovic, & Lichtenstein, 1977).

A feeling of confidence can be considered an essentially unanalyzed experience (Kahneman & Tversky, 1982b). There are thus two possible reasons for people appearing to be overconfident: They may have fundamentally inappropriate confidence, or they may have difficulty translating feelings of confidence into public expressions. There is evidence suggesting that people can have difficulty translating feelings of confidence into public expressions of confidence (Lichtenstein & Fischhoff, 1977), although data suggesting overconfidence have been obtained with different response schemes (Fischhoff et al., 1977). More important, there are findings indicating that people are overconfident because of incomplete analyses. Koriat, Lichtenstein, and Fischhoff (1980) had people choose their answers to difficult questions and list reasons for and against both the chosen answer and the rejected answer. They found that people focused on reasons supporting their chosen answers. Encouraging people to consider reasons against their answers resulted in more appropriate confidence levels. This phenomenon is similar to the finding, in syllogistic reasoning, that people tend to accept logically-invalid conclusions due to failure to consider alternative conclusions and to difficulty in generating contradictions to a preferred conclusion.

ESTIMATING RELATEDNESS

Understanding "what is related to what" is an important part of our knowledge of the world. As Crocker (1982) put it, "Knowing whether events are related, and how strongly they are related, enables individuals to explain the past, control the present, and predict the future" (p. 272). Research has been concerned with the question of how people estimate relatedness and how accurate their judgments are. Most relations that we encounter are imperfect, that is, there is error or uncertainty involved. For example, the heights of parents and their children are related—taller parents tend to have taller children, shorter parents tend to have shorter children—but knowing a parent's height would not enable you to predict the child's height without error.

The formal method for indexing relations or associations is to compute a correlation coefficient. Various formulas exist, but regardless of the particular formula, correlation coefficients range from $+1$ to -1, with zero an important mid-point. A correlation of zero means that two variables are simply unrelated to each other. For example, people vary in terms of how fast they can type and how much they like donuts, but these two things are not related. Knowing that a person likes donuts very much does not help predict his or her typing speed, and knowing that a person types slowly does not help predict that person's attitude toward donuts. When an association does exist, it might be positive or negative. For positive correlations, the general pattern may be described as high with high, low with low; for example, height and weight are positively correlated—taller people tend to be heavier, lighter people tend to be shorter. If the general pattern is reversed pairings—high with low, low with high—the correlation is negative. If a number of people had been drinking (varying amounts) at a party and then tried to perform a task requiring good motor coordination, you might well find that the more they had drunk, the lower their accuracy would be—a negative relation between amount of alcohol consumed and accuracy of motor performance. The sign of a correlation ($+$ or $-$) indicates what kind of relation exists, whereas the strength of the relation is indexed by the numerical value—the further from zero (which means no relation) and the closer to one (which means a perfect, error-free relation), the stronger is the relation. Thus, correlations of $+.2$, $+.4$, $-.6$, $+.8$ represent increasing strengths of association.

In research on this topic, people are shown some data—pairings of values on two variables—and asked to estimate the relation between the variables. A correlation coefficient can be calculated from the data and serves as the standard or correct answer. Table 9–4 shows some illustrative data concerning the relation between a hypothetical test result and a hypothetical disease. In reading the table, note that the number in each cell is a frequency count; in panel A the information is that there were 8 "yes-yes" pairs, 10 "no-no" pairs, and so on.

There are many reasons why people's intuitions about correlations might not agree with calculations using statistical formulas. One influence is memory, which we can illustrate with the data in panel A of Table 9–4. That panel tells us the frequency for every type of pairing. But suppose that a deck of cards were constructed,

Table 9-4. *Hypothetical data regarding a test result (positive or negative) and the presence or absence of a disease*

A			DISEASE PRESENT?		
			YES	NO	
		YES	8	4	
	POSITIVE TEST RESULT?				(correlation = +.33)
		NO	5	10	
B			DISEASE PRESENT?		
			YES	NO	
		YES	3	12	
	POSITIVE TEST RESULT?				(correlation = −.31)
		NO	10	10	
C			DISEASE PRESENT?		
			YES	NO	
		YES	15	5	
	POSITIVE TEST RESULT?				(correlation = .00)
		NO	9	3	

Note. Each entry is the number of times a test result/disease state combination has been observed. For example, in panel A, there were 8 cases of positive test result and disease present.

each card corresponding to a case or pairing, with the deck formed to match the frequencies in panel A (8 "yes-yes" cards, and so on). The deck is shuffled and then people are shown the deck, one card at a time, with no opportunity to make notes; under these conditions, people will get the frequency information contained in panel A but the manner in which they will receive it places considerable demands on their memories. Under memory-load conditions, people make errors in recalling the frequencies of different pairings (Shaklee & Mims, 1982). Even before making any judgment of relatedness, memory weaknesses leave people with inaccurate ideas of event frequencies. Shaklee and Mims note that, in everyday life, we do not get information about relations in nice, neat tables or even from (something equivalent to) flipping through decks of cards arranged to present data regarding just one possible association. Rather, we observe pairings distributed over time in the presence of a considerable amount of "noise"—information not relevant to a particular relation. Because of memory-load problems alone, we would expect people to have inaccurate impressions of the frequencies of various events, which will make it extremely difficult for them to make an accurate judgment of relatedness.

Even if given data in tabular form, thus eliminating problems of encoding and remembering event frequencies, people often make inaccurate judgments of relatedness. For many people who are not trained in statistics, the intuitive conception of correlation is different from what statistics dictates (Crocker, 1981). We will use Table 9–4 to discuss this issue, beginning with panel A. The correlation for these data is +.33, a modest positive correlation, which in this instance means that there is a tendency for the disease to be more likely with a positive test result than with a negative test result. The statistically-appropriate strategy requires using all four cells of the panel and comparing two probabilities or proportionate frequencies. For panel A, for the 12 positive test results, there are 8 cases of disease, or 67 percent, whereas there are 5 cases of disease for the 15 negative test results, or 33 percent. Because of the difference in these two percentages it is appropriate to say that positive test results tend to be associated with presence of disease. Turning to the other panels, we see that for panel B there is 20 percent disease for positive test results but 50 percent disease for negative test results, thus a negative relation. For panel C, there is 75 percent disease for either positive or negative test results, thus no relation between test outcome and disease state. To be correct, a person must do considerable processing and must compare probabilities; given what we know about the difficulties people have with probabilities, we should not be surprised that this correct strategy is relatively rare.

Two incorrect strategies that have been identified are the "single-cell" strategy and the "sum-of-diagonals" strategy. The single-cell strategy involves focusing on the "yes-yes" cell—if this is the highest frequency, infer a positive relation, if it is the lowest, infer a negative relation. A person using this strategy would have difficulty making a judgment for panel A since 8 is neither highest or lowest, would estimate a negative relation for panel B and a positive relation for panel C. As illustrated here, judgments based on the single-cell strategy will sometimes agree with the correct answer and other times be grossly inaccurate. The sum-of-diagonals strategy is more complex and will more often yield judgments that agree with the correct answer. This strategy involves adding the frequencies along the two diagonals and then comparing the sums; one finds the number of "similar pairings" ("yes-yes" + "no-no") and the number of "dissimilar pairings" ("yes-no" + "no-yes"), with the judgment based on the difference between sums. For panel A, this strategy yields 18 "similars" versus 9 "dissimilars" and a judgment of a positive relation; for panel B with 13 "similars" and 22 "dissimilars," a judgment of a negative relation; and for panel C, with 18 "similars" and 14 "dissimilars" a judgment of a slight positive relation.

Shaklee and Tucker (1980) constructed problems that would enable them to identify which strategy a person was using (including several others not described here). With data presented in tables, they found, among statistically-untrained adults, relatively little use of the single-cell strategy, with about one-third of subjects using the sum-of-diagonals strategy and another one-third following the correct, proba-bility-comparison strategy. When people viewed cases one at time, however, there was less use of the correct strategy and an increased use of the single-cell strategy (Shaklee & Mims, 1982). These findings indicate that not only do people have vary-ing conceptions of correlation, but also that higher and more realistic memory-load conditions lead both to errors in estimating event frequencies and to more use of less demanding and less adequate judgmental strategies.

Illusory Correlation.   We have discussed a few influences on people's judg-ments of relatedness when presented with relevant data. Although there are multi-ple reasons why subjective estimates may differ from objective correlations, there is a rough, general correspondence between the two. That is, although people may not notice modest objective correlations, their judgments of relatedness do tend to be higher when the objective correlation in the data is higher (Jennings, Amabile, & Ross, 1982). In other words, although people are generally not very good at detect-ing correlations in data presented to them, they are somewhat sensitive to large differences in objective correlations.

A seemingly contradictory phenomenon has been observed repeatedly, namely that people judge a substantial relation to exist when this belief is completely un-supported by the data. This phenomenon is known as *illusory correlation*—the belief that things are correlated when, objectively, they are not. The classic example was reported by Chapman and Chapman (1967, 1969), who found that both clinicians and college students believed that certain responses to psychological tests indicated particular psychodiagnoses, whereas objectively there was no association between these test responses and the diagnosis. A related concept is the *halo effect,* which is the tendency to rate individuals in a highly similar manner across different rating dimensions, with the result that the ratings are very highly correlated, much more so than the objective relations among the characteristics being rated (Cooper, 1981). An example would be rating school children who earn good grades as also better adjusted, better looking, nicer, more socially adept, and the like. Objectively, these characteristics are only weakly related.

It has been proposed that such illusory beliefs about correlations may have little or nothing to do with observing relevant data (we will qualify this statement shortly). Rather, these impressions arise from implicit theories held by people and stem from the use of the heuristics of representativeness and availability (Jennings, Amatrile, & Ross, 1982; Nisbett & Ross, 1980; Pollard, 1982). The use of representa-tiveness is well illustrated by the belief that people will behave very consistently across a variety of situations. Having observed a person behave in an honest (or friendly, or aggressive) manner in one situation, we are inclined to believe that the person will "always" behave that way; the objective evidence suggests that human behavior is far less consistent (Nisbett & Ross, 1980). One way in which availability plays a role is in terms of the ease with which reasons for correlations can be gener-ated. For example, it is relatively easy to imagine why people with sexual problems might report seeing more sexual content on projective tests, thus reporting sexual content and having sexual problems are believed to be correlated although, objectively, they are not (Chapman & Chapman, 1969).

For many associations about which people hold illusory beliefs, there may be no exposure to relevant data. Moreover, limited experience with relevant cases may serve to strengthen the illusory belief rather than correct it. A salient example—the one person with sexual problems who reported seeing many sexual objects on an inkblot test—could both initiate the belief and later be recalled as a supporting instance. With regard to any specific relation, people in everyday life encounter a limited and probably poor sample of experiences; in addition, once the belief exists, they may selectively sample confirming cases and encode ambiguous evidence as supportive of the illusory correlation (Crocker, 1981). These tendencies would lead to using the erroneous single-cell strategy when judging relatedness—recalling confirming examples and failing to consider the other categories that are critical for an accurate assessment. Evidence contradicting the assumed relation may be discounted (Crocker, 1981); indeed, it can be quite difficult to change illusory beliefs by presenting contradictory data (Chapman & Chapman, 1967, 1969).

MAKING CHOICES

Choosing, interpreted very broadly, is one of the most common activities of everyday life. In the most general sense, a choice or decision occurs whenever one of a set of alternatives is selected or followed; no awareness of the set or of the act of choosing is required. In these terms, a simple act like getting out of bed in the morning can be viewed as involving a large number of choices—not just get up or not, but also open right or left eye first or both simultaneously, lift head or move leg, move right or left leg, use side or end of bed as release point, and so on. From this perspective, we make perhaps hundreds of thousands of choices every day. Ordinarily, we associate decision-making with more deliberate behavior; the person (or organization), although not necessarily aware of how a choice is made, does have the task-orientation of making a choice. Of course, no one would suggest that all the formally-existing choices should be made deliberately. If a person, having made the initial decision to get out of bed, deliberated over the many, minor choices related to how to get out of bed, it is indeed possible that the day would be over with the person still in bed. The development of habits—relatively automatic ways of acting—can be seen as a way of freeing an individual's information-processing capacities for presumably more important activities. Although behaving automatically or "out of habit" has this advantage, it also can involve costs, since people can find themselves in situations or behavior patterns not to their liking because of failure to consider alternative courses of action. While the notion of implicit (automatic) decision-making is potentially interesting and important, most research has focused on more deliberate behavior where the task of making a choice is apparent.

Deciding can be viewed as based on some form of comparison among alternatives, each of which has multiple attributes or features. Some choices are "dominated." No matter how the alternatives are considered, one is superior to the others—a very easy choice, or, to some, "no choice at all." The more interesting cases are more complex and involve some uncertainty, as when each alternative has some assets and liabilities relative to the others. How such choices should be made and actually are made is a topic of continuing interest.

Expected-Utility Model. For decades, the dominant approach to decision-making has been expected-utility theory; interest in the theory dates back to the 1700s (Schoemaker, 1982). The simplest version of the theory (Schoemaker, 1982, lists nine variations) used expected monetary values and can be illustrated with choices among gambles (see Table 9–5). The expected value of a monetary gamble is calculated by multiplying the value of each alternative by its probability and summing these products across the alternatives. For gamble 1, for example, the expected monetary value is

$$(.5 \times \$12) + (.5 \times \$8) = \$10.$$

The essential notion is that the expected value of each gamble is determined, and that gamble with the highest expected value is chosen. According to this version of the theory, a decision-maker would be indifferent regarding the three gambles since each has the same expected monetary value, namely $10 or the amount required to bet.

Table 9–5. *On which gamble would you rather bet $10?*

Gamble 1:	50% chance that you get $12 and 50% chance that you get $8. (Expected value = $10)
Gamble 2:	75% chance that you get $12 and 25% chance that you get $4. (Expected value = $10)
Gamble 3:	10% chance that you get $28 and 90% chance that you get $8. (Expected value = $10)

Expected monetary-value theory proved too restrictive, and the general approach was modified in several ways to yield variations of expected-utility theory. The modifications take into account such things as the following: Monetary value and value-to-a-decision-maker are not related in a one-to-one fashion; in simple terms, the difference between one and two dollars is not the same, in many circumstances, as the difference between one hundred and one hundred and one dollars. Decisions may involve the use of subjective rather than objective probabilities. The features of the alternatives in many decisions do not have monetary value but do have some value to the decision-maker (In other words, all values cannot be translated into money).

The outcomes of these changes are different versions of expected-utility models. The common core of these models contains the following ideas (Einhorn & Hogarth, 1981):

1. The expected utility of an alternative is a weighted average of anticipated pleasures and pains.
2. Weights or probabilities and values are separate, but combine multiplicatively in determining expected utilities.
3. Choices are completely determined by expected utilities.

What this means is that, according to this approach, each alternative is evaluated in terms of some weighted combination of its good and bad aspects. Each alternative thus has an expected utility which takes into account its relatively positive and negative characteristics. Once the expected utilities of all alternatives have been determined, choosing is straightforward—in any choice, select the alternative with the highest expected utility. For a more concrete example, consider choosing a job. Assume that the relevant features of any job to the decision-maker are income, opportunity for advancement, the interest level of the work, fringe benefits, and ease of getting to and from work. Each of these features has some utility or value to a decision-maker (and they will vary from one to another). Each job thus will have some (overall, average) expected utility; the jobs can be ranked from highest to lowest in terms of expected utility, and choices will be determined by this rank ordering. Table 9–6 shows some hypothetical values for three jobs; for simplicity, it is assumed that all job features are equally weighted so that the expected utility of an alternative is the simple average of its values on the five dimensions.

Table 9-6 *Expected utilities for three hypothetical jobs.*

JOB	INCOME	OPPOR-TUNITY	INTEREST	BENEFITS	TRAVEL	EXPECTED UTILITY
Salesperson	9	5	2	2	3	4.2
Accountant	7	4	4	6	5	5.2
Teacher	5	3	7	6	8	5.4

Note: The numbers are arbitrary units reflecting the value to the decision-maker of a feature; higher numbers indicate greater value.

For any feature, the values shown in Table 9–6 reflect both the actual perceived characteristic of the job and the subjective value of that characteristic to the individual. For example, the value of 9 under "income" for salesperson represents the presumed value to the individual of the income anticipated from that job. As shown, each job has strengths and weaknesses; according to utility models these are all taken into account and can thus compensate for one another. For example, the low value of interest for salesperson is compensated by the high value on income, and so on. The overall value—the expected utility summed across features—is assumed to govern choice. This hypothetical decision-maker would choose the job of teacher because it has the highest expected utility.

Expected-utility models are commonly considered as standards for correct decision-making, although this position has been questioned (Einhorn & Hogarth, 1981; Lopes, 1981; Schoemaker, 1982). A different question is whether expected-utility models adequately describe actual decision-making. Here there is ample evidence that people frequently make choices that do not conform to the predictions of utility models (see Einhorn & Hogarth, 1981). There are many ways in which such discrepancies can occur. For example, the theory implies that features such as income and travel time can be placed on comparable scales (as in Table 9–6), but people may have difficulty doing so. If, in choosing among gambles like those in Table 9–5, people choose gamble 2 because they should win more often than they lose (ignoring how much would be won or lost) or select gamble 3 because a relatively large amount can be won (ignoring the probability of winning), they are not conforming to expected-utility principles. More generally, people have been observed to use a variety of other strategies for decision-making, some of which we will now discuss.

Noncompensatory Strategies.   A key feature of the expected-utility approach is that the evaluation of an alternative involves all its features (strengths and weaknesses), which can compensate for one another in determining overall utility. A variety of strategies exists in which features do not compensate or in which choices are based on less than the full set of features. The *maximax* strategy involves comparing alternatives on their best characteristics, with the alternative having the strongest best characteristic being chosen. Applied to the jobs in Table 9–6, this strategy leads to the choice of the salesperson job since its best feature, income, is the strongest of best features. Alternatively, the *minimax* strategy requires comparing alternatives' weakest features, with the alternative having the strongest weakest characteristic being chosen. Among the jobs, this strategy leads to the choice of the accountant's job. According to a *conjunctive* strategy, minimally acceptable values are set for each dimension and an alternative is selected only if its values exceed these minima on all dimensions. This strategy can lead to more than one acceptable alternative or no acceptable alternative, depending on the set of alternatives and the criteria that are established. For example, using the arbitrary job values in Table 9–6, setting the criteria as "at least three on every feature" results in both teacher and accountant being acceptable, whereas criteria of "at least five on every feature" produce no acceptable alternative.

Alternatives may be compared one feature at a time, as in Tversky's (1972) *elimination-by-aspects* theory. An aspect can be any sort of feature, such as automatic transmission for a car, "hotel-included" for a tour package, or salary over $20,000 for a job, the last being equivalent to setting criteria along dimensions. Aspects are considered in some order based probabilistically on perceived importance or preference. The first aspect is selected and all alternatives lacking this feature are eliminated from further consideration. If more than one alternative remains, the second aspect is considered and again used to eliminate alternatives, the process continuing until just one alternative remains. With this approach, or any other strategy in which features are considered successively, the order in which features are examined can influence the outcome of the choice process. Referring again to the hypothetical jobs in Table 9–6, if benefits were examined first with the desired aspect defined as "judged value of at least four," salesperson is eliminated and the choice will eventually be made between accountant and teacher. If in contrast, opportunity were considered first with the desired aspect equal to "judged value of at least four" teacher is eliminated and the choice reduces to salesperson versus accountant.

This is but a sample of the noncompensatory choice strategies that can be and are used. As we have seen, the use of such strategies can lead to the choice of an alternative that does not have the highest, overall expected value. If one defines "proper choice" as maximizing expected utility, such discrepancies can be viewed as errors in decision-making. Why might people not use the complete, compensatory evaluation of expected-utility theory? There are several possible and plausible reasons. Fundamentally, expected-utility models require that the probabilities of various outcomes be estimated and that the values of a wide variety of features be translated into comparable utility scales so that an overall expected utility can be generated for each alternative. We have already seen that people's intuitions about probabilities are often quite different from what probability theory dictates that they ought to be. Translating very different features into a common utility scale can be quite difficult. Expected-utility models also assume that people use the generated subjective probabilities and cross-dimensional utilities to do something akin to a multi-step computation, a complex procedure that may well be rejected, or not accomplished if attempted. Tversky (1972) suggests that people prefer decision strategies that provide a clear choice without estimating and computing, that are easy to understand and defend. Noncompensatory strategies tend to meet these needs. In addition, the use of a noncompensatory strategy may lead to choices identical to those dictated by expected-utility theory in many circumstances (Einhorn, 1970). That is, the decisions based on noncompensatory strategies and those based on compensatory strategies may, more often than not, be quite similar (see Einhorn, Kleinmuntz, & Kleinmuntz, 1979). In addition, focusing on the alternative that is chosen ignores a potentially-important factor, namely the cost of the process of deciding.

The Cost of Choosing.   Theories of decision-making tend to concentrate on the outcome—the characteristics of the alternatives selected and rejected. Yet a decision-maker must deal not only with the alternative but also with the act of choosing itself. As Einhorn and Hogarth (1981) point out, choices are made to direct future actions, and choosing implies commitment. Thus, although multiple options may exist prior to choosing, options are to some extent restricted after choice. This implies that choosing itself involves conflict—a cost—and that people may seek to reduce this cost by "deciding not to choose" or by limiting the amount of time and effort devoted to choosing.

It is generally believed, in our culture, that the more time and effort one invests in a decision, the better that decision will be—the more beneficial the choice will be (Christensen-Szalanaski, 1978, 1980). It is reasonable to suppose, however, that the relation between investment in a decision and quality of decision (expected benefit) follows a law of diminishing returns. That is, given that a certain amount of time, effort, and perhaps money has already been invested in decision-making, increasing the investment will produce decreasing improvements in the quality of the final decision. Under such circumstances, it can be argued that the optimal decision strategy is one that maximizes the difference between the benefit of the chosen outcome and the cost of deciding. That strategy is likely to be one which yields a choice that is less than the best alternative (when the cost of deciding is ignored). For example, suppose that you must choose a car to buy. The available cars can be ranked from best to worst *when everything is taken into account,*—car A best, car B second best, and so on. Your task is to gather information about the cars and evaluate it in some way so that you can choose a car. Suppose that ten hours of information gathering and evaluating would lead you to buy car B, but that one hundred hours would be needed for you to decide to buy car A. Looking only at the final outcomes, the ten-hour decision is not optimal—you wouldn't choose the best car. However, taking into account the (time and mental effort) costs of the decisions, it may well be that the ten-hour decision is the best one.

Christensen-Szalanski (1978, 1980) has found that people do take into account the cost of deciding—for example, in terms of time spent—in selecting a decision-making strategy. What, in addition to the essential conflict of choosing, affects the difficulty of making a decision? Two factors are the number of features of alternatives that need to be evaluated and the variability of differences among alternatives across features (Shugan, 1980). As we have noted earlier, when one alternative dominates others, choice is easy. In general, the more features that must be evaluated, and the more inconsistent the comparisons of alternative are across features, the greater the cost of choosing will be. Consequently, noncompensatory strategies, which tend to reduce the need to compare alternatives across multiple dimensions, can minimize the cost of deciding (Shugan, 1980). The general point is that, in a given situation, the benefit of choosing "the best alternative" needs to balanced against the cost of arriving at a decision.

Heuristics and Everyday Functioning

Throughout this chapter we have discussed research indicating that, when given reasoning and judgmental tasks, people often employ heuristic processes that result in responses deviating from a normative standard. The evidence suggests that human abilities to perform such tasks are rather poor, and one might well wonder how people can function successfully in the world with their biased and flawed processing. This question has received some attention from researchers, with two broad themes emerging. First, people may not be required to behave in everyday life as they are asked to perform in research environments. Second, people may acquire less-than-optimal modes of responding because ordinary living does not provide the conditions needed for identifying weaknesses in their approaches and for learning better strategies.

In a general sense, the demands of everyday living may be less stringent than the precise, normative standards applied in research on reasoning and judgment. For example, people may ordinarily be more concerned with accepting correct conclusions and rejecting incorrect conclusions, rather than focusing on the logical nature of the relation between a conclusion and its arguments. Similarly, as has been pointed out earlier in this chapter, it can be advantageous to identify potentially correct propositions even if, in doing so, one exhibits confirmation bias. Hogarth (1981) has proposed that many choices are made as part of a continuous process; thus a person may seek to make a decision that will lead to an improved position rather than trying to make the best possible choice. Over a series of decisions, it is possible to make corrections for "errors" that might have been made earlier. A person can use an "irrational" choice strategy which nonetheless leads to an acceptable outcome (Einhorn, 1980), and can be successful in competitive situations by making decisions that are better than the competitor's. Optimal choices are not strictly required (Hogarth, 1981).

Probability models that apply to judgments under uncertainty involve assumptions that people might sometimes be unwilling to make. In probability theory, a fixed source of outcomes is assumed and variations occur randomly. As Hogarth (1981) points out, such assumptions may be questionable in some circumstances. For example, if the profits of a company drop substantially from what they have been in the past, does this represent a random fluctuation (as probability theory would assume) or does it reflect some fundamental change in the company (a change in the source)? Under the first assumption, one would expect profits to return to the "established level," but under the second assumption, one would expect a continuation of poor profits (with some small random variations). In a similar vein, models of choice assume that preferences (values, utilities) are fixed, but people may view their own preferences as somewhat unstable, in which case attempting to make precise judgments would be unproductive (Hogarth, 1981).

These remarks should not be interpreted as meaning that the errors people make are unimportant. Rather, the point is that the heuristics people employ have some functional value in ordinary environments. Relatively simple cognitive strategies do have the advantage of reducing the "cost of thinking," and although simpler strategies do not regularly yield optimal outcomes, they tend to have some degree of accuracy (see, for example, Kleinmuntz & Kleinmuntz, 1981).

Einhorn (1980) has suggested that it is difficult for people to learn that there are weaknesses in their approaches to judgment. Judgments are made to direct actions, and people focus on the outcomes of their actions rather than on the structure of the task confronting them. Taking action can preclude gaining information necessary to evaluate the judgmental strategy, and the feedback received can be ambiguous or misleading. As one example, consider the case of selecting among applicants for a program involving some form of training—a management training

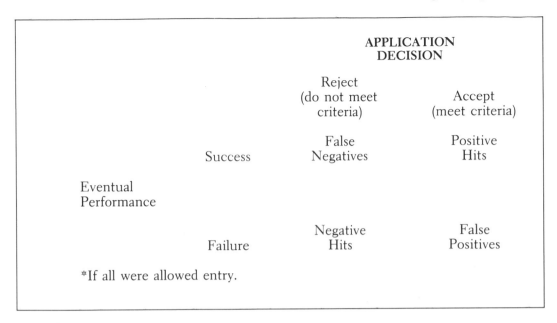

Figure 9-7 Categories needed to evaluate a selection strategy.

program, for example, or an officers' school, or graduate school. Whatever strategy is used to choose the applicants to be admitted, information about all four categories of applicants shown in Figure 9–7 is needed to evaluate that strategy properly (recall our earlier discussion of estimating relatedness).

To the extent that the strategy is accurate, the percentage of success among those accepted must be higher than the success percentage for those rejected. As Einhorn (1980) points out, those not chosen are not admitted and thus no information about their performance is available. The decision-maker is thus limited to information about percent success among those admitted. If the number of positive hits is relatively high and the number of false positives relatively low—the success rate among those accepted is high—the conclusion is likely to be that the strategy used to choose applicants is a good one. For example, if it were deemed satisfactory that, say, 70 percent of those accepted were eventually successful, this outcome would encourage future use of the selection strategy. Think of how this evaluation would change if those the strategy rejects had also been admitted and it were found that 90 percent of "rejectees" were successful! Clearly, knowing only the positive success rate can be misleading. A further complication is that, if the program is effective, it will increase the chances of success for those admitted to it. This results in an "inflated positive success rate" with respect to evaluating the selection strategy. To understand this point, imagine a treatment program so good that it makes successes of virtually everyone! Not knowing this (and not able to know this), the decision-maker interprets the very high rate of success among those accepted as support for the choice strategy. In fact, that strategy is irrelevant. As Einhorn (1980) remarks, when judgments lead to actions and actions lead to outcomes, feedback about the outcomes may be useless for evaluating and correcting a judgmental strategy.

Summary

Making judgments, arriving at conclusions, and deciding among alternatives are important activities which occur in many contexts. Logic and mathematics provide normative standards for assessing the accuracy of ordinary human performance; a frequent finding is that people's judgments and reasoning are less than optimal.

Syllogistic reasoning concerns the evaluation of the internal consistency of arguments—whether or not a conclusion necessarily follows from a set of premises. The most common error people make is to accept conclusions that do not follow logically from the premises. Syllogistic reasoning involves interpreting the premises, combining their meanings, and comparing possible conclusions to the combinations generated; errors may occur at any stage. People often misinterpret premises, do not always consider all possible combinations of the premises, and tend not to attempt to determine if a conclusion might be contradicted by a particular combination of the premises. People's beliefs can lead them to accept conclusions consistent with their beliefs and to reject inconsistent conclusions, rather than relating the conclusions to the premises; this belief—bias effect seems stronger with invalid syllogisms.

In attempting to determine if a given statement is empirically true or false, people tend to seek confirming evidence rather than potentially falsifying evidence. When the statement to be tested concerns a situation with which people are very familiar, their answers tend to be more accurate, not because they reason better but because they recall from past experience what to do in that situation. Although people tend to seek confirming evidence, they do typically make proper use of falsifying evidence if they should happen to encounter it.

Intuitions about uncertain events are often quite discrepant from answers based on mathematical probability theory. Probabilities are proportionate frequencies, but people often base "probability judgments" on simple frequencies. Outcomes are judged as more likely if, based on content, they appear representative or if they are easier to think of. People have exaggerated beliefs that small samples resemble the population from which they are taken, and that short, random series of events will "self-correct" when in fact they will not do so. Knowledge of an outcome appears to make it virtually impossible for people to judge accurately how well the outcome could have been predicted on the basis of only information available before the fact. Confidence in judgments is often much higher than is warranted by the accuracy of the judgments; overconfidence seems to stem from focusing on supporting evidence and from relative neglect of contradictory evidence. In estimating relations between uncertain events, many people use inadequate strategies which lead to grossly distorted views of statistical relations. The phenomenon of illusory correlation refers to incorrect beliefs that certain things are related; such beliefs seem to be based on semantic similarity rather than any form of empirical facts.

Expected-utility theory is a normative model of decision-making, according to which the value of each alternative is a weighted average of all its relevant characteristics and a decision is made by choosing the alternative with the highest expected value. Research shows that people often do not make choices in accordance with this model, for a variety of reasons. People tend to prefer noncompensatory strategies which, in any of several ways, base choices on selected features of the alternatives. For example, only best features or only worst features might be considered; alternatively, features might be used successively to eliminate alternatives until just one is left. People are also sensitive to the cost of choosing itself, and there can be conflict between simplifying choice and choosing "the best" alternative.

TEN

Cognitive Development

Outline

Consider for a moment the differences between a puppy and an adult dog, or between a kitten and an adult cat. In each case, the younger is smaller, perhaps cuter, not as well coordinated, and not quite as smart as the older organism. On the whole, however, the differences are not very striking. In contrast, the behavior of a human infant lying in a crib provides few clues to the vast repertoire of knowledge and skills which exist in adulthood. An arbitrary selection of "developmental achievements" is given in Table 10–1. Clearly, there are remarkable changes from infancy through childhood to adolescence and adulthood.

Table 10-1. *Illustrative examples of cognitive development.*

APPROXIMATE AGE	BEHAVIOR LIKELY TO BE OBSERVED
Birth	Reflexive sucking
3 months	Visual anticipation of future position of moving object
6 months	Prolonged repetition of actions (e.g., shaking a rattle)
8 months	Searching for hidden object if it has just been touched
8 months	Communicating with gestures
12 months	Laughing in anticipation of mother's playful kissing
15 months	Noticeable upset when parent leaves
20 months	Grouping objects on basis of function or color
2 years	Frequent production of two-word utterances
5 years	Understanding passive sentences
7 years	Understanding that amount of substance is unchanged when shape changes
8 years	Systematic construction of serial orders (e.g., sticks varying in length)
9 years	Understanding that weight of an object is unchanged when its shape is changed
14 years	Spontaneous use of proportional relations in problem solving
16 years	Generating all possibilities in a concrete "scientific experiment"

In previous chapters, we have discussed a variety of cognitive processes, dealing almost exclusively with the behavior of adults. In this chapter we will consider some of the ways in which cognitive processes change as individuals develop. When we contemplate a developmental process, we commonly think of changes taking place as an individual grows older that is, that behavior is related to age. However, "age" is a tricky variable; essentially, age is time since birth (or since conception for some purposes). Put bluntly, the age of a person who behaves in a particular way explains nothing by itself. Rather, changes in behavior with advancing age are the basic observations of development, and the researcher's job is to find explanations for those changes (Wohlwill, 1970). The particular age at which some behavior occurs may be of little importance; developmental theorists are often more interested in the order in which various kinds of behavior emerge. That is, the crucial question can be whether behavior X precedes, follows, or occurs simultaneously with behavior Y; the particular ages at which X and Y emerge may be theoretically irrelevant. Comparisons of children of different ages are often used in developmental research, but these comparisons are used more to study the ordinal relations between different behaviors than to identify "the age" at which something occurs. To summarize, age trends or age differences are often studied, but the trend itself is usually more important than the particular ages involved.

Consideration of what changes and how—and, indeed, of what does not change—over the course of development from infancy to adulthood is important for a well-rounded understanding of cognitive processes. In this chapter, we will present a selective survey of cognitive development, emphasizing the developmental aspects of the topics covered in earlier chapters. It is the case, however, that developmental theory and research differ in some important respects from standard research on cognitive processes using adult subjects. Therefore, before describing selected examples of developmental change, we will first discuss some special issues related to cognitive development.

General Issues

Developmental changes might occur for any of several reasons. The kinds of interpretations made of age trends tend to be different from those offered, say, for differences resulting from giving or not giving a hint in a study of problem-solving. There is no disagreement over the fact that there are massive differences between the behavior of infants and that of adult human beings. Nonetheless, the study of the changes that take place involves a number of complex issues, which we will briefly consider.

COMPETENCE AND PERFORMANCE

Any study of cognitive processes involves an assessment of what an individual *does* (performance). Developmental researchers often wish to infer what a person is capable of doing (competence) from performance. Inferring competence from performance is fraught with difficulties. Competence is typically defined rather abstractly, in terms of certain forms of knowledge. For example, one aspect of "knowing a language" is understanding its phrase structure rules (see Chapter 7). A researcher interested in determining if a person possesses such knowledge would try to devise a task which requires this knowledge. The desired situation is one in which competence can be inferred from success and lack of competence can be inferred from failure. Difficulties arise because performance on any cognitive task involves a number of processes, because there is often more than one way to assess performance on a task, and because any of a variety of tasks might be used to evaluate a particular kind of competence. In general, failure on a task might occur for reasons other than lack of competence, and it might be possible to achieve success by some means not involving the competence in question. Klahr and Wallace (1970), suggested that it might be impossible to devise tasks which correspond to the desired relation (success = competence; failure = incompetence).

On cognitive tasks, children usually perform worse than adults, and younger children worse than older children. Those who fail may "lack competence," but it should be clear that such inferences must be treated cautiously. Researchers have found that children might fail to accomplish one version of a task but succeed when the task is slightly modified. Under such circumstances, deciding whether the child is or is not "competent" is quite difficult. This issue will arise at several points later in the chapter.

NATURE-NURTURE

How are we to account for the massive changes that occur as an individual develops? It is tempting to try choosing between "biology" and "experience" as explanations for development, but the matter is much more complex. An individual has a particular genetic endowment but also lives in a particular environment, and both are important. Extreme examples illustrate the folly of trying to find one explanation: A kitten and a human infant exposed to the same environment will develop quite differently; a human infant who is fed but kept locked in a closet for life will not develop normal functioning. Setting aside extreme views, there are interesting and intricate questions to consider.

Flavell (1976) emphasizes the flexibility of the developing organism. There are alternative ways of developing any given cognitive skill, and thus a wide variety of environments may be developmentally interchangeable. Nonetheless, the question of what kinds of processes might develop remains for consideration. For example, a number of writers have proposed that, since "all" human beings acquire (some) language, human organisms must be endowed with a specific language-learning mechanism. This need not be so, however (see Lenneberg, 1969; Piaget, 1970). The species-specific acquisition of language can be viewed as one aspect of the acquisition of species-specific cognitive processes. In simpler terms, if language is peculiar to human beings (an issue of some debate), so are other cognitive accomplishments, and language development does not proceed independently of general cognitive development. (We will consider this issue later in the chapter.) Rather than postulating genetically determined, specific mechanisms for particular cognitive processes, it seems more sensible to think of a broader, more flexible endowment which, during the course of development, leads to the acquisition of increasingly complex cognitive skills.

A related issue is whether the rate of development is biologically fixed. Explanations of development in terms of maturational processes tend to imply that cognitive skills will not be acquired until the brain has sufficiently matured. Similarly, associating particular ages with certain accomplishments implies that one must "wait" until the child is the proper age to observe the behavior. Typically, such implications lead experience-oriented researchers to try very hard to produce the behavior in younger children, to emphasize the importance of experience. Resolving such conflicts is extremely difficult because of methodological problems (what performance demonstrates competence?) and theoretical uncertainties. It is well established that the brain changes during development, and it is easy to think of cognitive accomplishments as having to wait on the proper neural development. However, it is also true that different experiences affect the size, structure, and chemical composition of the brain (Rosenzweig, Bennett, & Diamond, 1972). Thus, there is a kind of basic ambiguity about the meaning of the fact that, say, five-year-olds have different brains and behave differently from one-year-olds. While it seems reasonable that neural growth places some limits on behavioral development, the nature of the brain-behavior relation is poorly understood.

Assimilation-Accommodation.   Cognitive development is best viewed as the result of complex biological and experiential influences. Development is not produced by "stamping in" environmental information on a passive, initially blank organism, nor is it the product of a predetermined unfolding of processes for which experience is essentially unimportant. In Piaget's influential account of cognitive development, great emphasis is given to the nature of the individual's interactions with the environment (see Flavell, 1976). Such interactions are necessarily two-sided affairs, affected both by the kind of information available in the environment and by the nature of the individual's existing cognitive structures. In dealing with the environment, a person takes into account the kind of information present in the environment but also interprets that information in the light of current knowledge. Piaget calls these two aspects of organism-environment interaction accommodation and assimilation, respectively.

Accommodation means taking into account the actual properties of the objects and events one encounters. *Assimilation* refers to interpreting objects and events in terms of one's current ways of thinking. These are not separate cognitive processes but two intertwined aspects of organism-environment interaction. For example, suppose a rough, outline drawing looks like a bird to you. This outcome depends equally on your having some existing idea of what birds look like and on the drawing having physical properties sufficient to enable you to perceive it as a bird. As a child repeatedly interacts with the environment, each new encounter leads to changes in knowledge. For example, in the course of encountering a variety of birds, accommodating to their particular characteristics while assimilating them into a *bird* concept, the child leaves each encounter with a slightly modified understanding of the concept. The cumulative effect of many encounters can be radically different cognitive structures.

The model of assimilation-accommodation raises two important questions: What processes or structures exist at the onset of development? To what extent can variation in environmental stimulation affect development?

With respect to the first question, it is clear that the minds of infants are not mere blank slates—the more we study infants, the more complex they seem to be. Because of the severe limitations on infants' activities, trying to assess their cognitive processes is very difficult. Researchers studying infant cognition are forced to be very inventive, using assessment techniques such as monitoring changes in sucking rate, heart rate, head-turning, and eye movements. A related problem concerns the proper interpretation of such measures. Nonetheless, researchers have obtained data suggesting that there is a considerable amount of cognitive activity in early infancy. Wertheimer (1961) presented a series of sounds randomly to the right or left of a newborn infant, finding that the infant looked in the correct direction (expected to see something?). Sroufe and Waters (1976) distinguished five different kinds of smiles exhibited by infants during the first eight weeks after birth. For example, at two weeks, a mouth-pulled-back smile occurs when low-level, modulated voices are heard; by four weeks, the mother's voice is especially effective at eliciting a bright, alert smile (a grin). By presenting both repeated pictures and novel pictures (mobiles hanging over a crib), researchers have found that infants less than two months old look more at repeated (familiar) items (Pick, Frankel, & Hess, 1975). Such findings indicate that very young infants possess at least rudimentary forms of attention, discrimination, memory, and intersensory coordination.

The second question concerns the effects of variation in environment. Two aspects of this issue will be considered. One involves the attempt to provide children younger than the "normative age" for some behavior with special experience, with the intent of facilitating the desired behavior. Such research has often been the response of "environmentalists" to the statement (presumably by "maturationists") that behavior X does not occur until children reach some "critical age." The purpose is to show that, with appropriate environmental stimulation, the target behavior will occur at an earlier age. As Kuhn (1974) has pointed out, such studies are beset by difficulties, including lack of agreement concerning the criteria for judging them successful. In addition, some experiments may begin with misguided premises. For example, is it reasonable to expect that an hour's special experience can take the place of a year or more of ordinary experience? Cognitive processes operate in real time and take time to emerge, even for adults who are considered to have completed maturation. Complex skills are likely to have simpler skills as prerequisites; providing the experience sufficient for the acquisition of the highest level will have no effect unless the prerequisite skills already exist. For example, it makes little sense to try to teach advanced calculus to an adult who has no background in mathematics, and it might take that person several years to acquire the prerequisite knowledge and skills. The analogy to cognitive development should be clear. The time that children seem to require in order to develop certain cognitive processes might be due in part to neural maturation and in part to the time needed to acquire component skills, maturational considerations aside. From this perspective, it is indeed remarkable that some short-term training studies have proven effective. The second aspect of this question, however, concerns the possible effects of a long-term environmental influence, namely, schooling.

Effects of Schooling.   A fairly large number of cognitive changes have been observed to take place roughly between the ages of five to seven years. In most industrialized, Western societies, children begin school at about age five. Therefore, a reasonable question is how much of the developmental change seen after age five is due to schooling, rather than being a result of the general (non-school) interaction of maturation and experience with the world. This question is virtually impossible to study in industrialized, Western societies because the vast majority of children attend school. Consequently, attempts to address this issue have involved research in societies where schooling is not so commonplace, comparing developmental trends for children who do or do not attend school.

One such study was performed by Wagner (1978), who compared the memory performance of schooled versus non-schooled, rural versus urban children in Morocco. One task required remembering the locations of seven animal drawings. First the cards were shown one at a time and placed face down, then a probe card was presented and the subject was required to point to the card (in the row of seven face-down cards) that had the same animal. A portion of Wagner's data is shown in Figure 10–1, where it can be seen that the trends for both schooled groups (rural and urban) exhibit improvement across ages whereas there is little or no change

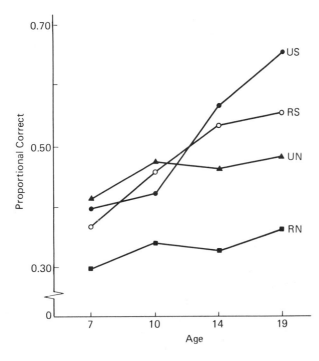

Figure 10-1. Total short-term recall (summed over serial positions). US = Urban/Schooled; RS = Rural/Schooled; UN = Urban/Non-schooled; RN = Rural/Non-schooled. (Source: Wagner, D.A. [1978]. Memories of Morocco: The influence of age, schooling, and environment on memory. *Cognitive Psychology, 10,* 1–28. Reprinted with permission of Academic Press, Inc.)

for the non-schooled groups. Stated differently, the gap between schooled and non-schooled children increased with "age" (increased schooling for the schooled subjects). Further analyses indicated that the differences were due to differential primacy effects, that is, the advantage due to schooling was limited to recall of items in the first few positions in the seven-item order. Primacy effects are attributed to the use of appropriate rehearsal techniques (see Chapter 3). On the basis of these and other data, Wagner (1978) concluded that schooling affects control processes in memory such as rehearsal or mnemonic techniques.

On the basis of a number of studies involving comparisons of schooled and non-schooled children, Cole and D'Andrade (1982) suggested that the effects of schooling will depend on the task that is presented. They noted that schools are rather special places where certain kinds of knowledge or processing are encouraged or required. In schools, there is a heavy emphasis on language, including the use of language to describe non-concrete or hypothetical events, as well as emphasis on using deliberate, task-relevant strategies (for example, rehearsal) and orderly classification schemes. For tasks where such knowledge and skills are relevant or even critical to performance, schooled children will outperform the non-schooled. For tasks where the content and requirements are common to everyday experience, schooling will not matter although performance will improve with age. On the whole, research on the effects of schooling suggests that at least some developmental changes depend on the kinds of experiences found in schools. The implication is that some aspects of cognitive development are not "universal"; that is, they are unlikely to emerge in any of a wide variety of "ordinary" life circumstances but rather require a particular kind of environment.

STAGES AND STRUCTURES

Is development a continuous process, or does an individual pass from one stage to another? Words such as "stage" or "phase" are frequently used in talking about development, often quite loosely. For example, parents commonly describe their children as "being in the negative stage" when the children regularly say "no" or refuse to do what they are told. (One might begin to wonder if a child who won't eat spinach is in the "anti-leafy-green-vegetable stage"!) What is meant by a stage of development? The term "stage" is used in two different ways in developmental theory. In its narrow sense, it refers to a distinct step in an acquisition process, a particular way of responding on some task. For example, in judging the amounts of liquids in containers, a child might be described as progressing from unsystematic responding (Stage 0), to using only height (Stage 1), to using "width" only when heights are equal (Stage 2), and so on to the final stage where the height and "width" of the liquid are appropriately combined. Although there are disagreements about the number or types of stages involved in some acquisitions and about the theoretical importance of stages in this sense, there are numerous instances in which this kind of stage-like progression has been observed (for example, Brainerd, 1978; Piaget, 1977; Siegler, 1981).

The more controversial meaning of "stage" is broader, referring to a general characterization of an individual's cognitive structures. At any point in development, a child is said to have a particular kind of "mind" or competence; the structures and processes of thought change qualitatively as a child moves from one stage to the next. The competence associated with a stage is broadly and abstractly defined, and presumably can be exhibited in a variety of ways—it should affect performance on a number of tasks. Without question, the most influential stage-theory of cognitive development is that of the Swiss psychologist-logician Jean Piaget. We will briefly consider this aspect of his theorizing.

Piaget's Theory.   Piaget is interested in what he terms genetic epistemology, the study of the formation and meaning of knowledge (Piaget, 1970). Thus, he is interested in the forms of competence that underlie cognitive performance. Piaget divides development into several periods and stages; each major segment is characterized by a distinct structure of knowledge processes. According to Piaget, there are three broad developmental periods: Sensory-motor, concrete operational, and formal operational. Each period has subdivisions called stages, and occasionally there are sub-stages as well; children are assumed to pass from stage to stage. A brief outline of Piaget's segmentation of development is shown in Table 10–2. In examining this outline, keep in mind that the ages shown are approximate; what is critical is the characterization of the stages and periods and the proposal that development proceeds in the order stated. It is important to note that Piagetian stages do *not* involve abrupt transitions from one complete cognitive structure to an entirely novel and complete cognitive structure. Rather, there is a point at which a child enters a particular stage and another point, several years later, where the stage is completed. As Flavell (1982) has suggested, the integrated cognitive structures associated with a stage might be expected to exist only at the completion of a stage.

Table 10-2.   *Outline of Piaget's view of cognitive development.*

SEGMENT	APPROXIMATE AGES	CHARACTERIZATION
Sensory-motor period	0– 2 years	Development of object permanence and sensory-motor schemes for dealing with objects in the immediate environment
Concrete-operations period	2–11 years	
Preoperational stage	2– 7 years	Gradual elaboration of mental process
Concrete-operational stage	7–11 years	Emergence of internalized, reversible operations for dealing with attributes of objects; formation of integrated groupings of operations
Formal-operations period	11–15 years	Emergence of abstract thought, hypothetical thinking; formation of completely integrated structure of mental operations

During the sensory-motor period, the infant moves from relatively undifferentiated, reflex-type behavior to a more systematic interaction with the immediate environment. The infant deals with whole objects rather than analyzing features of objects or using symbolic representations. Sensory-motor schemas are developed. A *schema* is whatever is repeatable and generalizable in an action. For example, the schema of "pulling" applies to a variety of specific action sequences. Piaget emphasized that schemas have a kind of logical character, involve sub-schemas and thus exhibit the rudiments of hierarchical classification or inclusion. For example, using a stick to move an object involves relating the hand to the stick, the stick to the object, and the object to its position in space. Extended action sequences involve ordered actions which Piaget viewed as the primitive basis of later linguistic and mathematical structures of order.

The ultimate accomplishment of the sensory-motor period is often considered to be the emergence of *object permanence*, which refers to the understanding that an object continues to exist when it is no longer in view and is interpreted as indicating the presence of representational thought. Infants' interactions with objects become increasingly sophisticated. Early on, an infant may cease attending to an object taken from its grasp; later, an infant might search for a hidden object only if it has just been held. Greatest sophistication is exhibited when, having seen an object hidden under a cup, the cup covered by a box and then withdrawn empty, the infant searches for the object under the box (Harris, 1975). Kopp, Sigman, and Parmelee (1974) studied the development of several behaviors during the sensory-motor period, including performance on an object-permanence task. As shown in Figure 10-2, there are substantial improvements in children's ability to search for hidden objects in a sophisticated way.

The concrete-operational stage is characterized by the child's becoming able to deal with attributes of objects in a more systematic fashion, to use symbolic representations, and to show what Piaget considers truly intellectual operations—internalized operations which are reversible and systematically related to each other. Included among concrete operations is the understanding of relations among classes—for example, that superordinate must be larger than subordinate categories. Also included is the understanding of relations among relations—for example, the understanding that, if A is greater than B and B is greater than C, it necessarily follows that A is greater than C.

In studies dealing with Piaget's concrete-operational stage, a great deal of attention has been given to conservation of concepts, which in his theory involves understanding that an operation can alter some attributes of an object while leaving other attributes unchanged. In general terms, conservation refers to the fact that the individual understands that something remains the same (is conserved) even though other things change. There are several levels of conservation. *Qualitative identity conservation* is shown by the recognition that an object remains the same object when some aspects of its appearance are altered. At a primitive level, infants who recognize *mother* as *mother* even though she has changed her clothes are conserving the concept of *mother*. Standard tests of qualitative identity conservation use ordinary objects such as balls of clay or water; if the clay is molded into a different shape or the water poured into a different sized container, this form of conservation is demonstrated by the child's understanding that "it's the same clay" or "it's the same water." Qualitative conservation is typically mastered during early childhood (roughly between the ages of two and six). Because qualitative conserva-

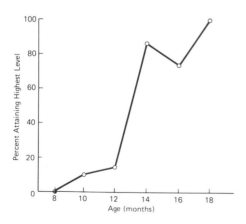

Figure 10-2. Performance on the hidden-object test. (Source: Kopp, C.B., Sigman, M., & Parmelee, A.H. [1974]. Longitudinal study of sensory-motor development. *Developmental Psychology, 10,* 687–695. Copyright 1974 by the American Psychological Association. Reprinted by permission of the publisher and author.)

tion is so obvious to adults, it might be worth emphasizing that, from the viewpoint of, say, a two-year-old, clay which is changed from a ball-shape to a sausage-shape isn't really the same clay it used to be!

The level of conservation that is important for Piaget's theory regarding concrete operations is *quantitative conservation*, which may involve either identity (one object) or equivalence (two objects). Quantitative identity conservation refers to the ability to understand that the *amount* of clay or water has not changed when the shape of the material or its container is altered. *Quantitative equivalence conservation* involves two distinguishable objects, initially judged to be equal with respect to some attribute; the child's task is to decide if that equivalence still holds when one object is transformed. The procedure for studying equivalence conservation for liquid amount is shown in Figure 10–3.

Two-object, quantitative equivalence conservation is more complex than single-object, quantitative identity conservation because to solve the equivalence problem, the child must both understand that the transformation (Step 2) did not change the amount of water (B = C) and remember the original equivalence (A = B). Notice that looking only at the presentation in Step 3 provides no useful basis for compar-

Step 1:

    Presentation:

Question: Same amount of water in the two glasses?
Child's response: Yes

Step 2: Water poured from glass B to glass C (transformation)

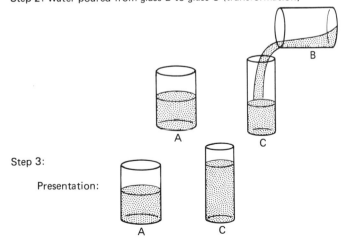

Step 3:

    Presentation:

Question: Same amount of water in the two glasses?
Child's response: Conserver — Yes. Nonconserver — No (likely to say glass C has more)

Figure 10–3. Testing equivalence conservation for liquid amount.

ing the amounts in the two glasses. It appears that quantitative identity conservation precedes quantitative equivalence conservation at least to some extent (Brainerd & Hooper, 1975). Illustrative age trends for the three kinds of conservation are shown in Figure 10–4.

Quantitative conservation is important for Piaget's theory because he considers it to be based on internalized, *reversible* operations that are characteristic of the stage of concrete operations. Two kinds of reversibility may be distinguished, simple reversibility (the amount of water is the same when poured from one glass to another because it could be poured back into the original glass and would be at the original level) or reciprocal reversibility (the water in glass C is taller than in glass B, but it is also thinner, and taller x thinner = same amount). Piaget requires a child to both make the correct judgment (that the amount is the same after transformation) and give an adequate explanation for the judgment (such as those given above). The argument for requiring an explanation is to ensure that the child understands the reason why transformation does not change amount. In contrast, Brainerd (1973) has strongly argued that conservation should be assessed solely in terms of correct judgments. The reason for this position is that a child might understand but have difficulty in adequately expressing that understanding in language. We will consider the relation between language and cognitive development later in this chapter; at this point, we can note that children are likely to be deemed "conservers" earlier in development if a judgments-only criterion is used.

In Piaget's view, the child with fully developed concrete operations has considerable intellectual skill, but further development is possible. Whereas concrete operations apply to attributes of objects and form several separate groupings, for-

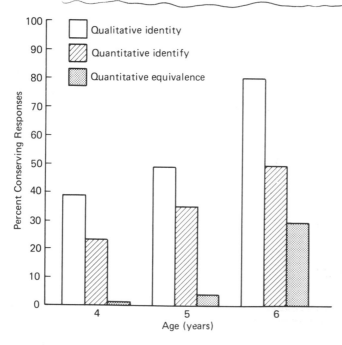

Figure 10-4. Age trends in conservation. (From data by Rybash, Roodin, & Sullivan, 1975. Courtesy of the author and Academic Press, Inc.)

mal operations apply to abstract entities such as propositions and constitute a single unified structure. Piaget characterizes the period of formal operations by truly hypothetical thinking, including formal logic and scientific reasoning. One feature of such thought is the use of a complete combinational system—the individual is able to "see all the possibilities." For example, the subject might be given five containers filled with colorless liquids, told that some combination of liquids will produce a colored mixture, and asked to produce the color. Interest lies in how the person goes about combining liquids. A concrete-operational child is expected to try a small number of combinations, perhaps pairings such as number one with number two, number two with number three, and so forth. The person having formal operations will systematically test all possible combinations, two at a time, three at a time, four at a time, and all five liquids mixed together in the attempt to find the one or more combinations that produce color. Performance on this task as well as others associated with formal operations changes markedly through adolescence (see Figure 10–5). Dealing with propositions, generating all possible combinations, and considering what might be true are all involved in syllogistic reasoning and proposition testing, as discussed in Chapter 9. Considering the many errors made by adults on such tasks, Neimark (1975) suggested that many people do not complete the stage of formal operations as proposed by Piaget.

Problems and Alternatives.   Although Piaget's theory has been influential for many years, problems with the approach have arisen. Keep in mind that we have merely sketched Piaget's theory here; the theory is enormously broad and covers many developmental topics. Perhaps because of its scope, there are many opportunities for weaknesses to be identified. In any case, as Flavell (1982) has stated, a number of developmental psychologists "now think that the theory may in vary-

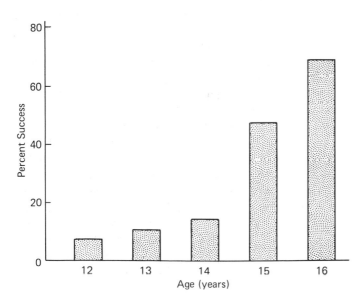

Figure 10-5. Development of an exhaustive system (with justification) for combining liquids. (From Experimental psychology: Its scope and method, edited by Paul Fraisse and Jean Piaget. VII—Intelligence by Pierre Oleron, Jean Piaget, Barbel Inhelder, & Pierre Greco. Translated by Therese Surridge. Copyright 1963 Presses Universitaires de France; English translation copyright Routledge & Kegan Paul, 1969. Reprinted by permission of Basic Books, Inc., Publishers.)

ing degrees be unclear, incorrect, and incomplete" (p. 2). The mental structures postulated by Piaget are quite abstract; hence, the connections between these structures and what children actually do are often elusive. Because of the emphasis on abstract mental structures in the theory, the competence-performance issue looms large. We have already mentioned the debates over the "most appropriate" way to make assessments. Investigators have demonstrated that performance on Piagetian tasks is influenced by a number of factors. For example, Rybash, Roodin, and Sullivan (1975) found that providing a memory aid for the initial A = B equivalence (see Figure 10–3) improved the performance of four- to six-year-olds on conservation of liquid amount. In Gelman's (1969) study, five-year-old *non*-conservers who received training in attending to relevant dimensions became conservers. As Gelman pointed out, the small amount of training could hardly have drastically "changed the children's minds." Rather, the results indicate that the children had initially failed the conservation test because they were attending to irrelevant dimensions (*not* because their "mental structures" were inadequate).

A related problem is that children frequently perform differently on tasks that, according to the theory, involve the same mental structures. For example, children succeed in conserving number before they conserve liquid or solid amount (Siegler, 1981). There is *not* a close relation between the development of competencies for two different versions of the "isolation of variables" task associated with formal operations. The influence of multiple factors on development and unevenness in patterns of development have been observed for the sensory-motor, concrete-operational, and formal operational periods (see for example, Corrigan, 1979; Martorano, 1977; Miller, 1976). When introducing Piaget's theory, we pointed out that the theory does *not* state that a child makes an abrupt change from one form of mental structures to an entirely-different form. Inconsistencies in patterns of development may, from the viewpoint of the theory, be attributed to "performance factors" (most of the processes discussed in this book would be relegated to the status of "performance factors"). However, as the number of inconsistencies and the number of factors influencing performance on Piagetian tasks increase, the value of talking about Piagetian stages diminishes. At the very least, the theory can be seen as ignoring a considerable amount of cognitive development.

The stages proposed by Piaget may be inappropriate, but there may still be a stage-like quality to cognitive development. As Flavell (1982) has stated, the overall question is "How homogeneous is the child's mind at any point in its development?" There might be stages of development other than those of Piaget's theory. For example, Case (1978) described a stage theory based on the idea that a child's information-processing capacity (working memory) undergoes qualitative changes during development. The merits of this approach remain to be determined. At the present time, there is abundant evidence suggesting heterogeneity in cognitive development, but the possibility of certain forms of homogeneity remains. Siegler (1981) has suggested that a child's behavior might be more consistent over a variety of tasks when all the tasks are novel for the child. When an acquisition process has been completed, homogeneity of behavior might be observed, that is, consistent use of stage-relevant processes might occur at the end of the stage (Flavell, 1982). In the broad middle of developmental sequences, on the other hand, heterogeneity of behavior is likely because the child's growing knowledge is more relevant to some tasks than to others. Theorists with an information-processing orientation (for example, Siegler, 1981) do not expect broad stage-like homogeneity, but others (for example, Flavell, 1982) speculate that there might be stage-like qualities of cognitive development that have not yet been identified.

Selected Aspects of Development

Even if there are no broad stages to cognitive development, the fact remains that tremendous changes occur from infancy to adulthood. In the remainder of this chapter, we will describe some of these changes, focusing on topics that seem to represent major aspects of development. As we have seen, infants process information, but not with the range or sophistication of older children or adults. From this perspective, the question is: What kinds of changes in which processes are responsible for most of the improvement that is commonly observed? Siegler (1983) points out that developmental trends might result from changes in "basic" processes such as attention and memory, from changes in task-interactive processes such as strategies, or from changes in general knowledge which in various ways will affect task performance. This section is clearly influenced by Siegler's (1983) presentation, and we will consider several possible sources of development.

ATTENTION AND ENCODING

The environment contains an immeasurable amount of potential information that may be encoded in a variety of ways. The manner in which an organism deals with such information has critical implications for success in environmental interactions. A key component of attentional processing is selectivity, and we shall see that selective responding undergoes a number of changes during development.

There is now abundant evidence that even very young infants exhibit selective attention. This evidence stems in large part from examinations of where infants look and how long they look at various displays, although other measures, for example, changes in heart rate, are also used. The central question is whether the infant shows differential responding, that is, looking more or longer at certain kinds of displays rather than others. Research has shown that very young infants (as well as older ones) prefer to look at moving patterns rather than stationary ones (see Pick, Frankel, & Hess, 1975), attend longer to reds and blues than to other hues and more to curved than to straight lines (see Kagan, 1976). Up to about two months of age, infants prefer to look at familiar (repeated) displays, whereas after two months infants prefer novel displays (Pick, Frankel, & Hess, 1975). Several investigators have presented black-and-white checkerboard patterns varying in complexity. With increasing age, infants prefer more complex patterns (Pick, Frankel, & Hess, 1975).

This is but a sample of the demonstrations of differential responding by infants; as Pick and co-workers (1975) pointed out, the infant's world is *not* the booming, buzzing, confusion that adults have often assumed it is. It is possible that infants' selectivity is a kind of reflex, with the response directly evoked by the occurrence of a stimulus. However, there is evidence indicating that infants' selective looking is an active process; for example, DeLoache, Rissman, and Cohen (1978) found that four-month-old infants, given a signal that something would be shown to the right or left, learned to look quickly where a display they preferred would be shown (the display occurring only *after* the infant looked). Other evidence supports the idea that infants actively influence what makes up their effective environment (Pick, Frankel, & Hess, 1975).

Although infants show some forms of active selection, it is still the case that their attention is strongly influenced by the kinds of stimulation they encounter. Of course, adults' attention is also drawn by certain types of stimulation—it is hard to ignore movement, or bright colors, or a sudden, loud sound. It is, however, clear that the young child's attention is more determined by environmental inputs than that of older children or adults. Wright and Vlietstra (1975) emphasize a distinction between *exploration* and *search*. Exploration is more spontaneous, unorganized, and governed by salient aspects of environmental objects and events. In contrast, search is more systematic and governed by the requirements of a task to be performed. These investigators propose that, through early childhood and well into middle childhood, there is a general shift from exploration to search behavior.

The difference between exploration and search is easily understood. Imagine yourself in a large and beautiful garden, just enjoying yourself; you might trace a rather irregular path as your attention is captured by the rose bushes, the flowering tree over here, the pretty bird over there, and so on. Compare this behavior to what you would do, in the identical setting, if you were trying to find the keys you had dropped somewhere along the way! Similar differences have been observed in the ways in which children look at and handle objects. Given an object to hold that cannot be seen (either "eyes closed" or with a cloth visually hiding the object), three-year-olds tend to play with it, knocking or pushing it, at best holding it while making primary contact with the palms of the hands. Six-year-olds tend to trace the outline of the object with their fingertips. There are also mixed patterns involving both palmar and finger contact, as well as variations in the thoroughness of the examination of the object. From roughly three to nine years of age, there is a progression from simple holding to partial examination to outline tracing and systematic search. Whereas young children typically use palmar contact, nine-year-olds seldom do so, employing finger contact almost exclusively. Corresponding to these differences, younger children tend to match held objects in terms of texture (available through palmar contact) whereas older children match by form.

Analogous observations have been made of children's visual scanning of pictures. For example, two pictures of house fronts might be shown, with the child asked to say if they are the same or different. Children under six seldom scan all of either picture, making same-difference judgments on the basis of incomplete information. In addition, patterns of scanning differ. A systematic way to compare the houses is to make successive fixations in corresponding locations on the two houses; for example, having looked at a window in the upper left-hand corner of one house, to look next at the upper left-hand corner of the other, and so on. Such systematic scanning is done by some five-year-olds and is quite common among six-year-olds (Wright & Vlietstra, 1975). There are many other examples of transitions from unsystematic exploration to more systematic search during early and middle childhood.

We have seen that there are developmental changes in the manner in which children seek and gain information from the environment and corresponding changes in the types of information that is acquired. There are related aspects of development which concern the ways in which children encode information when performing various tasks. A variety of evidence suggests a rough trend from dealing with complete objects to basing responses on one featural dimension to using information from multiple dimensions. We will begin with the first transition.

An example of materials that might be used to study encoding processes is shown in Figure 10-6. These materials would be the basis of a series of

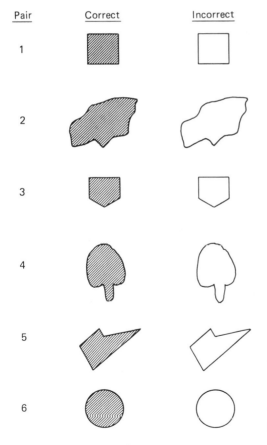

Pair	Correct	Incorrect
1		
2		
3		
4		
5		
6		

Figure 10-6. Materials used to study encoding processes.

discrimination-learning tasks. First the child would be shown pair 1 and asked to learn which item is "correct." The procedure is to present the pair, have the child choose an item, provide feedback (right or wrong), present the pair again, have the child again choose, again provide feedback, continuing this sequence until the child demonstrates knowledge of which item is correct by making several correct choices in succession. (In presenting the pair, the positions of the two items vary from trial to trial so that the child must learn to choose the correct item rather than, say, always picking what is on the left).

When the first pair-discrimination has been learned, the second is given, and so on through the series of pairs. Looking at the pairs in Figure 10–6, it is obvious to us that, in each pair, the shaded item is correct. With this knowledge, after learning a number of pairs, we would in essence know which item of the next pair is correct before receiving any feedback about that pair. In other words, we would have learned the concept "shaded is correct" (see Chap. 6). Having acquired this concept, an individual would make the correct choice on the very first presentation of subsequent pairs. This is precisely what older children and adults do, but younger children behave differently. Their choices on the first presentation of the pairs remain at chance levels even after they have learned a number of such pairwise discriminations. They learn each discrimination as an isolated task (Tighe & Tighe, 1978). When learning the first discrimination, they learn "this one's correct, the other one's wrong"; given the second pair, they again learn "this one's correct . . .," and so on through the series. They do not encode relations between feedback and separate features of the items. It is *not* that young children are incapable of distinguishing separate features of objects; indeed, drawing their attention to the features leads them to behave much like older children (Tighe & Tighe, 1978). What does happen is that, unaided, young children encode whole object-feedback relations rather than attending to individual featural dimensions.

Once children begin to base their responses on individual features or dimensions, they tend to use only one dimension at a time. For example, in judging the amounts of water in different-shaped glasses, four- to five-year-olds tend to use only the height of the water (Miller, 1973). Only some years later do they use both height and width (Siegler, 1981; recall our earlier discussion of conservation). There are many such judgments for which analogous transitions occur over time. In some instances there are intermediate steps, for example, using width, but only when heights are equal; vacillating between using height or width. Another facet of such "one-dimensional responding" is that children show preferences for some dimensions over others. Such preferences are dependent on the salience of the various dimensions of the materials presented—for example, striking differences in color or shape will be more salient than small differences—but there are also some consistent developmental trends. Three- and four-year-olds attend more to color than to visual form, with a preference for form appearing after age five. This pattern corresponds to that found for features encoded by touching objects—texture is preferred before shape. In both cases, the first-preferred dimension, color or texture, is often "all over" an object and thus accessible through gross, incomplete processing, whereas visual form and tactile shape require more systematic search (Wright & Vlietstra, 1975). When children exhibit dimensional preferences, their performance on cognitive tasks sometimes depends on whether a preferred or a non-preferred dimension is relevant to correct responding. For example, a child may be given a sorting task using objects which vary in both color and form. A form-preferring child is likely to perform better on the sorting task if form is made the basis for correct responding (Pick, Frankel, & Hess, 1975). The presence of salient or preferred dimensions that are irrelevant to correct responding disrupts the performance of younger children more than older children. It should be mentioned that adults also show preferences for some featural dimensions over others, but these preferences typically have no impact on their task performance (Dominowski, 1973).

We have presented just a sample of the many changes in attentional and encoding processes that take place during childhood. Differences in such processing might be an explanation for developmental trends in any of a wide variety of tasks. Although some selectivity is present even at birth, it is many years before children display systematic, task-relevant utilization of multiple features of objects and events.

LANGUAGE

One of the obvious and spectacular achievements of human beings is their acquisition of language. Many features of linguistic behavior were discussed in Chapter 7; here, we will focus on the relation between language development and (non-linguistic) cognitive development. Because of the complexity of language and the universal acquisition of a native language by normal children, it is tempting to suppose that language processing and development are separate from non-linguistic cognitive development. Researchers have found that young infants discriminate speech from non-speech sounds and, further, discriminate among speech sounds in ways that are strikingly similar to the phonetic differences of adult language (Miller & Eimas, 1983). A possible implication is that human infants possess some special language processor, although Miller and Eimas emphasize that this implication does not necessarily follow from their findings. Pinker (1979) evaluated two extreme positions: A. Language acquisition results from the operation of a general-purpose, rule-and-structure learning mechanism. B. Language acquisition rests on innate knowledge of the properties of natural languages. Pinker forcefully argued that neither extreme view can successfully explain language acquisition. Language development and non-linguistic cognitive development interact in some way, but the precise form of the relation remains to be determined. In our review, different kinds of language-cognition relations will be described.

The infant's exposure to language occurs in the context of everyday living and the input is primarily speech by adults. Most of the speech directed to young children consists of well-formed, simple sentences, which Pinker (1979) suggests might help them in forming hypotheses about language structure, because short sentences are easier to encode and remember. MacNamara (1972) emphasizes that speech is *about something* in everyday life and argues that infants try to understand "what is going on" and then use this derived meaning in an attempt to make sense of what is being said to them. MacNamara points out that during the first two years of life, infants generally know more about the world (their world) than about language; he shows how using non-linguistic meaning to comprehend language could lead to learning vocabulary and syntax. To illustrate this process, suppose you were abruptly deposited in the middle of a community whose inhabitants spoke a language you knew absolutely nothing about. In trying to figure out what people were saying, you would make use of many non-linguistic cues such as gestures, facial expressions, objects, actions, and reactions. This infant is in similar circumstances and may reasonably be supposed to use similar cues.

Meaning seems to dominate the linguistic behavior of young children. Early speech is commonly characterized as *holophrastic*—infants use single words to express entire ideas. Thus an infant might say "ball" to mean "the ball is rolling," "give me the ball," or "see the ball." Knowing a few words and using contextual information to derive meaning can help in comprehending longer expressions. Children tend to imitate well-formed, adult sentences in reduced form, that form representing a "core meaning." "Mommy will get you the ball" might come back as "Mommy ball." Two-year-olds respond just as well to distorted sentences—"Mommy clown to the show"—as to well-formed sentences—"Show the clown to Mommy" (Ginsburg & Koslowski, 1976).

Nelson (1974) argued that learning the name of something is the last step in the development of core concepts. If so, children should engage in consistent classification before "learning the words." To test this hypothesis, Nelson (1973) placed various collections of objects in front of children aged nineteen to twenty-two months; interest lay in whether or not the child would rearrange the objects into groups. The children had active vocabularies ranging from fifteen to over three-hundred words so that, from one set of categories to another, the number of children who knew possibly relevant labels varied greatly.

Two major results were obtained: First, children formed groups for which they did not have labels, supporting the hypothesis that core categorization precedes naming. Second, children were much more likely to form groups on some bases rather than others. Overall, Nelson's results suggested that functional concepts dominate the thinking of children in the early stages of language learning ("balls roll," "a hole is to dig"). Such results support the idea that sensory-motor development lays the foundation for language development (Piaget, 1970). One part of this notion is that the subject-object distinction of language is preceded by and based on the agent-action distinction contained in the sensory-motor schemas developed in the first year or so of life. Another part is that the development of representational thought (usually assessed through object-permanence tests) is a prerequisite for language acquisition. Although better performance on object-permanence tests tends to occur at *roughly* the same time as certain features of language appear (for example, two-word utterances), trying to find closer connections is virtually impossible because of the many ways in which object-permanence tests may be given and scored as well as the lack of clear criteria for "having language" (Corrigan, 1979).

As language development proceeds, children increase their vocabularies as well as the average length of the utterances they produce. Comprehension of language is greater than production—children nearly always understand more than they say. These aspects of language development are illustrated in a study by Goldin-Meadow, Seligman, and Gelman (1976), who studied language development in fourteen- to twenty-six-month-old children. Testing took place in the homes; in addition to recording the children's spontaneous speech, comprehension and production tests were given. Approximately seventy different toys were spread out on the floor. Comprehension of nouns and verbs was measured by asking the child to point to or to otherwise respond selectively to a named object (for example, "Where's the truck?") or by asking the child to perform the action indicated by a particular verb (for example, "Make the doll lie down"). Production was tested by having the experimenter select a toy and ask the child "What's this?" and by the experimenter performing an action, asking the child "What am I doing?" On the production test, children who consistently used idiosyncratic words—for example, "nite-nite" for "pillow"—were considered to have a production word for the object.

The authors identified two patterns of responding among their subjects. Children in the Receptive group comprehended from three to eight times as many nouns as they produced, produced no verbs at all (although they understood a fair number), and used few combinations in speaking. In contrast, those in the Productive group produced most of the nouns they understood, produced verbs (although not nearly as many as they understood), and generated more and longer combinations in their spontaneous speech. The authors proposed that the Receptive and Productive patterns represent different phases of language development, with the receptive phase preceding the productive phase. To test this hypothesis, they continued to study three Receptive children for several months, repeating the tests on a monthly basis. Several months later, each of these children produced most of the nouns they understood and began producing verbs and longer utterances, thus supporting the hypothesis.

The difference between comprehension and production appears in other aspects of language development as well. For example, young children overextend the meanings of some words when speaking, using a single word to convey the meanings of several different words. This behavior occurs even when the child understands the several meanings. For example, a child might call all four-legged animals "dogs" but, when told "Show me the dogs," select only dogs and not other animals (Clark, 1978). As Clark points out, producing language places different and somewhat greater demands on children, compared to comprehending speech directed toward them. Their communication strategies are fairly simple; having limited production capabilities, they nonetheless try to communicate and, in doing so, stretch the meanings of words. "Children may mean what they say, but they do not always mean what adults mean with the same words" (Clark, 1978, p. 956). Comprehension-production problems are hardly limited to two- and three-year-olds. For example, compared to second-grade children, kingergartners are less likely to notice that they have been given ambiguous or incomplete instruction and less likely to seek clarifying information when they do not understand a message (Flavell, Speer, Green, and August, 1981). In general, younger children are less sensitive to communication problems, whether they are sending or receiving information.

Comprehension and production skills develop throughout childhood, with comprehension leading production. These facts might pose problems for studies of non-linguistic cognitive development. Suppose a researcher wants to investigate what a child knows about something such as numerical amounts, liquid amounts, category relations, or ordering. To the extent that the task involves language, performance might reflect linguistic abilities rather than (or in addition to) the cognitive processes that are the main focus of the research. We mentioned earlier the debate over using judgments or explanations in assessing children's performance on various cognitive tasks; an argument for using judgments was that a child may fail to give a good explanation for linguistic rather than cognitive reasons. Siegel (1977) has argued that, at least for preschool children, language development lags behind corresponding cognitive development and that, in this sense, the two are independent. If so, one would expect children to perform better on nonverbal than on verbal tasks involving the same concepts.

One example of Siegel's research concerned numerical amounts. For studying numerical differences, children were shown, on each trial, two different sets of dots, for example a four-dot set and a five-dot set (over trials, both the numbers of dots and the left-right position of the bigger set were varied). For the *nonverbal* task, children were told simply that if they "picked the right one" in each pair, they would get a reward (candy, play money). For half the children, the "right one" was always the larger set; for the other children, the smaller set was "right." The question here was whether the children could learn to consistently choose the right set (keep in mind that the children had to respond on the basis of "bigger" or "littler" because any particular number of dots, for example, four, was "the big one" on some trials and "the little one" on others). For the *verbal* task, children were shown identical series of pairs of dot sets and asked, on each trial, "Which is the big one?" (For half the children, the question was always "Which is the little one?") The verbal task required children to respond to the words ("big," "little") but the nonverbal task did not have this requirement.

In Figure 10–7 you can see that four-year-olds performed better than three-year-olds. More important, however, are the data representing uneven performance—passing one task but failing the other (the middle of the figure). In both age groups, many children succeeded at the nonverbal task but failed the verbal task; hardly any showed the reverse pattern. Siegel (1977) observed this dominant pattern in children's performance on a variety of tasks. These findings led her to conclude that, for preschool children, a considerable amount of cognitive development precedes the corresponding language development.

A language provides a way of encoding objects and events, includes a symbol system for dealing with concepts not having clear perceptual referents, and incorporates a complex rule system in its grammar. By about the age of five, children show considerable mastery of their native language, including syntax, even though

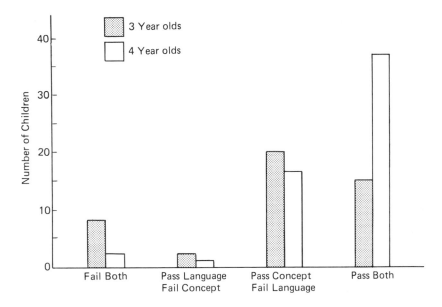

Figure 10-7. Performance on verbal and nonverbal tests of numerical amounts. (From Siegel, 1977. Adapted by permission of the author and Academic Press, Inc.)

their linguistic skills are still far from adult-like (Palermo & Molfese, 1972). Noting that five-year-olds' syntactical competence seems better developed than their ability to utilize non-language rules, Bruner, Olver, and Greenfield (1966) suggested that, from middle childhood on, language may guide cognitive development in significant ways. Structures and operations might be developed first in language and subsequently applied to a variety of contexts. There is evidence suggesting a changing relation between language and general cognition during development. Providing verbal cues to the correct responses does not help three-year-olds learn discriminations but is helpful for four-year-olds (Siegel, 1977), and verbal-rule instruction has been found to facilitate the performance of slightly older children on tasks such as tests of conservation (Beilin, 1976). Later in development and throughout life, language is the primary system for dealing with abstract concepts and relations.

MEMORY

Changes in memory processes, especially those related to short-term memory or working memory, have been proposed as playing a critical role in cognitive development for a long time. Tests of short-term memory are commonly included in tests of intellectual development and show clear developmental trends. For example, on digit-span tests, requiring a person to repeat a string of rapidly-presented digits, the length of strings that can successfully be repeated increases with age.

Because short-term processing of current information is involved in nearly all cognitive tasks, it is easy to understand why memory processes have been considered for a major role. Two proposals have received much attention: first, that the fundamental capacity of short-term memory increases with age; second, that younger children's basic information-processing is slower than that of older children and adults. We have already noted that there is ample evidence of age differences in *performance* on short-term memory tests; similarly, on a variety of speeded-processing tasks, slower performance has been observed in younger children (Wickens, 1974). However, inferring differences in basic capacities from such data is questionable because performance can be and is affected by many other factors, for example, by attention, organization, and relevant knowledge.

Consider the idea of changes in central processing speed. Chi (1977) points out that a distinction must be made between the speed with which a single mental operation is carried out and the speed with which a sequence of such operations is completed. The latter involves control processes, organization, and may be subject to many influences. With respect to individual processes, research using Sternberg's memory-scanning task has shown no differences between five and fourteen years of age in the time taken to make a single comparison (Chi, 1977). As you may recall from Chapter 3, in the Sternberg task a subject is shown a small number of items (the memory set), with the number varying from trial to trial, and then shown a probe item and asked to indicate as quickly as possible whether the probe was in the memory set. The slope of the function relating reaction time to the number of items in the memory set serves to estimate the speed with which a single comparison is made. In the studies cited by Chi (1978), slopes did not change with age. Chi concluded that there is no reason to assume age differences in central processing speed; rather, where processing speed differences are found, they are better explained in terms of different control processes being used by children and adults.

Similar comments apply to the idea that short-term memory capacity might increase with age; performance on short-term memory tests is affected by many factors. Perhaps the most dramatic demonstration was reported by Chi (1978), who compared children to adults on two short-term memory tasks, digit span and recall of the positions of chess pieces after a very brief presentation (see Chapter 8). The special feature of this study was that these children knew more about chess than the adults! A portion of Chi's results is shown in Figure 10–8. On the commonly-used digit-span test, the usual finding was obtained: the children performed less well than the adults. On the chess-memory test, however, the difference was strikingly reversed. These findings make it virtually impossible to believe that children simply have less memory capacity than adults. They also point to the importance of relevant knowledge of task materials to performance on cognitive tasks (a topic we will return to shortly).

On the basis of the existing evidence, there is no need to propose that there are developmental changes in fundamental short-term memory capacity or basic, central processing speed. This does *not* mean that age differences in memory performance are unimportant. Case (1978) has argued that processing limitations play

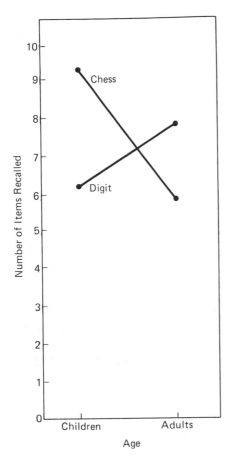

Figure 10-8. The amount of immediate recall for digits and chess stimuli. (Source: Chi, M.T., [1978]. Knowledge structures and memory development. In Siegler, R.S. [Ed.], *Children's thinking: What develops?* Hillsdale, New Jersey: Erlbaum.)

an important role in cognitive development, but these are functional limitations, not basic capacity limits. Younger children do process information more poorly than older children and adults. Case stresses that, as a child continues to employ a processing routine, it becomes increasingly automated, thus "freeing up" processing resources. In addition, processing efficiency can be improved by acquiring better strategies and relevant knowledge, topics to which we will now turn our attention.

STRATEGIES

A strategy is usually considered to be an organized, self-initiated activity that is engaged in to help performance on some task. In many situations, younger children are less likely than older children and adults to use strategies; if they do use strategies, these are likely to be less efficient (Siegler, 1983). We have already presented examples of such differences in discussing attentional processes. Given a search task, younger children are likely to explore the situation rather haphazardly whereas older children engage in more organized, task-relevant patterns of search

(Wright & Vlietstra, 1975). Younger children have greater difficulty in directing their attention toward task-relevant information and ignoring irrelevant information (Pick, Frantel, & Hess, 1975). The general implication is that the acquisition of more and better strategies is responsible for a considerable proportion of developmental trends in cognitive performance.

Much of the research on strategies has concerned performance on memory tasks. In Chapter 4 we pointed out that remembering is often affected by strategic activities—rehearsal, organization, retrieval, and so on. It is important to realize that much of our remembering is unintentional: children and adults remember many things that they never deliberately tried to remember. Thus, remembering does not necessarily require the use of any strategy, and age differences in memory performance do not necessarily result from differential use of strategies. For example, Perlmutter and Myers (1979) gave two- and four-year-old children a "remembering game" in which the children were asked to remember the names of familiar objects that were placed in a box. Several variations were employed. The test "list" might be categorized (three items from each of three categories) or uncategorized (nine items from nine different categories); a categorized list might be presented in a blocked fashion (first the three items from one category, then the three from another category, and so on) or presented randomly (items from different categories mixed together). With respect to recall of the objects' names, younger children recalled less than older children; both age groups recalled more from categorized lists; both age groups recalled more when categorized lists were blocked rather than randomly ordered in presentation. However, none of these effects appears to have anything to do with the use of memory strategies. Indeed, Perlmutter and Myers report that there were no indications of overt rehearsal and that, overall, the preschool children's memory performance could be considered nondeliberate. The results can be understood without reference to strategies. Semantic relations can be encoded rather automatically (categorized lists were recalled better) and are more readily elicited when same-category items are presented together; (blocking better than random presentation), and the older children know more about the categories than the younger children and thus recall more.

When older children are studied, strategy effects are commonly observed. The employment of rehearsal techniques varies greatly with age. For example, primacy effects (better recall of items presented early in a list) are attributed to the greater rehearsal that these items receive; differences in primacy effects have been found to account for most of the differences between nursery-school children and fifth-graders in list-recall (Allik & Siegel, 1976).

Rehearsal strategies have been studied by having subjects rehearse aloud. Kellas, McCauley, and McFarland (1975) presented children with lists of nine words, one at a time, and tape-recorded the children's vocalizations to assess rehearsal. The data, shown in Figure 10–9, clearly indicate greater rehearsal by older subjects, especially for items earlier in the list where the largest differences in recall are observed. Ornstein, Naus, and Liberty (1975) found that the kind of rehearsal used by younger and older children is different. Younger children (third-graders) tended

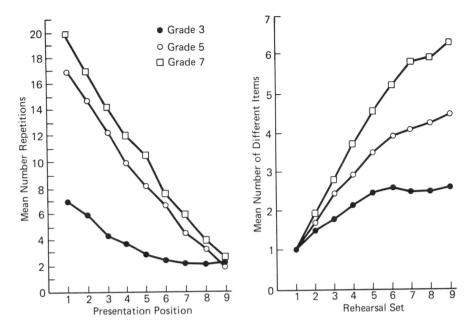

Figure 10-9. Mean repetitions and rehearsal set sizes for third, fifth, and seventh grades. (From Figure 1 in Kellas, McCauley, & McFarland, 1975. Courtesy of Academic Press, Inc.)

to rehearse just the item most recently presented or minimal combinations, whereas older children (sixth- and eighth-graders) used a cumulative rehearsal strategy resulting in integrated units. The difference can be illustrated as follows: If the series presented were "yard, cat, man, desk," a typical rehearsal pattern for a younger child after the presentation of "desk" would be "desk, desk, desk." For an older child it would be "desk, man, yard, cat, man, desk, cat, yard." An older child or adult is more likely to rehearse and to construct larger chunks by using a cumulative rehearsal strategy. Younger children can be taught rehearsal strategies, with a resulting improvement in memory, but they tend not to transfer the strategy to later tasks, rehearsing and remembering better only on the task for which they have been directly taught to rehearse (Hagen, Jongeward, & Kail, 1975).

Similar findings have been obtained in regard to organizational strategies. Moely, Olson, Halwes, and Flavell (1969) studied recall of the names of pictures which could be grouped into four categories—animals, furniture, vehicles, and clothing. During the study period, the child was shown the pictures arranged in an irregular circle with no two same-category members next to each other. Children were given two minutes to study the pictures and were told that they could move the pictures around if they liked. Interest lay in the extent to which children would group together pictures belonging to the same category.

Most of the children moved the pictures around during study, but kindergartners hardly ever grouped category members together; first- and third-graders were only slightly better, but the fifth-graders averaged about 60 percent grouping by categories during study. Given special instruction encouraging the use of a grouping strategy, younger children used the strategy just as often as the older children had done spontaneously, and recalled more items than without such instruction. In general, younger children do not spontaneously use organizational strategies even when they have the knowledge needed to organize the materials, but they can be taught to use such strategies to improve their memory performance (Naus & Ornstein, 1983).

This research demonstrates the important role played by strategies in understanding developmental trends in performance on cognitive tasks, but it also raises questions. Why are older children more likely to spontaneously use a strategy? Why do children sometimes use and sometimes not use an effective strategy? Why do children, especially younger children, who are taught a strategy fail to use it spontaneously on subsequent tasks? Two kinds of answers have been proposed to such questions, one focusing on what children know about their own cognitive processes and the other on what they know about the materials they are asked to work with. We will consider each idea in turn.

METACOGNITION

What people know about how (their own) cognitive processes operate is termed *metacognition* (cognition about cognitive processes). This topic has interest on its own merits but has potentially greater importance because metacognitive knowledge might explain the acquisition and use of cognitive strategies. Acquiring knowledge about how to think might well affect how one thinks which will affect how one performs on cognitive tasks (Brown & DeLoache, 1978).

Much of the research on metacognition has concerned memory, dealing with children's knowledge about memory. A landmark study was conducted by Kreutzer, Leonard, and Flavell (1975), who interviewed children of different ages, questioning them about remembering and asking them to explain their answers. Some of their findings are shown in Table 10–3.

The "savings" item assessed whether the child knew that prior learning would aid subsequent relearning even if a person could no longer recall the material. The child was told that two boys had to learn the names of all the birds in their city, that one boy had learned them last year but forgotten them while the other boy had never learned them. The child was then asked which boy would find it easier to learn the birds' names now, and why. Although the majority of children of all ages chose the relearner, older children were more likely to give an adequate justification for their choice. The "immediate-delay" item was intended to determine if children knew that forgetting can occur quite rapidly (loss from short-term memory). Childern were asked whether it would make a difference if they phoned immediately or got a drink of water first when someone had just told them a phone number to call. The results indicate that older children were more aware that information can be lost from memory quite rapidly. The children were also asked what they would do if they had to remember a phone number. Only the older children suggested rehearsal as a means of combatting forgetting.

Table 10-3. *Children's answers to questions about memory. (Adapted, with permission from data by Kreutzer, Leonard, & Flavell, 1975.)*

	Questions	GRADE LEVEL			
		K	*I*	*3*	*6*
A.	Savings				
	Percent choosing relearner	55	55	60	65
	Percent explaining choice	30	50	50	65
B.	Immediate-delay				
	Percent aware of loss	40	70	95	95
C.	Remembering phone number				
	Percent "write down"	55	55	80	45
	Percent "rehearse"	0	10	10	45
	Percent other/no answer	45	35	10	10
D.	Story-list				
	Percent "story easier"	50	75	100	85
	Percent explaining choice	15	20	70	80
E.	Opposition-arbitrary				
	Percent "opposites easier"	30	50	80	100

Other items tested children's knowledge of the advantages of organizational constraints in remembering material. They were asked whether it would be easier to remember a set of pictures that were merely presented ("list") or if they were told a story about the pictures. Another item involved asking the child whether it would be easier to learn a pair of words which were opposites or a pair of unrelated words (examples were used). It can be seen in Table 10–3 that other older children were more likely to be aware of the memory advantages which structural constraints provide.

Overall, the findings indicate that kindergartners do know some things about memory. They know that forgetting occurs, that a lot of material is harder to remember than a little material, that more study time is better than less study time, and that some things can be done to prevent forgetting/aid remembering. To aid remembering, the younger children tended to mention using external memory aids—writing things down, tying strings on fingers, asking other people—rather than referring to memory strategies such as rehearsal. Of course, there is a great deal that the younger child does not seem to know, and there is considerable growth in metamemory (knowledge about memory) during middle childhood, although the fifth-graders were far from experts.

What of the relation between metamemory and memory performance itself? Cavanaugh and Borkowski (1980) gave kindergarten to fifth-grade children both metamemory questions and a number of memory tasks. Although both metamemory and memory performance improved with age, finding closer relations was not generally possible. For example, children who appeared to lack relevant knowledge of metamemory often performed well on memory tasks, and those showing good metamemory frequently performed poorly on memory tasks. In existing data, only a weak relation seems to hold between metamemory and memory, and there are several possible reasons for this state of affairs. Cavanaugh and Perlmutter (1982) have criticized the concept of metamemory, arguing that it is used vaguely (precisely what counts as metamemory and what does not) and that specific predictions are elusive (which aspects of metamemory should, theoretically, be related to which aspects of memory?). Most studies of metamemory (but not all; see Siegler, 1983) employ evaluations of children's answers to questions, raising questions about the accuracy of the assessments. Recall from our discussion of language development that what a child says does not necessarily indicate what a child knows; thus, poor answers to metamemory questions might not mean poor knowledge. As Flavell and Wellman (1977) have suggested, a child might know a good strategy but choose not to use it, or have trouble executing it, or decide to use a different approach. Also, there is some inconsistency in performance and in metamemory-memory relations across memory tasks (Cavanaugh & Borkowski, 1980). Until these issues are clarified, the idea that metamemory development might explain memory development will remain promising, sometimes supported, and rather murky.

CONTENT KNOWLEDGE

Siegler (1983) observes that developmental psychologists have tended to focus on context-free processes—for example, attention, memory, strategies, metacognition—with relatively little consideration given to the role played by children's knowledge of specific domains. He suggests that children's acquisition of knowledge in various domains might be an important aspect of cognitive development.

With adults, it is clear that the amount and richness of a person's knowledge influences performance on relevant tasks. For example, Naus and Ornstein (1983) gave college students two types of word-lists to remember; one contained words from common, taxonomic categories (for example, animals, foods) while the other contained words related to the game of soccer. The students differed in their knowledge of soccer, thus there was a content-knowledge difference between "experts" and "novices," although the words were known to all students. On the taxonomic list there was no difference in recall between the two groups, but "soccer experts" recalled much more of the soccer-word-list than "novices." In Chapter 8, we discussed evidence showing both that novice and expert problem-solvers behave differently and that expertise applies to relatively specific domains, for example, chess, mathematics, car repair.

If adults' behavior is affected by knowledge of domains, it is eminently reasonable to suppose that children's behavior is similarly influenced. There are findings that suggest such effects. Bjorklund and Zeman (1982) found typical developmental trends from first to fifth grade for recall of taxonomic lists but minimal differences across age for recall of classmates' names. We have previously considered Chi's (1978) finding of a marked reversal of adult-(chess-expert) child differences in short-term memory, from recall of digits to recall of chess positions.

Naus and Ornstein (1983) pointed out that increased content knowledge can affect performance in two different ways. A richer, better organized semantic network may "automatically" lead to better performance—for example, useful relations might be more readily perceived and employed. Alternatively, a person might be more likely to use an effective strategy, or to use a more efficient strategy, when dealing with familiar, better understood materials. Naus and Ornstein cite evidence supporting both types of effects.

Emphasis on the role of content knowledge has two broad implications for understanding cognitive development. First, observed age differences in performance on cognitive tasks might be due in part to differences in content knowledge. It is quite difficult to present tasks that are equally familiar to children at all age levels, and there is a need to consider the possibility that performance differences might reflect older children's greater knowledge of task materials. Second, domain-specific knowledge effects may account for some of the heterogeneous patterns of behavior observed in children. When a child performs differently on tasks that involve similar processes, a possible explanation is that the unevenness in performance reflects variation in the child's knowledge of the task materials. Carmi (1981) suggests that children acquire knowledge that they can initially use only in rather narrow domains, with wider applicability contingent upon further, varied experience allowing interconnections to emerge. The idea is similar to that presented in our discussion of stages of development: Children may behave homogeneously across tasks when all the tasks are novel for them, then exhibit heterogeneity as they acquire task-relevant knowledge at varying rates, and still later show homogeneity again when slower-growing knowledge reaches the level attained earlier in other domains.

Keep in mind that content knowledge is just one of a number of influences on development. For example, children whose initial knowledge relevant to a task is quite similar have nonetheless be found to differ in acquiring additional knowledge because of differences in encoding potentially useful training information (Siegler, 1976, 1978). Finally, as Siegler (1983) cautions, research on this topic is itself in its infancy, and the precise role played by content knowledge in the course of cognitive development remains to be determined.

Summary

- Cognitive development concerns changes in cognitive processes, relations among these changes, and variables that influence those changes throughout the lifetime of human beings, with most attention paid to the period from birth to adulthood. It is important to distinguish between competence and performance, the latter often underestimating competence. Genetic and experiential factors influence development in a complex and intertwined fashion. Each environmental contact is interpreted in terms of existing structures (assimilation) and changes those structures (accommodation). Infants are more cognitively active than might at first be expected, showing rudimentary forms of attention, discrimination, and memory. Some aspects of cognitive development are strongly influenced by schooling rather than being a function of age or general experience.

It is convenient to talk of <u>stages</u> of development, although there is much controversy over the meaning and <u>validity</u> of broad stages. Piaget's theory is an influential stage theory in which development is divided into three broad periods, each having sub-stages. Infancy is characterized by sensory-motor development, including the acquisition of action schemas and increasingly sophisticated interactions with objects. Early and middle childhood are described as stressing the development of concrete operations, which allow the child to mentally manipulate features of objects in various ways. Adolescence is associated with the gradual emergence of formal operations, highly organized systems for dealing with abstract and hypothetical entities. Piaget's theory proposes broad stages defined in terms of underlying competence; research suggests that the theory ignores some important aspects of development.

• Young children's attention tends to be driven by environmental inputs and is thus very susceptible to interruption, whereas older children are able to engage in systematic, goal-oriented searches for desired information. Objects are encoded first as "whole entities," then in terms of one dimension at a time, and still later in terms of multiple features. The nature of encoding affects performance and learning in many task environments.

The relation between the acquisition of language and non-linguistic cognitive development is complex. Early on, general cognition is more developed than language and provides the basis for linguistic development. Young children possess concepts for which they do not yet have names, and children understand more than they exhibit in their speech. Preschool children may perform better on nonverbal than on verbal forms of a task. Once language is reasonably well acquired, however, it provides an encoding and symbol-manipulating system that strongly influences subsequent cognitive development.

Although there are clear differences between younger and older children (and between children and adults) on memory tasks, these differences appear to stem not from changes in basic memory capacities but from differences in what is known about the materials-to-be-remembered and the memory strategies that are used. Younger children tend not to use strategies or to use poor ones. They may not rehearse or may rehearse very inefficiently; they do not spontaneously employ organizational strategies, although they can use such techniques with some success if they are shown how to do so. Younger children know less than older ones about how their own cognitive processes function, and such metacognitive knowledge may be important for devising and using helpful task strategies. Also, younger children simply know less about the world and their knowledge is highly variable across content domains. It has been suggested that differences in content knowledge may be important for understanding both differences between younger and older children on many tasks and the uneven patterns of development that individual children exhibit.

ELEVEN

Practical Applications of Cognitive Psychology

Outline

In this book, we have attempted to sketch the dimensions of cognitive psychology and to highlight what we consider to be the most important contemporary areas of research. We have tried to show how a human being, conceived as an information-processing system, translates environmental information into a form upon which mental operations can be executed. After registering information perceptually, the system engages in at least the following processes. First, information is held veridically for some brief period of time in sensory memory. Rapidly, however, the information must be matched with some aspect of a person's knowledge of the world, a process known as pattern recognition. Pattern recognition may be largely automatic but it results in a sense of awareness about the current situation, including its comprehension and interpretation. Our awareness of the current situation is likely to be incomplete, however, because of a capacity limitation on the processing mechanism and the resulting necessity for selective attention.

We have seen how interpreted information is used consciously for a variety of purposes. Information that is processed superficially and acted upon immediately is quickly dropped from awareness and from memory. Other information may be processed over a more prolonged period of time, rehearsed and recirculated through the system. Under this circumstance, information persists through a time delay and is available for later use. But beyond this level, selected information can be processed deeply, so as to be integrated with our knowledge of the world and thus held indefinitely.

In a general sense, information processed through the system to a level of awareness and memory is used for purposes of deciding how to react to current circumstances. Very often, these decisions are based on more than just an immediate informational input. Indeed, decisions sometimes require that a person go beyond the information given, formulating reasonable inferences, constructing abstractions or concepts, developing hypotheses about possible actions, and in some cases creating original and practical solutions to problems.

Our presentation heretofore has been relatively abstract and theoretical. A reader may well wonder at this point about possible applications of basic cognitive research. Not to worry! There are plenty, beyond those mentioned in preceding chapters, and new applications of cognitive psychology are being discovered at a very rapid rate. We conclude this book by discussing some of these applications. While our primary goal will be to take the principles of previous chapters and show how they have been employed in the "real world," we will also introduce some important new findings from clinical research.

Implications for the Law

EYEWITNESS TESTIMONY

The following is a true story. Late one night, Assistant District Attorney William Schrager was observed acting "suspiciously" near a stalled car in Queens (New York) by two policemen (*Time*, April 2, 1973). The police noticed that Schrager fit the description of a man sought in connection with a series of sexual assaults. When Schrager failed to produce adequate identification, the police took him to a nearby station where he was booked and placed in several lineups along with a number of individuals to whom he bore no close resemblance. To his horror,

Schrager was identified by four different women as the person who had attacked them. Fortunately for Schrager, another man of very similar stature and looks later confessed to the crimes with which Schrager had been charged and he was released from custody.

There are a surprisingly large number of cases like Schrager's. Fortunately, most cases of misidentification are spotted promptly and dismissed. But on some occasions, individuals have been held in jail for some period of time on the basis of misidentification, and still other cases have gone all the way to the courtroom. In England, Lord Devlin's committee (Devlin, 1976) analyzed 347 court cases in which the only evidence against the accused was the identification of one or more eyewitnesses. Seventy-four percent of the cases resulted in conviction. Some of these convictions were later overturned because of demonstrated mistaken identification by prosecution witnesses.

Several psychological studies have addressed the question of the impact of eyewitness testimony on jury decision-making. In a classic example, Loftus (1974) presented subjects with a description of an armed robbery that resulted in two deaths. Some subjects heard a version of the case with only circumstantial evidence; 18 percent voted for conviction. Other subjects heard the same weak evidence plus an eyewitness identification; the conviction rate rose to 72 percent. There seems to be no doubt, then, that eyewitnesses are a potent source of influence on jurors. There is further evidence that such testimony, once offered, is difficult to discount. Loftus' study included a third group of subjects who heard the eyewitness discredited by the defense attorney on the grounds of very poor eyesight. With this group, the conviction rate dropped only slightly, to 68 percent. Moreover, Gorenstein and Ellsworth (1981) have shown that incorrect identification of a target person reduces the probability of later correct recognition of the real target.

Research in cognitive psychology applies directly to the question of eyewitness testimony. Cognitive psychology deals with the way people acquire information, store that information over some intervening period, and retrieve the information for purposes of description or report at a later time. Table 11–1, gives a list of factors operating during the acquisition, the storage, and the retrieval stages, that are known to influence the accuracy and completeness of a witness's account of an event.

Acquisition and Encoding of Information.   Information is acquired by a witness during the event itself. A study by Hollin and Clifford (1980) illustrates the typical methodology used to study the acquisition process. When investigators showed subjects a black and white videotape of an event staged by amateur actors. There were two versions of the film, both of which opened with a woman walking alone toward the camera. In the violent version, a man grabbed the woman's arm, forced her back against the wall, tore her purse from her grasp and ran away, leaving the woman alone and sobbing. In the non-violent version, the man approached the woman and asked for directions. After viewing the film, subjects were asked to recall the incident and to identify the man from a set of photographs. Accuracy

Table 11-1. *Factors affecting the memory of eyewitnesses.*

EVENT FACTORS	WITNESS FACTORS
Acquisition	Stress/Fear
Duration of event	Age
Frequency of viewing	Sex
Event complexity	Prior training
Violence	Expectation/Attitudes
Seriousness	Personality characteristics
Retention	
Length of retention	
interval	
Change in appearance	
Intervening photographs	
Post-event suggestions	
Retrieval	
Method of questioning	
Identification procedures	
Status of questioner	
Nonverbal communication	

Adapted from Loftus (1981).

of testimony was consistently and significantly poorer for the violent version of the film. This study shows that the stress or psychological arousal inherent in a situation can adversely affect the accuracy with which the event is encoded.

More directly relevant to the influence of arousal on encoding processes is a study by Johnson and Scott (1976). In the high arousal condition of this experiment, witnesses—naive subjects who waited alone in a reception room, ostensibly for an experiment to begin—overheard an increasingly acrimonious argument between two people in the next room. The altercation ended with one of the two bursting into the reception room shouting, "He wouldn't let me go," and leaving abruptly. In his hand was a knife covered with blood; electrical wires dangled from his upper arm. Witnesses in the low arousal condition also waited alone in the reception room. However, in this case, the witnesses overheard a routine conversation between the two individuals in the next room. Subsequently, one of them appeared momentarily with grease on his hands, holding a pen. He remarked, "Too bad, the machine broke" and left.

Overall, it was shown that more information about the episode was accurately recalled in the high than in the low arousal condition. Identification of the man leaving the room, however, was more accurate in the low arousal condition. Why did high arousal facilitate overall recall? One possibility is that subjects in the high arousal condition spent a good deal of their viewing time looking at the knife, not at the person. In fact, nearly all these subjects recalled the knife and could describe it in some detail. In contrast, the low arousal subjects paid less attention to the pen and more to their man, as he passed through the reception room. The study gives some reason to suspect the accuracy of eyewitness testimonies to violent crime.

A similar methodology has been used to address questions about age, sex, prior training, and intelligence, as these might effect a witness's encoding and memory. One question that is often asked is whether police officers, with a certain degree of training in observational techniques, are any better eyewitnesses than laypeople. Training can help people to be *sensitive* to certain details but has little or no effect on the encoding of details that were not especially well attended to. Police officers are trained to look for physical and behavioral clues that might escape the notice of a layperson. As an example, a police officer is more likely to take note of a piece of inappropriate clothing, such as a jacket worn on a warm day (suggesting the possibility of a concealed weapon). But, when it comes to face recognition, trained police officers do not seem to be any better than the rest of us.

Woodhead, Baddeley, and Simmonds (1979) evaluated an ongoing training course designed to improve encoding and subsequent face recognition. The training program, which had been operating for several months prior to the evaluation, involved an intensive study routine based on lectures, slides and film demonstrations, discussions, case history materials, and practice exercises. Although the program was both imaginative and enthusiastically taught, Woodhead and co-workers found no evidence that the training had any effect on the ability to remember photographed faces. No program currently available, no matter how intensive, seems to have much effect in improving the encoding of faces.

What about the age of the witness? Psychological research indicates a growth function for memory, with some possible deterioration in old age. It is generally thought that adults between the ages of twenty and sixty-five are much better than young children on memory tasks and somewhat better than the elderly. Since children are increasingly called upon to give evidence in court, their ability as eyewitnesses needs careful study. Marin, Holms, Guth, and Kovac (1979) compared four groups of subjects: kindergartners and first-graders, third- and fourth-graders, seventh- and eighth-graders, and college students. Subjects viewed a staged scenario in which a male adult entered the experimental room and, looking very upset, made some remarks to the experimenter. The entire interaction lasted only fifteen seconds. After a short delay, subjects were given a memory test for the details of the event and for the identity of the intruder. Two weeks later, subjects returned for a second memory test designed to assess the extent to which they picked up misleading information during the first interview and had encoded that information into memory. The results showed that recall of both correct and incorrect material increased with age. However, there was only a small and nonsignificant effect of age on the ability to answer specific questions accurately, on the ability to make accurate identifications from the photographs, and on susceptibility to leading questions. These minimal effects stand in sharp contrast to the generally accepted belief that young children are highly inaccurate and suggestible, and thus make poor witnesses.

The conventional wisdom is that old people, like children, have poor memories. Yet much of the evidence cited to support the decline of memory with advancing age comes from experiments using highly unrealistic material, such as lists of unrelated words or nonsense syllables, and may not generalize to natural memory. Fortunately, there have been some studies using naturalistic materials. For example, Byrd and Thomson (1979) compared college students and elderly subjects (over sixty-five years of age) on their memory for a seven-minute videotape of a purse-snatching incident. Older subjects were considerably poorer in their ability to remember the details of the videotape and their ability to identify the thief. This decrement seems to be primarily a matter of encoding, and is not attributable to poor eyesight or any other factors associated with old age. Thus, there may very well be good reason to question the adequacy of testimony provided by elderly witnesses.

Storage and Retrieval.   The most obvious factor affecting memory during the storage stage is length of time between the event and the test. Accuracy of recall or recognition tends to decline over the retention interval. But what is important about the retention interval is not the mere passage of time, but rather what happens during the interval. After an event, people talk about it, they overhear conversations about it, they may be asked leading questions by an investigator, or they may be required to examine photographs pertaining to the event. Any of these activities can cause interference with old information or can introduce new information into the witness's testimony.

In Chapter 4, we summarized the results of a variety of studies in which adult subjects were presented with a film of a complex event (for example, an accident) and subsequently questioned about that event. In some conditions of these experiments, questions were asked in such a way as to introduce misleading information. For example, a question might suggest the existence of a critical object that in fact did not exist. In one study, first mentioned in Chapter 4, subjects who had just watched a film of an automobile accident were asked, "How fast was the white sports car going when it passed the barn while travelling along the country road?" No barn actually existed, yet subjects who were asked this misleading question were substantially more likely to "recall" having seen the nonexistent barn than were subjects who had not been asked. Clearly, people do pick up later information related to an event, whether true or false, and integrate that information into their memory for the event. Such a process can significantly alter subsequent testimony.

The legal system is, of course, aware of the danger in leading questions and has established rules indicating when they can be used. While these rules of evidence provide protection in a courtroom, they are not operative during police examinations. The protection of the courtroom may be irrelevant if invalid information has been incorporated into memory during earlier improper questioning.

One other source of error in recall comes from the fact that the context at the time of recall (testimony) is typically different from the context in which the initial event was witnessed. Basic research on context effects has shown that a person's ability to remember information is heavily influenced by the relationship of the encoding or acquisition context for that information to its retrieval context (Tulving & Thomson, 1973; Smith, Glenberg, & Bjork, 1978). It is possible to enhance memory by reinstating the original event context. In a study by Malpass and Devine (1980), subjects viewed a staged act of vandalism. Five months later some of the subject-witnesses were reminded of the event in a detailed guided memory interview in which their feelings, their memories for details, and their immediate reactions were explored. Other subjects were not interviewed. When both groups of subjects tried to identify the vandal, those whose memory had been guided through the event were significantly more accurate.

LINEUPS AND THE THEORY
OF SIGNAL DETECTION

In a recognition memory experiment, subjects are first presented with a list of stimuli (for example, words or objects) and are later tested with a different set of stimuli from which they must choose the ones that appeared in the original set. Police lineups are recognition memory tests. On the basis of laboratory studies of recognition memory, we can guess that the composition of the lineup is extremely important. If the lineup has only two people in it, the witness has a fifty-fifty chance of picking out the suspect simply by guessing. With three people, the suspect has a one-third probability of being chosen by the witness on the basis of guessing alone. To cut down "chance" recognition, there should be a reasonable number of people in the lineup. Moreover, to insure reliability, several lineup tests, some with and some without the suspect, should be administered. Obviously, the witness should be given the opportunity in every case of responding "none of these" (Malpass & Devine, in press).

It is also important that those in the lineup resemble the suspect. This may seem to be a trivial point, but it was not properly appreciated by at least one police officer, who formed the lineup depicted in Figure 11–1. This lineup was used to test a witness to a crime who described the suspect as a young black male. Because there was only one black in the entire lineup, the witness was very likely to pick that individual as the guilty party. When asked about this particular lineup, the police officer claimed that the crime had been committed in a small town with hardly any blacks and he wanted a lineup that was "representative" of people in that town. But a lineup should not be so constituted that all possibilities except one can be eliminated on irrelevant grounds. The suspect must not be picked out simply by default. Much of what psychologists have learned about recognition memory tests can be applied directly to the construction of lineups. Proper construction of lineups can help to improve the fairness of such a procedure to both witness and suspect.

The theory of signal detection has a direct application to police lineups. The eyewitness is asked to decide which of several persons matches a particular memory trace. Each suspect either is (signal) or is not (noise) the same individual actually seen at the scene of the crime. The witness can either say "Yes, that's the person",

Figure 11-1. Lineup similar to the one used in a small town in Michigan to test a witness who had described a black assailant.

or "No, that's not the one." These possibilities create the four situations outlined in Figure 11–2.

If the witness's criterion for a "yes" response is influenced by a desire to protect society from criminals, it might be set too low, resulting in a high rate of false alarms and an increase in the likelihood that an innocent person will be identified. Setting the criterion too high, perhaps in the interest in protecting the innocent, might result in letting the actual criminal go. Ellison and Buckhout (1981) developed a decision analysis of eyewitness identification along these lines. They argue that, in a lineup, witnesses must take two decision steps, first answering the question "Is the suspect in the lineup?" and, second (given an affirmative answer), "Which one?" Ellison and Buckhout argued that witnesses generally have a low response criterion for the first question and, therefore, are more likely to say "Yes" than "No". This bias, coupled with the fact that recognition memory is highly error-prone, makes lineups unreliable, they conclude.

	State of the World	
Witness's Response	Signal (This is the criminal)	Noise (An innocent person)
"Yes, this is the criminal"	Hit	False Alarm
"No, this is not the one"	Miss	Correct Rejection

Figure 11–2. Signal detection analysis of eyewitness identification.

The probability of erroneous identification is enhanced if precautions are not taken against techniques that capitalize on witness biases. For example, a person who is dressed differently from others in the lineup, who has been seen in the presence of one or more police officers prior to the lineup, or who is in any other way different from the rest, is more likely to be chosen by the witness. Any kind of uniqueness on the part of the suspect can lead a person, even one who had not witnessed the crime, to select that suspect if invited to do so.

What techniques are available to reduce the magnitude of a witness's response bias? Three are suggested by Ellison and Buckhout. First, do not confuse confidence in recognition with good memory. As Deffenbacher (1980) has suggested, there might be little or no correlation between confidence and memory in these identification tasks. Second, inform the witness that the suspect may not be in the lineup. This will produce a more nearly optimal criterion setting. Third, take steps to insure that all individuals in the lineup are as similar as possible in dress, in demeanor, and in other ways that are not relevant to the crime. While increased similarity will tend to reduce the hit rate, it has a far larger effect on false alarm rate, resulting in a net increase in overall sensitivity in the task.

ROLE-PLAYING AND TESTIMONY

In the courtroom, witnesses are called either for the defense or for the prosecution. Thus, in a sense, the witness plays a social role, being partisan to one side or another in a dispute. It is conceivable that the role one is asked to assume and the expectations it carries with it may be a source of error in the presentation of testimony—that a person asked to testify for the defense will (possibly unwittingly) give information biased in favor of the defense. To examine this possibility, Vidmar and Laird (1983) asked subjects to view a complex stimulus event after which they were to testify in a simulated trial. Between the event and the trial, subjects were divided into three groups. One group was told that they would provide testimony on behalf of the plaintiff; another was to give testimony on behalf of the defendant; the third group was to testify on behalf of the court. Oral testimony in the simulated trial was shown to be biased in the first two, adversary role conditions. These biases were exhibited by particular inflections in the voice of the witness and by the choice of words, but not by the omission of facts. Thus, while these roles did not affect any of the objective evidence, the way facts were presented was changed. Style of presentation might cause judges or juries to draw inaccurate conclusions.

Other Applications of Memory Research

Much of cognitive psychology today is the study of human memory. Research has shown that remembering is not the passive stamping in of information, but rather that there are several kinds of memory with many processes involved. A central theme is that remembering what or how well depends on how material is processed. In Chapter 4 we discussed mnemonic techniques, such as the method of loci, which have been shown to sometimes produce large increases in memory performance. An implication is that memory, rather than being completely fixed, is changeable. Indeed, some have argued that skills in memorization ought to be taught early, just as skills in reading and writing are taught. One interesting application of memory research concerns work with mentally-retarded individuals.

HELPING THE MENTALLY RETARDED

Training in strategies for memorizing produces particularly impressive increments in memory for mentally retarded subjects. The work of Beaumont and Butterfield (1977) illustrates these effects. Adolescent mentally retarded subjects were first given an opportunity to proceed at their own pace through a set of to-be-remembered materials. Under these circumstances, retarded individuals typically did not take time to rehearse items, but moved quickly through the entire set of materials. As a consequence of poorly distributed and utilized study time, their performance was only 50 percent of the average achieved by normal individuals. Beaumont and Butterfield then proceeded to train their retarded adolescents in the study strategies typically used by successful normal individuals. These techniques included trying to form associations between items, trying to create subgroups of items, rehearsing those items together, and pacing slowly through the materials. These techniques are generally designed to create chunks of materials or large, well-organized cognitive units, which we have seen in other circumstances to be extremely helpful in committing materials to memory. The effect of this procedure was to improve the performance of adolescent retardates to a level roughly comparable to the memory performance of normal individuals of the same age.

What this study demonstrates is that one can improve the performance of individuals who appear otherwise to suffer a memory deficit. There have been similar demonstrations of this phenomenon with retardates younger than those studied by Beaumont and Butterfield, and with senior citizens who show a deterioration of memory. The main point of this work is to demonstrate that strategies, plans, or mnemonics for learning new material and committing it to long-term memory can be mastered, under proper training conditions, even by individuals with poor memory and poor intellectual skills. Of course, in addition to the strategy, what is required is the desire to learn and the willingness to invest the effort required to integrate new information with prior knowledge.

LEVELS OF PROCESSING
AND CONTEXT-DEPENDENT MEMORY

Two particularly powerful principles of memory have emerged from laboratory research in the past ten years. The levels-of-processing principle (Craik & Lockhart, 1972) states that the amount of information recalled is a function of the type of processing engaged in during initial learning or encoding. More specifically, the deeper the processing, the better the recall. Shallow processing, such as an examination of material for its orthographic characteristics, yields poor retention for those materials. Deeper processing, such as some involvement with the meaning or semantic characteristics of the material, is more durable.

The second principle is Tulving and Thomson's (1973) encoding specificity hypothesis. This principle states that the encoding operation utilized during initial learning determines what retrieval cues will be effective at recall. Thus, reinstating the circumstances of initial encoding and inducing the subject to engage in similar processing operations at the time of recall will maximize the amount recalled.

Allen Baddeley (1982) has shown how these two principles of memory can be used to help explain a variety of real-world observations. We will summarize briefly one of these applications, that to the phenomenon of amnesia.

Amnesia is not a well-defined clinical category. Its most striking feature is that patients appear to forget events of their daily lives almost as fast as they happen. Often they are unable to tell where they are at any moment, what day of the week it is, who the President of the U.S. is, what they had for dinner last night, or to supply any of the many details of memory a normal person can supply with minimal effort. These symptoms can arise from any of a variety of causes, including most importantly various kinds of damage to the brain.

Baddeley and Warrington (1973) explored the hypothesis that the defect of amnesic patients is associated primarily with long-term memory and with inadequate semantic encoding procedures. In one study, they showed that amnesics were no different from normal individuals in their use of phonological (superficial) codes, but inferior in using categorical and visual-spatial codes. Other researchers have confirmed that patients with amnesia due to alcohol-induced brain deterioration are similarly inferior to normal individuals in their use of semantic retrieval cues.

On the basis of this evidence, Baddeley concluded that the levels-of-processing principle provides a possible interpretation of the amnesic deficit. Amnesics simply do not encode material at a level deep enough to leave a durable trace in long-term memory. But there is more to amnesia than just a simple failure to encode deeply enough. Baddeley (1982) conducted an additional experiment in which amnesic patients were aided in encoding verbal materials at a semantic level. His induction procedure was successful in improving subsequent recall, but amnesics were still inferior to normal people treated in a similar way. Thus, one needs to look for additional factors that may be involved in amnesia.

One possible factor is the role of consciousness in memory. The argument is that amnesics might learn or encode material in much the same way as normal people but fail to remember that they had done so. Following others, Baddeley suggests an interesting analogy between amnesia and the phenomenon of "blind sight." Certain patients with damage in the visual area of the cerebral cortex are unable to report consciously on material presented to parts of their visual field, even though, when forced to guess, they can identify that material correctly. In other words, in "blind sight" the information is available, but the patient is not aware of it. Baddeley argues that amnesic patients might learn and acquire new material normally, and be able to use it subsequently, but at the same time not be aware of what they have learned nor be able to perform tasks that depend on awareness.

To what extent might the occurrence of learning in the absence of conscious remembering be peculiar to amnesia? Mendell and Mayes (1981) asked both normal and amnesic patients to search cartoons for particular objects. Over many trials, both groups became faster at locating critical objects, giving evidence of learning. When tested after a delay of seven weeks the amnesics continued to show rapid performance, indicating that they had retained whatever skill they had learned. Nonetheless, they were unable to recognize the relevant cartoons. Controls showed the same effect when tested after a much longer delay (1.5 years), indicating that the loss of awareness is not peculiar to amnesia, but might be characteristic of the weakening of memories in general.

Baddeley concludes that the major deficit associated with amnesia lies partly in a failure to process materials at various levels, but more importantly in whatever process it is that contributes to persistent awareness of previous experiences. When we say that amnesic patients have difficulty remembering what they had for breakfast or any other recent incident in their lives, we mean to attribute this inability as much to a lack of awareness as to the unavailability of encoded information in memory. The fact that amnesics might "know" what they had for breakfast could very well show up in the breakfast selections that they make the next day.

IS EXCEPTIONAL MEMORY REALLY EXCEPTIONAL?

In Chapter 1, we cited the extraordinary performances of memory experts and others capable of unusual mental feats. Ericsson and Chase (1982) suggest that these performances might not be as exceptional as they first appear and might well be within the capacity of most normal human beings. In fact, they argue that expert performance is largely attributable to extensive practice and a willingness to invest the effort that extensive practice requires. Chase and Simon (1973) estimate, for example, that the skill of chess masters is based on over 10,000 hours of practice. The mental calculations of Professor Aitken (see Chapter 1) rested on a lifetime of practice with numerical problems. Luria's memory expert, S, was educated in a school system that relied almost completely on rote memorization.

Still, what evidence is there that normal individuals have a similar capacity? Ericsson and Chase point to the fact that, normally, memory for prose is many times better than for nonsense material. Our short-term memory for the exact wording of sentences, for example, is markedly greater than our short-term memory for unrelated words (Aaronson & Scarborough, 1977). In fact, without any special training, people recall sentences of up to fourteen words perfectly about half the time (in contrast, our span for unrelated words is about six). If words average five letters in length, then this level of memory performance for sentences converts to approximately seventy letters recalled, a feat numerically comparable to that of the digit expert, SF (see Chapter 1). Both the performance of SF and normal sentence memory can be explained by reference to essentially the same mechanisms. As a consequence of practicing and using the language over a prolonged period of time, we develop means for chunking letters into higher-order meaningful units (words), and then combining words into even higher-order units such as phrases, simple sentences, compound sentences and the like. A normal person's memory for prose exceeds short-term memory capacity to the extent that the person has knowledge of the semantics and syntax of the language which can be used both in encoding and subsequent retrieval. People who have spent many years building up their language skills have acquired an extensive verbal knowledge base in long-term memory that can be used for effective storage and retrieval of new information. SF appears to be able to chunk digits in much the same way that all of us chunk letters into words.

Thus Ericsson and Chase argue that exceptional memory is a skill based on learned cognitive mechanisms and processes, developed through extensive practice and experience. Exceptional memory can be accommodated within the basic abilities and limits of the normal cognitive system. The suggestion is that any one of us willing to invest the time and effort can improve memory performance within any selected domain.

Applications in Education

PROCESSING INFORMATION IN TEXTBOOKS AND LECTURES

A main task for any student is to extract the "right" information from a text or lecture and to learn it well enough to perform successfully on tests given some time later. We can assume that college students have automated lower-level reading and listening skills and thus can devote full attention to comprehension. Still, it appears that the "average student's" study habits could be improved. While there are no magical methods for becoming an outstanding student, research findings do provide some helpful suggestions.

Extracting Information from Texts.   Poor grades are often attributed to inadequate study—the student who reads a chapter just once is unlikely to learn much. Yet, if left strictly to their own devices, students do not seem to improve much from repeatedly reading course material. Crouse (1974) allowed students to study material until they felt ready to take a test and to repeat the study-and-test cycle up to a total of five tests. The students showed virtually no improvement as a function of repeated study.

Students also underestimate how much they can learn from a text. In one study, some students were told to read a given set of materials so that they would "do their best" on a test, while others were told to read so that they could score 90 percent correct on the test. Students given the higher goal both thought they would and really did score higher on the test, as shown in Table 11–2. Those given the higher goal studied longer when length of study time was optional, but the higher

Table 11-2   *Percent correct: Subjects' estimates and test scores. (From data in table 2, LaPorte & Nath, 1976.)*

GOAL	ESTIMATED BEFORE READING	ESTIMATED AFTER READING	TEST PERFORMANCE
90% Correct	64%	58%	56%
"Do your best"	47%	38%	40%

goal instructions also led to better performance when study time was controlled, indicating that setting the higher goal led in some sense to better processing of the material (LaPorte & Nath, 1976).

Learning from a text can be improved if the reader engages in appropriate activities before and after reading. Acquisition of text information is aided by utilizing those cues that provide advance information about the content of the material (Glaser & Resnick, 1972). Such cues will be present in varying degrees from one text to another, and even from section to section, but there are some organizing cues that appear in any text. Before reading a chapter, a student would be well advised to examine the chapter outline and the chapter summary (if provided). Skimming the chapter, attending to section and paragraph headings, will also provide an idea of the structure of the material. Such activities prior to reading give the student a context for the material and provide some attention-directing clues. Similar ideas apply to reading smaller sections such as paragraphs—most paragraphs contain a sentence, often but not necessarily the first, which reasonably summarizes what the paragraph is about.

If a passage has been read through once, what can be done to improve learning and retention of the material? We have seen that merely reading it again probably will not help much—assuming, of course, that the first reading was an honest effort. A technique which does improve subsequent test performance is having students work together, taking turns asking and answering questions about the material (Frase & Schwartz, 1975). The trick is to construct questions to cover as much of the material as possible and also to form networks among ideas presented in different places (sentences, paragraphs within a section) rather than merely to "parrot" textual material in a rote-learning manner. Generally, integrative questions have been found to facilitate retention more than simpler, rote-learning questions (Rickards & DiVesta, 1974).

According to the Kintsch and van Dijk (1978) analysis of text, propositions or idea units are organized hierarchically, with the more important propositions represented higher in the hierarchy. Support for this analysis comes from the observation that higher-order propositions are better recalled than those lower in the hierarchy. Such results are also consistent with the intent of textbook writers, which is to communicate the main points in their text, if nothing else.

The Kintsch-van Dijk analysis raises an interesting question about study habits. If all that the writer intends is to communicate main ideas, and if they are all that the student remembers, what is the point of including lower-order propositions or details within the text? One answer is that not all the information in a text needs to be carried around in memory. The text continues to be available as a reference and the student will have an easy time accessing the right details if he or she has the general ideas clearly in mind before starting. Another possible answer is that inclusion of details may help to support memory for the main points of the text.

Reder and Anderson (1980) listed a number of arguments for and against the inclusion of details within a text. On the basis of this listing, they, with the assistance of their colleagues, arrived at the intuitive prediction that details support overall memory for text. To discover whether their intuitions were correct, they undertook a series of experiments to determine whether a person's memory for information has better after reading a text chapter or after spending the same amount of time on the summary of that chapter. The data from seven separate experiments all supported the conclusion that learning from summaries is at least as good as reading the original text, even when the test of memory is delayed as much as one year (see Table 11–3). Those who studied summaries did better with questions taken directly from the text and with inference-type questions that required the subject to combine facts. Even more impressive was the fact that performance on a transfer task (examining the ability of students to learn new, related material) was better after reading the summary. Summaries maintained their advantage over chapters even when the main points in the text were underlined.

Table 11–3. *Proportion correct answers to questions asked at various times after study.*

TEST	STUDY MATERIAL	
	SUMMARY	TEXT
Immediate	.793	.693
One week	.675	.600
Six months-one year	.595	.575

Data from Reder & Anderson (1980).

Thus, Reder and Anderson disconfirmed their intuitive hypothesis. Apparently, the supporting information provided by details does not contribute to memory for the main points in the text. Apparently, subjects do better on summaries because they can devote their entire study time to the main points of the text, not having to spend part of that study time on details contained in the chapter. It is possible also that students provide their own elaborations and details when studying the summary.

Reder and Anderson do not take this evidence as a recommendation against the use of full-blown textbooks. They allow for the possibility that the text can serve a variety of purposes beyond those provided by a summary. For example, students are likely to gain a better appreciation of the field as a whole from a complete text.

Also, there is no guarantee that, outside of the laboratory, a student would spend as much time going over a summary as he or she would going over a complete chapter (a necessity if the total time hypothesis is to apply). But the main point still remains: If the amount of study time is fixed and the aim is to score well on an examination, then devoting that time to an intensive examination of a well-written summary will provide better test performance than distributing the time over the entire text.

Extracting Information from Lectures. Lectures present students with an overlapping but substantively different information-processing task from that involved in reading a textbook. Whereas a textbook can be read at one's own pace, can be reviewed if desired, and need not be read exactly as ordered, a lecture occurs once with information presented at the rate chosen by the lecturer and with little or no opportunity for repetition. Of course, tape-recording a lecture provides a student with a partial record and some opportunity for review. However, for most students, comprehending a lecture presents a considerably more difficult information-processing task than reading a text covering the same material.

What can students do to get more out of lectures? Note-taking is the typical method. But is the effort worthwhile? It depends. Taking notes on what has been said and listening to what is being said compete for a person's limited resources for processing information. Rather than trying to listen and take notes "at the same time," it is better for students to listen for a time and then have a brief "blank period" in which to take notes (Aiken, Thomas, & Shennum, 1975). If a lecture proceeds too quickly and continuously, the lecturer could be asked to pause periodically so that notes can be recorded.

While it might plausibly be argued that the act of note-taking itself is beneficial because it results in deeper, more elaborate processing of the lecture material, this effect is typically not observed. Beneficial effects are obtained only when students engage in further processing, such as rewriting notes in their own words, and reviewing them prior to a test (Carter & Van Matre, 1975). Reviewing notes before a test obviously provides some repetition of the information in the notes and, in effect, shortens the retention interval for that information. In addition, reviewing notes might promote memory retrieval of lecture information not in the notes.

A sense of humor is positively regarded in our society. Lecturers often try to inject humor into their lectures, and students seem to like humorous lectures and lecturers. A little humor can have social benefits, but one might wonder whether humorous lectures are better or worse than serious lectures with respect to learning. Overall, injecting humor seems to have little impact on students' performance. Kaplan and Pascoe (1977) compared several versions of a lecture on personality theory and personality assessment. One version was serious; in a corresponding "lighter" version, humorous examples were used to illustrate the main concepts of the lecture; in a third version humorous comments were interjected that did not bear directly upon the concepts under discussion. The use of humorous examples of concepts tended to result in better test performance on questions related to those concepts but poorer performance on the remaining items. In terms of total test performance, the different versions were equivalent. These results suggest that a lecturer can effectively use humor to direct students' attention to important points in a lecture and to induce deeper processing of the target material. Doing so does not necessarily lead to better learning of lecture material overall, however.

Some researchers have used memory for classroom lectures as a means for testing psychological theories of memory in a natural setting. Kintsch and Bates (1977) conducted two experiments on their students' ability to recognize statements from a prior classroom lecture (See Table 11-4). Three types of statements were tested—statements concerning (1) major topics in the lecture, (2) details of the lecture, and (3) nonessential or extraneous matters, such as jokes or announcements. Memory for all three types of statements was high both two days and five days after the lecture. With a two-day delay, there was still a considerable amount of verbatim memory; after five days, basically only the gist remained. Over both retention intervals, extraneous remarks were remembered best and there was no significant difference between major topic and details. The fact that extraneous sentences were remembered best is not surprising, since these items were designed especially to differ both in content and in affect (especially the jokes) from the lecture. This is an example of a familiar phenomenon called the von Restorff effect, in which unique elements of all kinds tend to be remembered better than nonunique elements.

Table 11-4. *Mean recognition scores for lecture sentences actually spoken (old), paraphrases of lecture sentences, and control sentences (new) as a function of sentence type*

	TEST SENTENCE		
Spoken Sentence Type	*Old*	*Paraphrase*	*New*
Major Topic	2.92	2.42	1.78
Detail	2.85	2.29	1.37
Extraneous	3.31	1.79	79

Data from Kintsch & Bates (1977).

What was surprising was that the topic sentences were not remembered better than the details, a difference that would have been predicted from earlier laboratory work in which it had been observed that macropropositions have a much higher probability of recall than detail statements (Kintsch and van Dijk, 1978). Kintsch and Bates suggest that the outcome might be attributable to a difference in the way the lecturer and the student organized the material. A well-remembered detail statement might in fact have been that student's organizing macroproposition. Another possibility is that the macropropositions identified by the lecturer were too abstract, leading the listener to re-formulate them more concretely using less abstract details. Unfortunately, the Kintsch and Bates study does not give a basis for deciding whether either of these interpretations is true. Thus, for the time being, it is not clear whether or to what extent lecture and text materials are organized differently in the memory of the recipient. Memory for both types of material is consistent, however, in the sense that gist persists in time while verbatim information fades.

THE USE OF PRIOR KNOWLEDGE

There have been many investigations of how expertise in various domains affects problem-solving, comprehension, and memory. In general, the results illustrate the importance of previous knowledge for understanding the significance of new facts and events. But how do people become experts? This is a question of obvious significance on which there is relatively little factual information.

One of the first things a beginner has to master in any new domain is a technical vocabulary. We might suggest that a new learner adopt mnemonic techniques for learning this vocabulary; Atkinson and Raugh (1975) have shown that such techniques have considerable benefit in learning a new language. But mnemonic techniques do not help a person to understand the significance of facts. They promote rote learning, but rote learning, without understanding, does not make for expertise in a field.

Bransford, Stein, Vye, Franks, Auble, Mezynski, and Perfetto (1982) undertook a series of experiments on how learners acquire an understanding of facts in a new field. Their research addressed two basic questions: What are successful learners doing that less successful learners do not do? Can the performance of less successful learners be improved by modifying their cognitive processes?

To study the difference between successful and less successful learners, Bransford and his co-workers undertook some observations on fifth-graders learning new subject matter. These observations lead them to conclude that successful learners take a much more active role in the learning process. They ask questions of themselves and of their teacher. They actively scan pictures and text relevant to the new area. They try to compare different concepts or examples of different concepts. They attempt to relate new information to things that they already know. In contrast, less successful students are relatively passive and engage primarily in reading and rereading materials that are given to them.

The notion of levels-of-processing is no doubt involved in the development of expertise. Information must be processed at a semantic level if it is to be retained in durable form. Thus, it is important for new learners to attend to the semantic properties of new material with which they are presented. But semantic processing assumes that the learner already has a semantic network into which the new sentence is easily fit or to which it can easily be related; in fact, the new learner in any domain may have a quite poor semantic network. Even though the new learner can understand the meaning of the words he or she reads, thus processing them at a semantic level, he or she has little prior knowledge that can be used to elaborate on these terms and thereby support or secure their meaning. (Consider the terms quasar, binary pulsar, neutron star, and super nova. While you may have some sketchy knowledge of these terms, you are unlikely to understand their relationships unless you happen to be an astrophysicist.) Semantic processing will be of relatively little help in the absence of relationships provided by prior knowledge—the type of knowledge possessed by experts.

Stein and Bransford (1979) showed that elaboration within a sentence that enhances the significance—and therefore reduces the arbitrariness—of the relationship between terms in the sentence materially aids memory. Elaborations of this type are called *precise* by Stein and Bransford. Bransford and his co-workers suggest that the major difference between experts and novices in any domain is the extent to which the experts can spontaneously supply precise elaboration for terms that they read or hear. In other words, experts can embellish new material using their prior knowledge, while novices cannot. These investigators suggest that spontaneous generation of precise elaboration may also be the major factor that differentiates more successful from less succcessful learners.

In a series of experiments, Bransford and his colleagues provided empirical evidence on their hypothesis. First, they showed that self-generated elaborations had powerful effects on memory in fifth-graders and that the more successful students spontaneously produced a greater number of precise elaborations than the less successful. Second, they showed that less successful students who received training demonstrated a large increase in the precision of their elaborations and a corresponding increase in their performance on a memory test. Third, the more successful fifth-grade learners were able to judge whether or not the relationship specified in a sentence was arbitrary or not, and on the basis of that judgment to estimate the difficulty they would have in learning the material. Less successful learners were less accurate in their judgments, although, once again, training facilitated their ability both to make the judgments and to remember the new material.

These results offer strong support for the elaboration hypothesis. Experts differ from novices in the extent of their knowledge and their ability to use that knowledge as a means of elaborating precisely on new information that is presented. Better learners, overall, have a greater ability to benefit from precise elaboration and therefore are more likely to become experts than poorer learners. However, techniques for making precise elaborations can be provided, by training, for less successful learners. These techniques have considerable promise in improving the learning ability of all students, thus increasing their likelihood of becoming expert in some domain.

THE MEASUREMENT OF INTELLIGENCE

The first test of intelligence was constructed around the turn of the century by a French psychologist, Alfred Binet, in an effort to identify school children who might benefit from special educational programs. This initial test, and those that quickly followed, were extremely successful for their purpose. Over the years, the tests were elaborated and expanded to cover a variety of different aspects of intelligence, such as verbal ability, memory, reasoning and performance manipulations, and to be applicable over a wide range of ages. The intelligence quotient (IQ), a measure of general intelligence, was defined as a composite of scores on a variety of sub-scales. Today, the IQ has become interchangeable with the concept of intelligence itself, and for some good reasons. There are relatively high correlations between IQ and other supposed measures of intelligence such as academic or occupational success.

Most psychologists have assumed that underlying performance on intelligence tests, is one basic general ability—or at most a very few such abilities. Analysis of the correlations between individual tests suggest that they can be categorized or clustered into a smaller number of factors. There is some disagreement about how many factors are involved, but, generally, psychologists agree that there is a factor for verbal ability, another for reasoning, a third for visual or spatial ability, and possibly others. The approach to this issue has been strictly empirical, designed to identify through paper-and-pencil measurement certain subabilities which, taken together, constitute our general or global concept of intelligence.

Recently, an alternative point of view on intelligence has been derived from research in cognitive psychology. This point of view defines intelligence in terms of cognitive processes and structures and is based on an analogy between intelligent behavior and the behavior of computers. Like a computer, a human being has an internal representation (knowledge) of the external world. In addition, human beings have certain processes (like computer programs) that can operate on that representation. How effectively a person performs in any given situation depends upon the extent to which the internal representation matches the external world and the adequacy of the program that operates on that representation. Individual differences in intelligence are to be understood in terms of differences in cognitive structures (representations) and cognitive processes (programs).

Robert Sternberg of Yale University is one cognitive psychologist who adheres to this approach. Sternberg (1977) uses problems of analogy as a basic analytic tool. Analogies have the form A is to B as C is to ___ . For example, *table* is to *furniture* as *knife* is to ___ . In some analogy problems, a number of alternatives are provided to fill in the blank. So, for example, in the preceding analogy, *animal, vehicle, weapon,* and *vegetable* might be the alternatives to be chosen from. How is such a problem solved? Sternberg argues that a person goes through a step-by-step approach in which the analogy is broken down into sub-problems, each of which requires its own solution. In other words, problem-solving is defined in terms of more primitive information-processing components such as pattern recognition, or retrieving the meaning of terms, and memory searches, or determining the relation between pairs of terms. The subject is said to be guided by a strategy that defines an order in which rudimentary processing components are to be executed. Sternberg calls this approach "componential analysis."

Having identified the component parts of an overall strategy for analogy problems, Sternberg then attempted to control the strategy by presenting analogies in parts. By selecting the parts appropriately, Sternberg could measure the time it took individuals to complete various portions or components of the strategy. These estimates could then be combined so as to predict the time required to solve the problem when it was presented in its usual way, with all aspects shown at once. This form of analysis has been used to study the strategies that people use in a wide variety of traditional IQ tests.

One of Sternberg's major assumptions is that tests correlate to the extent that they rely upon the same underlying strategy or strategy components. Thus, if one can identify communalities in required strategy across tasks, then one can predict the size of correlations in performance between two tasks. These process or component communalities are the basis for the so-called factors or abilities identified in earlier, more traditional studies of intelligence.

Earl Hunt of the University of Washington has taken a somewhat different approach to the analysis of cognitive components of intelligence. Hunt (1983) places special emphasis on the exchange of information among memory systems. Three categories of activity—pattern recognition, short-term memory processes, and long-term memory processes—have been studied extensively by Hunt.

Pattern Recognition.   To review briefly, pattern recognition is the identification of an object as a member of a particular class. Lexical access, in which the meaning of a word is retrieved from long-term memory, is a special case of pattern recognition. Lexical access is the initial step toward comprehension of written or spoken material. As we have seen in previous chapters, several tasks have been developed to measure the time it takes to execute lexical access. In an identification task, the subject is asked to determine whether a string of letters is a word or not. In a matching paradigm, two words are presented and the subject is asked to decide whether the two words are the same or belong to the same category. In verification studies, a person might be asked to verify some relationship between two terms. Subjects typically perform these tasks with low error rate. The primary measure of performance is time to correct response. Correlations across these tasks are high, indicating the existence of a single memory access process underlying competence in the pattern recognition aspect of cognition.

Short-term Memory Processes.   There is evidence for at least two types of code, linguistic and visual-spatial, in short-term memory. Individuals differ in their facility with these two codes. Asking subjects to verify phrases as descriptions of simple pictures is commonly used as a measure of facility with linguistic codes. Research using this paradigm has shown that the time required to verify a phrase or sentence changes as a function of its complexity. It takes longer, for example, to verify a negative sentence than it does a positive sentence. There are rather sizeable differences among individuals in their performance in this task, however, and those differences correlate with more traditional measures of verbal ability.

The mental rotation paradigm has been used to study visual-spatial code in short-term memory (see Chapter 4). In this task, two shapes are presented at different angles or orientations and the task is to decide whether the two figures are identical or mirror images. Time required to make this judgment is a linear function of the difference in orientation. Thus, this task measures, in some sense, the speed with which a person can mentally manipulate a visual representation. This task also shows wide individual differences, but there is virtually no correlation between performance in mental rotation (the visual-spatial representation), and in sentence verification (the linguistic representation).

Long-term Memory Processes. Tasks that tap the input of information and the manipulation of memory codes in short-term memory entail relatively simple cognitive processes. Nonetheless they correlate significantly with traditional measures of intelligence and perhaps can account for as much as 25 percent of the variance on traditional tests of intelligence. But there is certainly more to intelligence than can be captured by these rudimentary tasks. A paradigm used by Hunt to study information in long-term memory is the verbal comprehension task in which a brief paragraph or story is presented to the subject who is then asked a series of questions about it. For adults, there is a strong correlation between comprehension after listening and comprehension after reading. Reading and spoken comprehension are not highly correlated in young children, however. Reading comprehension lags considerably behind listening comprehension until children are about nine years old. It seems possible that lexical access for visual material is slower to develop than that for auditory material. Once these two skills are perfected, however, individual differences in comprehension processes apply equally well to both reading and listening.

Hunt has been able to demonstrate important individual differences in modes of problem representation. In a study using the sentence verification paradigm, instead of presenting the descriptive phrase and the picture together, the phrase was displayed first and remained in view until subjects indicated that they had comprehended it. Then the picture was displayed and the subject verified the description. Subjects reported adopting one of two forms of representation. "Verbalizers" first memorized the phrase; then they described the picture to themselves; finally they compared the picture description to the memorized phrase. "Imagers" read the sentence, generated an image of the expected picture, and then compared the image to their percept. These two forms of representation produced large differences in verification times. Verbalizers were slow overall and were markedly affected by sentence complexity. Imagers responded rapidly overall and showed no effect of sentence complexity. Verification times of verbalizers correlated highly with traditional tests of verbal ability, while verification times of imagers correlated with traditional tests of visual-spatial ability.

To summarize, intelligence, from the point of view of a cognitive psychologist, can be understood by determining the requirements of a given task, how people represent knowledge appropriate to that task, and how they use cognitive processes to operate on those representations so as to complete the task. Individual differences in intelligence are traceable to individual differences in cognitive processes and knowledge representations. To understand how intelligence contributes to performance on a given task, one must be able to identify the relevant processes and structures required by that task. Intelligence tests of the future will be more firmly linked to the theories of cognitive psychology. These tests will measure not only the scope of a person's knowledge, but the rudimentary structuring and processing of that knowledge.

Applications in Clinical Psychology

Psychopathology or mental illness is one of society's most pressing problems. To make any kind of progress, we need to understand better its origins and manifestations. To the cognitive psychologist, schizophrenia is a particularly interesting category of psychopathology. Although there are several distinguishable types of schizophrenia, a single theme carries through all of them: schizophrenic individuals tend to be different from normal individuals on cognitive tasks. As a consequence, schizophrenia is often described as a "thought disorder." A close examination of some of the cognitive deficits associated with the condition may help us to understand schizophrenia and psychopathology better.

SELECTIVE ATTENTION

Selective attention is the ability to focus upon information from one source and to ignore potentially interfering information from other sources. It is the process by which a person maintains heightened awareness of a limited range of available stimulation. Because schizophrenic individuals appear to be highly distractable, it is often suggested that they suffer an attentional deficit. Let us examine this possibility.

Selective attention is often studied by means of a dichotic listening task that requires the listener to shadow one of two messages while ignoring the other. Schneider (1976) administered such a task to two groups of schizophrenic patients, one paranoid and the other nonparanoid. (Paranoia is characterized by beliefs that are clearly unfounded, grandiose, persecutory, hallucinatory, and/or bizarre.) Interestingly, Schneider found that neither schizophrenic group was generally inferior to normal subjects in accuracy of shadowing. He did observe, however, that the content of the distracting message was quite important. When that message touched on a topic that pertained to the subject's delusions, performance on the shadowed message decreased substantially.

Schneider interpreted his results to imply that the attentional mechanisms of schizophrenic individuals are *not* impaired. The finding that schizophrenics make a significant number of errors when they are presented with personalized distractors is entirely consistent with distraction effects of personalized messages in normal individuals. Although other studies have confirmed these results (Straube & Germer, 1979), it is important to note that Schneider's subjects were only recently diagnosed and had never been previously hospitalized for their condition. Other investigators (for example, Korboot & Damiania, 1976) have reported that chronic schizophrenics, individuals who have been repeatedly hospitalized, do exhibit a marked slowness of mental processes, which becomes apparent in abnormally poor shadowing at a high rate of item presentation.

Pogue-Geile and Oltmanns (1980) undertook a follow-up to Schneider's work, administering an unexpected recall test after the shadowing task was completed. Shadowing accuracy, verbatim recall, and constructive shadowing errors were the three dependent measures of interest. According to the experimenters' definition, a constructive shadowing error occurs when the subject reproduces the essence of the message but not its detail. These errors presumably reflect the schema employed by the listener while perceiving and anticipating the passage. In addition to schizophrenic and normal individuals, two affectively disordered groups, manic and depressive patients, were used in the study.

None of the patient groups differed significantly from the normal subjects in shadowing accuracy either with or without a competing irrelevant message. All subjects committed constructive shadowing errors, indicating that schizophrenics use semantic and syntactic information in the message to anticipate in the same way normal individuals do. Interestingly, however, schizophrenics inserted more semantically irrelevant words than any of the other groups of subjects. Moreover, the presence of distractors interfered with the schizophrenics' ability to recall the content of relevant passages to a much greater degree than it did for any of the other three groups (see Table 11–5). Thus, although the schizophrenics perceived the message as accurately as normal individuals, as indexed by shadowing, and utilized the syntactic and semantic structure of the message to facilitate shadowing, they did not encode the content of the message into memory as well. Conceivably then, for schizophrenics, processes responsible for encoding and/or retrieval are especially vulnerable to distractors. This may derive from a resource allocation problem. That is, schizophrenics may find it necessary to allocate most or all of their resources to the shadowing task, leaving less for encoding, relative to normal individuals. It is important to note that the recall deficit due to distraction was unique to schizophrenics in this study. Manics and depressives were relatively unaffected by the competing message. This is obviously an observation of great significance,

Table 11-5. *Mean percent correct responses.*

	TASK			
	Shadowing		*Recall*	
Group	Neutral Condition	Distracting Condition	Neutral Condition	Distracting Condition
Schizophrenic	67.5	59.6	50.0	30.0
Depressed	62.4	62.7	57.5	58.1
Manic	66.8	62.7	63.1	66.3
Normal	72.5	76.3	75.6	79.9

Data from Pogue-Geile & Ottmanns (1980).

and could be an important clue to the basis of the distinction between affective and thought disorders.

ITEM MEMORY

Schizophrenics show deficits in a variety of memory tasks, in addition to the one just described. For example, Oltmanns and Neale (1975) demonstrated an increasing difference between schizophrenic patients and normal subjects as the material to be remembered increased in length. Normal subjects tend to organize a stimulus series into chunks, if at all possible, because chunks can be stored and recalled as single items. The importance of such a coding strategy increases with the length of the series. Schizophrenic patients have difficulty with the spontaneous use of such organizational processes, limiting their ability to create manageable chunks.

The isolation of such a specific deficit in schizophrenia provides a useful clue to the origin of gross, clinical symptomatology. Schizophrenic patients often show an inability to concentrate on discourse, either in text or in dialogue. The problem might, once again, be traceable to a deficit in organizational abilities—in this case those required for the comprehension of discourse. This possibility led Oltmanns and Neale to suspect that internally generated distraction (intruding thoughts) might in fact be responsible for the patients' deficit in organizational processes.

Russell, Consedine, and Knight (1980) compared schizophrenics and normal subjects on tasks that required either visual or memory search. Subjects searched visual displays varying in the number of letters they contained (one, five, or fifteen letters), indicating whether or not the display contained a designated target letter. The target was drawn from a memorized set of one, three or six letters. Russell and colleagues analyzed their data in terms of a model first proposed by Schneider and Shiffrin (1977). In this model, memorized items, selected from active short-term memory, are compared sequentially to each of the displayed items for purposes of making a match/no match decision. If no match is found, a new memory item is selected and the sequence is repeated. This process continues until a match is found, at which point a response is executed, or until the memory set is exhausted. Schneider and Shiffrin found that the response times of normal subjects were well described by a linear increasing function of the number of comparisons between displayed and memorized items, that is, the product of memory set × display size. The intercept of this function reflects processes involved in the initiation of a search and in response time. The slope is affected primarily by the comparison and match processes.

Response times of both schizophrenics and normals increased linearly with the product of the number of memorized items in the target set and the number of displayed letters. On the whole, however, the intercepts and the response times of schizophrenics were higher than those of normal controls. There was no difference between groups in slope. The investigators suggest that schizophrenics are retarded in processes associated with response production but not in a variety of processing stages involved in the comparison of displayed and memorized information. They propose that future research on cognitive deficits in schizophrenia should not neglect response processes.

Cognitive deficits in schizophrenic patients seem to center around the use of conscious organizational processes in short-term memory. Frame and Oltmanns (1982) point out that most of these studies have been conducted during a psychotic episode; few investigators have studied whether or not memory and attentional performance improves with remission. These experimenters reported a longitudinal study of short-term memory in schizophrenics, with measures taken both during a psychotic episode and after significant clinical improvement, and in both the presence and absence of distractors. On the basis of previous research, they hypothesized that schizophrenics' performance would deteriorate in the presence of distraction but that relief from clinical symptomatology would be accompanied by improved memory. Eight schizophrenics, eight depressed patients, and eight normal control subjects were asked to recall short word strings. Results showed that, even though schizophrenics were significantly better in recall just prior to discharge than they were shortly after admission, they were still inferior to both depressives and normal control subjects. Thus, memory deficit seems to be a continuing attribute of the schizophrenic individual.

MEMORY FOR DISCOURSE

There is considerable evidence in the cognitive psychology literature on the differences between memory for word lists and memory for sentences and text. Among the important considerations for this difference is the parsing of word strings into syntactic and semantic units in sentences. Moreover, in listening to sentences, subjects tend to abstract the gist and to make inferences from the gist based on their personal knowledge of the world. These factors, among others, affect sentence memory but are nonoperative in word lists.

The studies of schizophrenics' memory discussed thus far have focused on word lists. In general, they suggest that the internal representation of words, when it develops, is probably intact and normal in schizophrenic individuals. Schizophrenics are poor in remembering word lists largely because of inefficient or unavailable organizational encoding processes. The recall deficit is corrected in part more or less automatically by relief from clinical symptomatology, but can also be remediated by inducing subjects to engage in appropriate organizational processes during encoding (Koh, 1978).

Studies of comprehension and memory for discourse are particularly likely to test the schizophrenic deficit since discourse failures are one of the most outstanding characteristics of schizophrenic thinking. In fact, the classical descriptions of the schizophrenic thought disorder have focused on the lack of idea organization in these patients' language. Schizophrenics appear to have lost the ability to put thoughts in a logical order and, as a consequence, incoherent combinations of ideas are often expressed. Schizophrenic speech represents those fragmentary ideas connected in a generally illogical way. The lack of semantic integration in schizophrenic language may be in part a reflection of poor integration in the comprehension, in the encoding, or in the retrieval processes that apply to language stimuli.

Koh, Marusarz, and Rosen (1980) reported a study designed to determine whether factors similar to those described above influence the schizophrenic subjects' memory for sentences as well as for word lists. They initially determined that the schizophrenics' free recall of short sentences was significantly worse than that of normal subjects. Then, all subjects were induced to engage in an orienting task that required the formation of meaningful and correct sentences out of scrambled word strings. This task was followed by an unexpected test of recall. In this test, schizophrenics did as well as the normal subjects. Moreover, the structural aspects of recall were precisely the same in the two groups. Thus it appears, just as with word lists, that if schizophrenics are induced to engage in the proper syntactic-semantic encoding operation, they develop a representation for the material in memory that is normal in all respects.

Studies of sentence memory have shown that people normally notice the relations among words provided by both semantic and syntactic rules; they form an integrated representation of these structures, embedded in the larger context of world knowledge. Tests of memory reveal the effects of integration as much as, or more than, they reveal the words or the surface structure originally presented. Because schizophrenic patients appear to be less able than normal people to take advantage of organization without external prodding or inducement, they are likely candidates for exhibiting a deficit in integrative processing.

A research paradigm developed by Bransford and Franks (1972) seems particularly well suited to testing this integration deficit hypothesis. Bransford and Franks presented normal subjects with sentences that varied in the number of simple ideas they contained. An integration of these simple ideas across sentences would produce a complex idea or mini-story. Subjects heard sentences from several different mini-stories, presented in a haphazard order. Subsequently, they were given an unexpected recognition task in which they had to decide whether each of a set of sentences was in the original acquisition series or not. The results of this study demonstrated that normal subjects integrate ideas across sentences and form the equivalent of a prototype sentence for each story in the original acquisition set. This prototype sentence, which contains all the simple ideas heard in the acquisition series, is used as a basis for deciding whether sentences presented in the recognition test are new or old sentences. On this basis, subjects can easily reject as new any test sentence that combines ideas from two or more different mini-stories or introduces new ideas not contained in any of the acquisition sentences. Bransford and Franks also discovered that the greater the number of integrated ideas included in a test sentence, the higher the probability that the subject would accept it as an old sentence—whether or not it was in fact an old sentence.

Knight and Sims-Knight (1979) reported a study using the Bransford-Franks paradigm to study the integration deficit in schizophrenia. They found that normal subjects and nonpsychotic patients exhibited recognition patterns reflecting the organization of simple ideas into mini-stories. Their response patterns were entirely consistent with those observed by Bransford and Franks. Schizophrenic patients, however, were incapable of distinguishing sentences that violated the relationships within mini-stories from those that did not. Only those schizophrenic patients who had only a single psychotic episode, and whose premorbid history was good to excellent showed any evidence of idea integration. Patients with chronic illness and a poor premorbid history were essentially unable to use the interrelationships among ideas to organize their representation of the material or to respond normally on the recognition test. The authors suggest that these patients have difficulty abstracting any complex idea from ordinary discourse. They show the discourse failure often spoken about in the clinical treatment of schizophrenics. Thus, unless some external guidance or inducement is provided, schizophrenics are likely to exhibit idea integration failure when trying to understand anything but the simplest of spoken or written discourse.

In a follow-up to their study of the schizophrenic deficit in sentence integration, Knight and Sims-Knight (1980) examined whether the integration process would work for schizophrenics when the task involved a somewhat less complex integration process. For this purpose, they used a parallel research paradigm developed by Franks and Bransford (1971). Subjects were presented with a series of visual, letter-like forms that were simple spatial transformations of a selected arbitrary base pattern. That is, a simple base pattern was used to generate each of the acquisition stimuli through simple transformations (see discussion in Chapter 5). These stimuli were presented to three different groups of schizophrenics (acute [single episode] patients with a good premorbid history, acute patients with a poor premorbid history, and chronic schizophrenics), to a non-psychotic patient group, and to a normal control group.

After initial presentation of the acquisition stimuli, subjects were given a previously unannounced recognition task. All subjects gave evidence of representing and remembering the stimuli in an integrated fashion. That is, the base pattern was "remembered" best and other stimuli were remembered in an order reflecting their transformational distance from the base. Thus it appears that schizophrenics, even those with chronic illness or with a poor premorbid history, are capable of organizing or integrating disparate stimuli when the task is simple enough. Combined with earlier results, these data suggest that the extent of the problem that schizophrenics have with integrative memory is affected by the nature of the stimuli and by the difficulty of the integration process. The evidence suggests that the ability to abstract the basic meaning within a set of simple visual stimuli is intact in schizophrenics, but that their processing of complex event information, especially in the verbal mode, is deficient.

AUTOBIOGRAPHICAL MEMORY

Studies using sentences or text clearly have an advantage over studies using word lists as investigations of natural memory processes. But an even more significant step in that direction has been taken in recent work on autobiographical memory, that is, memory for previous personal experiences that can be independently documented (see Chapter 4). One such study has recently been reported in the clinical literature.

This study, by Clark and Teasdale (1982), addressed the question of mood state and its effect on the accessibility of memories. Recent research has shown that, for normal people, memories of positive experiences are less accessible in experimentally-induced depressed mood states than in experimentally-induced states of elation (Bower, 1981). Conversely, memories of negative experiences tend to be more accessible in induced depressed mood states. Cognitive theories of depression (see for example, Beck, 1976) imply that negative thoughts with certain types of content play an important role in the origins and maintenance of clinical depression. Thus, the finding that depressed moods are associated with an increase in the accessibility of negative thoughts could be of considerable clinical importance.

There is little rigorous experimental evidence on memories in the clinically depressed patient. The study by Clark and Teasdale attempts to rectify this deficiency by studying the effects of variations in depression on the accessibility of positive and negative memories. Depressed patients were tested at two different times during a single day. On one of these occasions they were substantially more depressed than on the other. On each occasion, they retrieved past real-life experiences associated with certain stimulus words presented by the experimenter. At the end of a series of tests, they rated these experiences on a happiness scale both in the context of the original experience itself and in the context of the memory provoked. Clark and Teasdale found that unhappy memories were more likely to be retrieved on more depressed occasions than on less depressed occasions. Just the opposite was found for happy experiences. The current tone of a recalled experience was more likely to be rated as less positive than the original tone if the test was administered during a period of depression. The results of this study are summarized in Table 11-6. Thus, the effects of natural variations in clinical depression were found to be essentially the same as the effects of the experimentally-induced changes in mood. Moreover, the results of investigations of experimentally

Table 11-6. *Effects of mood on memory.*

	OCCASION	
	More Depressed	Less Depressed
Total number experiences recalled	18.1	17.8
Mean recall latency (sec)	8.60	7.17
Happy memories (%)	37.7	51.3
Unhappy memories (%)	52.3	36.7
Mean happiness rating	−.34	.35
Latency for happy memories (sec)	7.94	6.70
Latency for unhappy memories (sec)	8.76	7.21

Data from Clark & Teasdale (1982).

manipulated mood on memory accessibility in normal individuals can safely be generalized to clinical depression. Clark and Teasdale found that happiness ratings given to a particular experience tend to be distorted by current mood state. Thus it appears that mood may have two independent effects. First, it influences the selection of emotional material for entry into consciousness. Second, it effects how pleasing or upsetting that material will be, once it has entered consciousness.

The outcome of this research suggests a vicious cycle that is likely to contribute to the maintenance and deepening of depression once it has started. Depression, through its effects on memory accessibility, increases the likelihood of negative thoughts, thus causing further depression (Beck, 1976). What is needed to change the pattern is some means of introducing positive life events into the cycle. Alternatively, some method might be found for blocking negative thoughts. It is of interest to note that some patients report a total absence of thoughts during extreme depression. Thus, there may be an automatic psychological mechanism to prevent deterioration in mood beyond a certain point. In any case, psychological treatment for this condition should benefit from the development of methods for modifying the negative bias of thoughts and memory on depression.

Final Comment

Human beings have both profited and suffered in significant ways from our growing knowledge in the physical sciences about how energy and matter are structured and processed. Out of this knowledge we have built grand machines that warm and cool, that roll and fly, that compute and communicate. The human mind has been more resistant than the physical world to scientific analysis. It has been slow to give up its secrets to those who research it. But, in the last twenty years, some answers have been forthcoming. Through research in cognitive psychology, we are beginning to understand how the mind works and, as we do, to see increasingly broad uses for this knowledge.

The examples of applied cognitive psychology discussed in this chapter have been simple, limited, and imprecise, reflecting the limitations of the field at the present time. But as our scientific knowledge accumulates, application should become increasingly more common, clear, and valuable. What has been done so far is a promising start. We look for even greater contributions in the future. We hope that at least some of you who have read this book will be among those responsible for the next generation of work in applied cognitive psychology.

References

Aaronson, D., & Scarborough, H.S. (1977). Performance theories for sentence coding: Some quantitative models. *Journal of Verbal Learning and Verbal Behavior, 16*, 277–303.

Adams, J. A. (1976). *Learning and memory: An introduction.* Homewood, Ill.: Dorsey

Adams, J. L. (1979). *Conceptual blockbusting: A guide to better ideas* (2nd ed.). New York: W. W. Norton.

Adelson, B. (1981). Problem solving and the development of abstract categories in programming languages. *Memory & Cognition, 9*, 422–433.

Aiken, E. G., Thomas, G. S., & Shennum, W. A. (1975). Memory for a lecture: Effects of notes, lecture rate, and informational density. *Journal of Educational Psychology, 67*, 439–444.

Alba, J. W., & Hasher, L. (1983). Is memory schematic? *Psychological Bulletin, 93*, 203–231.

Allen, R., & Reber, A.S. (1980). Very long term memory for tacit knowledge. *Cognition, 8*, 175–185.

Allik, J. P., & Siegel, A. W. (1976). The use of the cumulative rehearsal strategy: A developmental study. *Journal of Experimental Child Psychology, 21*, 316–327.

Allport, G.W., & Postman, L. J. (1958). The basic psychology of rumor. In E. E. Maccoby, T. M. Newcomb, & E. L. Hartley (eds.), *Readings in social psychology* (3rd ed.). New York: Holt, Rinehart, & Winston.

Anderson, B. F. (1975). *Cognitive psychology.* New York: Academic Press.

Anderson, J. R. (1976). *Language, memory and thought.* Hillsdale, N.J.: Erlbaum.

Anderson, J. R. (1978). Arguments concerning representations for mental imagery. *Psychological Review, 85*, 249–277.

Anderson, J. R. (1983). A spreading activation theory of memory. *Journal of Verbal Learning and Verbal Behavior, 22*, 261–295.

Anderson, J. R. (1984). Spreading activation. In J. R. Anderson & S. M. Kosslyn (Eds.), *Tutorials in learning and memory.* San Francisco: W. H. Freeman.

Anderson, J. R. & Bower, G. H. (1973). *Human associative memory.* Washington, D.C.: V. H. Winston & Sons.

Anderson, J. R., Kline, P. J., & Beasley, C. M. (1979). A general learning theory and its applications to schema abstraction. In G. H. Bower (Ed.), *The psychology of learning and motivation* (Vol. 13). New York: Academic Press.

Anisfeld, M., & Knapp, M. E. (1968). Association, synonymity, and directionality in false recognition. *Journal of Experimental Psychology, 77*, 171–179.

Anthony, W. S. (1973). Learning to discover rules by discovery. *Journal of Educational Psychology, 64*, 325–328.

Atkinson, R. C., & Raugh, M. R. (1975). An application of the mnemonic keyword method to the acquisition of a Russian vocabulary. *Journal of Experimental Psychology: Human Learning and Memory, 104*, 126–133.

Atwood, M. E., Masson, M. E. J., & Polson, P. G. (1980). Further explorations with a process model for water jug problems. *Memory & Cognition, 8*, 182–192.

Atkinson, R. C., & Shiffrin, R. M. (1968). Human memory: A proposed system and its control processes. In K. W. Spence & J. T. Spence (Eds.), *The psychology of learning and motivation: Advances in research and theory,* (Vol. 2). New York: Academic Press.

Atkinson, R. C., & Shiffrin, R. M. (1971). The control of short-term memory. *Scientific American, 225*, 82–90.

Baddeley, A. D. (1966a). Short-term memory for word sequences as a function of acoustic, semantic, and formal similarity. *Quarterly Journal of Experimental Psychology, 18*, 362–365.

Baddeley, A. D. (1966b). The influence of acoustic and semantic similarity on long-term memory for word sequences. *Quarterly Journal of Experimental Psychology, 18*, 302–309.

Baddeley, A. D. (1978). The trouble with levels: A reexamination of Craik and Lockhart's framework for memory research. *Psychological Review, 85,* 139–152.

Baddeley, A. D. (1982). *Your memory: A user's guide.* New York: Macmillan.

Baddeley, A. D. (1982). Domains of recollection. *Psychological Review, 89,* 709–729.

Baddeley, A. D., & Warrington, E. K. (1973). Memory coding and amnesia. *Neuropsychologia, 11,* 159–165.

Bahrick, H. P. (1984). Semantic memory content in permastore: Fifty years of memory for Spanish learned in school. *Journal of Experimental Psychology: General, 113,* 1–29.

Bar-Hillel, M. (1980). What features make samples seem representative? *Journal of Experimental Psychology: Human Perception and Performance, 6,* 578–589.

Bar-Hillel, M., & Falk, R. (1982). Some teasers concerning conditional probabilities. *Cognition, 11,* 109–122.

Barsalou, L. W. (1983). Ad hoc categories. *Memory & Cognition, 11,* 211–227.

Bartlett, F. C. (1932). *Remembering: A study in experimental and social psychology.* New York: Macmillan.

Beaumont, J. N., & Butterfield, E. C. (1977). The instructional approach to developmental cognitive research. In R. V. Kail and J. W. Hagen (Eds.). *Perspectives on the development of memory and cognition.* Hillsdale, N.J.: Erlbaum.

Beck, A. T. (1976). *Cognitive therapy and the emotional disorders.* New York: International Universities Press.

Begg, I., & Denny, J. P. (1969). Empirical reconciliation of atmosphere and conversion interpretations of syllogistic reasoning errors. *Journal of Experimental Psychology, 81,* 351–354.

Beilin, H. (1976). Constructing cognitive operations linguistically. *Advances in Child Development and Behavior, 11,* 68–106.

Bekerian, D. A., & Bowers, J. M. (1983). Eyewitness testimony: Were we misled? *Journal of Experimental Psychology: Learning, Memory and Cognition, 9,* 139–143.

Bellezza, F. S., Cheesman, F. L., & Reddy, B. G. (1977). Organization and semantic elaboration in free recall. *Journal of Experimental Psychology: Human Learning and Memory, 3,* 539–550.

Berlin, B., & Kay, P. (1969). *Basic color terms: Their universality and evolution.* Berkeley: University of California Press.

Bjork, E. L., & Healy, A. F. (1974). Short-term order and item retention. *Journal of Verbal Learning and Verbal Behavior, 13,* 80–97.

Bjork, R. A. (1975). Short-term storage: The ordered output of a central processor. In F. Restle, R. M. Shiffrin, N. H. Castellan, H. R. Lindeman, & D.

B. Pisoni (Eds.), *Cognitive theory* (Vol. 1). Hillsdale, N. J.: Erlbaum.

Bjorklund, D. F., & Zeman, B. R. (1982). Children's organization and metamemory awareness in the recall of familiar information. *Child Development, 53,* 799–810.

Blumenthal, A. L. (1967). Prompted recall of sentences. *Journal of Verbal Learning and Verbal Behavior, 6,* 203–206.

Boring, E. G. (1950). *A history of experimental psychology.* New York: Appleton-Century-Crofts.

Bourne, L. E., Jr. (1970). Knowing and using concepts. *Psychological Review, 77,* 546–556.

Bourne, L. E., Jr. (1974). An inference model of conceptual rule learning. In R. Solso (Ed.), *Theories in cognitive psychology.* Washington, D.C.: Erlbaum.

Bourne, L. E., Jr. (1979). Stimulus-rule interaction in concept learning. *American Journal of Psychology,* 3–17.

Bourne, L. E., Jr. (1982). Typicality effects in logically defined concepts. *Memory & Cognition, 10,* 3–9.

Bourne, L. E., Jr., Dodd, D. H., Guy, D. E., & Justesen, D. R. (1968). Response-contingent intertrial intervals in concept identification. *Journal of Experimental Psychology, 76,* 601–608.

Bourne, L. E., Jr., Ekstrand, B. R., & Dominowski, R. L. (1971). *The psychology of thinking.* Englewood Cliffs, N.J.: Prentice-Hall.

Bourne, L. E., Jr., & Restle, F. (1959). A mathematical theory of concept identification. *Psychological Review, 66,* 278–296.

Bower, G. H. (1970). Analysis of a mnemonic device. *American Scientist, 58,* 496–510.

Bower, G. H. (1973). How to . . . . uh . . . remember! *Psychology Today,* 63–70.

Bower, G. H. (1978). Interference paradigms for meaningful propositional memory. *American Journal of Psychology, 91,* 575–585.

Bower, G. H. Mood and memory. (1981). *American Psychologist, 36,* 129–148.

Brainerd, C. J. (1973). Judgments and explanations as criteria for the presence of cognitive structures. *Psychological Review, 79,* 172–179.

Brainerd, C. J. (1978). The stage question in cognitive-developmental theory. *Behavioral and Brain Sciences, 1,* 173–213.

Brainerd, C. J., & Hooper, F. H. (1975). A methodological analysis of developmental studies of identity conservation and equivalence conversation. *Psychological Bulletin, 82,* 725–737.

Bransford, J. D., & Franks, J. J. (1971). The abstraction of linguistic ideas. *Cognitive Psychology, 2,* 331–350.

Bransford, J. D., & Johnson, M. K. (1973). Considerations of some problems of comprehension. In W. G. Chase (Ed.), *Visual information processing.* New York: Academic Press.

Bransford, J. D., Stein, B. S., Vye, N. J., Franks, J. J., Aubel, P.M., Mezynsky, K. J., & Perfetto, G. A. (1982). Differences in approaches in learning: An overview. *Journal of Experimental Psychology: General, 111,* 390–398.

Briggs, G., E. (1957). Retroactive inhibition as a function of the degree of original and interpolated learnings. *Journal of Experimental Psychology, 53,* 60–67.

Brink, T. L. (1980). Idiot savant with unusual mechanical ability: An organic explanation. *American Journal of Psychology 137,* 250–251.

Broadbent, D. E. (1954). The role of auditory localization in attention and memory span. *Journal of Experimental Psychology, 47,* 191–196.

Broadbent, D. E. (1957). A mechanical model for human attention and immediate memory. *Psychological Review, 64,* 205–215.

Brooks, L. (1978). Nonanalytic concept formation and memory for instances. In E. Rosch B. B. Lloyd (Eds.), *Cognition and categorization.* Hillsdale, N. J.: Erlbaum.

Brown, A. L., & DeLoache, J. S. (1978). Skills, plans, and self-regulation. In R. S. Siegler (Ed.), *Children's thinking: What develops?* Hillsdale, N.J.: Erlbaum.

Brown, J. (1958). Some tests of the decay theory of immediate memory. *Quarterly Journal of Experimental Psychology, 10,* 12–21.

Brown, R., & Kulik, P. (1977). Flashbulb memories. *Cognition, 5,* 73–99.

Brown, R. W. (1976). Reference in memorial tribute to Eric Lenneberg. *Cognition, 4,* 125–153.

Brown, R. W. (1977). In reply to Peter Schönbach. *Cognition, 5,* 185–187.

Brown, R. W., & Lenneberg, E. H. (1954). A study in language and cognition. *Journal of Abnormal and Social Psychology, 49,* 454–462.

Brown, R., & McNeill, D. (1966). The "tip of the tongue" phenomenon. *Journal of Verbal Learning and Verbal Behavior, 5,* 325–337.

Bruce, D., & Clemons, D. M. (1982). A test of the effectiveness of the phonetic (number-consonant) mnemonic system. *Human Learning, 1,* 83–93.

Bruner, J. S., Goodnow, J. J., & Austin, G. A. (1956). *A study of thinking.* New York: Wilcy.

Bruner, J. S., Olver, R. R., & Greenfield, P. N. (1966). *Studies in cognitive growth.* New York: Wiley.

Burke R. J. (1969). A comparison of two properties of hints in individual problem solving. *Journal of General Psychology, 81,* 3–21.

Burke, R. J. (1970). Near success and solution persistence in individual problem solving. *Journal of General Psychology, 82,* 133–138.

Burke, R. J., & Maier, N. R. F. (1965). Attempts to predict success on an insight problem. *Psychological Reports, 17,* 303–310.

Burke, R. J., Maier, N. R. F., & Hoffman, L. R. (1966). Functions of hints in individual problem solving. *American Journal of Psychology, 79,* 389–399.

Byrd, M., & Thomson, D. M. (1979). Age differences in eyewitness testimony. Unpublished manuscript, University of Toronto.

Campbell, D. T. (1960). Blind variation and selective retention in creative thought as in other knowledge processes. *Psychological Review, 67,* 380–400.

Cantor, N., Mischel, W., & Schwartz, J. C. (1982). A prototype analysis of psychological situations. *Cognitive Psychology, 14,* 45–77.

Carmi, G. (1981). The role of context in cognitive development. *Quarterly Newsletter of the Laboratory of Comparative Human Cognition, 3,* 46–54.

Carroll, J. B., & Casagrande, J. B. (1958). The function of language classifications in behavior. In E. E. Maccoby, T. Newcomb, & E. L. Hartley (Eds.), *Readings in social psychology* (3rd ed.). New York: Holt, Rinehart, & Winston.

Carter, J. F., & VanMatre, N. H. (1975). Note taking versus note having. *Journal of Educational Psychology, 67,* 900–904.

Case, R. (1978). Intellectual development from birth to adulthood: A Neo-Piagetian interpretation. In R. S. Siegler (Ed.), *Children's thinking: What develops?* Hillsdale, N.J.: Erlbaum.

Cash, W. S., & Moss, A. J. (1972). Optimum recall period for reporting persons injured in motor vehicle accidents. Public Health Service, DHEW, Pub. No. (HSM) 72–1050, April.

Cavanaugh, J. C., & Perlmutter, M. (1982). Metamemory: A critical examination. *Child Development, 53,* 11–28.

Cavanaugh, J. C., & Borkowski, J. G. (1980). Searching for metamemory-memory connections: A developmental study. *Developmental Psychology, 16,* 441–453.

Ceraso, J., & Provitera, A. (1971). Sources of error in syllogistic reasoning. *Cognitive Psychology, 2,* 400–410.

Cermak, L. S., & Reale, L. (1978). Depth of processing and retention of words by alcoholic Korsakoff patients. *Journal of Experimental Psychology; Human Learning and Memory, 4,* 165–174.

Chapman, I. J., & Chapman, J. P. (1959). Atmosphere effect re-examined. *Journal of Experimental Psychology, 58,* 220–226.

Chapman, L. J., & Chapman, J. (1967). Genesis of popular but erroneous psycho-diagnostic observations. *Journal of Abnormal Psychology, 72,* 193–204.

Chapman, L. J., & Chapman, J. (1969). Illusory correlation as an obstacle to the use of valid psycho-diagnostic tests. *Journal of Abnormal Psychology, 74,* 271–280.

Charness, N. (1981). Aging and skilled problem solving. *Journal of Experimental Psychology: General, 110,* 21–38.

Chase, W. G., & Ericsson, K. A. (1981). Skilled memory. In J. Anderson (Ed.). *Cognitive skills and their acquisition.* Hillsdale, N.J.: Erlbaum.

Chase, W. G., & Simon, H. A. (1973). Perception in chess. *Cognitive Psychology, 4,* 55–81.

Cherry, E. C. (1953). Some experiments on the recognition of speech with one and two ears. *Journal of the Acoustical Society of America, 25,* 975–979.

Chi, M. T. H. (1977). Age differences in the speed of processing: A critique. *Developmental Psychology, 13,* 543–544.

Chi, M. T. (1978). Knowledge structures and memory development. In R. S. Siegler (Ed.), *Children's thinking: What develops?* Hillsdale, N.J.: Erlbaum.

Chomsky, N. (1957). *Syntactic structures.* The Hague: Mouton.

Chomsky, N. (1965). *Aspects of the theory of syntax.* Cambridge, Mass.: MIT Press.

Christensen, P. R., Guilford, J. P., & Wilson, R. C. (1957). Relations of creative responses to working time and instructions. *Journal of Experimental Psychology, 53,* 82–88.

Christensen-Szalanski, J. J. J. (1978). Problem solving strategies: A selection mechanism, some implications, and some data. *Organizational Behavior and Human Performance, 22,* 307–323.

Christensen-Szalanski, J. J. J. (1980). A further examination of the selection of problem-solving strategies: The effects of deadlines and analytic aptitudes. *Organizational Behavior and Human Performance, 25,* 107–122.

Christensen-Szalanski, J. J. J., & Beach, L. R. (1982). Experience and the base-rate fallacy. *Organizational Behavior and Human Performance, 29,* 270–278.

Cimbalo, R. S., & Laughery, K. R. (1967). Short-term memory: Effects of auditory and visual similarity. *Psychonomic Science, 8,* 57–58.

Clark, D. M., & Teasdale, J. D. (1982). Diurnal variation in clinical depression and accessibility of memories of positive and negative experiences. *Journal of Abnormal Psychology, 91,* 87–95.

Clark, E. V. (1978). Strategies for communicating. *Child Development, 49,* 953–959.

Cofer, C. N. (1984). Comments on "Semantic memory content in permastore: Fifty years of memory for Spanish learned in school" by Bahrick. *Journal of Experimental Psychology: General, 113,* 30–31.

Cohen, D. B. (1979). Remembering and forgetting dreaming. In J. F. Kihlstrom & F. J. Evans (Eds.), *Functional disorders and memory.* Hillsdale, N.J.: Erlbaum.

Cole, M., & D'Andrade, R. (1982). The influence of schooling on concept formation; Some preliminary conclusions. *Quarterly Newsletter of the Laboratory of Comparative Human Cognition, 4,* 19–26.

Collins, A. M., & Loftus, E. F. (1975). A spreading-activation theory of semantic processing. *Psychological Review, 5,* 85–88.

Collins, A. M., & Quillian, M. R. (1969). Retrieval time from semantic memory. *Journal of Verbal Learning and Verbal Behavior, 8,* 240–247.

Collins, A. M., & Quillian, M. R. (1972a). Experiments on semantic memory and language comprehension. In L. W. Gregg (Ed.), *Cognition in learning and memory.* New York: Wiley.

Collins, A. M., & Quillian, M. R. (1972b). How to make a language user. In E. Tulving & W. Donaldson (Eds.), *Organization of memory.* New York: Academic Press.

Coltheart, M. (1975). Iconic memory: A reply to Professor Holding. *Memory & Cognition, 3,* 42–48.

Conrad, C. (1972). Cognitive economy in semantic memory. *Journal of Experimental Psychology, 92,* 49–54.

Conrad, R. (1964). Acoustic confusions in immediate memory. *British Journal of Psychology, 55,* 75–84.

Conrad, R., & Hull, A. J. (1964). Information, acoustic confusion, and memory span. *British Journal of Psychology, 55,* 429–432.

Conrad, R., & Hull, A. J. (1968). Input modality and the serial position curve in short-term memory. *Psychonomic Science, 10,* 135–136.

Cooper, L. A., & Shepard, R. N. (1973). Chronometric studies of the rotation of mental images. In W. G. Chase (Ed.), *Visual information processing.* New York: Academic Press.

Cooper, W. H. (1981). Ubiquitous halo. *Psychological Bulletin, 90,* 218–244.

Corrigan, R. (1979). Cognitive correlates of language: Differential criteria yield differential results. *Child Development, 50,* 617–631.

Cowan, N. (1984). On short and long auditory stores. *Psychological Bulletin, 96,* 341–370.

Cox, J. R., & Griggs, R. A. (1982). The effects of experience on performance in Wason's selection task. *Memory & Cognition, 10,* 496–502.

Craik, F. I. M., & Lockhart, R. S. (1972). Levels of processing: A framework for memory research. *Journal of Verbal and Verbal Behavior, 11,* 671–684.

Craik, F. I. M., & Tulving, E. (1975). Depth of processing and the retention of words in episodic memory. *Journal of Experimental Psychology, 104,* 268–294.

Craik, F. I. M., & Watkins, M. J. (1973). The role of rehearsal in short-term memory. *Journal of Verbal Learning and Verbal Behavior, 12,* 599–607.

Crocker, J. (1981). Judgment of covariation by social perceivers. *Psychological Bulletin, 90,* 272–292.

Crothers, E. (1979). *Paragraph structure inference.* Norwood, N.J.: Ablex.

Crowder, R. G. (1971). The sound of vowels and consonants in immediate memory. *Journal of Verbal Learning and Verbal Behavior, 10,* 587–596.

Crowder, R. G. (1975). Inferential problems in echoic memory. In P.M. A. Rabbitt & S. Dornic (Eds.), *Attention and performance* V. London: Academic Press.

Crowder, R. G. (1982). Decay of auditory memory in vowel discrimination. *Journal of Experimental Psychology: Learning, Memory, and Cognition,* 8, 153–162.

Crowder, R. G., & Morton, J. (1969). Precategorical acoustic storage (PAS). *Perception & Psychophysics,* 5, 365–373.

Crouse, J. H. (1974). Acquisition of college course material under conditions of repeated testing. *Journal of Educational Psychology,* 66, 367–372.

Cunningham, T. F., Healy, A. F., & Williams, D. M. (1984). The effects of repetition on short-term retention of order information. *Journal of Experimental Psychology: Learning, Memory, and Cognition,* 10, 575–597.

Cutting, J. E. (1982). Plucks and bows are categorically perceived, sometimes. *Perception & Psychophysics,* 31, 462–476.

Darwin, C. J., & Baddeley, A. D. (1974). Acoustic memory and the perception of speech. *Cognitive Psychology,* 6, 41–60.

Davies, G. J., Shepherd, J. W., & Ellis, H. (1979). Effects of interpolated mug shot exposure on accuracy of eyewitness identification. *Journal of Applied Psychology,* 64, 232–237.

Deffenbacher, K. (1980). Eyewitness accuracy and confidence: Can we infer anything about their relationship? *Law and Human Behavior,* 4, 243–260.

deGroot, A. D. (1965). *Thought and Choice in Chess.* The Hague: Mouton.

DeLoache, J. S., Rissman, M. W., & Cohen, L. B. (1978). An investigation of the attention-getting process in infants. *Infant Behavior and Development,* 1, 11–25.

Deutsch, J. A., & Deutsch, D. (1966). *Physiological psychology.* Homewood, Ill.: Dorsey.

Devlin, Hon. Lord Patrick. (1976). Report to the Secretary of State for the Home Department of the Departmental Committee on Evidence of Identification in Criminal Cases. London: H.M. Stationery Office.

Dickstein, L. S. (1978). Error processes in syllogistic reasoning. *Memory & Cognition,* 6, 537–543.

Dodd, D. H., & Bradshaw, J. M. (1980). Leading questions and memory: Pragmatic constraints. *Journal of Verbal Learning and Verbal Behavior,* 19, 695–704.

Dominowski, R. L. (1969). The effect of pronunciation practice on anagram difficulty. *Psychonomic Science,* 16, 99–100.

Dominowski, R. L. (1972). Effects of solution familiarity and number of alternatives on problem difficulty. *Journal of Experimental Psychology,* 95, 223–225.

Dominowski, R. L. (1973). Requiring hypotheses and the identification of unidimensional, conjunctive, and disjunctive concepts. *Journal of Experimental Psychology,* 100, 387–394.

Dominowski, R. L. (1974). How do people discover concepts? In R. L. Solso (Ed.), *Theories of cognitive psychology: The Loyola Symposium.* Potomac, Md.: Erlbaum.

Dominowski, R. L. (1977). Reasoning. *Interamerican Journal of Psychology,* 11, 68–77.

Dominowski, R. L. (1981). Comment on "An examination of the alleged role of 'fixation' in the solution of several 'insight' problems" by Weisberg and Alba. *Journal of Experimental Psychology: General,* 110, 199–203.

Dominowski, R. L., & Ekstrand, B. R. (1967). Direct and associative priming in anagram solving. *Journal of Experimental Psychology,* 74, 85–86.

Dominowski, R. L., & Jenrick, R. (1972). Effects of hints and interpolated activity on solution of an insight problem. *Psychonomic Science,* 26, 335–338.

Dooling, D. J., & Christiaansen, R. E. (1977). Levels of encoding and retention of prose. In G. H. Bower (Ed.), *The psychology of learning and motivation* (Vol 11). New York: Academic Press.

Drewnowski, A. (1978). Detection errors on the word *the*: Evidence for the acquisition of reading levels. *Memory & Cognition,* 6, 403–409.

Duncan, C. P. (1961). Attempts to influence performance on an insight problem. *Psychological Reports,* 9, 35–42.

Duncan, C. P. (1966). Effect of word frequency on thinking of a word. *Journal of Verbal Learning and Verbal Behavior,* 5, 434–440.

Duncan, C. P. (1973). Storage and retrieval of low-frequency words. *Memory & Cognition,* 1, 129–132.

Duncker, K. (1945). On problem-solving. *Psychological Monographs,* 58, 5, (Whole No. 270).

Dyer, J. C., & Meyer, P. A. (1976). Facilitation of simple concept identification through mnemonic instruction. *Journal of Experimental Psychology: Human Learning and Memory,* 2, 489–496.

Ebbinghaus, H. (1964). *Memory: A contribution to experimental psychology.* New York: Dover. (Originally published 1885.)

Eimas, P. D. (1975). Auditory and phonetic coding of the cues for speech: Discrimination of the [r-l] distinction by young infants. *Perception & Psychophysics,* 18, 341–347.

Einhorn, H. J. (1970). The use of nonlinear, noncompensatory models in decision making. *Psychological Bulletin,* 73, 221–230.

Einhorn, H. J. (1980). Learning from experience and suboptimal rules in decision making. In T. S. Wallsten (Ed.), *Cognitive processes in choice and decision behavior.* Hillsdale, N.J.: Erlbaum.

Einhorn, H. J., & Hogarth, R. M. (1981). Behavioral decision theory: Processes of judgment and choice. *Annual Review of Psychology, 32,* 53–88.

Einhorn, H. J., Kleinmuntz, D. N., & Kleinmuntz, B. (1979). Linear regression *and* process-tracing models of judgment. *Psychological Review, 86,* 465–485.

Ekstrand, B. R. (1972). To sleep, perchance to dream (about why we forget). In C. P. Duncan, L. Sechrest & A. W. Melton (Eds.), *Human memory: Festschrift in honor of Benton J. Underwood.* New York: Appelton-Century-Crofts.

Ekstrand, B. R., & Dominowski, R. L. (1968). Solving words as anagrams: II. A clarification. *Journal of Experimental Psychology, 77,* 552–558.

Elio, R. & Anderson, J. R. (1981). The effects of category generalizations and instance similarity on schema abstraction. *Journal of Experimental Psychology: Human Learning and Memory, 7,* 397–417.

Elio, R., & Healy, A. F. (1982). Deep-structure syntactic relations: To-be-retrieved information and retrieval cues in prompted sentence recall. *Language and Speech, 25,* 221–242.

Ellison, K. W. & Buckout, R. (1981). *Psychology and criminal justice.* New York: Harper & Row.

Erickson, J. R. (1978). Research on syllogistic reasoning. In R. Revlin & R. Mayer (Eds.), *Human reasoning.* Washington, D.C.: Winston Wiley.

Ericsson, K. A., & Chase, W. G. (1982). Exceptional memory. *American Scientist, 70,* 607–614.

Ericsson, K. A., Chase, W. G., & Faloon, S. (1980). Acquisition of a memory skill. *Science, 208,* 1181–1182.

Ericsson, K. A., & Simon, H. A. (1980). Verbal reports as data. *Psychological Review, 87,* 215–251.

Estes, W. K. (1972). An associative basis for coding and organization in memory. In A. W. Melton & E. Martin (Eds.), *Coding processes in human memory* (pp. 161–190). Washington, D.C.: Winston.

Estes, W. K. (1976). The cognitive side of probability learning. *Psychological Review, 83,* 37–64.

Estes, W. K., & Taylor, H. A. (1964). A detection method and probablistic models for assessing information processing from brief visual displays. *Proceedings of the National Academy of Sciences of the United States of America, 52,* 446–454.

Evans, J. St. B. T. (1972). Interpretation and matching bias in a reasoning task. *Quarterly Journal of Experimental Psychology, 24,* 193–199.

Evans, J. St. B. T. (1977). Linguistic factors in reasoning. *Quarterly Journal of Experimental Psychology, 29,* 297–306.

Evans, J. St. B. T., Barston, J. L., & Pollard, P. (1983). On the conflict between logic and belief in syllogistic reasoning. *Memory & Cognition, 11,* 295–306.

Fillmore, C. J. (1968). The case for case. In E. Bach & R. T. Harms (Eds.), *Universals in linguistic theory* (p.p. 1–88). New York: Holt, Rinehart, & Winston.

Fink, R. S., & Dominowski, R. L. (1974). Pronounceability as an explanation of the difference between word and nonsense anagrams. *Journal of Experimental Psychology, 102,* 159–160.

Fischhoff, B. (1975). Hindsight = foresight: The effect of outcome knowledge on judgment under uncertainty. *Journal of Experimental Psychology: Human Perception and Performance, 1,* 288–299.

Fischhoff, B. (1977). Perceived informativeness of facts. *Journal of Experimental Psychology: Human Perception and Performance, 3,* 349–358.

Fischhoff, B., Slovic, P., & Lichtenstein, S. (1977). Knowing with certainty: The appropriateness of extreme confidence. *Journal of Experimental Psychology: Human Perception and Performance, 3,* 552–564.

Fisher, D. L. (1981). A three-factor model of syllogistic reasoning: The study of isolable stages. *Memory & Cognition, 9,* 496–514.

Flavell, J. H. (1976). *Cognitive development.* Englewood Cliffs, N.J.: Prentice-Hall.

Flavell, J. H. (1982). On cognitive development. *Child Development, 53,* 1–10.

Flavell, J. H., Speer, J. R., Green, F. L., & August, D. L. (1981). The development of comprehension monitoring and knowledge about communication. *Monographs of the Society for Research in Child Development, 46,* No. 5.

Flavell, J. H., & Wellman, H. M. (1977). Metamemory. In R. V. Kail & J. W. Hagen (Eds.), *Perspectives on the development of memory and cognition.* Hillsdale, N.J.: Erlbaum.

Fletcher, C. R. (1981). Short-term memory processes in text comprehension. *Journal of Verbal Learning and Verbal Behavior, 20,* 564–574.

Fletcher, C. R. (1984). *Strategies for the allocation of short-term memory during comprehension: A comparative analysis.* Unpublished Doctoral Thesis, University of Colorado, Boulder.

Fodor, J. A., & Bever, T. G. (1965). The psychological reality of linguistic segments. *Journal of Verbal Learning and Verbal Behavior, 4,* 414–420.

Fodor, J. A., Bever, T. G., & Garrett, M. F. (1974). *The psychology of language.* New York: McGraw-Hill.

Fraisse, P., & Piaget, J. (Eds.). (1969) *Experimental psychology: Its scope and method, VII. Intelligence.* New York: Basic Books.

Frame, C. L., & Oltmanns, T. F. (1982). Serial recall by schizophrenic and affective patients during and after psychotic episodes. *Journal of Abnormal Psychology, 91,* 311–318.

Franks, J. J., & Bransford, J. D. (1971). Abstraction of visual patterns. *Journal of Experimental Psychology, 90,* 65–74.

Frase, L. T., & Schwartz, B. J. (1975). Effect of question production and answering on prose recall. *Journal of Educational Psychology, 67,* 628–635.

Freedman, J. L., & Loftus, E. F. (1971). Retrieval of words from long-term memory. *Journal of Verbal Learning and Verbal Behavior, 10,* 107–115.

Freeman, G. L. (1931). Mental activity and the muscular process. *Psychological Review, 38,* 428–447.

Frey, P., & Adesman, P. (1976). Recall-memory for visually presented chess positions. *Memory & Cognition, 4,* 541–547.

Fried, L. S., & Holyoak, K. J. (1980). *Induction of category distributions: A framework for classification learning.* Unpublished manuscript, University of Michigan.

Fry, D. B., Abramson, A. S., Eimas, P. D., & Liberman, A. M. (1962). The identification and discrimination of synthetic vowels. *Language and Speech, 5,* 171–189.

Fulgosi, A., & Guilford, J. P. (1968). Short-term incubation in divergent production. *American Journal of Psychology, 81,* 241–246.

Gagné, R. M., & Smith, E. C., Jr. (1962). A study of the effects of verbalization on problem solving. *Journal of Experimental Psychology, 63,* 12–18.

Gardner, G. T. (1973). Evidence for independent parallel channels in tachistoscopic perception. *Cognitive Psychology, 4,* 130–155.

Gardner, R. A., & Runquist, W. N. (1958). Acquisition and extinction of problem-solving set. *Journal of Experimental Psychology, 55,* 274–277.

Garner, W. R. (1974). *The processing of information and structure.* New York: Wiley.

Garner, W. R. (1976). Interaction of stimulus dimensions in concept and choice processes. *Cognitive Psychology, 8,* 98–123.

Garner, W. R. (1978). Aspects of a stimulus: Features, dimensions, and configurations. In E. Rosch & B. B. Lloyd (Eds.), *Cognition and categorization.* Hillsdale, N.J.: Erlbaum.

Garrett, M., Bever, T., & Fodor, J. (1966). The active use of grammar in speech perception. *Perception & Psychophysics, 1,* 30–32.

Gelman, P. (1969). Conservation acquisition: A problem of learning to attend to relevant attributes. *Journal of Experimental Child Psychology, 7,* 67–87.

Getty, D. J., & Howard, J. H., Jr. (Eds.). (1981). *Auditory and visual pattern recognition.* Hillsdale, N.J.: Erlbaum.

Gick, M. L., & Holyoak, K. J. (1980). Analogical problem solving. *Cognitive Psychology, 12,* 306–355.

Gilani, Z. H., & Ceraso, J. (1982). Transfer and temporal organization. *Journal of Verbal Learning and Verbal Behavior, 21,* 437–450.

Gilhooly, K. J., & Falconer, W. A. (1974). Concrete and abstract terms and relations in testing a rule.

Quarterly Journal of Experimental Psychology, 26, 355–359.

Ginsburg, H., & Koslowski, B. (1976). Cognitive development. *Annual Review of Psychology, 27,* 29–61.

Glanzer, M., & Cunitz, A. R. (1966). Two storage mechanisms in free-recall. *Journal of Verbal Learning and Verbal Behavior, 5,* 351–360.

Glaser, R., & Resnick, L. B. (1972). Instructional psychology. *Annual Review of Psychology, 23,* 207–276.

Glass, A. L., & Holyoak, K. J. (1975). Alternative conceptions of semantic memory. *Cognition, 3*(4), 313–339.

Gleason, H. A. (1961). *An introduction to descriptive linguistics.* New York: Holt, Rinehart, & Winston.

Glucksberg, S., & Weisberg, R. W. (1966). Verbal behavior and problem solving: Some effects of labeling upon availability of novel functions. *Journal of Experimental Psychology, 71,* 659–664.

Goldin-Meadow, S., Seligman, M. E. P., & Gelman, R. (1976). Language in the two-year-old. *Cognition, 4,* 189–202.

Gorenstein, G., & Ellsworth, P. (1981). Effect of choosing an incorrect photograph on a later identification by an eyewitness. *Journal of Applied Psychology, 65*(5), 616–622.

Greene, E., Flynn, M. S., & Loftus, E. F. (1982). Inducing resistance of misleading information. *Journal of Verbal Learning and Verbal Behavior, 21,* 207–219.

Greeno, J. G. (1973). The structure of memory and the process of solving problems. In R. L. Solso (Ed.), *Contemporary issues in cognitive psychology.* Washington, D.C.: V. H. Winston & Sons.

Greeno, J. G. (1977). Process of understanding in problem solving. In N. J. Castellan, D. B. Pisoni, & G. R. Potts (Eds.), *Cognitive theory* (Vol. II). Hillsdale, N.J.: Erlbaum.

Greeno, J. G. (1978). Natures of problem-solving abilities. In W. K. Estes (Ed.), *Handbook of learning and cognitive processes.* Hillsdale, N.J.: Erlbaum.

Griggs, R. A., & Cox, J. R. (1982). The elusive thematic-materials effect in Wason's selection task. *British Journal of Psychology, 73,* 407–420.

Grudin, J. (1980). Processes in verbal analogy solution. *Journal of Experimental Psychology: Human Perception and Performance, 6,* 67–74.

Guyotte, M. J., & Sternberg, R. J. (1981). A transitive-chain theory of syllogistic reasoning. *Cognitive Psychology, 13,* 461–525.

Hagen, J. W., Jongeward, R. H., Jr., & Kail, R. V., Jr. (1975). Cognitive perspectives on the development of memory. In H. Reese (Ed.), *Advances in child development and behavior* (Vol. 10). New York: Academic Press.

Hammerton, M. A. (1973). A case of radical probability estimation. *Journal of Experimental Psychology, 101,* 252–254.

Hampton, J. A. (1982). An investigation of the nature of abstract concepts. *Memory & Cognition, 9,* 149–156.

Harris, P. L. (1975). Development of search and object permanence during infancy. *Psychological Bulletin, 82,* 332–344.

Hartley, J., & Homa, D. (1981). Abstraction of stylistic concepts. *Journal of Experimental Psychology: Human Learning and Memory, 7,* 33–36.

Hasher, L., & Zachs, R. T. (1979). Automatic and effortful processes in memory. *Journal of Experimental Psychology: General, 108,* 356–388.

Haviland, S. E., & Clark, H. H. (1974). What's new? Acquiring new information as a process in comprehension. *Journal of Verbal Learning and Verbal Behavior, 13,* 512–521.

Haygood, R. C., & Bourne, L. E., Jr. (1960). Effects of intermittent reinforcement of an irrelevant dimension and task complexity upon concept identification. *Journal of Experimental Psychology, 60,* 371–375.

Haygood, R. C., & Bourne, L. E., Jr. (1965). Attribute- and rule-learning aspects of conceptual behavior. *Psychological Review, 72,* 175–195.

Healy, A. F. (1976). Detection errors on the word *the:* Evidence for reading units larger than letters. *Journal of Experimental Psychology: Human Perception and Performance, 2,* 235–242.

Healy, A. F. (1978). Poor communication in psycholinguistics: Review of four new textbooks. *Journal of Psycholinguistic Research, 7,* 477–492.

Healy, A. F., & Cutting, J. E. (1976). Units of speech perception: Phoneme and syllable. *Journal of Verbal Learning and Verbal Behavior, 15,* 73–83.

Healy, A. F., & Levitt, A. G. (1978). The relative accessibility of semantic and deep structure syntactic concepts. *Memory & Cognition, 6,* 518–526.

Healy, A. F., Oliver, W. L., & McNamara, T. P. (1982). *Detecting letters in continuous text: Effects of display size.* Paper presented at the 23rd Annual Meeting of the Psychonomic Society, Minneapolis, Minnesota.

Healy, A. F., & Repp, B. H. (1982). Context independence and phonetic mediation in categorical perception. *Journal of Experimental Psychology: Human Perception and Performance, 8,* 68–80.

Heider, E. R. (1972). Universals in color naming and memory. *Journal of Experimental Psychology, 93,* 10–20.

Helsabeck, F., Jr. (1975). Syllogistic reasoning: Generation of counterexamples. *Journal of Educational Psychology, 67,* 102–108.

Henle, M. (1962). On the relation between logic and thinking. *Psychological Review, 69,* 366–378.

Herrmann, D., & Neisser, U. (1978). An inventory of everyday memory experiences. In M. M. Gruneberg, P. E. Morris, & R. N. Sykes (Eds.), *Prac-*

tical Aspects of Memory (pp. 35–51). New York: Academic Press.

Hiew, C. C. (1977). Sequence effects in rule learning and conceptual generalization. *American Journal of Psychology, 90,* 207–218.

Higbee, K. L. (1977). *Your memory: How it works and how to improve it.* Englewood Cliffs, N.J.: Prentice-Hall.

Hinton, G. E., & Anderson, J. A. (1981). *Parallel models of associative memory.* Hillsdale, N.J.: Erlbaum.

Hock, H. S., & Schmelzkopf, K. F. (1980). The abstraction of schematic representations from photographs of real world scenes. *Memory & Cognition, 8,* 543–554.

Hogarth, R. M. (1981). Beyond discrete biases: Functional and dysfunctional aspects of judgmental heuristics. *Psychological Bulletin, 90,* 197–217.

Holding, D. H. (1975). Sensory storage reconsidered. *Memory & Cognition, 3,* 31–41.

Holding, D. H., & Reynolds, R. I. (1982). Recall or evaluation of chess positions as determinants of chess skill. *Memory & Cognition, 10,* 237–242.

Hollin, C. R., & Clifford, B. R. (1980). *The effect on eyewitness memory of the nature of the witness incident.* Unpublished manuscript, Northeast London Polytechnic, London.

Homa, D., Sterling, S., & Trepel, L. (1981). Limitations of exemplar based generalization and the abstraction of categorical information. *Journal of Experimental Psychology: Human Learning and Memory, 7,* 418–439.

Houston, J. P., Bee, H., Hatfield, E., & Rimm, D. C. (1979). *Invitation to psychology.* New York: Academic Press.

Howard, D. (1983). *Cognitive psychology: Memory, language and thought.* New York: Macmillan.

Hull, C. L. (1920). Quantitative aspects of the evolution of concepts. *Psychological Monographs* (Whole No. 123).

Hunt, E. (1983). On the nature of intelligence. *Science, 219,* 141–146.

Hunt, E., & Love, T. (1972). How good can memory be? In A. W. Melton & E. Martin (Eds.), *Coding processes in human memory.* Washington, D.C.: Winston.

Hunter, I. M. L. (1968). Mental calculation. In P. C. Wason & P. N. Johnson-Laird (Eds.), *Thinking and reasoning.* Middlesex, England: Penguin Books, Ltd.

Hupp, S. C., & Mervis, C. B. (1982). Acquisition of basic object categories by severely handicapped children. *Child Development, 53,* 760–767.

Hyde, T. S., & Jenkins, J. J. (1969). Differential effects of incidental tasks on the organization of recall of a list of highly associated words. *Journal of Experimental Psychology, 82,* 472–481.

Intraub, H. (1979). The role of implicit naming in pictoral encoding. *Journal of Experimental Psychology: Human Learning and Memory, 5,* 78–87.

Jacobs, M. K., & Dominowski, R. L. (1981). Learning to solve insight problems. *Bulletin of the Psychonomic Society, 17,* 171–174.

James W. (1890). *The principles of psychology.* New York: Henry Holt.

Jeffries, R., Polson, P. G., Razran, L., & Atwood, M. E. (1977). A process model for missionaries-cannibals and other river-crossing problems. *Cognitive Psychology, 9,* 412–440.

Jenkins, J. G., & Dallenbach, K. M. (1924). Obliviscence during sleep and waking. *American Journal of Psychology, 35,* 605–612.

Jenkins, J. J. (1974). Remember that old theory of memory? Well, forget it! *American Psychologist, 29,* 785–795.

Jennings, D. L., Amabile, T. M., & Ross, L. (1982). Informal covariation assessment: Data-based versus theory-based judgments. In D. Kahneman, P. Slovic & A. Tversky (Eds.), *Judgment under uncertainty: Heuristics and biases.* Cambridge: Cambridge University Press.

Johnson, C., & Scott, B. (1976). *Eyewitness testimony and suspect identification as a function of arousal, sex of witness, and scheduling of interrogation.* Presented at the meeting of the American Psychological Association, Washington, D.C.

Johnson, D. M., Parrott, G. R., & Stratton, R. P. (1968). Production and judgment of solutions to five problems. *Journal of Educational Psychology Monograph Supplement, 59,* No. 6, Part 2.

Johnson-Laird, P. N., & Steedman, M. (1978). The psychology of syllogisms. *Cognitive Psychology, 10,* 64–99.

Johnson-Laird, P. N., & Wason, P. C. (1970). A theoretical analysis of insight into a reasoning task. *Cognitive Psychology, 1,* 134–148.

Johnston, J. C., & McClelland, J. L. (1974). Perception of letters in words: Seek not and ye shall find. *Science, 184,* 1192–1194.

Johnston, W. A., & Heinz, S. P. (1978). Flexibility and capacity demands of attention. *Journal of Experimental Psychology: General, 107,* 420–435.

Kagan, J. (1976). Emergent themes in human development. *American Scientist, 64,* 186–196.

Kahneman, D., & Henik, A. (1981). Perceptual organization and attention. In M. Kubovy & J. R. Pomerantz (Eds.), *Perceptual organization.* Hillsdale, N.J.: Erlbaum.

Kahneman, D., & Tversky, A. (1972). Subjective probability: A judgment of representativeness. *Cognitive Psychology, 3,* 430–454.

Kahneman, D., & Tversky, A. (1973). On the psychology of prediction. *Psychological Review, 80,* 237–251.

Kahneman, D., & Tversky, A. (1982a). On the study of statistical intuitions. *Cognition, 11,* 123–142.

Kahneman, D., & Tversky, A. (1982b). Variants of uncertainty. *Cognition, 11,* 143–158.

Kaplan, R. M., & Pascoe, G. C. (1977). Humorous lectures and humorous examples: Some effects upon comprehension and retention. *Journal of Educational Psychology, 69,* 61–65.

Katz, A. N., & Paivio, A. (1975). Imagery variables in concept identification. *Journal of Verbal Learning and Verbal Behavior, 14,* 284–293.

Kellas, G., McCauley, C., & McFarland, C. E., Jr. (1975). Developmental aspects of storage and retrieval. *Journal of Experimental Child Psychology, 19,* 51–62.

Kellogg, R. T. (1980). Feature frequency and hypothesis testing in the acquisition of rule governed concepts. *Memory & Cognition, 17,* 297–303.

Kellogg, R. T. (1980). Is conscious attention necessary for long term storage? *Journal of Experimental Psychology: Human Learning and Memory, 6,* 379–390.

Kellogg, R. T. (1982). Hypothesis recognition failure in conjunctive and disjunctive concept-identification tasks. *Memory & Cognition, 19,* 327–330.

Kellogg, R. T., Robbins, D. W., & Bourne, L. E., Jr. (1983). Failure to recognize previous hypotheses in concept learning. *American Journal of Psychology, 96,* 179–199.

Kellogg, R. T., Robbins, D. W., & Bourne, L. E., Jr. (1978). Memory for intratrial events in feature identification. *Journal of Experimental Psychology: Human Learning and Memory, 4,* 256–265.

Kendler, H. H., & Kendler, T. S. (1961). Effect of verbalization on reversal shifts in children. *Science, 134,* 1619–1620.

Kendler, H. H., & Kendler, T. S. (1962). Vertical and horizontal processes in problem solving. *Psychological Review, 69,* 1–16.

Kintsch, W. (1970). Models for free recall and recognition. In D. A. Norman (Ed.), *Models of human memory.* New York: Academic Press.

Kintsch, W. (1974). *The representation of meaning in memory.* Hillsdale, N.J.: Erlbaum.

Kintsch, W., & Bates, E. (1977). Recognition memory for statements from a classroom lecture. *Journal of Experimental Psychology: Human Learning and Memory, 3,* 150–159.

Kintsch, W., & Keenan, J. (1973). Reading rate and retention as a function of the number of propositions in the base structure of sentences. *Cognitive Psychology, 5,* 257–274.

Kintsch, W., & van Dijk, T. A. (1978). Toward a model of text comprehension and production. *Psychological Review, 85,* 363–394.

Kintsch, W., & Vipond, D. (1979). Reading comprehension and readability in educational practice and psychological theory. In L. G. Nilsson (Ed.), *Perspectives on memory research.* Hillsdale, N.J.: Erlbaum.

Klahr, D., & Wallace, J. G. (1970). An information processing analysis of some Piagetian experimental tasks. *Cognitive Psychology, 1,* 358–387.

Klatzky, R. L. (1975). *Human memory: Structures and processes.* San Francisco: W. H. Freeman.

Kleinmuntz, D. N., & Kleinmuntz, B. (1981). Decision strategies in simulated environments. *Behavioral Science, 26,* 294–305.

Knight, R. A., & Sims-Knight, J. E. (1979). Integration of linguistic ideas in schizophrenics. *Journal of Abnormal Psychology, 88,* 191–202.

Knight, R. A., & Sims-Knight, J. E. (1980). Integration of visual patterns in schizophrenics. *Journal of Abnormal Psychology, 89,* 623–634.

Koh, S. D. (1978). Remembering of verbal materials by schizophrenic young adults. In S. Schwartz (Ed.), *Language and Cognition in Schizophrenia.* Hillsdale, N.J.: Erlbaum.

Koh, S. D., Marusarz, T. L., & Rosen, A. J. (1980). Remembering of sentences by schizophrenic young adults. *Journal of Abnormal Psychology, 89,* 291–294.

Köhler, W. (1925). *The mentality of apes.* London: Routledge & Kegan-Paul.

Kopp, C. B., Sigman, M., & Parmelee, A. H. (1974). Longitudinal study of sensory-motor development. *Developmental Psychology, 10,* 687–695.

Kopp, J., & Lane, H. (1968). Hue discrimination related to linguistic habits. *Psychonomic Science, 11,* 61–62.

Korboot, P. J., & Damiani, N. (1976). Auditory processing speed and signal detection in schizophrenia. *Journal of Abnormal Psychology, 85,* 287–295.

Koriat, A., Lichtenstein, S., & Fischhoff, B. (1980). Reasons for confidence. *Journal of Experimental Psychology: Human Learning and Memory, 6,* 107–118.

Kotovsky, K., & Simon, H. A. (1973). Empirical tests of a theory of human acquisition of concepts for sequential events. *Cognitive Psychology, 4,* 399–424.

Krauth, J. (1982). Formulation and experimental verification of models in propositional reasoning. *Quarterly Journal of Experimental Psychology, 34,* 285–298.

Kreutzer, M. A., Leonard, S. C., & Flavell, J. H. (1975). An interview study of children's knowledge about memory. *Monographs of the Society for Research in Child Development, 40* (1, Serial No. 159).

Kroll, N. E. A., Parks, T., Parkinson, S. R., Bieber, S. L., & Johnson, A. L. (1970). Short-term memory while shadowing: Recall of visually and of aurally presented letters. *Journal of Experimental Psychology, 85,* 220–224.

Kuhn, D. (1974). Inducing development experimentally: Comments on a research paradigm. *Developmental Psychology, 10,* 590–600.

Langendoen, D. T. (1970). *Essentials of English grammar.* New York: Holt, Rinehart, & Winston.

LaPorte, R. E., & Nath, R. (1976). Role of performance goals in prose learning. *Journal of Educational Psychology, 68,* 260–264.

Lee, C. L., & Estes, W. K. (1981). Item and order information in short-term memory: Evidence for multilevel perturbation processes. *Journal of Experimental Psychology: Human Learning and Memory, 7,* 149–169.

LeMay, E. H. (1972). Anagram solutions as a function of task variables and solution word models. *Journal of Experimental Psychology, 92,* 65–68.

Lenneberg, E. H. (1969). On explaining language. *Science, 164,* 635–643.

Levine, M. (1966). Hypothesis behavior by humans during discrimination learning. *Journal of Experimental Psychology, 71,* 331–338.

Levine, M. (1975). *A cognitive theory of learning.* Hillsdale, N.J.: Erlbaum.

Liberman, A. M., Cooper, F. S., Shankweiler, D. P., & Studdert-Kennedy, M. (1967). Perception of the speech code. *Psychological Review, 74,* 431–461.

Liberman, A. M., Harris, K. S., Hoffman, H. S., & Griffith, B. C. (1957). The discrimination of speech sounds within and across phoneme boundaries. *Journal of Experimental Psychology, 54,* 358–368.

Lichtenstein, S., & Fischhoff, B. (1977). Do those who know more also know more about how much they know? *Organizational Behavior and Human Performance, 20,* 159–183.

Lichtenstein, S., Slovic, P., Fischhoff, B., Layman, M., & Combs, B. (1978). Judged frequency of lethal events. *Journal of Experimental Psychology: Human Learning and Memory, 4,* 551–578.

Linton, M. (1982). Transformation of memory in everyday life. In U. Neisser (Ed.), *Memory observed.* San Francisco: W. H. Freeman.

Loewi, O. (1960). *Perspectives in Biology and Medicine.* Chicago: University of Chicago Press.

Loftus, E. F. (1974). On reading the fine print. *Quarterly Journal of Experimental Psychology, 27,* 324.

Loftus, E. F. (1979). *Eyewitness testimony.* Cambridge, Mass.: Harvard University Press.

Loftus, E. F. (1981). Eyewitness testimony: Psychological research and legal thought. In M. Tonry & N. Morris (Eds.), *Crime and justice: An annual review of research.* Chicago: University of Chicago Press.

Loftus, E. F. (1983). *Misfortunes of memory.* Philosophical Transactions of the Royal Society, London, B 302, 413–421.

Loftus, E. F. (1984). Eyewitnesses: Essential but unreliable. *Psychology Today,* pp. 22–26.

Loftus, E. F., & Loftus, G. R. (1980). On the permanence of stored information in the human brain. *American Psychologist, 35,* 409–420.

Loftus, E. F., Miller, D. G., & Burns, H. J. (1978). Semantic integration of verbal information into a visual memory. *Journal of Experimental Psychology: Human Learning and Memory, 4,* 19–31.

Lorayne, H., & Lucas, J. (1974). *The memory book.* New York: Ballantine Books. (Published in paperback by Stein and Day Publishers, New York, 1975.)

Lopes, L. L. (1981). Decision making in the short run. *Journal of Experimental Psychology: Human Learning and Memory, 7,* 377–385.

Lopes, L. L. (1982). Doing the impossible: A note on induction and the experience of randomness. *Journal of Experimental Psychology: Learning, Memory, and Cognition, 8,* 626–636.

Lucy, J. A., & Shweder, R. A. (1979). Whorf and his critics: Linguistic and non-linguistic influences on color memory. *American Anthropologist, 81,* 581–608.

Lung, C. T. & Dominowski, R. L. (1985). Effects of strategy instructions and practice on nine-dot problem solving. *Journal of Experimental Psychology: Learning, Memory, and Cognition,* in press.

Luria, A. R. (1968). *The mind of a mnemonist* (L. Solotaroff, Trans.). New York: Basic Books.

MacNamara, J. (1972). Cognitive basis of language learning in infants. *Psychological Review, 79,* 1–13.

Maier, N. R. F. (1940). The behavior mechanisms concerned with problem solving. *Psychological Review, 47,* 43–53.

Maier, N. R. F., & Janzen, J. C. (1968). Functional values as aids and distractors in problem solving. *Psychological Reports, 22,* 1021–1034.

Maier, N. R. F., & Janzen, J. C. (1969). Are good problem-solvers also creative? *Psychological Reports, 24,* 139–146.

Malin, J. T. (1979). Information-processing load in problem solving by network search. *Journal of Experimental Psychology: Human Perception and Performance, 5,* 379–390.

Malpass, R. S., & DeVine, P. G. (1980). *Guided memory in eyewitness identification.* Unpublished manuscript, State University of New York, Plattsburgh.

Mandler, J. M. (1983). Representation. In J. H. Flavell and E. M. Markman (Eds.), *Cognitive development* (pp. 420–494). New York: Wiley.

Manske, M. E., & Davis, G. A. (1968). Effects of simple instructional biases upon performance in the unusual uses test. *Journal of General Psychology, 78,* 25–33.

Manktelow, K. I., & Evans, J. St. B. T. (1979). Facilitation of reasoning by realism: Effect or non-effect? *British Journal of Psychology, 70,* 477–488.

Marin, B. V., Holmes, D. L., Guth, M., & Kovac, P. (1979). The potential of children as eyewitnesses: A comparison of children and adults on eyewitness tasks. *Law and Human Behavior, 3,* 259–306.

Martin, R. C., & Caramazza, A. (1980). Classification in well defined and ill defined categories: Evidence for common processing strategies. *Journal of Experimental Psychology: General, 109,* 320–353.

Martorano, S. C. (1977). A developmental analysis of performance on Piaget's formal operations tasks. *Developmental Psychology, 13,* 666–672.

Mayer, R. E. (1975). Information processing variables in learning to solve problems. *Review of Educational Research, 45,* 525–541.

Mayer, R. E. (1982). Different problem-solving strategies for algebra word and equation problems. *Journal of Experimental Psychology: Learning, Memory, and Cognition, 8,* 448–462.

Mayer, R. E., & Greeno, J. G. (1972). Structural differences between learning outcomes produced by different instructional methods. *Journal of Educational Psychology, 63,* 165–173.

Mayer, R. E., Stiehl, C. C., & Greeno, J. G. (1975). Acquisition of understanding and skill in relation to subjects' preparation and meaningfulness of instruction. *Journal of Educational Psychology, 67,* 331–350.

Mayzner, M. S., & Tresselt, M. E. (1962). Anagram solution times: A function of word transition probabilities. *Journal of Experimental Psychology, 63,* 510–513.

McClelland, J. L., & Rumelhart, D. E. (1981). An interactive activation model of context effects in letter perception: Part 1. An account of basic findings. *Psychological Review, 88,* 375–407.

McDowall, J. (1979). Effects of encoding instructions and retrieval cuing on recall in Korsakoff patients. *Memory & Cognition, 7,* 232–239.

McGeoch, J. A. (1942). *The psychology of human learning.* New York: Longmans, Green & Co.

McNeill, D., & Lindig, K. (1973). The perceptual reality of phonemes, syllables, words, and sentences. *Journal of Verbal Learning and Verbal Behavior, 12,* 419–430.

Medin, D. L., & Schaffer, M. M. (1978). A context theory of classification learning. *Psychological Review, 85,* 207–238.

Mednick, S. A. (1962). The associative basis of the creative process. *Psychological Review, 69,* 220–232.

Mehler, J. (1963). Some effects of grammatical transformations on the recall of English sentences. *Journal of Verbal Learning and Verbal Behavior, 2,* 346–351.

Melton, A. W., & Irwin, J. M. (1940). The influence of degree of interpolated learning on retroactive inhibition and the overt transfer of specific responses. *American Journal of Psychology, 53,* 173–203.

Mervis, C. B., & Crisafi, M. A. (1982). Order of acquisition of subordinate, basic, and superordinate categories. *Child Development, 53,* 258–266.

Meudell, P., & Mayes, A. (1981). The claparede phenomenon: A further example in amnesics, a demonstration of a similar effect in normal people with attenuated memory, and a reinterpretation. *Current Psychological Research, 1,* 75–88.

Meyer, D. E. (1970). On the representation and retrieval of stored semantic information. *Cognitive Psychology, 1*, 242–300.

Meyer, D. E. (1975). Long-term memory retrieval during the comprehension of affirmative and negative sentences. In R. A. Kennedy & A. L. Wilkes (Eds.), *Studies in long-term memory*. London: Wiley.

Miller, G. A. (1956). The magical number seven, plus or minus two: Some limits on our capacity for processing information. *Psychological Review, 63*, 81–97.

Miller, J. L., & Eimas, P. D. (1983). Studies on the categorization of speech by infants. *Cognition, 13*, 135–166.

Miller, J. R., & Kintsch, W. (1980). Readability and recall of short prose passages: A theoretical analysis. *Journal of Experimental Psychology: Human Learning and Memory, 6*, 335–354.

Miller, P. H. (1973). Attention to stimulus dimensions in the conservation of liquid quantity. *Child Development, 44*, 129–136.

Miller, R. R. & Marlin, N. A. (1979). Amnesia following electroconvulsive shock. In J. F. Kihlstrom & F. J. Evans (Eds.), *Functional disorders of memory*. Hillsdale, N.J.: Erlbaum.

Miller, S. A. (1976). Nonverbal assessment of Piagetian concepts. *Psychological Bulletin, 83*, 405–430.

Milner, B. (1959). The memory defect in bilateral hippocampal lesions. *Psychiatric Research Reports, 11*, 43–52.

Milner, B. (1966). Amnesia following operation on the temporal lobes. In C. W. M. Whitty & O. L. Zangwill (Eds.), *Amnesia*. London: Butterworths.

Minsky, M. A. (1975). A framework for representing knowledge. In P. H. Winston (Ed.), *The psychology of computer vision*. New York: McGraw-Hill.

Miyawaki, K., Strange, W., Verbrugge, R., Liberman, A. M., Jenkins, J. J., & Fujimura, O. (1975). An effect of linguistic experience: The discrimination of [r] and [l] by native speakers of Japanese and English. *Perception & Psychophysics, 18*, 331–340.

Moely, B. E., Olson, F. A., Halwes, T. G., & Flavell, J. H. (1969). Production deficiency in young children's clustered recall. *Developmental Psychology, 1*, 26–34.

Moerk, E. L. (1975). Piaget's research as applied to the explanation of language development. *Merrill-Palmer Quarterly of Behavior and Development, 21*, 151–169.

Moray, N. (1959). Attention in dichotic listening: Affective cues and the influence of instructions. *Quarterly Journal of Experimental Psychology, 11*, 59–60.

Morishima, A., & Brown, L. F. (1977). A case report on the artistic talent of an autistic idiot savant. *Mental Retardation, 15*, 33–36.

Morton, J., Crowder, R. G., & Prussin, H. A. (1971). Experiments with the stimulus suffix effect. *Journal of Experimental Psychology Monograph, 91*, 169–190.

Morton, J., Hammersley, R., & Bekerian, D. A. (1983). *Headed records: Framework for remembering and its failures*. Unpublished manuscript, M.R.C. Applied Psychology Unit, Cambridge, England.

Murdock, B. B., Jr. (1962). The serial position effect of free recall. *Journal of Experimental Psychology, 64*, 482–488.

Murphy, G. L., & Smith, E. E. (1982). Basic level superiority in picture categorization. *Journal of Verbal Learning and Verbal Behavior, 21*, 1–20.

Mynatt, C. R., Doherty, M. E., & Tweney, R. D. (1978). Consequences of confirmation and disconfirmation in a simulated research environment. *Quarterly Journal of Experimental Psychology, 30*, 395–406.

Mynatt, C. R., Doherty, M. E., & Tweney, R. D. (1977). Confirmation bias in a simulated research environment: An experimental study of scientific inference. *Quarterly Journal of Experimental Psychology, 29*, 85–95.

Nairne, J. S., & Healy, A. F. (1983). Counting backwards produces systematic errors. *Journal of Experimental Psychology: General, 112*, 37–40.

Nairne, J. S., & Walters, V. L. (1983). Silent mouthing produces modality- and suffix-like effects. *Journal of Verbal Learning and Verbal Behavior, 22*, 475–483.

Naus, M. J., & Ornstein, P. A. (1983). Development of memory strategies: Analysis questions, and issues. *Contributions to Human Development, 9*, 1–30.

Neely, J. H. (1982). The role of expectancy in probability learning. *Journal of Experimental Psychology: Learning, Memory, and Cognition, 8*, 599–607.

Neimark, E. D. (1975). Intellectual development during adolescence. In F. D. Horowitz (Ed.), *Review of child development research* (Vol. 4). Chicago: University of Chicago Press.

Neimark, E. D., & Wagner, H. (1964). Information-gathering in diagnostic problem solving as a function of number of alternative solutions. *Psychonomic Science, 1*, 329–330.

Neisser, U. (1967). *Cognitive psychology*. New York: Appleton-Century-Crofts.

Neisser, U. (1981). John Dean's memory: A case study. *Cognition, 9*, 1–22.

Neisser, U. (1982). *On the trail of the tape-recorder fallacy*. Paper presented at the American Association for Advancement of Science, Annual Meeting, Washington D.C.

Neisser, U. (1984). Interpreting Harry Bahrick's discovery: What confers immunity against forgetting? *Journal of Experimental Psychology: General, 113*, 32–35.

Neisser, U., & Weene, P. (1962). Hierarchies in concept attainment. *Journal of Experimental Psychology, 64*, 640–645.

Nelson, D. L., Reed, V. S., & Walling, J. R. (1976). Pictorial superiority effect. *Journal of Ex-

perimental Psychology: Human Learning and Memory, 2, 523–528.

Nelson, K. (1973). Some evidence for the cognitive primacy of categorization and its functional basis. *Merrill-Palmer Quarterly of Behavior and Development, 19,* 21–39.

Nelson, K. (1974). Concept, word, and sentence: Interrelations in acquisition and development. *Psychological Review, 81,* 267–285.

Nelson, T. O. (1977). Repetition and depth of processing. *Journal of Verbal Learning and Verbal Behavior, 16,* 151–171.

Neumann, P. G. (1974). An attribute frequency model for the abstraction of prototypes. *Memory & Cognition, 2,* 241–248.

Neumann, P. G. (1977). Visual prototype formation with discontinuous representation of dimensions of variability. *Memory & Cognition, 5,* 187–197.

Newell, A., & Simon, H. A. (1972). *Human problem solving.* Englewood Cliffs, N.J.: Prentice-Hall.

Newstead, S. E., & Griggs, R. (1983). Drawing inferences from quantified statements: A study of the square of opposition. *Journal of Verbal Learning and Verbal Behavior, 22,* 535–546.

Nickerson, R. S. & Adams, M. J. (1979). Long-term memory for a common object. *Cognitive Psychology, 11,* 287–307.

Nisbett, R. E., & Ross, L. (1980). *Human inference: Strategies and shortcomings.* Englewood Cliffs, N.J.: Prentice-Hall.

Norman, D. A., & Rumelhart, D. E. (1975). *Explorations in cognition.* San Francisco: W. H. Freeman.

Oltmanns, T. F., & Neale, J. M. (1975). Schizophrenic performance when distractors are present: Attentional deficit or differential task difficulty? *Journal of Abnormal Psychology, 84,* 205–209.

Omohundro, J. (1981). Recognition vs. classification of ill-defined category exemplars. *Memory & Cognition, 9,* 324–331.

Ornstein, P. A., Naus, M. J., & Liberty, C. (1975). Rehearsal and organizational processes in children's memory. *Child Development, 46,* 818–830.

Osherson, D. N., & Smith, E. E. (1981). On the adequacy of prototype theory as a theory of concepts. *Cognition, 9,* 35–58.

Paivio, A. (1971). *Imagery and verbal processes.* New York: Holt, Rinehart, & Winston.

Paivio, A. (1975). Perceptual comparisons through the mind's eye. *Memory & Cognition, 3*(6), 635–647.

Paivio, A. (1978). Mental comparisons involving abstract attributes. *Memory & Cognition, 6,* 199–208.

Paivio, A., Yuille, J. C., & Madigan, S. A. (1968). Concreteness, imagery, and meaningfulness values for 925 nouns. *Journal of Experimental Psychology Monograph Supplement, 76,* (1, Pt. 2).

Palermo, D. S., & Molfese, D. L. (1972). Language acquisition from age five onward. *Psychological Bulletin, 78,* 409–428.

Pavlov, I. (1927). *Conditioned reflexes.* London and New York: Oxford University Press.

Penfield, W., & Perot, P. (1963). The brain's record of auditory and visual experiences. *Brain, 86,* 595–696.

Penfield, W., & Roberts, L. (1959). *Speech and brain mechanisms.* Princeton, N. J.: Princeton University Press.

Perlmutter, M., & Myers, N. A. (1979). Development of recall in 2- to 4-year-old children. *Developmental Psychology, 15,* 75–83.

Peterson, C. R., & Beach, L. R. (1967). Man as an intuitive statistician. *Psychological Bulletin, 68,* 29–46.

Peterson, L. R., & Peterson, M. J. (1959). Short-term retention of individual verbal items. *Journal of Experimental Psychology, 58,* 193–198.

Pezdek, K. (1977). Cross-modality semantic integration of sentence and picture memory. *Journal of Experimental Psychology: Human Learning and Memory, 3,* 515–524.

Pezkek, K., & Miceli, L. (1982). Life-span differences in memory integration as a function of processing time. *Developmental Psychology, 18,* 485–490.

Piaget, J. (1970). *Genetic epistemology.* New York: W. W. Norton.

Piaget, J. (1977). *The development of thought: Equilibration of cognitive structures.* New York: Viking Penguin.

Pick, A. D., Frankel, D. G., & Hess, V. L. (1975). Children's attention: The development of selectivity. In E. M. Hetherington (Ed.), *Review of child development research* (Vol. 5). Chicago: University of Chicago Press.

Pinker, S. (1979). Formal models of language learning. *Cognition, 7,* 217–284.

Pogue-Geile, M. F. and Oltmanns, T. F. (1980). Sentence perception and distractability in schizophrenic, manic, and depressed patients. *Journal of Abnormal Psychology, 89,* 115–124.

Poincaré, H. (1913). Mathematical creation. In *The foundations of Science.* (G. B. Halsted, Trans.). New York: Science Press.

Polich, J. M., & Schwartz, S. H. (1974). The effect of problem size on representation in deductive problem solving. *Memory & Cognition, 2,* 683–686.

Pollard, P. (1982). Human reasoning: Some possible effects of availability. *Cognition, 12,* 65–96.

Posner, M. I., Goldsmith, R., & Welton, K. E., Jr. (1967). Perceived distance and the classification of distorted patterns. *Journal of Experimental Psychology, 73,* 28–38.

Posner, M. I., & Keele, S. (1968). On the genesis of abstract ideas. *Journal of Experimental Psychology, 77,* 353–363.

Postman, L. (1975). Verbal learning and memory. *Annual Review of Psychology, 26,* 291–335.

Postman, L., & Stark, K. (1969). Role of response availability in transfer and interference. *Journal of Experimental Psychology, 79,* 168–177.

Postman, L., Stark, K., & Fraser, J. (1968). Temporal changes in interference. *Journal of Verbal Learning and Verbal Behavior, 7,* 672–694.

Potter, M. C. (1976). Short-term conceptual memory for pictures. *Journal of Experimental Psychology: Human Learning and Memory, 2,* 509–522.

Potter, M. C., & Levy, E. I. (1969). Recognition memory for a rapid sequence of pictures. *Journal of Experimental Psychology, 81,* 10–15.

Potts, G. R. (1974). Storing and retrieving information about ordered relationships. *Journal of Experimental Psychology, 103,* 431–439.

Pylyshyn, Z. W. (1973). What the mind's eye tells the mind's brain: A critique of mental imagery. *Psychological Bulletin, 80*(1), 1–24.

Raaijamakers, J. G. W., & Shiffrin, R. M. (1981). Search of associative memory. *Psychological Review, 88,* 93–134.

Reason, J., & Mycielska, K. (1982). *Absent-minded? The psychology of mental lapses and everyday errors.* Englewood Cliffs, N. J.: Prentice Hall.

Reber, A. A., & Allen, R. (1978). Analogical and abstraction strategies in synthetic grammar learning: A functionalist interpretation. *Cognition, 6,* 189–221.

Reber, A. S., Kassin, S. M., Lewis, S., & Canter, G. (1980). On the relationship between implicit and explicit modes in the learning of a complex rule structure. *Journal of Experimental Psychology: Human Learning and Memory, 6,* 492–502.

Reder, L. M., & Anderson, J. R. (1980). A comparison of texts and their summaries: Memorial consequences. *Journal of Verbal Learning and Verbal Behavior, 19,* 121–134.

Reed, S. F., Ernst, G. W., & Banerji, R. (1974). The role of analogy in transfer between similar problem states. *Cognitive Psychology, 6,* 435–450.

Reed, S. K. (1972). Pattern recognition and categorization. *Cognitive Psychology, 3,* 383–407.

Reed, S. K. (1973). *Psychological processes in pattern recognition.* New York: Academic Press.

Reich, S. S., & Ruth, P. (1982). Wason's selection task: Verification, falsification, and matching. *British Journal of Psychology, 73,* 395–405.

Reicher, G. M. (1969). Perceptual recognition as a function of meaningfulness of stimulus material. *Journal of Experimental Psychology, 81,* 275–280.

Reitman, J. S. (1971). Mechanisms of forgetting in short-term memory. *Cognitive Psychology, 2,* 185–195.

Reitman, J. S. (1974). Without surreptitious rehearsal, information in short-term memory decays. *Journal of Verbal Learning and Verbal Behavior, 13,* 365–377.

Reitman, W. R. (1965). *Cognition and thought.* New York: Wiley.

Revlin, R., Leirer, H., Yopp, H., & Yopp, R. (1980). The belief-bias effect in formal reasoning: The influence of knowledge on logic. *Memory & Cognition, 8,* 584–592.

Revlin, R., & Leirer, V. O. (1980). Understanding quantified categorical expressions. *Memory & Cognition, 8,* 447–458.

Revlis, R. (1975). Two models of syllogistic reasoning: Feature selection and conversion. *Journal of Verbal Learning and Verbal Behavior, 14,* 180–195.

Reznick, J. S., & Richman, C. L. (1976). Effects of class complexity, class frequency, and pre-experimental bias on rule learning. *Journal of Experimental Psychology: Human Learning and Memory, 2,* 774–782.

Rickards, J. P., & DiVesta, F. J. (1974). Type and frequency of questions in processing textual material. *Journal of Educational Psychology, 66,* 354–362.

Rips, L. J. (1975). Inductive judgments about natural categories. *Journal of Verbal Learning and Verbal Behavior, 14,* 665–681.

Rips, L. J., Shoben, E. J., & Smith, E. E. (1973). Semantic distance and the verification of semantic relations. *Journal of Verbal Learning and Verbal Behavior, 12,* 1–20.

Roberge, J. J. (1982). Linguistic factors in conditional reasoning. *Quarterly Journal of Experimental Psychology, 34,* 275–284.

Ronning, R. R. (1965). Anagram solution times: A function of the "Rule-out" factor. *Journal of Experimental Psychology, 69,* 35–39.

Rosch, E. (1974). Universals and cultural specifics in human categorization. In R. Breslin, W. Lonner, & S. Bochner (Eds), *Cross-cultural perspectives on learning.* London: Sage Press.

Rosch, E. H. (1973). Natural categories. *Cognitive Psychology, 4,* 328–350.

Rosch, E. H. (1975). Cognitive representations of semantic categories. *Journal of Experimental Psychology: General, 104,* 192–233.

Rosch, E. H., & Mervis, C. B. (1975). Family resemblances: Studies in the internal structure of categories. *Cognitive Psychology, 7,* 573–605.

Rosch, E. H., Mervis, C. B., Gray, W. D., Johnson, D. M., & Boyes-Braem, P. (1976). Basic objects in natural categories. *Cognitive Psychology, 8,* 382–439.

Rosenzweig, M. R., Bennett, E. L., & Diamond, M. C. (1972). Brain changes in response to experience. *Scientific American, 226,* 22–29.

Ross, J., & Lawrence, K. A. (1968). Some observations on memory artifice. *Psychonomic Science, 13,* 107–108.

Roth, E. M., & Mervis, C. B. (1983). Fuzzy set theory and class inclusion relations in semantic categories. *Journal of Verbal Learning and Verbal Behavior, 22,* 509–525.

Roth, E. M., & Shoben, E. E. (1983). The effect of context on the structure of categories. *Cognitive Psychology, 15,* 346–379.

Rothenberg, A. M. (1982). *The emerging goddess: The creative process in art, science, and other fields.* Chicago: University of Chicago Press.

Rozin, P., Poritsky, S., & Sotsky, R. (1971). American children with reading problems can easily learn to read English represented by Chinese characters. *Science, 171,* 1264-1267.

Rumelhart, D. E. (1977). *Introduction to human information processing.* New York: Wiley.

Rumelhart, D. E. (1977). Toward an interactive model of reading. In S. Dornic (Ed.), *Attention and performance VI.* Hillsdale, N. J.: Erlbaum.

Rumelhart, D. E., Lindsay, P. H., & Norman, D. A. (1972). A process model for long-term memory. In E. Tulving & W. Donaldson (Eds.), *Organization of memory.* New York: Academic Press.

Rundus, D. (1971). Analysis of rehearsal processes in free recall. *Journal of Experimental Psychology, 89,* 63-77.

Rundus, E., & Atkinson, R. C. (1970). Rehearsal processes in free-recall: A procedure for direct observation. *Journal of Verbal Learning and Verbal Behavior, 9,* 99-105.

Russell, P. N., Consedine, C. E., & Knight, R. G. Visual and memory search by process schizophrenics. *Journal of Abnormal Psychology,* 1980, 89, 109-114.

Rybash, J. M., Roodin, P. A., & Sullivan, L. F. (1975). The effects of a memory aid on three types of conservation judgments. *Journal of Experimental Child Psychology, 19,* 358-370.

Safren, M. A. (1962). Associations, sets, and the solution of word problems. *Journal of Experimental Psychology, 64,* 40-45.

Sanders, G. S., & Simmons, W. L. (1983). Use of hypnosis to enhance eyewitness accuracy: Does it work? *Journal of Applied Psychology, 68,* 70-77.

Savin, H. B., & Bever, T. G. (1970). The nonperceptual reality of the phoneme. *Journal of Verbal Learning and Verbal Behavior, 9,* 295-302.

Schank, R. C. (1982). *Dynamic memory; A theory of reminding and learning in computers and people.* Cambridge: Cambridge University Press.

Schank, R. C., & Abelson, R. (1977). *Scripts, plans, goals, and understanding.* Hillsdale, N. J.: Erlbaum.

Scheerer, M., Rothmann, E., & Goldstein, K. (1945). A case of "idiot savant": An experimental study of personality organization. *Psychological Monographs, 58,* Whole No. 269.

Schneider, S. J. (1976). Selective attention in schizophrenia. *Journal of Abnormal Psychology, 85,* 167-173.

Schneider, W., & Shiffrin, R. M. (1977). Controlled and automatic human information processing: I. Detection, search, attention. *Psychological Review, 84,* 1-66.

Schoemaker, P. J. H. (1982). The expected utility model: Its variants, purposes, evidence, and limitations. *Journal of Economic Literature, 20,* 529-563.

Schoenfeld, A. H., & Herrmann, D. J. (1982). Problem perception and knowledge structure in expert and novice mathematical problem solvers. *Journal of Experimental Psychology: Learning, Memory, and Cognition, 8,* 484-494.

Schwartz, S. H. (1971). Modes of representation and problem solving: Well evolved is half solved. *Journal of Experimental Psychology, 91,* 347-350.

Shaklee, H., & Mims, M. (1982). Sources of error in judging event covariations: Effects of memory demands. *Journal of Experimental Psychology: Learning, Memory, and Cognition, 8,* 208-224.

Shaklee, H., & Tucker, D. (1980). A rule analysis of judgments of covariation between events. *Memory and Cognition, 8,* 459-467.

Shannon, C. E., & Weaver, W. (1949). *The mathematical theory of communication.* Urbana: University of Illinois Press.

Shanteau, J. (1978). When does a response error become a judgmental bias? Commentary on 'Judged frequency of lethal events.' *Journal of Experimental Psychology: Human Learning and Memory, 4,* 579-581.

Shaughnessy, J. J., & Mand, J. L. (1982). How permanent are memories for real life events? *American Journal of Psychology, 95,* 51-65.

Sheehan, P. W., & Tilden, J. (1983). Effects of suggestibility and hypnosis on accurate and distorted retrieval from memory. *Journal of Experimental Psychology: Learning, Memory, and Cognition.*

Shepard, R. N., & Cooper, L. A. (1982). *Mental images and their transformations.* Cambridge, Mass.: MIT Press.

Shepard, R. N., & Metzler, J. (1971). Mental rotation of three-dimensional objects. *Science, 171,* 701-703.

Shephard, J. W., & Ellis, H. D. (1973). The effect of attractiveness on recognition memory for faces. *American Journal of Psychology, 86,* 627-633.

Shiffrin, R. M., & Cook, J. R. (1978). Short-term forgetting of item and order information. *Journal of Verbal Learning and Verbal Behavior, 17,* 189-218.

Shiffrin, R. M., & Gardner, G. T. (1972). Visual processing capacity and attentional control. *Journal of Experimental Psychology, 93,* 72-82.

Shiffrin, R. M., & Geisler, W. S. (1973). Visual recognition in a theory of information processing. In R. L. Solso, (Ed.), *Contemporary issues in cognitive psychology: The Loyola symposium.* Washington, D.C.: V. H. Winston & Sons.

Shugan, S. M. (1980). The cost of thinking. *Journal of Consumer Research, 7,* 99-111.

Shulman, H. G. (1971). Similarity effects in short-term memory. *Psychological Bulletin, 75,* 399-415.

Siegel, L. S. (1977). The relationship of language and thought in the preoperational child: A reconsideration of nonverbal alternatives to Piagetian tasks. In L. S. Siegel & C. J. Brainerd (Eds.), *Alternatives to Piaget: Critical essays on the theory.* New York: Academic Press.

Siegler, R. S. (1976). Three aspects of cognitive development. *Cognitive Psychology, 8,* 481-520.

Siegler, R. S. (1978). The origins of scientific reasoning. In R. S. Siegler (Ed.), *Children's thinking: What develops?* Hillsdale, N. J.: Erlbaum.

Siegler, R. S. (1981). Developmental sequences within and between concepts. *Monographs of the Society for Research in Child Development, 46,* No. 2.

Siegler, R. S. (1983). Information-processing approaches to development. In H. Mussen (Ed.), *Carmichael's manual of child psychology.* New York: Wiley.

Simon, H. A., & Hayes, J. R. (1976). The understanding process: Problem isomorphs. *Cognitive Psychology, 8,* 165–190.

Simon, H. A., & Reed, S. K. (1976). Modeling strategy shifts in a problem-solving task. *Cognitive Psychology, 8,* 86–97.

Slovic, P., & Fischhoff, B. (1977). On the psychology of experimental surprises. *Journal of Experimental Psychology: Human Perception and Performance, 3,* 544–551.

Smith, E. E. (1976). Theories of semantic memory. In W. K. Estes (Ed.), *Handbook of learning and cognitive processes* (Vol. 5). Hillsdale, N. J.: Erlbaum.

Smith, E. E., & Medin, D. L. *Categories and concepts.* Cambridge, Mass.: Harvard University Press, 1981.

Smith, E. E., Shoben, E. J., & Rips, L. J. (1974). Structure and process in semantic memory: A featural model for semantic decisions. *Psychological Review, 81,* 214–241.

Smith, S. M., Glenberg, A., & Bjork, R. A. (1978). Environmental context and human memory. *Memory & Cognition, 6,* 342–353.

Sperling, G. (1960). The information available in brief visual presentations. *Psychological Monographs, 74,* 1–29.

Sperling, G. (1963). A model for visual memory tasks. *Human Factors, 5,* 19–31.

Sperling, G. (1967). Successive approximations to a model for short term memory. *Acta Psychologica, 27,* 285–292.

Spiro, R. J. (1977). Remembering information from text: The "state of schema" approach. In R. C. Anderson, R. J. Spiro, & W. E. Montague (Eds.), *Schooling and the acquisition of knowledge.* Hillsdale, N. J.: Erlbaum.

Spiro, R. J. (1980). Accommodative reconstruction in prose recall. *Journal of Verbal Learning and Verbal Behavior, 19,* 84–95.

Spoehr, K. T., & Corin, W. J. (1978). The stimulus suffix effect as a memory coding phenomenon. *Memory & Cognition, 6,* 583–589.

Sroufe, L. A., & Waters, E. (1976). The ontogenesis of smiling and laughter: A perspective on the organization of development in infancy. *Psychological Review, 83,* 173–189.

Stein, B. S., & Bransford, G. D. (1979). Constraints on effective elaboration: Effects of precision and subject generation. *Journal of Verbal Learning and Verbal Behavior, 18,* 769–777.

Stern, L. D. (1981). A review of theories of human amnesia. *Memory & Cognition, 9,* 247–262.

Sternberg, R. (1977). *Intelligence, information processing, and analogical reasoning.* Hillsdale, N. J.: Erlbaum.

Sternberg, R. J. (1977). Component processes in analogical reasoning. *Psychological Review, 31,* 356–378.

Sternberg, S. (1966). High-speed scanning in human memory. *Science, 153,* 652–654.

Sternberg, S. (1967). Retrieval of contextual information from memory. *Psychonomic Science, 8,* 55–56.

Sternberg, S. (1969). Memory-scanning: Mental processes revealed by reaction-time experiments. *American Scientist, 57,* 421–457.

Sternberg, S. (1975). Memory scanning: New findings and current controversies. *Quarterly Journal of Experimental Psychology, 27,* 1–32.

Stratton, R. P., Parrott, G. L., & Johnson, D. M. (1970). Transfer of judgment training to production and judgment of solutions on a verbal problem. *Journal of Educational Psychology, 61,* 16–23.

Straube, E. R., & Germer, C. K. (1979). Dichotic shadowing and selective attention to word meaning in schizophrenia. *Journal of Abnormal Psychology, 88,* 346–353.

Sweller, J., & Levine, M. (1982). Effects of goal specificity on means-end analysis and learning. *Journal of Experimental Psychology: Learning, Memory, and Cognition, 8,* 463–474.

Taplin, J. E. (1975). Evaluation of hypotheses in concept identification. *Memory & Cognition, 3,* 85–96.

Taplin, J. E., & Standenmeyer, H. (1973). Interpretation of abstract conditional sentences in deductive reasoning. *Journal of Verbal Learning and Verbal Behavior, 12,* 530–542.

Theios, J., Smith, P. G., Haviland, S. E., Traupmann, J., & Moy, M. C. (1973). Memory scanning as a serial self-terminating process. *Journal of Experimental Psychology, 97,* 323–336.

Thomas, J. C., Jr. (1974). An analysis of behavior in the hobbits-orcs problem. *Cognitive Psychology, 6,* 257–269.

Thorndike, E. L., & Lorge, I. (1944). *The teacher's word book of 30,000 words.* New York: Columbia University Press.

Tighe, T. J., & Tighe, L. S. (1978). A perceptual view of conceptual development. In R. D. Walk & H. L. Pick, Jr. (Eds.), *Perception and experience.* New York: Plenum.

Trabasso, T., & Bower, G. H. (1968). *Attention in learning.* New York: Wiley.

Treisman, A. M. (1960). Contextual cues in selective listening. *Quarterly Journal of Experimental Psychology, 12,* 242–248.

Treisman, A., & Geffen, G. (1967). Selective attention: Perception or response? *Quarterly Journal of Experimental Psychology, 19,* 1–17.

Tulving, E. (1972). Episodic and semantic memory. In E. Tulving & W. Donaldson (Eds.), *Organization of memory*. New York: Academic Press.

Tulving, E. (1983). *Elements of episodic memory*. Oxford: Oxford University Press.

Tulving, E., & Arbuckle, T. Y. (1963). Sources of intratrial interference in immediate recall of paired associates. *Journal of Verbal Learning and Verbal Behavior, 1*, 321–334.

Tulving, E., & Pearlstone, Z. (1966). Availability versus accessibility of information in memory for words. *Journal of Verbal Learning and Verbal Behavior, 5*, 381–391.

Tulving, E., & Thomson, D. M. (1971). Retrieval processes in recognition memory: Effect of associative context. *Journal of Experimental Psychology, 87*, 116–124.

Tulving, E., & Thomson, D. M. (1973). Encoding specificity and retrieval processes in episodic memory. *Psychological Review, 80*, 352–373.

Tversky, A. (1972). Elimination by aspects: A theory of choice. *Psychological Review, 79*, 281–299.

Tversky, A., & Kahneman, D. (1971). Belief in the law of small numbers. *Psychological Bulletin, 76*, 105–110.

Tversky, A., & Kahneman, D. (1973). Availability: A heuristic for judging frequency and probability. *Cognitive Psychology, 5*, 207–232.

Tversky, A., & Kahneman, D. (1980). Causal schemata in judgment under uncertainty. In M. Fishbein (Ed.), *Progress in social psychology*, Hillsdale, N. J.: Erlbaum.

Underwood, B. J. (1948a). Retroactive and proactive inhibition after five and forty-eight hours. *Journal of Experimental Psychology, 38*, 29–38.

Underwood, B. J. (1948b). "Spontaneous recovery" of verbal associations. *Journal of Experimental Psychology, 38*, 429–439.

Underwood, B. J. (1949). Proactive inhibition as a function of time and degree of prior learning. *Journal of Experimental Psychology, 39*, 24–34.

Underwood, B. J. (1957). Interference and forgetting. *Psychological Review, 64*, 49–60.

van Dijk, T. A., & Kintsch, W. (1983). *Strategies of discourse comprehension*. New York: Academic Press.

Van Duyne, P. C. (1974). Realism and linguistic complexity in reasoning. *British Journal of Psychology, 65*, 59–67.

Vidmar, N. & Laird, N. (1982). Adversary social roles: The efforts of witnesses communication of evidence and the assessments of adjudicators. *Journal of Personality and Social Psychology, 44*, 888–898.

von Wright, J. M. (1972). On the problem of selection in iconic memory. *Scandinavian Journal of Psychology, 13*, 159–171.

Wagner, D. A. (1978). Memories of Morocco: The influence of age, schooling, and environment on memory. *Cognitive Psychology, 10*, 1–28.

Warnick, D. H., & Sanders, G. S. (1980). The effect of group discussion on eyewitness accuracy. *Journal of Applied Social Psychology, 10*, 249–259.

Wason, P. C. (1968). On the failure to eliminate hypotheses—a second look. In P. C. Wason & P. N. Johnson-Laird (Eds.), *Thinking and reasoning*. Baltimore: Penguin.

Wason, P. C., & Johnson-Laird, P. N. (1972). *Psychology of reasoning: Structure and content*. Cambridge, Mass.: Harvard University Press.

Wason, P. C., & Shapiro, D. (1971). Natural and contrived experience in a reasoning problem. *Quarterly Journal of Experimental Psychology, 23*, 63–71.

Watkins, M. J. (1979). In C. R. Puff (Ed.), *Memory organization and structure*. New York: Academic Press.

Watson, J. B. (1913). Psychology as a behaviorist views it. *Psychological Review, 20*, 158–177.

Weinberg, H. I., Wadsworth, J., & Baron, R. S. (1983). Demand and the impact of leading questions on eyewitness testimony. *Memory & Cognition, 11*, 101–104.

Weisberg, R. W., & Alba, J. W. (1981). An examination of the alleged role of "fixation" in the solution of several "insight" problems. *Journal of Experimental Psychology: General, 110*, 169–192.

Welker, R. L. (1982). Abstraction of themes from melodic variation. *Journal of Experimental Psychology: Human Perception and Performance, 8*, 435–447.

Wertheimer, M. (1961). Psychomotor co-ordination of auditory-visual space at birth. *Science, 134*, 1692.

Wertheimer, M. (1982). *Productive thinking*. Chicago: University of Chicago Press.

Wetherick, N. E. (1970). On the representativeness of some experiments in cognition. *Bulletin of the British Psychological Society, 23*, 213–214.

Wetherick, N. E., & Dominowski, R. L. (1976). How representative are concept attainment experiments? *British Journal of Psychology, 67*, 231–242.

Whitely, S. E., & Barnes, G. M. (1979). The implications of processing event sequences for theories of analogical reasoning. *Memory & Cognition, 7*, 323–331.

Whorf, B. L. (1956). *Language, thought, and reality: Selected writings of Benjamin Lee Whorf*, J. B. Carroll (Ed.). New York: John Wiley.

Wickelgren, W. A. (1968). Sparing of short-term memory in an amnesic patient: Implications for a strength theory of memory. *Neuropsychologia, 6*, 235–244.

Wickens, C. D. (1974). Temporal limits of human information processing: A developmental study. *Psychological Bulletin, 81*, 739–755.

Wingfield, A. (1979). *Human learning and memory: An introduction*. New York: Harper & Row.

Wingfield, A., & Byrnes, D. L. (1981). *The psychology of human memory.* New York: Academic Press.

Wohlwill, J. F. (1970). The age variable in psychological research. *Psychological Review, 77,* 49–64.

Wood, G. (1978). The knew-it-all-along effect. *Journal of Experimental Psychology: Human Perception and Performance, 4,* 345–353.

Woodhead, M. N., Baddeley, A. D., & Simmonds, D. C. V. (1979). On training people to recognize faces. *Ergonomics, 22,* 333–343.

Wright, J. C., & Vlietstra, A. G. (1975). The development of selective attention: From perceptual exploration to logical search. *Advances In Child Development and Behavior, 10,* 195–239.

Wulff, F. (1922). Uber die Veränderung von Vorstellungen. *Psychologische Forschung, 1,* 333–373.

Yarmey, A. D. (1973). I recognize your face but I can't remember your name: Further evidence on the tip-of-the-tongue phenomenon. *Memory & Cognition,* 287–290.

Author Index

Subject Index